The New Rich in China

Three decades of reform in the People's Republic of China have resulted in the emergence of new social groups. These have included new occupations and professions that have been generated as the economy has opened up and developed and, most spectacularly given the legacy of state socialism, the identification of those who are regarded as wealthy. However, although China's new rich are certainly a consequence of globalisation, there remains a need for caution in assuming either that China's new rich are a middle class, or that if they are they should immediately be equated with a universal middle class.

Including sections on class, status and power; entrepreneurs, managers, and professionals; and lifestyle *The New Rich in China* investigates the political, socio-economic and cultural characteristics of the emergent new rich in China, the similarities and differences to similar phenomenon elsewhere, and the consequences of the new rich for China itself. In doing so, it links the importance of China to the world economy and helps us understand how the growth of China's new rich may influence our understanding of social change elsewhere. This is a subject that will become increasingly important as China continues its development, and private entrepreneurship continues to be encouraged. As such, *The New Rich in China* will be an invaluable volume for students and scholars of Chinese studies, history and politics, and social change.

David S. G. Goodman is Professor of Contemporary China Studies at the University of Technology, Sydney. In the 1990s he created the project to examine *The New Rich in Asia*, also published by Routledge.

The New Rich in China

Future rulers, present lives

**Edited by
David S. G. Goodman**

Routledge
Taylor & Francis Group

LONDON AND NEW YORK

First published 2008
by Routledge
2 Park Square, Milton Park, Abingdon, Oxon OX14 5RN

Simultaneously published in the USA and Canada
by Routledge
270 Madison Avenue, New York, NY 10016

Routledge is an imprint of the Taylor & Francis Group, an informa business

© 2008 Editorial selection and matter, David S. G. Goodman; Individual
chapters, the contributors

Typeset in Times New Roman by
Taylor & Francis Books
Printed and bound in Great Britain by
TJ International Ltd, Padstow, Cornwall

British Library Cataloguing in Publication Data
A catalogue record for this book is available from the British Library

Library of Congress Cataloging-in-Publication Data
The new rich in China : future rulers, present lives / edited by
David S. G Goodman.
    p. cm.
    1. Middle class–China.   2. Wealth–China.   3. Social classes–
China.   4. Social change–China.   5. Power (Social sciences)–China. I.
Goodman, David S. G.
    HT690.C55N49 2008
    305.5′50951–dc22   2007045216

ISBN 978-0-415-45564-0 (hbk)
ISBN 978-0-415-45565-7 (pbk)
ISBN 978-0-203-93117-2 (ebk)

Contents

Illustrations

Tables

Figures

Contributors

Beatriz Carrillo Garcia is lecturer in Asian Studies at the University of Technology, Sydney and a member of the UTS China Research Centre. She researches social change in contemporary China and is currently working on two projects: one on problems of health care provision; the other on the evolution of the interaction between the new rich and the state. She is the author of *Small town North China: Rural labour and social inclusion* (2008.)

Carolyn Cartier works on cultural economy and city-region formation in South China and is Associate Professor of Geography at the University of Southern California. She is the author of *Globalizing South China* (2001); and 'Origins and Evolution of a Geographical Idea: The Macroregion in China' in *Modern China* (2002). She is also the co-editor of *The Chinese Diaspora: Place, Space, Mobility and Identity* (2003).

Minglu Chen teaches China studies at the University of Guadalajara, Mexico; and is an associate of the UTS China Research Center. She is the author of *Tiger Girls: Women and Enterprises in the People's Republic of China* (2008.) Her current research is concerned with women and social change in China.

Ivan Cucco is a PhD candidate in China Studies, UTS. His main research interest is the application of network analysis and complex systems theories to study the process of institutional transformation in China. His current research projects investigate the functioning of professional labor markets in Nanjing, and the development of Farmer's Economic Cooperative Organisations in three Chinese provinces (Shanxi, Jiangsu and Zhejiang).

Stephanie Hemelryk Donald is Professor of International Studies, UTS and a member of the UTS China Research Centre. She has published work on global media, children's film culture, city branding and the politics of film in the Asia Pacific. She is currently undertaking research into class, taste, reading and choice in China; mobile youth culture in Sydney, and cosmopolitanism and belonging in Europe and Asia.

Louise Edwards is Professor of China Studies at UTS, a member of the UTS China Research Centre and Convener of the Australian Research Council's Asia Pacific Futures Research Network. Her most recent book is *Gender, Politics and Democracy: Women's Suffrage in China* (2008). Other publications include *Men and Women in Qing China* (1994, 2001), *Censored by Confucius*, (1996) (with Kam Louie) and three edited volumes with Mina Roces: *Women in Asia: Tradition, Modernity and Globalization* (2000); *Women's Suffrage in Asia* (2004); and *The Politics of Dress in Asia and the Americas*. Her current research includes an exploration of women and war in China.

David S. G. Goodman is Professor of Contemporary China Studies at UTS and a member of the UTS China Research Centre. The editor of *The New Rich in Asia* in 1996, recent publications include *China's Campaign to 'Open Up the West'* (2004) and *China's Communist Revolutions* (2002). Current research projects include a study of the interactions between the state and the new rich at county level in contemporary China (with Beatriz Carrillo and Minglu Chen.)

Yingjie Guo is a senior lecturer in Chinese Studies UTS and a member of the UTS China Research Centre. His research is related to nationalism in contemporary China and the domestic political impact of China's WTO membership. He is the author of *Cultural Nationalism in Contemporary China: The Search for National Identity under Reform* (2003) and co-author of *Nationalism, National identity and Democratization in China* (2000).

Colin Hawes is a senior lecturer in Law at UTS and a member of the UTS China Research Centre. His research focuses on Chinese business law, corporate culture and legal reform, especially the ways in which legal and business structures have been imported to China and transformed to fit the Chinese social and political context.

Elaine Jeffreys is a senior lecturer in China Studies UTS and a member of the UTS China Research Centre. She received a PhD in Political Science from the University of Melbourne. Elaine is the editor of *Sex and Sexuality in China* (2006) and author of *China, Sex and Prostitution* (2004). Her current research is on the regulation of new sexual behaviors in the People's Republic of China.

Wanning Sun is an Associate Professor at Curtin University, Australia. She was Visiting Professor at State University of New York, Binghamton (2005–6). She researches on media, migration, and gendered mobility. Her works include *Leaving China* (2002); *Media and the Chinese Diaspora* (2006); and *Maid in China: Media, Morality and the Cultural Politics of Boundaries.*

Beibei Tang is a PhD student in Sociology at the The Australian National University. Her dissertation is focused on the status attainment of

China's urban middle class, and social stratification and mobility dynamics in transitional China.

Luigi Tomba is a political scientist with the Australian National University, College of Asia and the Pacific, Department of Political and Social Change. His research focuses on China's urban politics and governance, community building, labor reform, social stratification, social conflicts and class. He is co-editor of *The China Journal*, and his publications include *Paradoxes of Labour reform: Chinese Labour Theory and Practice from Socialism to the Market* (2002), and *East Asian Capitalism: Conflicts, Growth and Crisis* (2002).

Xiaowei Zang teaches sociology at City University of Hong Kong and is the author of *Children of the Cultural Revolution* (2000), *Elite Dualism and Leadership Selection in China* (2004), and *Ethnicity and Urban Life in China* (2007).

Jingqing Yang is Senior Lecturer in China Studies at UTS and a member of the UTS China Research Centre. His research interests include Chinese healthcare system, health reform, sociology of professions and professional ethics.

Zheng Yi is a research fellow at the Institute for International Studies, UTS and a member of the UTS China Research Centre. She received her PhD from the Program of Cultural and Critical Studies, University of Pittsburgh, USA, and was previously an Agora Fellow at the Advanced Studies Institute of Berlin, Germany; a Senior Fellow at the Advanced Studies Institute of Budapest, Hungary; a post-doctoral Fellow at the Porter Institute for Comparative Poetics; and a lecturer in the Department of East Asian Studies, Tel Aviv University. Her most recent Publication is: *The Transformation of a Sublime Aesthetics: from Edmund Burke to Guo Moruo* (2008).

Preface

The wealth of China's economy, and the individuals driving and benefiting from its growth, have been matters of increasing importance and profile around the world during the last twenty years. In the early 1990s this development was seen very much in the context of apparently significant economic development generally in East and Southeast Asia. At that time the Australian Research Council established a Special Research Centre at Murdoch University in Western Australia that was specifically designed to examine the emergence of the New Rich in Asia and the consequences for both the countries of the region and Australia. It produced a series of studies – also published by Routledge – that set a benchmark for both theoretical and empirical research into the topic, and essentially set the agenda for further research internationally.

Fifteen years on China's new rich have achieved an increasingly higher profile in the popular consciousness as that country's economic growth has proceeded apace. There remains a need for further understanding and conceptualisation of the new rich, the environment from which they have emerged and the forces that have shaped their existence as well as the consequences, for both China and the rest of the world. The latter includes not only the practical political and economic consequences but also the impact on the world of knowledge, in particular understandings of social change.

The project to examine the new rich in China in greater depth has been an undertaking of the UTS China Research Centre. The production of this volume resulted from a chance conversation with one of the eventual participants, Xiaowei Zang (City University, Hong Kong) who provided the initial encouragement. The project was then joined by a further ten participants at the UTS China Research Centre: the Director, Louise Edwards; Stephanie Hemelryk Donald; Elaine Jeffreys; Yingjie Guo; Colin Hawes; Jingqing Yang; Beatriz Carrillo Garcia; Minglu Chen; Zheng Yi; and Ivan Cucco. Discussions among this lively and enthusiastic group led to further invitations being extended to Carolyn Cartier (from the University of Southern California), Wanning Sun (Curtin University), and Luigi Tomba and Beibei Tang (ANU), all close associates of the UTS China Research Centre.

Research for this project has its origins, as already noted, in a project supported by the Australian Research Council. Subsequent research into different aspects of China's new rich has also been supported by the Australian Research Council through individual grants: Stephanie Hemelryk Donald for 'The Cultivation of Middle Class Taste: reading, Tourism and Education Choices in Middle Class China' (DP0665537); David S. G. Goodman for 'Shanxi province in reform' (A10010001) and for 'China's Qinghai Province: migration, colonisation and the contest for political space' (A00103610); David S. G. Goodman and Minglu Chen for 'China's invisible economic leadership: women in family enterprises' (DP0344767); Luigi Tomba for 'Communities and New Patterns of Social Stratification in a Chinese City' (DP662894); and Wanning Sun for 'Maid in China: Gendered Mobilities, Internal Migration, and the Translocal Imagination' (DP 0451492). Carolyn Cartier undertook research in South China supported by a US CIES-Fulbright Fellowship.

David S. G. Goodman
UTS, October 2007

Abbreviations

ACWF	All China Women's Federation
AWE	Association of Women Entrepreneurs
CASS	Chinese Academy of Social Sciences
CEPA	Closer Economic Partnership Agreement
CEO	Chief Executive Officer
CCP	Chinese Communist Party
CGSS	China General Social Survey
COFCO	China National Cereals, Oils & Foodstuffs Corporation
DTC	Diamond Trading Company
FDI	Foreign Direct Investment
GDP	Gross Domestic Product
HKTB	Hong Kong Tourist Board
HKTDC	Hong Kong Trade Development Council
HR	Human Resources
IVS	Individual Visit Scheme
KPI	Key Performance Indicators
NBS	National Bureau of Statistics
NHTDZ	Nanjing High-tech Industrial Development Zone
NPC	National People's Congress
PRC	People's Republic of China
PSD	Public Security Department
PSU	Public Service Unit
R&D	Research and Development
SDRC	State Development Research Commission
S&T	Science and Technology
SINOPEC	China Petroleum Company
SOE	State Owned Enterprise
SYNJ	*Shenyang Nianjian* (Shenyang Yearbook)
TCM	Traditional Chinese Medicine
TVE	Town and Village Enterprise
UTS	University of Technology, Sydney
Xinhua	New China News Agency
YPC	Yangzi Petrochemical Corporation
Yuan	Dollar. US$ = 7.56 *yuan* Renminbi (PRC Currency).

Introduction

The new rich in China: the dimensions of social change

David S. G. Goodman and Xiaowei Zang

Three decades of reform since 1978 in the People's Republic of China (PRC) have resulted in the emergence of new social groups. These include new occupations and professions generated as the economy has opened up and developed, and most spectacularly given the legacy of state socialism, the identification of those who are regarded as wealthy. According to a mid-2007 report from *Xinhua* (the New China News Agency) 6.15 percent of the population (80 million people) had an annual income between 60,000 *yuan* and 500,000 *yuan* (*Xinhua* 18 June 2007) as against an average annual income of 11,759 *yuan* for urban and 3,587 *yuan* for rural residents in 2006 (*Xinhua* 6 May 2007). Colloquially within the PRC these 'new rich' are referred to most commonly as *xingui* (the new rich), *xinfu* (new wealth), or *dakuan* (big spender); but also more variedly in terms that highlight their political and social impact as well such as *zhongchan jieji* (middle class), *xin zibenjia* (new capitalists), and *xinrui* (new blade) or that return to pre-1949 terms such as *xinquangui* (the new influential) and *fuhao* (the rich and powerful).

China's new rich are certainly a consequence of globalisation, as that country has become not simply integrated with the world economy, but in many ways the focus of every other country's globalisation. They are though less certainly to be regarded as the PRC manifestation of a universal middle class. It may be convenient to interpret China's new rich in this way. Middle class implies markets, democracy, consumerism and 'people like us.' At the same time, as was pointed out in the early 1990s when 'The New Rich in Asia' were first identified, it remains far from self-evident that China's new rich are a middle class quite like or in the same ways that middle classes occur elsewhere (Goodman and Robison 1992; Robison and Goodman 1996a).

The contributions to this volume are designed to examine the political, socio-economic and cultural characteristics of the emergent new rich in China, the similarities and differences to similar phenomena elsewhere, and the consequences for China itself. In the process they highlight the complex composition and conceptualisation of both the new rich and the middle class. Some of those who have benefited materially from economic growth and development have already become significant power-holders and it would appear that wealth is in the process of becoming an increasingly important component of political power. On the other hand, not all the middle class are the middle market, not all the new rich are fabulously wealthy, and neither status nor power is so crudely determined. The research presented in this volume underscores the need to appreciate that individual behaviour is often driven as much by subjective factors such as perceptions of status and status difference and ideas of class and class identity, as by more objective socio-economic structures. Moreover, while aspects of China's socio-economic development are reminiscent of similar processes elsewhere, the research that follows also emphasises that there are local dimensions to ideology and organisation, economic structure, social history and cultural construction that play a significant role in the analysis and explanation of social change.

The New Rich

Inequality and real disposable income have both increased in the PRC in ways that were unimaginable when the reform era started. In 1978, the PRC was one of the most egalitarian societies in the world. A standard index of inequality is the Gini Coefficient that ranges from 0 (perfect equality) to 1. In 1978, the PRC Gini Coefficient was 0.22, one of the most equal ever recorded (Adelmen and Sunding 1987). By 2007 it had become one of the most unequal, with a Gini Coefficient of 0.496 (*Xinhua* 17 January 2007) alongside Brazil, Zambia and Uganda. A sign of this inequality is that by 2006, despite a relatively low average annual income, 12 percent of global sales of luxury handbags, shoes, jewellery, and perfume were to be found in the PRC and the Chinese were being described as 'the third-biggest high-end buyers on earth' (Ford 2007; Jones 2007; Roberts and Balfour 2006).

Several groups have been the major beneficiaries, as well as to a large extent the drivers of this massive transformation. In academic reflections on social stratification and class formation in the PRC's post-1978 era (published both inside and outside the PRC) they are variously defined as the 'relatively well off and educated', 'middle income', 'wealthy', 'high achievers', 'the economic elite', 'an affluent strata', 'the middle strata', 'middle class people', 'middle-class citizens', 'middle-income earners', 'the middle classes', 'the bourgeoisie and middle class', and 'an emerging strata of new rich', or simply some variant of the colloquial terms for 'the new rich' and for the most part these different labels have been used interchangeably (Cai 2005b: 777; A. Chen 2002: 401, 404, 408–9, 416–7; Lee 2002: 220; Liu 2006: 506–7; Tomba 2004: 3–4, 7, 18; Tsai 2002: 1, 132; Xiao 2003: 62; Yang 2006: 155). One explanation for this variety is the broad consensus that the new rich are a disparate group including not only economic (and to some extent political) elites but also the petty bourgeoisie and professionals (A. Chen 2002: 403–4, 408, 411; A. Chen 2003a: 54; A. Chen 2003b: 155; Liu 2006: 507; Tomba 2004: 4–5; 7–8).

Scholars both inside and outside the PRC have focused attention on entrepreneurs and professionals, though there are differences in the range of groups they identify as the new rich. Scholars outside China identify the new rich in terms of business people generally, but also sometimes including small-scale entrepreneurs; contract-based managers of state enterprises; professors and senior scientists; stockbrokers; estate agents; senior employees in major banks and other financial institutions; managers and white collar workers of foreign and large private companies; and lawyers, accountants, singers, fashion models, designers, and athletes (A. Chen 2003a: 54; Goodman 1996: 225; Xiao 2003: 62). Scholars and media commentators inside the PRC include scientific development entrepreneurs; Chinese managerial staff working in foreign firms in China; middle and high-level managerial staff in state-owned financial institutions; professional technicians in various fields especially in intermediary firms; and some self-employed private entrepreneurs in their identification of China's new rich (Five Groups 2002).

The idea of the new rich points to the importance of wealth and highlights the impact of economic growth on other aspects of social, political and cultural change. There are various social groups who can generally and collectively be regarded as the new rich. It is a broad idea – the beneficiaries of economic growth – rather than a precise social group or distinct analytical category. The new rich are not all by any means super rich. Just as there are hierarchies of political power and status, so too there are gradations of wealth. Understanding the interactions amongst these hierarchies of wealth, power and status helps explain the dynamics of Chinese society and the exercise of political power.

As the earlier mention of luxury goods sales highlights, patterns of consumption matter to marketing executives outside China not least since the new rich are a symbol of wealth creation on a massive scale. The PRC's GDP increased from US$147.3 billion in 1978 to US$2.7 trillion in 2007, having in 2005 become the fourth largest economy in the world (Xu Binglan 2007). At the same time, growing inequality and the implications for the PRC's society and politics matter to cadres and scholars (inside and outside China) seeking to understand the social forces economic growth has unleashed. Scholars have written extensively on the underprivileged groups and the needy such as laid-off state workers (Cai 2002; Cai 2005a; F. Chen 2000; Lee 2002; Liu and Wu 2006; Solinger 2002; M Wang 2004) and rural inhabitants (Cartier and Rotheberg-Aalami 1999; C Fan 2004; Yan, Hugo and Potter 2005; Yao, Zhang and Hanmer 2004; Zhang and Wan 2006). There has also been research concerned with those who have benefited most from economic growth, including for example studies of private entrepreneurs (A. Chen 1999; Dickson 2003; Krug 2004; Tsai 2002; Wank 1999) and Chinese employees in foreign firms (Pearson 1997; Santoro 2000).

Research into China's new rich to date has been uneven and perhaps necessarily inconclusive. There is little agreement on the factors explaining the generation of wealth, or the relationships between economic and political power, let alone the consequences for the future. There has been only a limited interest in the component elements of the new rich other than private entrepreneurs and Chinese employees in foreign firms. The most obvious lesser-considered social categories include both state managers and professionals (A. Chen 2002; Goodman 1999; Tsai 2005). Despite their importance for understanding social and economic dynamics there has been almost no attention paid to the family life and consumption patterns of different elements of the new rich.

Much of the research on the new rich has concentrated on the consequences for regime change, and this is not an insignificant concern. There would though seem to be a case for that focus to be placed in a wider perspective that considers conceptual problems of identification alongside questions of agency and behaviour. Who precisely are the new rich who have gained so much from the post-1978 market reforms? How have they amassed their enormous assets? What has been the role of the Party-state in wealth creation? What are the potential political consequences from the emergence of China's new rich? How have key stratification factors such as gender and ethnicity influenced the probabilities of mobility into elite status? Have the beneficiaries of market reforms been awarded social recognition and status compatible to the levels of economic successes they have attained? What are their cultural values, status aspirations, and consumption patterns? Have they simply made a fetish of money, or developed an obsession with Chinese folk religions, or acquired a taste for other belief systems?

There is an inherent comparativist dimension to addressing these issues. Reference to the concept of the middle class draws attention to an earlier European experience. Another concept often used to explain the development of the PRC since 1978 is that it is 'transitional.' This refers to processes of rapid social change and the dramatic reconfiguration of social and economic interests that other countries have experienced, especially those associated with the evolution of authoritarianism and the collapse of communist party-states (Konrad and Szelenyi 1979; Polanyi 1957; Szelenyi 1978).

Building on this comparativist intellectual tradition, Victor Nee's research has not only set the agenda for those studying China as a transitional system but also highlighted the structures encouraging the emergence of the new rich (Nee 1989, 2005). In a redistributive economy, the production and allocation of resources are determined by and thus biased toward those who redistribute: in the PRC before 1978 this was the cadres and officials of the Party-state. In the process of market transition, direct producers gain property rights over their products through the market link between producer and consumer. Nee accordingly develops three hypotheses. The first is the market power thesis. This suggests that market power over resources would increase at the expense of the state's redistributive power since exchange in the market is based on contracts instead of government fiat. As a result, the returns to direct producers should be higher than the returns to redistributors such as CCP cadres and government officials. The second is the market incentive thesis. This indicates that the market would produce incentives to direct producers since they could exchange their labour power and products for greater benefit than would accrue to cadres through redistribution. Market incentives entail a direct link between rewards and labour, and between labour and human capital. The expected result is then diminishing rewards for the redistributive power of CCP cadres and government officials. The third is a market opportunity thesis. This highlights the role of political mobility as the only avenue for upward mobility in the socialist redistributive economy. In contrast, market transition creates alternatives so that entrepreneurship becomes a key variable of status attainment, and human capital becomes increasingly important in career mobility.

Using data collected from China's rural areas, Nee found declining returns to political capital and increasing rewards for entrepreneurship and human capital as measured by educational attainment. Later, Nee found that cadre households were more likely than average households to enjoy upward mobility in market reforms. He explains that this finding does not suggest there is no transition to the market since (almost) everyone has become better off with reform. Cadres' incomes have risen together with the deepening of market reforms. Many cadre families have taken advantage of their political capital to become entrepreneur families (Nee 1991, 1996; Nee and Yang 1999; Nee and Matthews 1996).

These findings are usually accepted by researchers concerned with China's rural development. Political office, human capital, and private entrepreneurship are identified as the keys to wealth creation. (Chin-Jou Chen 2004, 2006; Peng 2004; Walder 2002a, 2002b; Walder and Zhao 2006). When attention turns to the urban environment, Nee's analysis of transition seems in need of a slight modification. Scholars have found that entrepreneurship and human capital have been two key variables in wealth creation among urban residents (Bian and Logan 1996; Bian 2002; Parish and Michelson 1996; Walder 1996; Zang 2002, 2003). Yet, in contrast to Nee's line of argument, others put greater importance on the redistributive power aspects of post-1978 stratification in urban China. There is some scepticism about the speed of the transformative power of the market since it seems that the main beneficiaries of economic reforms have been individuals with political capital, such as CCP cadres and government officials. This view is rather persuasive since China's reforms have been conducted within the framework of the Party-state and its 'work-unit' (*danwei*) system, which had been the main focus of production and redistribution in urban China. Individuals with political capital were located in strategic positions in the redistributive system and so could take advantage of the vast resources controlled by the work-unit for private profits.

These observations about path dependency highlight China's distinctiveness as a social system in transition. The Party-state has presided over, adapted to, and provided the framework for reform even where it has not actually led processes of change. One consequence is that China's new rich are not readily separable from the Party-state as a social, political or even economic force. Another consequence is to question the rigidity of the equation between economic growth and political change. The Party-state is changing but there is so far no evidence of any factors promoting its disappearance. On the contrary, as the chapters in this volume clearly highlight, there is every evidence of a solid community of interest having been developed between the new rich and the Party-state.

The middle class

One way to see the new rich is as a result of the PRC's transition from state socialism; another that features prominently in the literature on recent social change in the PRC is to describe the new rich as the middle class or classes. One clear difficulty with this equation is that the idea of class in general, let alone the notion of the middle class, is much contested. As the chapters in the first section of this volume discuss in greater detail, class may be related varyingly to economic structures, income, patterns of consumption, value concerns and lifestyles, and often bewilderingly in multiple dimensions at the same time. The concept of the middle class covers a range of historical phenomena and attracts a number of other definitions and concerns along the way. One middle class was the early capitalists of the early industrial revolution in Northwest Europe during the first half of the nineteenth century, the bourgeoisie between the aristocracy and the towns-people. Another has been the state and capitalist enterprise sponsored managers and professionals of the managerial revolution during the first half of the twentieth century, between the capitalists and the workers. More recently, the term has been applied to the vast majority of consumers in late capitalist industrialised societies, between the rich and the poor.

Research and media commentary in China have suggested that the middle class 'refers to a group of people with stable incomes who are capable of purchasing private houses and cars, and who can afford the costs of education and holidays'. Elsewhere it has been suggested that the PRC middle class includes mainly 'professionals who work in middle management positions' (Jones 2007). Some scholars outside the PRC have described its middle classes as a 'social stratum lying above ordinary working people but still not the richest' (Cai 2005a: 778; A. Chen 2002: 404; Xiao 2003: 62). Others have pointed out that in the social sciences 'the middle class is usually more broadly or ambiguously defined. It is not limited to small entrepreneurs and business people, but also covers many other professions that typically require good education, receive high pay, and have some particular consumption habits' (Chen 2002: 408). Still others have argued that the middle classes 'appear amorphous and lack the cohesiveness required by the traditional definitions of class, they appear increasingly to shape their status around a new set of collective interests, especially in their modes of consumption and access to resources' (Tomba 2004: 3).

Some scholars outside the PRC have complained that the concept of the 'middle class' is too broad to be a useful instrument (Tsai 2005: 1). Others have queried the relevance of the concept of class at all in this context. It is argued that the use of terms related to social class outside the PRC relate to issues of inequality and hierarchy, understood in terms of occupation, income and wealth. In the Chinese context, these conceptualisations are less meaningful because of the role of the CCP and its officials (A. Chen 2002: 408). Revolution too has bequeathed a different legacy in the PRC:

> In the West, the term refers more to a social status than a strictly cir-cumscribed class and is therefore quite subjective. The majority of the population in many industrial democracies prefer to assign themselves to the middle-class category. By contrast, for historical and practical reasons, most Chinese urban citizens tend to identify themselves as the working class
>
> (A. Chen 2002: 410)

Thus, some scholars simply 'bypass the ontologically ambiguous category of the middle class by focusing instead on the specific actors that constitute the preponderance of China's economic structural transformation' such as entrepreneurs or middle-income professionals (Tsai 2005: 1132).

Despite these uncertainties, there have been attempts to develop 'objec-tive' measurements to study the PRC's middle class. One approach is to focus on cash income. For example, Chen An has pointed out that based on his investigations of wage schemes and sources of income for several trades and professions in some affluent provinces, an annual income between 100,000 and 700,000 *yuan* would qualify a household as a middle class family in urban China (A. Chen 2002: 410). Similarly, in 2004, Tomba identified middle class professional families in Beijing as those with a 'household budget of 8,000–10,000 *yuan* a month, considering that in 2001 only about 11 percent of the city's employed population had salaries above 2,000 yuan a month' (Tomba 2004: 21). In 2006, Edward characterised China as a 'three-peaked' society with a small upper-class whose consump-tion level is estimated (in US$) 'as $5,500 per person per annum, a middle-class averaging $2,000 per person per annum, and a still sizable poor class living predominantly near the $2-a-day line' (Edward 2006: 1679). Media writers in the West supported this approach to measurement, arguing in 2006 that the urban middle class in the PRC are those with an annual income of about US$5,000 per capita. This amount is modest by Western standards, but in China '$5,000 buys a lifestyle that would cost four times as much in America' (Ford 2007).

In 2002, some research in China calculated that 'a characteristic young family' would have needed on a monthly basis 1,500–5,000 *yuan* for food and beverage; 600–1,500 *yuan* for medical insurance; 300–5,000 *yuan* for education; 500–1,000 *yuan* for communication and transportation; 1,000–5,000 *yuan* for clothes and beauty treatment; and 600–3,500 *yuan* for sports and entertainment activities. As a result, this source suggested that the characteristic young family needs to earn at least 10,000 *yuan* per month if they wanted to lead a standard 'middle class' life. For a mid-level middle class family, the couple needed to earn 20,000 *yuan* per month, while 40,000 *yuan* a month was necessary to provide an upper middle class lifestyle (Five Groups 2002).

One problem in any attempt to identify the middle class in this way is the difficulty in estimating the disposable income of Chinese citizens due to the tendency to under-report earnings for taxation purposes. Wealth is usually deeply hidden and its actual amount hardly known. Cash income is usually only one component of any remuneration package. State firms and agencies provide heavily subsidised home-purchasing schemes to their employees. Tomba has argued that 'the importance of income levels is overshadowed by the distorted access to housing' since at the present stage of China's development 'higher salaries and a better bargaining power in the labour market would not be enough to account for the dramatic rise in status and consumption levels experienced by some employees and professionals' (Tomba 2004: 15). The patterns of housing acquisition are also proving to be decisive in changing the lifestyles and consumption abilities of the professional middle-class' (Cai 2005a: 780).

Some scholars have thus suggested that home ownership can be used as a key criterion to define economic elite status in urban China today (Cai 2005a; Hu and Kaplan 2001; Li and Wu 2006; Tomba 2004; Wang Ya Ping 2000; Wu Fulong 2004). 'Housing is perhaps the most important asset of most families, including those of the middle class' (Li and Niu 2003: 5). 'On the open market, in 2002 an average apartment of 80 square metres cost around 33 times the average yearly disposable income of a Beijing household!' In a situation 'where the gap between housing prices and income remains wide, people with a privileged access to the state's distribution policies have managed to carve out lifestyles well beyond their means and that this phenomenon has contributed more to the emergence of prestigious residential communities than has the acquisition of wealth' (Tomba 2004: 6). Hence, 'housing has become a major discriminant between social actors, and that it often determines social status more than income does' (Tomba 2004: 11).

A definition of middle class in terms of home ownership has the beauty of simplicity but a potential bias is the fact that the vast majority of urban working families are homeowners. 'By the early 2000s, about 70 percent of urban households in China owned their homes' (Cai 2005a: 779). It is however unlikely that these homeowners are all middle class families.

Indeed the government has offered real estate developers free or cheap land and reduced fiscal charges on the condition that they must sell a portion of the housing units at a discounted price to lower-income 'households with a yearly income below 60,000 *yuan*, who have no property of their own and who have been occupying substandard rental housing' (Tomba 2004: 18). Operationalisation of the definition of the PRC middle class in terms of home ownership is also difficult because of technical matters such as variations in housing size, location, and prices.

One PRC commentator proposed (in 2004) that an urban household could not be classified as a middle class family without assets valued between 150,000 and 300,000 *yuan* (Xin 2004). Elsewhere the level was estimated (in 2006) at an annual household income of between 80,000 and 1 million *yuan* and family assets of between 800,000 and 8 million *yuan*. This source claimed that about 4 percent of the wealthy had an annual household income of 400,000–1,000,000 *yuan*; 15 percent, 200,000–400,000 *yuan*; and the remaining 81 percent, 80,000–200,000 *yuan* (*The People's Daily* 13 January 2006). The French bank BNP Paribas Peregrine suggested (in 2002) that a middle class household would report an 'annual average income of 75,000 *yuan* and assets of 310,000 *yuan*' (Xin 2004).

In addition to issues of definition and measurement, the size of the middle class has been a subject of considerable speculation. One writer has argued that 'without income taxation data as the basis of calculation, it is hard to determine precisely the real size of the Chinese bourgeoisie ... For the same reasons as for the bourgeoisie, a precise assessment of the proportion of China's middle class is almost impossible.' (A. Chen 2002: 409–10). Another writer has stated that even with concrete benchmarks, it is still 'difficult to pinpoint how many Chinese are middle class' (Chin-Jou Chen 2006: 55).

There are those writers and commentators though who are more optimistic about their ability to assess the size of the PRC's middle class. In 2003, The Chinese Academy of Social Sciences (CASS) released a report that suggested China's middle class represented 19 percent of the total population in that year, having risen one percentage point every year since 1999. If this trend continues, the report states 'middle class' people in China would account for 40 percent of the total population in 2020 (Middle Stratum 2004). Similarly, the PRC State Statistical Bureau claimed that about 13 percent of urban households (24.5 million households, or 75 million people) would become middle stratum families in 2005. The number would amount to 25 percent in 2010 (57 million households and 170 million people). The French bank BNP Paribas Peregrine asserted that the number of 'middle class' households in China stood at 50 million in 2002. 'The figure is expected to rise to 100 million in 2010, with each household having an annual average income of 150,000 yuan and assets of 620,000 yuan' (Xin 2004). Elsewhere it has been predicted that 700 million Chinese would join the middle class by 2020 compared with less than 100 million today (Ford 2007).

In contrast, some researchers outside the PRC are more conservative in their estimates, claiming that China's middle class, though growing, is still very small by international standards. According to one 'Even by the most generous yardsticks, China remains far from being a society of the middle class' (D. Yang 2006: 155–6). Another researcher has argued that the new rich 'cannot exceed 12 million in China. Including all the family members, middle-class people should number between 35–45 million. They constitute 9–11 percent of the urban population, but may not exceed 4 percent nationwide' (A. Chen 2002: 410).

In sum, the identification of the middle class in the PRC is clearly hotly contested. Even so, it is equally obvious that at present the size of the middle class is severely limited, however it may be defined. Even within the ranks of those identified in various ways as being middle class there remain huge differences between on the one hand, the super rich, and on the other, those who are comfortably off.

Private entrepreneurs

Private entrepreneurs have been one of two core elements in China's emergent new rich. Not surprisingly their activities have attracted considerable research, which has identified the 'social, economic, and political influence disproportionate to size' private entrepreneurs have wielded 'particularly at local levels' (Hong 2004: 23). They have played a central role in the transition of the formerly centrally planned economies to market economies, and as a result the emergence of private entrepreneurs has been regarded as one of the most dramatic changes that the post-1978 economic reforms have engendered (Guo 2004; Kim 2005; McMillan and Woodruff 2002).

It is broadly agreed that the first group of new rich to emerge from market reforms was the small-scale individual business people (*getihu*) during the late 1970s and early 1980s. They were mainly urban unemployed and small-scale business people who were uneducated, limited in economic scale and activity and not permitted to employ more than seven workers. Wealth accumulation during this period relied heavily on small trade speculation (Gold 1991; Hershkovitz 1985; Young 1995). They were followed into the ranks of the new rich by entrepreneurs based in rural township and village enterprises (TVEs) from the early 1980s to the early 1990s who rapidly developed China's manufacturing base. Starting during the 1990s, a third group of successful entrepreneurs emerged from the construction and resources industries, and they were rapidly followed by others engaged in more speculative activities such as real estate and finance, especially stock market related (Tomba 2004: 5; Hong 2004: 26–7).

The popular explanation for the success of China's entrepreneurs has always been their personal attributes and mindsets, based on hard work, resilience, and self-help. Some scholars have argued that the hardships of the pre-1978 era produced a generation of entrepreneurs who are inured to hard work, willing to endure hardship, and eager to pursue opportunity. They learned from the hard knocks and hard work in their early careers. With diligence and attention to regulations, business trends, and competitors on an ongoing basis, they have been able to seize business opportunities, provide for new customer needs, and make new resources available. The successful PRC entrepreneurs appear passionate, committed, observant, driven, talented, and relentless. They have been invariably described as 'self-made men and women' (A. Chen 2002: 413; Djankov *et al.* 2006a: 348; Hong 2004: 26; Santoro 2000: 265; Sull and Wang 2005; Szelenyi and Kostello 1996: 1082; Tomba 2004: 5; K Yang 2004: 371).

Cross-national research has shown that compared to non-entrepreneurs, both Russian and Chinese entrepreneurs have more entrepreneurs in their families and among childhood friends; value work more relative to leisure; and have higher wealth ambitions. Russian entrepreneurs have had a better educational background and their parents are more likely to be the members of the Communist Party than their Chinese counterparts. In comparison, Chinese entrepreneurs are more risk-taking and greedy, and have more entrepreneurs among their childhood friends than the Russians (Djankov *et al.* 2006b: 352).

The economic successes of PRC entrepreneurs has been explained through reference to their social capital, broadly defined in terms of their people skills and extensive networks with major players in the market economy. An example of the consequences of this line of argumentation is entrepreneurs' access to loans and investments. Research has found that 'strong ties between entrepreneurs and venture capitalists have significant direct effects on investment process decisions such as contractual covenants, investment delivery, and venture valuation' (Batjargal and Liu 2004: 159).

The role of the state in the growth of private entrepreneurship has also been emphasised. It is argued that:

> the rise of the urban private economy as part of the reform package has been mostly a product of the Party-state policy and placed under tight government control ... the nascent entrepreneurial class in a situation in which political protection and favor proved, if not crucial, important for its economic successes ... Throughout the reform process, therefore, China's private businesses must rely heavily upon arbitrary political power to survive and prosper.
>
> (A. Chen 2002: 405–6)

The Chinese Party-state's influence on the fortunes of private entrepreneurs is a matter of some debate. Some scholars have argued that market reforms in urban areas can be seen as decentralised marketisation in which substantial regulatory power is delegated from the central government to local governments. One consequence has been that laws are often non-existent or not enforceable. Thus, entrepreneurs face constant risks of expropriation and discrimination since they cannot rely on the legal system to protect their private property. Another consequence is that local government has been empowered to decide a wide-range of issues such as the freedom from formal regulatory frameworks, informal levies, intellectual property rights protection, and the use of local resources. Local officials have not been reluctant to exploit their empowerment to regulate entrepreneurial behaviour, both to increase local fiscal revenue or for personal gain (Bai *et al.* 2006; Bardhan 1997; Gibb and Li 2003).

Some researchers have highlighted the prevalence of cronyism and bureaucratic rent seeking in the reform era, where private entrepreneurs have had to maintain intricate networks of mutual obligations with local power holders for survival and growth. The private economy has been under-girded by social networks that have converted power into wealth. 'Entrepreneurs set up a special coffer to feed the officials, who use part of the "donated" money to bribe their superiors for job security or promotion.' In turn, they let the entrepreneurs enjoy business favours, tax-breaks, regulatory rulings, and other supports from local officials. Local officials have strong 'incentives to boost the private economy, whose profits they share as part of hidden personal income.' Accordingly:

> A large portion, if not a majority, of the bourgeois have prospered from the commercial privileges deriving from political lineage. They are essentially a parasitic appendage of corrupt and unrestricted political power and have a taken-for-granted personal stake in preventing regime change
>
> (Root 1996: 741)

Other research has emphasised that local government officials have influenced the growth of private entrepreneurship not only as referee but also as active players in market activities. Media commentators have written that more than 90 percent of the new rich are 'children of senior Communist Party officials. In Guangdong province, 12 of the major property-development companies are owned by the offspring of senior officials. In booming Shanghai, nine of the 10 largest property companies are reportedly owned by senior officials' children' (Jones 2007: 17). These companies have seemingly thrived upon their political resources through insider information, tax exemptions, and business concessions.

Research has generally highlighted the ways in which officials, if not the Party-state per se, is involved in enterprise development. There are claims that a large number of local officials in positions of authority have their own private companies registered under the names of family members. There are also claims that officials tend to reciprocate favours by granting privileges and benefits to one another's enterprises under their jurisdiction. It is also observed that entrepreneurs with higher social status enjoy better protection of their private property (A.Chen 2002: 419; Tomba 2004: 4; Tsai 2005: 1136; Bai *et al.* 2006; Dickson 2003; Wank 1999). At least one scholar has asserted that officials as 'parasitic' entrepreneurs might outnumber the genuinely self-made entrepreneurs (A.Chen 2002: 411).

There are three key characteristics about the development of private entrepreneurship to be derived from even such a brief overview. The first is that many private entrepreneurs are involved in small-scale businesses that do little more than clear their costs. The second is that there is a developmental aspect to the evolution of private enterprises during the reform era. In the early years, individual businesses were smaller and less complex than the private enterprises emerging during the late 1990s and into the twenty-first century. The third is that the relationships between enterprises and politics, and between entrepreneurs and the Party-state are both close and ambiguous. The extent of this proximity and the nature of this relationship is a major topic explored in many of the contributions to this volume.

Professionals and managers

In addition to private entrepreneurship, human capital has become a key determinant of entry to the new rich since the beginning of the 1990s. This largely explains the growth of large numbers of professionals and managers in the PRC. Professionals and skilled employees had been seen as 'perennial under-achievers well into the reform era.' With the passage of time 'the picture of the high achievers has become more complex and has begun to include a larger group of urban professionals and skilled employees in both the public and private sector' (Tomba 2004: 10–11).

Human capital became a key determinant of individual economic successes after 1990 for a variety of reasons. One explanation may be found in market mechanisms: Nee's market transition theory argues for increasing returns to human capital such as education and skills as the market economy becomes more established in China. Indeed, it has been noted that shortages

> in specific areas of expertise contributed to the competitiveness of professionals' salaries. Analysis of salaries in different professions shows that skills often provide higher remuneration than administrative responsibility. High-in-demand occupations such as telecommunication technicians (42,305 yuan/year), software engineers (33,201 yuan/year) and even bank clerks (24,100 yuan/year) today earn higher salaries than the average state factory director (24,070 yuan/year)
>
> (Tomba 2004: 21)

In addition, some professionals were able to take second jobs since their expertise and special skills were in great demand – a part explanation of why their disposable income might be higher than their nominal salaries.

Global capitalism has been recognised as another key element in increasing the returns for human capital. One PRC commentary claimed that

> Since China's entry to the World Trade Organisation, the compensation for a range of talented people has generally risen by a considerable margin, especially for people working in high-tech industries. Experts estimate that people with high-level skills in international finance and trade, the IT industry, medical and biological industries and foreign languages will be in great demand. As a result, the price of talent will certainly soar. Moreover, the differences in levels of compensation will continue to grow for people with similar levels of education but who work in different professions or have different capabilities
>
> (Five Groups 2002)

Scholars outside the PRC have noted that interaction between foreign and Chinese firms increases the use of meritocratic hiring and promotion practices and enhances respect for the rule of law (Guthrie 1999; Rosen 1999). As a result international trade and investment 'helps create a middle class with power and interests independent of the state' since multinational corporations such as Motorola and General Motors have invested huge sums of capital in China 'in the hopes of capturing consumer and business markets'. In order to attract and retain talented workers, these foreign firms have paid wages far above the norm and offered a high-quality working environment, thereby creating a middle class meritocracy in the PRC. Their workforces include the young, the skilled, and educated workers. 'In China today, an MBA is replacing membership in the Communist Party as a qualification of success for young, talented, and ambitious men and women.' These middle class employees acquire 'wealth, status, and power through individual merit and hard work rather than through Communist Party connections' (Santoro 2000).

Some scholars have argued that the state has also played a role in the rising trend toward meritocracy in China since it has developed a desire to foster a more efficient and dynamic bureaucracy. Merit-based hiring procedures have been extended from elite recruitment at the national level throughout the system down to local levels, especially with regard to positions that require formal credentials and expertise (Lee 1991; Walder 1995; Zang 2001; Zang 2004). Employment is education-driven and employees in public administrative units 'are recruited today on the basis of examinations and educational credentials' (Tomba 2004: 10–11). Moreover, the government has repeatedly raised the salaries, improved work conditions, and professionalised the appointment process for officials (Tomba 2004: 25).

This emphasis on a state-driven meritocracy is however not universally accepted. Others maintain that it is unsubstantiated and they have even downplayed the role of market mechanisms in the growth of middle class professionals in China. Instead, they have argued that the emergence of middle class professionals

> has been as much the outcome of the social engineering project of the contemporary reformist state and its agencies as it has been a consequence of the opening up of the economy and society ... the emergence of a professional middle class was also the consequence of intensive, ideologically justified and coordinated policymaking, which manifested itself in a steep rise in public sector salaries and a protection of the welfare privileges of the skilled, publicly employed urban population
> (Cao 2004)

There can be no doubt that state intervention has led to a heavily subsidised home purchase scheme for employees in the public sector. Housing has become very expensive in urban China. Buying a home has become a major concern for anyone wishing to climb the ladder of social status in China today. The link between public employment, the state and the status achievement is also often explicitly central to the experience of homeowners in China. Those with a relatively high status position in the public sector have been privileged (either directly or indirectly) in the access to real estate assets and have formed the mainstream of the propertied class in China due to assistance from state-owned real-estate developers and state commercial banks. It has been found that 'high-income households in Beijing have a higher than average number of their members employed in the state sector, as well as a higher level of education and professional training' (Tomba 2004: 16–7).

Future rulers, present lives

This Introduction has considered past research on China's new rich. In the process, it has attempted to outline the social and historical background against which their emergence should be considered, as well as some of the key concepts which surround discussion of the phenomenon. In the pages that follow the various authors build on that foundation to examine in separate sections how the new rich interact with structures of class, status, and power; the development of specific component parts of the new rich; and selected aspects of new rich life-style and behaviour.

The first section on *Class, Status and Power* considers the political, ideological, social and cultural impact of the new rich. All four of the chapters in this section are centrally concerned with the issues of class identity and formation, though approaching the topic from different perspectives. In the process, each engages with the wider literature in the social sciences and cultural studies, in particular interrogating the dynamics of class.

David Goodman examines the extent to which the PRC's new rich are the new middle class, as is often claimed, concluding that social change has been much more complex. He interrogates the role and characteristics of the middle class through the evidence of a series of surveys of new rich entre-preneurs in different parts of the PRC (Zhejiang, Shanxi, Qinghai, Sichuan, and Hainan Provinces) since the early 1990s. He points out that somewhat paradoxically the PRC produced a managerial state-sponsored middle class from the 1950s on, with an enterprise-developing middle class only emer-ging after the mid-1980s. Moreover, in terms of hierarchies of wealth, status and power he argues that the new rich represent not just a significant com-ponent of the current ruling class, but perhaps more significantly highlight the dimensions for the long-term future.

Yingjie Guo investigates the paradoxes inherent in the ideological formations of a communist party encouraging capitalist development. Through a tex-tual analysis of the pronouncements on class and social change emanating from both the Party-state and academics and political commentators in the PRC he both acknowledges the difficulties in squaring the Marxist circle, and yet at the same time provides a deeper insight into the political pro-cesses involved. Capitalism can be encouraged if it is led by a 'middle class' because the term not only implies the greatest good of the greatest number and entails description of an olive-shaped social structure, it also speaks to an essential egalitarianism inherent within the Chinese Communist movement.

Xiaowei Zang points out that while questions of stratification and mobi-lity in the PRC have been some of the most researched in recent years, there has been relatively little enquiry into the status acquisition of the new rich. His chapter details the ways in which in contrast to other societies wealth acquisition in the PRC has not been accompanied by increased social status. Indeed, on the contrary there has been the development of considerable 'wealth hatred'. Zang examines this phenomenon and concludes (somewhat reinforcing Guo's point in the previous chapter) that there is a social reluc-tance to accept the legitimacy of extremes of individual wealth. While this 'wealth hatred' may be the immediate and short-term product of the tran-sition to a market economy, it remains the case that in that short-term many others in society feel short-changed by the activities of private entre-preneurs whatever the wider benefits.

Stephanie Hemelryk Donald and Zheng Yi move from a consideration of 'taste structure' (as manifested in educational choices) to a discussion of how class is constructed in a post-socialist society. They focus on the con-struction of the idea of 'the middle market' (again reinforcing the central point of Guo's earlier chapter) to explain how taste is both formulated and legitimated. The analysis identifies an alternative (non-CCP) materialism that replaces political activism with middle class contentment. The PRC's new rich may be a middle class (and that remains contested) yet even so they are not a middle class as elsewhere with commitment to values such as liberal democracy and even apathy.

The second section of the volume turns to focus on *Entrepreneurs, Man-agers and Professionals*. The chapters in this section deal in some detail with specific elements of the new rich, but there are common experiences and concerns. Regardless of occupation and the relationship to entrepreneurial activities, human capital development is central to any analysis of the new rich. Similarly the influence of and interaction with the Party-state cannot be ignored in seeking to understand the development of enterprises, and the behaviour of owners, managers and professionals. A concern with status is possibly a more interesting common theme that faces the entrepreneurs, managers and professionals. Entrepreneurs are worried about how to gain a status they think they lack; managers and professionals to retain status they see slipping away; and women to work their ways carefully through male status concerns (especially their husbands).

Colin Hawes examines how the CEOs and other senior executives of China's large corporations, both state-controlled and privately-managed, are not content to be seen merely as materially rich: they also wish to become culturally rich too, and to raise the cultural level of their employees and even of their customers. Hawes provides various reasons for this fixation of corporate executives on culture, which range from business factors and traditional Chinese concepts of the 'scholar merchant' (*rushang*) to government pressure on CEOs to improve their firms' corporate culture and to find a new role for Party organisations within their corporations.

Beatriz Carrillo also deals with entrepreneurs searching for social status and recognition. She examines the development of small and medium scale entrepreneurs in a North China county (Hongtong County, Shanxi Province) where coal mining and associated industries dominate. Carrillo's analysis builds on Zang's earlier examination of entrepreneurs' failure to attract the high status that wealth generation and indeed enterprise bring in other societies. In the case of Hongtong the 'dirty' nature of money making is exacerbated by the physical dirtiness of the coal industry. One way forward attempted by successful entrepreneurs is to use their surplus to develop new initiatives in industries in 'clean' or socially useful activities, such as schools and hospitals.

Minglu Chen raises questions of gender and examines a special cohort within China's New Rich – women entrepreneurs. She reports on interviews with women in Shanxi, Hainan and Sichuan Provinces. The chapter explains the dynamic connections between these women's accumulation of personal wealth, their role in local politics, and their continued commitment to certain 'traditional values'. It illustrates that while signifying a new degree of participation in the public domain, the increased personal wealth of these women, and their participation in local politics, has not freed them from the traditional gendered expectation that women should keep to the private domain. At the same time though her research also shows that wealth has loosened the interviewees' subservience to both household tasks and their husband (and his family). Family though remains crucial to understanding the dynamics of women's role in enterprise development. One important suggestion from this research is the role of family-based networks of power at the local level.

Ivan Cucco and Jingqing Yang both examine the careers of professionals in the rapidly changing socio-economic environment. Ivan Cucco considers the professionalisation of managers and technical specialists, particularly in the high-tech, post-manufacturing enterprises of Nanjing. Despite superficial similarities with Burnham's managerial elite, this research argues that China's current professional classes have modes of organisation and places in the economic hierarchy that deliver markedly less autonomy. On the contrary, particularly in the absence of welfare capitalism and with current emphases on managerialism, Cucco identifies the professional classes as the mechanism for bridging the public-private divide.

While Cucco places the new professionals, especially human resource managers, in the ranks of the new rich, Jingqing Yang in his study of university professors, doctors and lawyers is more circumspect. Yang explores the institutional and policy changes that have affected the economic development of professionals in the reform era, seeing this development in its historical context, considering first the economic conditions of intellectuals and professionals in the pre-reform era, and then the general decline of the economic status of professionals in the reform era and the opportunities that economic reform has presented. He analyses the development of each of the three professions in turn, identifying the paths that lead most usually to individual wealth, emphasising that individual wealth for professors and doctors is highly contingent. It is only in the legal profession that individual wealth is likely to remain legitimate and obtainable, and even then only for a small minority or practitioners under specific circumstances.

The third and final section deals with aspects of the *Lifestyle* of the new rich. This section is necessarily less than comprehensive in its description of new rich activities, and the issues they face as they make their life choices. Relatively absent is leisure, a rapidly growing area of activity, and the international outreach of the new rich. For example, in Kalmar in Sweden, the two have recently begun to be combined as infrastructure is being developed to attract and entertain China's new rich. As Donald and Zheng outlined in an earlier chapter, the search for status, and the sense of a performative middle class taste permeate these various accounts of new rich activities. Most importantly there is a strong self-consciousness of middle class making.

Luigi Tomba and Beibei Tang examine the impact of housing reform in one specific area of Shenyang, in Northeast China, a former rust-belt, heavy industrial area. It focuses on the transformative power of the new rich, who produce value through consumption: in this case by turning a rapidly becoming run-down district of the city and turning it into a new rich ghetto. It firmly identifies the community of interest that brings the local levels of the Party-state together with the new rich, with the former effectively preferring the new, white-collar, professional and entrepreneurial urban elites to the area's more traditional working class.

Jewellery is associated with wealth and in her chapter Carolyn Cartier examines the demand for fine jewellery and diamonds generated by China's new rich. This is most definitely not about ordinary jewellery though, or the all-class love affair with old gold. The point of Cartier's chapter is to emphasise the design and fashion consciousness elements of these high-level jewellery artefacts, and in the process both place and the internationalised nature of the business are important. For a PRC member of the new rich, Shanghai is the place to buy to impress, yet from Shanghai it is often still Hong Kong; even though that is changing rapidly. Moreover, there is a cosmopolitan edge to these cultural negotiations, and yet one in which it is the cosmopolitan Chinese who has pride of place.

Louise Edwards challenges recent notions that despite economic growth there has been little change in the workings of the Chinese state. Stability in the overarching political structure does not mean stasis in the relationship between the people and the Party-state. In particular, as she argues that, through a case study of recent activism on women's issues, a new space has emerged for issue-based politics, as the result of the new rich's perception of their political engagement with the Party-state. Issue-based politics, such as campaigns against sexual violence, female infanticide or domestic violence, serve to consolidate broad regime stability by presenting each problem as discrete and solvable within the current political structures. Far from being challenged by these movements, the CCP may not simply treat their activism as an exercise in repressive tolerance, but rather be prepared to see that the activists' goals may fit well into the Party's agenda to encourage greater 'social harmony'.

While domestic servants have come to be very much one marker of middle class status in contemporary China, the maid is often absent from the consciousness of the new rich in whose household they often live, as well as work. In her chapter that describes life in the new rich home, centring on the role of domestic service, Wanning Sun explains both the indispensability and invisibility of the maid. 'Dirt' is the key to understanding: the maid is there to clear up the dirt and take on the less clean tasks; at the same time, the maid is an interloper, a source of disease and dirt that may come into the home as the not-quite-family member enters the house or apartment. As Sun reminds the reader through her comparative perspectives on social change in other countries at earlier times, one becomes middle class by behaving middle class, and one way to do that is to employ domestic servants.

The final chapter deals with the relationships between money, sexual morality and gender. Following on from Xiaowei Zang's earlier chapter, and with a more specific focus, Elaine Jeffreys highlights how the new rich have become seen as both the most advanced productive forces in the PRC but also its most serious moral corrupters. She argues that the new rich cannot be regarded as replacement for the CCP in the vanguard of progressive social change under these conditions.

The new rich have already had a substantial impact not only on China's economic development, but also on its social and political environment, as the chapters in this volume demonstrate. The speed of change remains rapid, making change difficult to identify, understand and manage. This volume represents a first detailed look at China's new rich. There remain though many elements of the new rich, their activities and behaviour to be considered in further detail. These include the new rich in the rapidly emerging financial sector; not only in banking and insurance, but also those associated with stock markets in Shanghai and Shenzhen. As already noted, new forms of consumption, particularly in the luxury goods markets and leisure industries are increasingly the focus of the new rich's disposable income. It is also clear that the new rich are moving beyond their domestic boundaries to engage internationally for business, life and leisure in new and different ways.

Part I
Class, status and power

1 Why China has no new middle class

Cadres, managers and entrepreneurs[1]

David S. G. Goodman

The prime beneficiaries and the agents of the rapid economic growth in the People's Republic of China (PRC) since the early 1980s have been a whole range of new entrepreneurs who in large and small ways; in retail, manufacturing and services; have invented, invested, owned, and managed their way to varying degrees of wealth. Since the late 1980s and early 1990s, these entrepreneurs have been increasingly described as China's new 'middle class' or 'middle classes' by academic and more general media commentators outside the PRC (Glassman 1991; White, Howell and Shang 1996; Goodman 1999a; Lardy 2007). In the process a parallel is clearly being implied between the PRC's socio-economic development since the late 1970s and the consequences of industrialisation in Europe over a longer period starting at the beginning of the nineteenth century.

While the rhetoric of convergence between once apparently widely divergent social and economic systems is comforting, and is an oft-repeated subtheme inside and outside the PRC, this assumption of equivalence is also easily rushed. The middle class is not a simple concept but is made up of different elements and is itself often regarded as stratified: one clear reason that reference is also often made to the middle classes in the plural. Interestingly the middle classes are now generally seen in industrialised societies as the large, middle sectors of contemporary hierarchies of economic wealth, social status and political power, identified as much by their consumption and adherence to style as in socio-economic terms (Robison and Goodman 1996a).

Current conceptualisations of the middle classes are related to but somewhat different from the emergence of the concept of middle class, and its origins, in the European context. Though the concept is necessarily complex, it can be broadly reduced to two general and historically determined definitions: the bourgeoisie, and (separately) the managers of the modern state. Starting with the early nineteenth century, the bourgeoisie were a new middle class created by the process of industrialisation. They were the captains of industry whose ownership of the means of production – extraction, processing and manufacturing activities – drove industrialisation, and they became a middle class because they were neither the landed aristocracy on the one hand, nor ordinary townspeople on the other. As industrialisation deepened towards the end of the nineteenth and beginning of the twentieth centuries both economic enterprises and the modern state itself became more complex, producing managerial and professional classes. These too were a new middle class because while they neither owned capital nor controlled the state, they served either or both and derived their income and status from service and management rather than ownership of the means of production (Burnham 1972).

In both cases the significance of these new middle classes is as much if not more political as it is social and economic. The demand for a widening of the franchise and the emergence of liberal democracy during the first half of the nineteenth century in Northwest Europe are often seen as necessary results of the emergence of the bourgeoisie. The managerial revolution of the first half of the twentieth century is part and parcel of the development of mass society, mass politics and the welfare state (Kornhauser 1959; Galbraith 1967).

While the PRC has clearly seen the emergence of new categories of entrepreneurs, the key question is the extent to which these new rich can be identified as the equivalent of the middle classes in other, earlier socio-economic contexts (Pearson 1997; Wank 1999; Guthrie 1999; Dickson 2003a). There is certainly a growing discourse of middle classness in domestic self description of social change in the PRC (Qin 1999; Li 2004; Zheng 2004a; Zheng 2004b; Lu 2002; *Xinhua* 18 June 2007) as well as (as already noted) from the outside. To some extent and from some perspectives regardless of socio-economic construction the assumption of middle class behaviour, especially in patterns of consumption, is not just reasonable it is also to be expected as a function of globalised commercialisation. Gucci, Loewe and Louis Vuitton are brands targeted at the wealthy consumer in Shanghai and Beijing as much as in Milan, London and New York.

At the same time, there is room for caution lest too much is read into the PRC's processes of social change. Identification of middle class behaviour in the contemporary PRC does not necessary entail an equation with earlier middle classes in other societies, and it is clearly just as necessary to isolate differences as well as similarities. In particular, there are three aspects of the emergence of the PRC's new rich categories of entrepreneurs – which separately highlight their relationship to social status, economic wealth and political power – that suggest they are less the new middle class than a future central part of the ruling class. In a sense, the PRC had a managerial revolution before a bourgeois revolution (though of course history does not start in 1949) with the creation of managerial and professional classes as part of the development of the modernising state during the 1950s. Certainly the entrepreneurs of the post-1978 era include not just the comfortably well off but also more dramatically the rich and the super-rich. At the same time, they have been and remain unlike the European bourgeoisie of the first half of the nineteenth century in the extent to which they have emerged from and have close relationships with the established political system.

The PRC and the middle class

It is considerably easier to regard the new rich of the post-1978 PRC as equivalent to a European or North American middle class if modernisation is dated only from the post-Mao era. However, the sustained economic development experienced since the early 1980s is not China's first taste of modernisation. Though modernisation is clearly a contested concept, in broad terms it is possible to identify three eras of industrialisation and modernisation in China's twentieth century experience.

The Republican Era saw sustained attempts at modernisation in various parts of China under both warlord rule and colonial influence (Spence 1990; Sheridan 1975; Gillin 1967; Kapp 1973; Henriot 1993). This included the development of the iron and steel industry, large-scale coal mining, a machinery industry, a textile industry, financial institutions, shipping and railways, as well as an exceptionally large cigarette industry. Largely because much of this economic activity was externally sourced, owned or supported, by the early 1920s some of China's various economies were considerably better integrated into the world economy than was to be the later case from 1937 through to 1978 (Richardson 2005). Even mountainous counties some distance from the coast, such as Liaoxian in North China's hinterland (on the borders of Shanxi and Hebei Provinces) were supplying products to external markets by the 1930s (Xu and Chen 1992: 556).

Of probably greater importance to understanding the most recent political economy of change, the establishment of the PRC once the new regime was secured ushered in a renewed and sustained industrialisation and modernisation, after the dislocation of the 1930s and 1940s. The years from 1952 to 1978 were not without their economic problems, notably during the early 1960s when the economy threatened to implode in the wake of the Great Leap Forward, or during the height of the Cultural Revolution when production was impeded. Nonetheless, the PRC economy achieved an overall 6 percent per annum growth rate throughout the Mao-dominated era (Ma 1990: 6).

At the heart of this growth was the development of a modern state, including the construction of communications networks, and the provision of education, health and welfare infrastructure, if more focussed on the urban than the rural areas. Certainly the bourgeoisie and generally the large-scale owners of property were dispossessed during a series of campaigns designed to ensure the socialisation of the means of production during 1952–5 (Gardner 1969). At the same time the 1950s saw the growth of managerial and professional occupations in the service of the new state, its administration and economic management, who in many ways can be regarded as the backbone middle classes of the PRC: clearly not a term that would have been employed in the PRC itself during an era dominated by the ideological formulations of Marxism-Leninism-Mao Zedong Thought. They were and to a large extent still remain, both socially and individually, those who were the instruments of the state and capital as opposed to strategic decision-makers or front-line producers.

The establishment and development of the new state required a sizeable force of officials. While considerable attention always focuses on the cadres and leading cadres who peopled the Party-state, the new bureaucracy also engendered a large army of lower order officials and administrators, referred to in Chinese as 'petty cadres' (*xiao ganbu*) (Barnett 1967). To a large extent these petty cadres were the essence of the bureaucratic state established by the Chinese Communist Party (CCP). The more senior cadre positions were most usually filled by those who had joined the CCP and the revolution before the end of the War of Resistance in 1945. As the Communist movement grew during the Civil War these individuals attained positions of leadership which then transferred to the new state in and after 1949 as the CCP expanded from North and Northeast China to occupy the whole of the country and they effectively became the new ruling class (Teiwes 1967; Goodman 1980; Bo 2002). Under their leadership, the Party-state had responsibility not only for state administration and regulation of social life, it also provided social and welfare services, and ran the economy. Economic production was completely state directed even though only part of the economy was managed immediately through government departments. The officials, administrators and managers who staffed this extensive bureaucracy were initially hired locally during the early 1950s and while that practice continued, it was supplemented by the allocation of university students on graduation to positions anywhere in the PRC (Whyte and Parish 1984).

Alongside and sometimes overlapping with the bureaucracy of state socialism the new state also ensured the further development of the professions, which expanded way beyond their beginnings in the Republican Era. Teachers, doctors and engineers were the most numerous as the modernising state expanded its activities and reach. At the same time, the 1950s also saw the emergence of career paths for other professions including lawyers and economists, albeit heavily politicised. These intellectual middle classes were precisely those who were criticised during the Cultural Revolution in the late 1960s for having become the 'stinking ninth category of counter revolutionaries'. Many lost their positions and possessions, at least temporarily until the 1970s, were sent to the countryside or the front-line-of-production for 're-education' and some were physically abused (Esherick, Pickowicz and Walder 2006; MacFarquhar and Schoenhals 2006).

The PRC's drive for further industrialisation and modernisation after 1978 appealed to and to some extent relied on these managerial middle classes and their families. Just as the reputations of leading cadres removed during the Cultural Revolution, and sometimes the individuals themselves, came for the most part to be gradually restored through the 1970s, so too middle class reputations rose again. The process of restoring their positions in society and employment had already started well before Mao's death in September 1976. However, the late 1970s saw a more complete and explicit restoration, often including the payment of reparations. Education and training were generally put back on the agenda by the Party-state as it sought economic growth, and the various types of professional knowledge and expertise were to be once again mobilised to the PRC's developmental goals.

Entrepreneurs and enterprise development

The identification of professional and managerial middle classes in the PRC does not necessarily mean that the entrepreneurs to have emerged as a result of the economic reforms introduced since 1978 are not also middle class. It does however require that they be examined as such more closely both in terms of the PRC's development and in the wider comparative context. In particular, it draws attention to the specific characteristics of the new entrepreneurs as a middle class, and their relationship to the professional and managerial classes. Clearly, these two broad social categories may have much in common, not the least of which is a shared set of life-style aspirations, including living in one's own house, having a car, ensuring private education for one's children and engaging in leisure time activities that may include holidays elsewhere (Goodman 1998). It is also possible that members of the pre-1978 professional and managerial middle classes transformed themselves into new-style entrepreneurs during the 1980s. At the same time, acknowledgment that there has been and remains a state-sponsored professional and managerial middle class does suggest that the new entrepreneurs may not only be a different kind of middle class but also that the processes of middle class formation and conceptualisation in the PRC may be somewhat different to those that occurred in the earlier European context.

Since the early 1990s, a series of interviews of entrepreneurs have been undertaken in different parts of China. These have included surveys in Hangzhou during 1991–3 (Goodman 1996); Shanxi Province during 1996–8 (Goodman 2001) and 2000–2 (Goodman 2006); Qinghai Province during 2001–3 (Goodman 2005); and in Jiaocheng County, Shanxi during 2003–4 Qiongshan City, Hainan during 2004, and Mianyang City, Sichuan Province during 2004–5 (Goodman 2007). Entrepreneurs have been asked about their social backgrounds (and that of their families), their careers and their entrepreneurial activities. In terms of middle class formation, there are three clear conclusions highlighted in each set of interviews. The first is that the new entrepreneurs are a complex and not a simple social category, including not only owner-operators in the private sector but also managers of state-, collectively-, privately-, and foreign-owned enterprises, as well as oftentimes confusing combinations of these various sub-categories (Nee 1992). The second relates to the wealth of the new entrepreneurs. While there were some disastrously unsuccessful entrepreneurs and others who were only of moderate wealth, many were not just comfortably well off by the standards of their local economy when interviews were conducted, but were clearly the rich and the super-rich. This conclusion draws attention to the parallels between the contemporary new entrepreneurs in the PRC and the nineteenth century European bourgeoisie. The third overall conclusion limits such arguments by highlighting the close institutional and associational links between the new entrepreneurs and the Party-state: they are neither independent of nor excluded from the political establishment, which on the contrary seeks actively to incorporate them if there is no pre-existing relationship.

The notion of any *ab initio* industrialisation in the PRC since 1978 is rapidly dispelled by consideration of the processes that generated new entrepreneurs in the reform era. The model of a single individual who has an idea, seeks capital, and establishes an enterprise to develop an invention or innovation is only broadly applicable in the PRC (Krug 2004). Broadly speaking the new enterprises that have emerged during the last three decades have emerged in one of four ways, differentiated by source of the initial capital and resources.

Historically, the introduction of greater measures of market determination and the development of new types of enterprise started in the rural areas, or more accurately the sub- and peri-urban rural districts of cities. Through the 1980s and 1990s Town and village enterprises (TVEs) became the mainstay of the collective sector of the economy, and grew out of rural economic activities and perceptions of spare labour or other forms of underutilised capacity (Oi 1989; Henriot and Lu 1996; White 1998; Oi 1999; Whiting 2001; Yep 2003). In the Hangzhou area, one village transformed its machinery workshop, which had access to wire products, into a production line for using wire to produce elaborate gift cards for the Japanese market. It was soon so successful that the production line became a large-scale factory and the village ceased agricultural production. In Yuci (in Shanxi Province) another village agricultural machinery workshop turned to aluminium radiator production; in Yingchuan (also in Shanxi) surrounded by coal-mining, coal by-products, particularly plastics, were produced. These enterprises and their development were led by local individuals, often the former workshop manager or some other level of local leadership who was able to mobilise their fellow villagers. Though technically managers and not owners of the TVEs, many behaved economically, socially and politically as if they were.

The state sector of the economy saw similar processes at work. The previous system of state socialism had been characterised by large-scale production and inherent economic inefficiencies. Increasingly after 1984, economic reform inevitably resulted in managers seeking economic efficiencies and partly in consequence new opportunities to use the assets they controlled. In a variety of ways, state assets were developed or built on to produce an economic return. Often subsidiary companies operating in the collective sector of the economy were established by the state owned enterprises or department of the state administration (Blecher 1991; Duckett 1998; You 1998).

In North China an iron and steel works at the start of the reform era was a complex organisation that like other large-scale, state-owned enterprises at that time attempted to meet most of the social and welfare needs for its workforce and their dependents. The enterprise had canteens, farmlands to supply the canteens and trucks to transport the agricultural produce to the canteens. Before reform little attention was paid to the low level of economic activity generated by the canteens or the trucking department since they fulfilled their allotted tasks of feeding the workforce and transporting produce to the canteens once a day. With reform, each of these activities was hived off as a separate company, technically owned by the parent state-owned enterprise, but under the control of the previous management who had been assigned to the new collective sector enterprise. Each was provided with a contract to provide services as before but now in order to survive they also had to find additional moneymaking work in the open market. In Hangzhou, the now PRC-wide famous *Wahaha* drink and food company was born from the non-profitable print shop of a secondary school when its managers realised to survive they had to not just diversify but find new economic activities.

Though many of the collective sector enterprises were established by state owned parent enterprises, the reallocation of state assets in these ways also sometimes left less than clear distinctions between ownership and management. State sector enterprise managers who led the way in reforming their companies clearly remained as managers whatever their level of emotional investment in the newly developed undertakings. Managers of new collective sector enterprises that had grown out of state assets on the other hand often, like their semi-rural counterparts, behaved in many ways like owners. In Hangzhou on one occasion, one such entrepreneur was asked if the state assets that had been effectively reassigned to their new style enterprise had been repaid in any way. The response was clear: 'There's no need. These were previously All-people's assets, and we are the people.'

There certainly are private sector owner-operators who have developed their businesses from nothing based on an innovative idea or perceived market opportunity (Young 1995; Garnaut and Song 2003; Dickson 2003a). In the various surveys undertaken since the early 1990s, they have been found in all industrial sectors and activities, including mining and heavy industry, as well as light industry, processing, retail and service industries. In general, most private sector owner-operators remain small-scale. As their business grows and they wish to scale-up the pressure for access to factors of production – investment capital, land, labour and political permission – essentially dictates that the successful private entrepreneur has to surrender part of their equity to local government and incorporation as a collective sector enterprise. As with TVEs and those companies that have developed from within the state sector and state administration, the potential for confusion over ownership and control is often high.

In Hangzhou during the late 1980s, a disgruntled workshop technician left his job to branch out on his own, reckoning that even if his income went down he would be happier working for himself. He established a series of beehives and produced honey, which he sold himself to local restaurants and hotels. After two years, he had managed to pay off his debts and save some capital so he decided to establish his own restaurant. This in turn was a great success leaving him after three years with capital to invest further in a new undertaking. Thinking he would like to move into manufacturing, he looked around for a product, finally deciding to establish a food-processor manufacturing plant. (He had found the machine mentioned in the translation of a Graham Green novel and not knowing what it was had investigated further, realising that there was or would probably be a market in China). Unfortunately as a private entrepreneur he had no access to bank loans and had been denied land to build his factory by the local authority. It was not until he accepted the invitation by the local government to cooperate (and surrender half his equity) in the development of a new collective sector enterprise that he was able to proceed.

In Jiexiu County, Shanxi, Li Anmin, now President and General Manager of the Antai International Enterprise Group Company and one of the province's richest individuals established a coke production company as a private enterprise in 1984. He had been the village accountant in his home village and invested 3,000 *yuan* of his own money, employing 27 of his neighbours. Within ten years the enterprise had become a collective stock company through cooperation with local government and equity from Li's fellow villagers. By the mid-1990s, the company had expanded into other activities, including cement, clothing and retail, employing 3,500 people (Liu *et al.* 1989: 302).

The fourth and final way in which new enterprises have been established is through foreign investment. The scope for foreign investment has been episodically increased since the mid-1980s leaving relatively few areas of the economy totally restricted though regulation remains high. From milk production in Shanxi Province, to luxury wool production in Qinghai Province, to manufacturing in Jiaocheng (Shanxi) and Hangzhou, and retail and services in Qiongshan (Hainan Province) foreign investment has occurred where there are economic opportunities and known relations to the local economy. Somewhat confusingly, state sector enterprises, TVEs, collective sector enterprises, and private companies have all established joint venture operations with external partners. There is equally a variety of ownership relationships attending these foreign funded enterprises. Though all have entrepreneurial managers, in many cases they are not the originator of the idea leading to cooperation.

Entrepreneurs and wealth

Estimating the wealth of the PRC's entrepreneurs is not an easy task. Most have proven themselves understandably somewhat reticent to discuss their wealth at interview. As with business people almost universally there is a tendency to minimise income and earnings because of taxation or local fee regulation. The political climate for business people has certainly improved over the years, and dramatically since the first interviews were conducted in 1991 before Deng Xiaoping had undertaken his 'Inspection Tour of the South' which reignited the pace of economic reform the following year (Goodman 1994a: 113). Nonetheless, the PRC remains a Communist Party-state governed by an ideology which has within recent memory come down very hard not only on business people but on individuals engaging in economic activities for personal profit.

All the same the available evidence would seem to suggest that the new entrepreneurs occupy a position of considerable wealth (Croll 2006: Ch.4). Their patterns of conspicuous consumption were already becoming apparent during the 1990s, in housing, private education for their children, clothing and food (Davis 2000c; Fraser 2000; Lu 2000). Anecdotally these seem to have increased dramatically since 2000 particularly in the growth of leisure activities in the metropolises of Guangdong, Shanghai, Tianjin and Beijing.

Although the entrepreneurs interviewed have generally been reluctant to provide details of their income or earnings, during research in Shanxi in 1996–7 some four in five of those questioned were prepared to estimate their monthly cash income: salary plus bonuses, and additional payments. Table 1.1 provides details of average estimates adjusted to an annual basis and differentiated by categories of entrepreneur and enterprise ownership or management. Members of the professional classes (mainly doctors and lawyers) were interviewed as part of the same research, and their average annual cash income is also provided, together with the provincial average income per capita for 1997.

Table 1.1 Entrepreneurs cash income: Shanxi Province, 1996–7 (yuan)

Category of entrepreneur	Annual cash income
Manager, State owned enterprise	18,627
Manager, collective sector enterprise	17,388
Owner, private enterprise	37,200
Manager, foreign funded enterprise	18,000
Professional	3,700
Provincial average income per capita (1997)	4,762

Source: Interviews, Shanxi 1996–7 (47 managers, state-owned enterprises; 56 managers, collective sector enterprises; 51 owners, private enterprises; 7 managers, foreign-funded enterprises; 11 professionals)

The differences in average earnings between the various categories of the new entrepreneurs and ordinary people indicated in this table are clearly large. Owner-operators in the private sector would seem to have cash earnings almost eight times the provincial average income per capita, and other categories of the new entrepreneurs earn just under four times the provincial average. In Hangzhou in the early 1990s the differences between the new rich and the provincial average was estimated at about 12:1 so these ratios are somewhat lower and may be accounted for by the earlier stage of development of the Shanxi Provincial economy, which had considerably less foreign investment and light industrial development.

Necessarily these figures have to be treated with caution, not simply because of the methods of data gathering, but also as indicators of wealth. Business people often have cost-less (to them personally) access to resources and effectively subsidised income not available to others. Under state socialism, and even under state socialism in transition, similar benefits of food, housing, education, access to transport (especially use of cars) and holidays also applied to almost all those working within the Party-state. It is for example, extremely unlikely that the professionals interviewed during 1996–7 and whose average cash earnings are reflected in Table 1.1 would have had a lower than average standard of living, and would be more likely to share the life-style aspirations of those they came into contact with within the Party-state if not across all the categories of new entrepreneurs.

Another way of attempting to estimate the wealth of the new entrepreneurs would be to consider the flows of money that they control and are ultimately responsible for. Table 1.2 provides details of information revealed through interviews with entrepreneurs in Shanxi (1996–8) about enterprise profits after tax, and in Qiongshan (2004) and Mianyang (2005) about

Table 1.2 Indicators of economic scale: average enterprise profits or turnover (*yuan*)

Location	Date of Interviews	Average income per Capita		
Shanxi	1996–8	4,762 (1997)	Average enterprise profits after tax State enterprises Urban collectives Rural collectives Private enterprises	*Yuan million* 24.3 29.8 4.2 0.3
Qiongshan	2004	12,697	Average enterprise annual turnover	24.0
Mianyang	2005	8,383	Average enterprise annual turnover	58.0

Source: Interviews, Shanxi 1996–8 (230 interviewees); Qiongshan, 2004 (53 interviewees); Mianyang, 2005 (56 interviewees)

annual enterprise turnover. The figures for each locality are contrasted with the appropriate local average income per capita at the time the interviews were undertaken. While the figures presented in Table 1.2 must also be treated with caution, they do serve to underline the key position of the new entrepreneurs in terms of wealth creation, and to indicate considerable disparities in terms of at least wealth management between entrepreneurs and the rest of the population.

Of course, this is not to argue that all entrepreneurs are fantastically wealthy. Those who have been interviewed over the years including a number on the edge of bankruptcy, and at least one once private entrepreneur who was being bailed out by the local government because he was a large-scale employer whose business was in trouble. Others were simply not successful or just ran very modest businesses. Typically, single retail outlets, beauty salons and one-person service industry activities were private enterprises of a small business type to be found almost universally around the world. The averages detailed in Tables 1.1 and 1.2 are derived from a range of earnings and turnover. The Shanxi 1996–7 interviews for example found a private entrepreneur whose annual personal cash income was estimated as low as 3,000 *yuan*, and several others with estimated cash earnings in excess of 70,000 *yuan*.

Entrepreneurs and the Party-state

By any standard, economic development in the PRC – whether in the 1950s or later in the 1980s – fits well into the pattern of late industrialisation identified as having been established by Germany, Japan and Russia during the late nineteenth century. In these countries the state played a central role in industrialisation, as opposed to the laissez-faire capitalism of the earlier European experience based on the protection of the role of the individual outside the state (Kurth 1979). With very few exceptions (White 1998) most research on the socio-economic changes of PRC reform since 1978, and particularly that related to industrialisation (Solinger 1991) highlights the centrality of the Party-state in generating change. Debate centres on the extent to which the Party-state is itself involved in entrepreneurial activities, as opposed to supporting the economic activities of enterprises and entrepreneurs (Blecher 1991; Blecher and Shue 1999; Oi 1999; Duckett 1998).

The relationship between the new entrepreneurs and the Party-state is generally very close, in a number of different ways. Quite apart from the delivery of the policy settings that have made change possible and the government arrangements at the local level that support such development, many of the enterprises for which they are now responsible have grown out of Party-state activities; where new entrepreneurs did not already participate formally in the activities of the Party-state, particularly at leadership levels, they have now found themselves fully incorporated; and many new entrepreneurs would appear to depend on family networks of influence grounded in the Party-state. Remarkably, these networks of relationships and influence even extend to small-scale business people in the private sector of the economy.

As already indicated in the description of the processes of enterprise development during the reform era, it is clear that a large proportion of the new companies either have emerged from the Party-state or have become subject to close local government involvement as they have grown. Ownership relations may be complex and confused, but the continued growth of the subsidiaries of state sector enterprises, state administration-run economic activities, as well as of a collective sector whose theoretical status is long since challenged, provide ample evidence of the continued importance of the economic relationship between the new entrepreneurs and the Party-state outside of the formal plan. For the last decade it has certainly seemed more sensible to regard the collective sector of the economy as the local government sector, rather than as was previously the case that part of the PRC state economy not fully regulated by the central planning process.

One of the consequences of the growth of the collective sector is that the ranks of the new entrepreneurs contain many who have come directly from the professional and managerial middle classes. In the Shanxi Province interviews of 1996–8, 72 percent of the state enterprise managers interviewed had come from a professional or managerial career, as had 79 percent of the managers of urban collectives, 62 percent of managers of rural collectives and 42 percent of private enterprise owner-operators. In interviews of women entrepreneurs in Jiaocheng (2003–4) 19 percent had previously been employed in professional or managerial work. 19 percent of the women entrepreneurs interviewed in Qiongshan (2004) had a similar background, though in Mianyang (2004–5) the figure was 36 percent.

As might be expected given both the structures of state socialism and the ways in which enterprise formation has occurred, a substantial proportion of those working professionally or managerially before becoming entrepreneurs had been employed within the Party-state. At the same time, as already noted, it has been possible for private entrepreneurs to establish themselves independently and to develop their business activities quite successfully before being required to cooperate with local government or other arms of the Party-state if they desired to maintain a growth trajectory. One of the costs expected of private entrepreneurs following this path is that they will take up the challenge of local leadership positions. Often the deal is quite explicit. One coal mine developer in Shanxi told at interview how he not only had to surrender half his equity to the local (county) government in order to be permitted to establish his enterprise (although he argued that the company in his view remained private and his property) but had to be prepared to join the CCP (which he had steadfastly refused to do up until that point) and to hold a leadership position on the county CCP committee.

The requirement on the new entrepreneurs is not always so formal or to fill such an important leadership position within the Party-state. Certainly there has been a growing imperative for successful business people to join the CCP, and indeed one of the key aspects of Jiang Zemin's principle of 'The Three Represents' (incorporated into Party ideology at the 16th CCP Congress in 2002) was the recognition that business people should be both able and encouraged to join the CCP, for the first time since 1955. Most of those who had started out as small-scale private entrepreneurs and grown their business through cooperation with local government would have subsequently been expected to join the CCP though not necessarily to assume positions of leadership. At the same time, there are other ways in which successful new entrepreneurs are encouraged to participate in and support the Party-state, notably through being recognised as provincial and national model entrepreneurs and having their experiences well publicised for emulation through the media, as well as being elected as deputies to county, provincial and national people's congresses. Amongst those interviewed many had been feted as model entrepreneurs, and there were several who had been elected as deputies to provincial people's congresses and two who had been elected to the national people's congress: a one-time university bio-chemist who had returned to his home town in Shanxi to establish an enterprise based on developing coal by-products; and the man who had led the development of the luxury wool processing industry in Qinghai Province.

Although it would seem logical to assume that many of the enterprises to have been established in the era of reform are owned or established by leading cadres, or at least that leading cadres engage in such processes, the evidence of the various interviews undertaken since 1991 is that this has rarely been the case. While it is conceivable that the methods of interviewee selection would have largely precluded the possibility of encountering leading cadres as entrepreneurs, the amount of time spent in fieldwork in given locations and the degree of familiarity developed would have most likely provided some pointers and information to activities of that kind had they been present. There was no such anecdotal evidence generated.

At the same time though, it would appear to be the case that family ties to leading cadres in the Party-state do appear to be important to the process of enterprise formation. The evidence from the Shanxi Province interviews undertaken during 1996–8 is that there is a definite three generation pattern. Leading cadres are generally recruited on intellectual merit from amongst the peasantry, as has long been CCP practice under the PRC. They do their jobs and retire but it is their children who go on to become business people, in particular building on the local relationships and networks of influence that their parents have developed (Goodman 2000). As one entrepreneur who had developed a medium-sized iron and steel plant on a green field site in the locality where his father had been CCP secretary for many years said at interview, when asked about why he had joined one of the state sponsored democratic political parties and not the CCP. 'Why should I join the CCP? My father owns the village.'

Certainly, all the interviews suggest quite strongly that while it is not necessary for the new entrepreneurs to be CCP members themselves it is extremely helpful for close family members to have been members of the CCP and to have been part of the Party-state. Even allowing that the samples chosen for the interviews cannot be held directly representative of either the population as a whole or even necessarily the entrepreneurs in each locality, the proportions of those whose families were linked into various networks of influence of this kind is too high to be ignored. Currently about 5.4 percent of the total population of the PRC is a member of the CCP, though the proportion was somewhat lower during the 1990s.

In the Shanxi 1996–8 interviews, 60 percent of the private enterprise owner-operators were not members of the CCP themselves, but 39 percent had at least one parent who was; 35 percent of the 'managers' of collective sector enterprises were not themselves members of the CCP but again 39 percent had at least one parent who was. Similar proportions are to be found in the other interviews. In Jiaocheng in 2003–4 only 24 percent of the entrepreneurs themselves were either members of the CCP or had some other direct connection to the Party-state, as opposed to 42 percent of their fathers. In Qiongshan (2004) similarly only 23 percent of those interviewed were members of the CCP or had a direct Party-state connection, compared to 40 of their fathers. In the Mianyang interviews (2004–5) the proportions were somewhat higher: 35 percent of those interviewed were members of the CCP or directly involved in the Party-state, while 50 percent of their fathers were. In the Jiaocheng interviews, 58 percent of those interviewed had either a father or a father-in-law (the interviewed entrepreneurs were all women) who were members of the CCP; in Qiongshan the proportion was 55 percent, and in Mianyang 66 percent.

New entrepreneurs and the middle class

Inevitably social change in the PRC is both *suis generis* and reminiscent of processes that have occurred in other political systems. The complications, from a comparative perspective, in analysing the PRC is that the starting point for recent change has been a late industrialising state socialist system that has chosen to introduce market reforms. Ownership, management and control are intertwined in ways that cut across previous analyses of middle (or indeed any other) class behaviour.

On the one hand, the new entrepreneurs are not a middle class of the same kind as the long established professional and managerial class. While many come from managerial backgrounds and occupy positions that revolve around their control of enterprises, many have a far greater emotional investment in their own personal position in the enterprise than this term usually implies. Nor for the most part do new entrepreneurs generally represent the middle-income sections of the population. On the other hand, to the extent that a rising middle class may act with economic development to become the backbone of the ruling class, then it is possible to see similar processes in formation in the PRC. The difference of course is that the PRC remains a Communist Party-state and that the new entrepreneurs far from being excluded have been targeted for incorporation into the political establishment, where they did not emerge from those ranks in the first place.

These observations highlight the objectives of the various discourses of middle classness to be found both inside the PRC and outside. Within the PRC there is a clear ideological constraint in promoting and wealth economic growth, even as the third decade of such policy settings draws to an end. Promoting the new entrepreneurs and the new rich as the new middle classes is somewhat more egalitarian and certainly generally more acceptable than describing them as the super-wealthy or the new bourgeoisie.

Encouraging the development of the new middle classes is also generally a way of promoting individual initiative and self-driven economic growth, as well as wealth creation. In society as a whole, it is probably more comfortable as well as generally more acceptable for individuals to articulate their middle class aspirations than those of being an A-list mega-star. Certainly specifically described middle class aspirations can be portrayed as and allied to modernisation and desirable life-styles through the mass media of communication.

Outside the PRC it does sometimes seem that those who are attempting to interpret its development really do want to be able to find the middle class in its contemporary social change. While a full explanation of that phenomenon lies elsewhere, one clear possibility is that the PRC's transformation is seen as hopeful by those who see an equation between industrialisation and economic development on the one hand and the emergence of a peace-ensuring liberal democracy on the other. The argument that these are people 'just like us' is very seductive, especially if it is delivered without any hint of irony.

Note

1   Research has been supported by the following grants from the Australian Research Counsil: 'Shanxi Province in Reforms' (A10010001); 'Qinghai Province: migration, colonisation and the contest for political space' (A1001003610); and 'China's invisible economic leadership' (DP0344767).

2 Class, stratum and group

The politics of description and prescription

Yingjie Guo

Chinese analysts are agreed that the destratified Chinese society before 1978, comprising two classes (workers and peasants) and one stratum (intellectuals), has stratified into much more complex structure as a result of three decades of reform. This fundamental change has been the subject of burgeoning research in the last decade or so, which has sparked a nation-wide debate on China's actual and ideal social configurations. The most contentious question in the debate is whether stratification is creating relations of conflict and how it is impacting on the country's socio-political order. Though the answers differ vastly, there have been two interrelated trends: One is the increasing downplay of social polarisation; the other is the gravitation of interest towards the middle classes by various names.

Since 2002, interest in the middle classes, and the new rich, has evolved into something approaching a fetish. Not only that, there have been increasingly more claims that a middle class or middle stratum has actually emerged in China (Lu *et al.* 2002; Zheng 2002; Zhang *et al.* 2005; Chen Xiaoya 2002a and 2002b; Luo 2002; Chen *et al.* 2004; Zhou 2005; and He Li 2006). Comments to that effect have prompted sensational writers to announce that China has entered 'the age of the middle class' (Xu 2002). According to Lu *et al.*, as of 2001, 80 million people belonged to the middle stratum of society (2002: 29–30). But Xu Jiang (2002) and Chen *et al.* (2004) estimated that the Chinese middle class was 350 million strong in 2001 and 450 million strong in 2002.

Party-state officials and official media, too, have contributed to the middle class fetish, despite their unease about the term. As early as 2001, the State Information Centre added fuel to the fire by claiming that 200 million Chinese would enter the 'middle stratum' between 2001 and 2006, (*Xinxi shibao* 21 July 2001). In the same year, the forecast of Long Yongtu, then deputy trade minister, made the country buzz with excitement again. By his calculation, China's 'middle-income groups' (*zhongdeng shouru qunti*) by 2010 would include 400 million people (*Xinhua*, 1 December 2001). More recently, the Economic Research Institute of the State Development and Reform Commission has stated that there are about 100 million people in China who can be categorized as 'the middle class group' (*Xinhua* 10 May 2007).

The estimates differ not least because the pundits are not talking about the same thing. Some speak of 'classes'; others, of 'strata'; and still others, of 'groups'. The construction of these categories, accompanied by contestation and conflation, is not simply a matter of academic concern but also one with wider implications. For it is related to the socio-political context and competing values, theories, paradigms and ideological positions. From a constructivist perspective, China's newly devised class schemes are no different from other social facts which, once brought under scrutiny, are no longer available as a topic in their own right, that is as something to be described and explained, but 'instead become an accomplishment of the accounting practices through and by which they are described and explained' (Zimmerman and Weider 1971: 293–4; Colin 1997: 3).

The effect of extrinsic factors on Chinese class schemes can be seen, first of all, from the fact that the shift of academic attention from social polarisation to the middle classes has taken place regardless of much evidence that China has become a highly polarised society and that social conflict is on the rise (Macroeconomic Research Group 2000; *Jingji da cankao* 18 July 2000; Sun 1994 and 2003; Wu and Perloff 2004; Harvey 2006; Zhou 2005; Li Peilin *et al.* 2007; Zhu 2007). It is thus plausible to argue that the shift is not so much attributable to changing realities as to alternative ways of approaching the subject.

To start with, the trend is related to the consensus among Chinese elites of varying persuasions that the middle class or stratum can only be a good thing. The consensus has consolidated since the Chinese Communist Party's (CCP) adoption of a policy aimed at 'controlling the growth of the upper stratum of society, expanding the middle, and reducing the bottom' at its 16th national conference in 2002 (Jiang 2002), and particularly because of the Party's recent emphasis on 'harmonious society'. In addition, it has much to do with the dilemma of China's political elites and social scientists struggling with the various manifestations of the new rich and the new poor. The dilemma is detectable in official communications and academic literature, which typically refer to the poor as 'disadvantaged' groups (*ruoshi qunti*) rather than an underclass and rarely treat the rich as a separate grouping but as interchangeable with the middle class or part of it.

The socio-political context and contestation have added a complex political dimension to the description of social groupings and structures, and descriptions have become entangled in webs of theories, paradigms and ideological positions, as well as prescriptions for idealised social configurations. The 'middle class' in particular, is not so much a uniform, unproblematic concept or an actual, homogeneous grouping as a hodgepodge of intermediate groups, an embodiment of desirable values, and a shorthand for new progressive actors, the mainstream of a harmonious well-off society, or new masters of the country in place of the working class.

New masters of the country: the middle class replaces the working class

There can be no doubt that the CCP's shift from continuous revolution under Mao to economic development and wealth creation in the reform era has dramatically transformed social relations and altered the status order in the country. In Mao's China, the proletariat was said to be the most progressive force of history and the embodiment of the most advanced forces of production. Together with the peasants, they were the 'masters of the country' and constituted 'the regime's only, or surely, most legitimate, political actors' (Solinger 2004: 54–55). Today, the key players in China's socialist market economy are those who generate material wealth by producing, providing and consuming goods and services.

Despite that shift, the current constitutions of the Party and state still define the CCP as the vanguard of the proletariat guided by Marxism, Leninism and Mao-Zedong-Thought, and the PRC as a socialist state under the people's democratic dictatorship led by the proletariat and based on the alliance of the workers and peasants. In one of his keynote speeches in 1989, Jiang Zemin reiterated that the CCP was 'the class organisation of the Chinese working class' and that 'the working class needs the Party and the Party cannot do without the working class' (Jiang in Zhang, 1995: 1673). Though his position on the issue was moderated later, it was not advisable for him, or any other Party leader, to forsake the Party's revolutionary mandate.

However, the reality in the reform era is quite different. In the words of Blecher, 'China's workers have lost their world' (Blecher 2002: 283). Or, as Solinger has put it more strongly, the Chinese proletariat has shifted from master in name and privilege to mendicant (2004: 50). Some may disagree with Blecher and Solinger on this account, but there is no denying that large sections of the working class have lost their privilege and joined the new poor since losing their 'iron rice bowl' and becoming detached form the CCP's historical mission.

The size of these social categories will depend on the definition of poverty. According to official statistics, as of January 2007, China had 23.65 million people below the official poverty line, earning less than 85 US dollars a year (*Xinhua* 18 June 2007). If the poor include the recipients of the government's 'basic subsistence' payments (*dibao*), their number approaches 35 million (*China Civil Affairs Yearbook* 2006). The situation is bleaker in the vast western region, where 9 percent of rural residents and 13.5 percent of urban residents lived below the poverty line in 2006 (Zhao *et al.* 2007: 77). If one counts the unemployed, estimated at a dozen million to 100 million, and those among the 120 million or so migrant workers who are poorly paid or owed wages on a regular basis, the number of the poor increases considerably.[1]

The plight of the new poor may or may not be related to natural inequalities of personal endowments, but they are justified to hold the Party responsible and demand that it live up to its own claims, as it is the CCP which has set in motion and presided over a reform that has taken away their job security and social welfare. The CCP's dilemma was exemplified when, in rising to a defence of a worker brought to trial for leading a violent factory walk-out, a prominent lawyer argued that in the past 'the Communist Party stood alongside the workers in their fight against capitalist exploitation, whereas today the Communist Party is fighting shoulder to shoulder with cold-blooded capitalists in their struggle against the workers' (Cody 2004b).

In the eyes of these and other victims of reform, socialism and the leadership of the proletariat have probably become meaningless, except as a reminder of the CCP's ideological inconsistency or as grounds for challenging the Party. From the Party's viewpoint, it does not matter at all whether the proletariat loses its status as the most progressive force of history; it is all the better that the poor working class no longer constitutes the core of society. For the Party's new mission is economic development, which requires advanced productive forces and consumers with ample purchasing power rather than revolutionary forces ready to wage class struggle. The mission has therefore entailed a fundamental shift from a primary concern with the working class to the principal creators of wealth.

But it remains important for the CCP to pretend that it has not betrayed its own class base or abandoned its ideology. In this regard, it has been plagued by a couple of remarkable contradictions, namely dissynchronised structures of value and a dissynchronised value-environment nexus. The former is exemplified by glaring ideological inconsistencies and the latter by the ideology's failure to legitimise the trial-by-error arrangements by which the Party-state has been adapting to the socio-economic environment. If one agrees with Chalmers Johnson that values and the requirement of environmental adaptation both determine a social structure and produce conflicts within it (Johnson 1966: 35) the contradictions may well be seen as sources of tension and structural determinants of Chinese society.

Instead of revamping the Party and state constitutions in response to new realities, the CCP has chosen to paper over the inconsistencies by redefining key concepts by a sleight of hand. Hence, socialism is no longer characterised by public ownership but by 'three advantages', that is, it should be 'advantageous to the development of productive forces, to increasing the comprehensive strength of a socialist nation, and to raising people's standards of living' (Deng 1993: 372). And the 'vanguard of the proletariat' is accordingly transformed into a Party that represents advanced productive forces, the whole nation, and advanced culture.

Once the advancement of productive forces becomes its overriding objective, the CCP is freed from the shackles of socialist relations of production, or the basic principles of Chinese socialism, as productive forces, or the ability to use tools to act upon nature, define individuals' relations with nature instead of class relations and are ideologically neutral (Guo

2004: 41). It is also able to sever its ideological bond with the working class. Non-socialist forms of ownership are then accepted and encouraged, and the new clarion call is 'to get rich is glorious'. Moreover, the CCP has to throw open its doors to private businesspeople (Jiang 2001), although the latter cannot be fully trusted but 'must be educated and guided', like the national bourgeoisie in the 1950s.[2]

Ideological revision has been contested vigorously by the old left. In September 1992, for example, a *Xinhua* editorial included a warning inserted by leftist ideologue Gao Di that 'While carrying out reform and opening up to the outside world, we must ask ourselves whether we are practising socialism or capitalism' (Fewsmith 2001: 53). Deng Liqun, a key spokesman of the left, struck out again in 1994, asserting that a new bourgeoisie had already taken shape as a class in itself (Fewsmith 2001: 169). Jiang's theory drew even more fire from leftists, who accused him of weakening the Party's social base and changing the colour of the Party (Lam 2001; Dickson 2004: 152–153).

Leftists within the CCP are certainly not the only ones to find a new bourgeoisie in the ranks of the new rich. Overseas writers, such as So and Dickson, have argued that 'a cadre-capitalist class has emerged to monopolise economic capital, political capital, and social/net capital in Chinese society' (So 2003: 478). There is also a class of 'red capitalists' in China (Dickson 2003a). The irony of the CCP recruiting the new rich has also been noted by no small number of Party theorists (Lin 14 July 2001).

The CCP can only deny the existence of such a class. As early as the 1990s, Deng Xiaoping stated that 'we will not allow a new bourgeoisie to take shape' (1993: 172), that 'if a bourgeoisie has emerged, we must have gone astray' (1993: 110–11). Yet, as much depends on how 'bourgeoisie' is defined, Deng's statement is meaningless. Indeed, the CCP's mouthpieces have routinely stressed that today's private entrepreneurs are not capitalists, because they were originally members of the working class, and work under a political system opposed to exploitation (*The People's Daily* 17 February and 25 April 2001). This is not a convincing argument, to say the least, and it betrays the Party's dilemma over the new rich. The dilemma is compounded by the common perception that the rich got rich dishonestly or unscrupulously, and by what the Chinese media call the 'original sin' of the rich; many were guilty of suspect or unlawful deals in the early days of their business (Wang Junxiu 2007).

In contrast, Hu Jintao and Wen Jiabao have steered away from ideological debates, focusing instead on practical problems, such as education, health care and social welfare. Nevertheless, they are clearly interested in a different kind of society from that which emerged in the previous decades. Their well-known model is a 'harmonious society' as well as a '*xiaokang* society' ('an all-round well-off society'[3]). The model has been variously interpreted as harmonious *xiaokang* for the majority (*dazhong xiaokang*), middle-income *xiaokang*, or middle-class *xiaokang*, and so on. It has entailed the 'second redistribution of social wealth' to balance social justice and economic efficiency, unlike the first in the early days of reform, which focused on efficiency without taking social equality seriously.

This new social blueprint has drawn more attention to the middle reaches of society and encouraged the middling of wealth. At the same time, it has also highlighted the current status of the new rich and the working class. The former may be recognised as legitimate players in wealth creation, but cannot be described as the backbone of the socialist market economy due to ideological constraints and negative popular perceptions. The latter have become a disadvantaged grouping, a burden to the government, and a source of instability and unrest, rather than one that constitutes the 'masters of the country'. Their best prospect is to move out of poverty and get rich if they can. Unless they do, their status in society remains lowly, in contrast to the rising middle classes, the new masters of the country.

Naming the middle classes: conflation and contestation

While Chinese elites are united on the importance of the middle reaches of society, there is much dispute over names, most notably '*jieji*' (class), '*jieceng*' (stratum) and '*qunti*' (group). The water is muddied by three major factors. Firstly, it is not easy to tell if the terms are singular or plural. Secondly, these words are often translated into 'class' in English. Finally, the Chinese words for 'middle' include '*zhongchan*' (middle-propertied), '*zhongjian*' (intermediate) or '*zhongdeng*' (middle range), and if class, stratum and group are modified by those words, then nine synonymic phases are possible, most of which are in wide circulation. In China's discursive context, these phrases have different political overtones and may or may not refer to the same groupings, and the use of different terms is part of the contestation over the constitution of the middle class and its implications for China.

For the mass media inside and outside China, naming the middle class seems to be a straightforward matter; it refers to what analysts call middle class, middle stratum, intermediate group or any other variant. There are academics too who take the same approach (Zheng 2002; Zhang Wanli *et al.* 2005; Chen Xiaoya 2002; Luo 2002; Li and Niu 2003; Chen *et al.* 2004; He Li 2006). There are still others who consider 'class', 'stratum' and 'group' to be more or less equivalent or undistinguishable, as can be seen from common expressions such as 'class/stratum', 'class and stratum', 'class or stratum', 'class (stratum)', 'stratum (class)', 'middle class group', and 'middle income stratum group'. Because of conceptual conflation and confusion, 'middle class' appears to have become a standard term by default.

By contrast, some analysts deliberately distinguish between the various concepts, particularly between 'class' and 'stratum', as much is at stake. The word 'class' appears almost exclusively in five collocations in contemporary Chinese: 'unpropertied class' (proletariat), 'peasant class', 'middle class', 'propertied class' (bourgeoisie), and 'petit propertied class' (petit bourgeoisie).

The first two are still acceptable, although they have turned into academic jargon and are rarely found in official communications or daily conversations. The last is not used in serious academic discussions but mostly heard in joking remarks about bohemian or yuppie tastes and lifestyles. These three terms are the least controversial. It is a different story with 'bourgeoisie' and 'middle class'. The former, as already noted, cannot be attached to any group with official endorsement, while the latter is controversial for ideological reasons, though both *Xinhua* (The New China News Agency) and the *China Daily* now use the term.

From the CCP's viewpoint, the middle class is a problematic concept and grouping. For one thing, 'middle class' in English versions of the works of Marx and Engels was sometimes translated into '*zichan jieji*' (bourgeoisie), causing much confusion about how the class was perceived by the communist pioneers (Liu 2006). To this day, the *Modern Chinese Dictionary* still defines 'middle class' as 'middle-ranking bourgeoisie'. For another, Mao equated the 'wavering middle class' with 'national bourgeoisie', and most of the groups now included in the middle class would fall into the categories of 'national bourgeoisie' or 'petit bourgeoisie' in Mao's classification (1991: 3).

Worse still, some Marxist writers dismiss the middle class as a dubious Western concept and look upon China's middle class fetish as a sign of Western influence eroding China's political system. Influential Party theorists Qing Lianbin and Zheng Bijian, for example, have criticised the uncritical adoption of Western terminology and the classification of intellectuals and other white-collar workers as middle class. That practice, Zheng stresses, 'is bound to degrade, weaken and obliterate the working class' (11 July 2001). Qing argues similarly that the privileging of the middle class in the West is meant to cover up class struggle and write off the working class (2001: 24). According to Zheng, that is why the CCP refuses to use the term 'middle class'; otherwise, it will fall into the trap set by subversive forces.

That is no doubt an extreme view. But it underlines a prevalent sense of unease amongst Party theorists and establishment intellectuals about dramatically different 'class maps' which fail to square with CCP orthodoxy. If, for example, the intellectuals in all the new professions are considered middle class, it does mean, as Zheng feared, that they are separated from the working class, into which Deng Xiaoping elevated them in the late 1970s. It also raises many questions about China's polity. The questions might be irrelevant to the average Chinese or academics dwelling on the middle class alone without referring to its relationship with any other groupings, but Party theorists must find plausible answers. It is no easy job given the CCP's allegiance – perfunctory as it may be – to Marxism, as well as the workers and peasants.

For these reasons, those steeped in the Marxist approach to class analysis cannot easily come to terms with the middle class as a concept and a social reality and mostly opt for 'middle stratum', 'intermediate groups', 'middle-income stratum', 'middle-income groups', and so on. Many social scientists prefer these terms too, although for somewhat different reasons. For analysts who work within official frameworks, these categories are advantageous in that they can be accommodated within the established class schemes. One way of accommodation is to treat 'stratum' and 'group' as constituent groups of classes. It is thus possible for white-collar occupational aggregates to be labelled 'middle strata', while those located in the middle range in terms of income, purchasing power and so on may be called either 'strata' or 'groups'.

In this case, 'stratum' and 'group' are more or less interchangeable, the only difference being that the former can be a layer of a bigger structure and the latter, a smaller unit or a largely self-standing grouping classified on the basis of common interest or other characteristics. At any rate, what matters is that these categories are confined within the proletariat and peasantry and are therefore counted, theoretically, as members of the working class. In consequence, the constitutional polity of the PRC gains a measure of credibility and consistency, and social stratification, regardless of its scope and extent, can only be conceived to be intra-class stratification. If there is any conflict among any of the constituent strata, it is a resolvable 'internal contradiction' rather than one that leads to class warfare.

The problem with that approach is obvious: some new social groups or strata simply do not fit in the working class. Many businesspeople and entrepreneurs, for instance, not only rank among the richest in the country but also own a large amount of property and control the means of production within their enterprises. Moreover, if the extraction of surplus value constitutes exploitation (as many Marxists would argue) it is logical to see them as exploiters and their employees as exploited. It is surely not easy to convince the exploiters and exploited that they belong to the same class, not to mention the fact that very few in China are keen to identify themselves socially as working class these days. Even if exploitation and conflict are explained away, there is really no point in this exercise other than maintaining a semblance of ideological consistency.

A politically safe option is to acknowledge that some portions of the population no longer belong to the working class and have aggregated into new strata or groups in the middle reaches of society, while maintaining that these transitional formations do not constitute classes per se or significantly change China's two-class social structure (Qing 2001: 25; Guo Zhenshu 2003: 37; Wu 2004; Shen 2003). This approach makes a virtue of being vague about the position of the separate groups and their future prospect, but it goes against the quest for clarity and certainty and therefore holds little appeal to hard-headed academics.

Another alternative, which has predominated in academia in recent years, is to discard the concept of class – except for the middle class – break up the two-class structure, and rearrange all identified social groupings into a new hierarchy of strata. This alternative is called 'stratum analysis' as opposed to class analysis. Those who take this approach have turned their back on 'class' not because it has become an outmoded concept that is 'ceasing to do any useful work for sociology' (Pahl 1989: 710) or 'an increasingly redundant issue' (Holton and Turner 1989: 194) but because they believe, like Margaret Thatcher, that 'Class is a communist concept', that 'it groups people as bundles and sets them against one another.'[4]

Moreover, class struggle has cost countless lives and caused suffering to millions of Chinese. Little wonder then that, since the 1980s, Chinese intellectuals called for a 'farewell to revolution' – to the violent act of one class toppling another (Li Zehou 1994; Li and Liu 1995). The thrust of the slogan is, primarily, the rejection of historical materialism, as it posits a model of society divided by classes and fraught with class conflict. In a historical materialist view, individuals are moulded as social beings by the material conditions of their production and divided into classes based on their relationship to the means of production (Marx and Engels 1968: 32). The principal classes do not play complementary roles but occupy different or diametrically opposed positions in relations of exploitation, domination and subordination. Hence, Engels speaks of 'these warring classes of society' (Engels 1934: 37). And in the eyes of Marxists, class struggle is not a bad thing, for 'No antagonism, no progress.' (Marx 1955: 61).

The rejection of revolution has been carried on in the last decade by social scientists and translated into specific ways of reconceptualising social structure and analysing social classes which depart from Marxist approaches, so that society cannot be conceived as comprising warring classes and class struggle cannot be said to constitute the motive force of history. For those social scientists, the Marxian concept of 'class' is merely a political instrument for identifying the motive force of the Chinese revolution and its enemies, whereas 'stratum' is a new 'sociological concept' to be used in the analysis and description of actual social structures (Lu *et al.* 2002: 2; Chen *et al.* 2004; Li Chunling 2005; Jia 2005).

However, 'stratum' is by no means as apolitical as Chinese sociologists claim; in fact, there is a common perception in China that class analysis is indicative of adherence to Marxist and socialist principles and stratum analysis amounts to rejection of these principles (Li Chunling 2005, 100–101). In that sense, 'class' and 'stratum' are not only hallmarks of oppositional, analytical paradigms but also a watershed between Marxism and subversive ideologies. Advocates of stratum analysis typically defend themselves by asserting that they are not anti-Marxist, that they prefer 'stratum' simply because 'class' cannot be understood differently in China from established connotations (Li Chunling 2005, 100–101; Chen *et al.* 2004; Jia Gaojian 2005). They are right about Chinese conceptions of class, but they are by no means pro-Marxist.

What ultimately sets 'strata' and 'classes' apart is that the former are hierarchical or gradational rather than relational. That is, a stratum is envisioned as a layer of a hierarchical structure, and its relationship with other strata is gradational, as determined by the possession of economic and cultural capital. Since it is not defined in reference to its direct structural relationship to processes of production and exchange, the dynamics and actualities of class relations that Marxists envision are ignored, and the constructed structure might be one of inequality but not one of exploitation and domination. In other words, relations of conflict are bypassed in the construction and antagonism is defined out of 'stratum'. Furthermore, the issue of class consciousness and action, which is central to Marx's work, is circumvented when a stratum is devised on the basis of objective indexes, such as income, occupation, consumption, education, and life styles.

From objective to subjective middle classes

Of all the indexes with which Chinese middle classes are classified, the most essential is income. This has much to do with the Chinese word '*zhongchan*' (middle-propertied) and the fact that income is probably the most reliable and quantifiable parameter of the economic position of individuals and households. For the same reason, consumption is also crucial to most schemes. A third index is occupation, which is related to both income and prestige. Education is considered important too, but only if it is positively correlated with income, consumption, and lifestyles.

As might be expected, the advertiser's image of the middle class is mostly associated with consumption and lifestyles. As Li Lin writes:

> the moment ones opens the newspaper, turns on the TV, or walks into a street, one comes face to face with the lifestyle of the 'middle class': big mansions, private cars, fashion, jewellery, famous watches, banquets, tenpin bowls, golf courses, pubs, and every new trend and every form of fashion, entertainment and luxury are all marked as 'middle class'.
>
> (Li Lin 2005: 63)

The advertiser's message is simple: If you want to be regarded as middle class, you must own and do these things, which, constructed as they may be, become objectified as hallmarks of the middle class.

In contrast, income predominates in official schemes. In a 2005 survey, for example, the National Bureau of Statistics (NBS) defined middle-income households as having an annual income between 60,000 and 500,000 *yuan* (*Xinhua* 18 June 2005). In a more recent report by the Economic Research Institute of the State Development and Reform Commission (SDRC) the 'middle-income group' included individuals earning 34,000–100,000 *yuan* per annum and members of households with a total annual income of 53,700–160,000 *yuan* (*Xinhua* 10 May 2007). Those who earn more or less than this group fall into the categories of high- or low-income groups. Evidently, neither the NBS nor the SDRC refers to 'middle class', but their term 'middle-income group' was translated into 'middle class group' in

English, for instance, by *Xinhua* and is often transformed into 'middle class' in the Chinese media.

Unlike advertisers and government agencies, most academic schemes use composite criteria. The best-known and most elaborate scheme is that of Lu Xueyi and his colleagues at the Institute of Sociology of CASS (Lu *et al.* 2002). Based on a nation-wide sample, the team identified a 'modern' social structure comprising three gradational but otherwise unrelated strata (upper, middle and lower), which were further divided into ten sub-strata. These include Party-state cadres, middle- and high-ranking managers of large and medium-sized enterprises, private entrepreneurs, technical and academic professionals, public servants and office workers, employees of the service sector, manual and semi-manual workers, agricultural workers, and the unemployed and semi-unemployed in urban areas.

Using the same dataset, Li Chunling (2005: 490–507), a member of the CASS team, later classified as 'income middle class' those who had a monthly income ranging from 233.45 *yuan* to 1,250.02 *yuan*. The five middle-stratum occupational categories in the 2002 report were labelled 'occupational middle class'. The consumption index was the ownership of major durables, such as 1) coloured TV sets, refrigerators, washing machines, telephones, mobile phones, stereos, DVD players, air conditioners, and microwaves (1 point per item); 2) computers, video cameras, pianos, and motor bikes (4 points per item); and 3) cars (12 points per item). Those who scored 6 points or above qualified as 'consumption middle class'.

The only operationalised subjective classification criterion was self-identification; respondents who considered themselves middle class fell into the category of 'self-identified middle class'. Some data was collected about the subjects' satisfaction with China's socio-economic situation and their perceptions with respect to the benefits of reform and to social equality, but the responses were not differentiated along class or stratum lines, although there was an expected division between the winners and losers in the reform (Li Chunling 2005: 339–340).

Overall, 24.6 percent qualified as middle class by income, 15.9 percent by occupation, 35 percent by consumption, and 46.8 percent by status. Surprisingly, there were some relatively low levels of education behind these figures – 89.9 percent of those who were identified as middle class by income only had a senior high school education or below. The figures for the other definitions were similar – 75.3 percent of those identified as middle class by occupation, 89 percent of those identified as middle class by consumption, and 92.4 percent of those identified as middle class by status. This clearly does not resonate well with the perception that the middle class boasts high levels of education. It is also worth noting that 41.1 and 38.1 percent of the blue-collar workers and 11.5 and 18.3 percent of the farmers in the sample qualified as middle class in terms of income and consumption. Even more blue-collar workers (50 percent) and farmers (40 percent) considered themselves middle class.

It is evident then that the Chinese middle class identified by the CASS sociologists is rather mixed, ranging from farmers and blue-collar workers to the new rich. In terms of income and consumption, the range is too broad and flexible to give a clear idea about an individual's socio-economic position. As an example, there is little comparison between a rich business-man driving a new Mercedes and a middle-class blue-collar worker with a motor bike plus a coloured TV and a DVD player. It is also possible that the self-identified middle class are in error concerning their social status.

Certainly, the CASS scheme is only one of many. Other eminent sociologists, most notably Xiao Wentao (2001), Li Qiang (2001: 18–19), Zhang Wanli *et al.* (2005) and Zhou Xiaohong (2005) have also devised their own middle class schemes, but these differ little from the CASS scheme and are far less sophisticated. In any case, although one can easily modify the quantitative indexes of income and consumption, expand or reduce the range of middle class occupational aggregates, or have alternative categories, it is difficult to construct a clear-cut and homogeneous middle class. This raises many questions: Does such a diverse, objective aggregate as the CASS scheme constitute a grouping? If so, is the grouping a class? Is it inevitable for collective consciousness and values to emerge from a grouping or class? Is there such a thing as class without agency?

These are both theoretical and empirical questions. Theoretically, class can be defined with respect to positions within the technical division of labour or the positions within the social division of labour (Abercrombie and Urry 1983: 109; Wright 1979). Alternatively, a distinction can be made between a 'class in itself' and a 'class for itself', one which exists as a historical reality and one which has acquired a consciousness of its identity and a capacity to act (Marx 1955: 195; Bendix and Lipset 1967). This is the subject of an enormous body of literature. For the purpose of this chapter, suffice it to say that a class separable from agency is a problematic concept. As Giddens has put it, if classes become social realities, 'this must manifest in the formation of "common patterns of behaviour and attitudes"' and 'differentiated class "cultures" within a society' (1973: 111 and 134).

In fact, most Chinese analysts are not just interested in objective but also subjective dimensions of the middle classes. There is even a habitual tendency to fall back on Marxian structural determinism and to take it for granted that social structures of various kinds naturally generate common values and collective consciousness and lead to interest aggregation and collective action. This reasoning moves from structure to consciousness and then to action. It is therefore incumbent on them to demonstrate empirically the attitudinal and behavioural characteristics of the middle classes. Yet few analysts have gone beyond self-identification and small-sample interviews in their investigation of middle class subjectivity, and searches in CNKI and qikan.com, two of the largest journal databases in the PRC, failed to bring up any in-depth analyses which allow generalisations about the subjective dimension of the middle classes as a whole.

Despite the lack of convincing evidence, however, commentators rarely refrain from making claims about the subjective attributes of what can at best be described as the objective middle classes. Liberal thinkers and democracy advocates, for instance, insist that the middle class, like civil society, is a driving force for liberalisation and democratisation (Chen Shujuan *et al.* 2005: 163; Chen Xiaoya 2002a; He Li 2006; He 2004; Huang 2003: 15; Ma 1999: 110; Sheng 2005). Economists and sociologists argue that a large middle class with stable purchasing power is indispensable to economic growth (Chen Dongdon 2004; Chen Xiaoya 2002a; Li Yinin cited in Lin Li 2005: 64; Tan Yin 2001; and Wu Jinglian and Xiao Zhuoji, cited in Chen *et al.* 2004).

China's social scientists are emphatic that a stable society is an olive-shaped structure rather than a pyramid-shaped distribution and that the middle classes should be the mainstream of a modern society (Dong 2003: 19; Huang 2003: 15; Li Qiang 2001: 19–20; Lu Hanlong 2005; Lu *et al.* 2002; Qin Yan 2002; Su 2004: 20; Zhang Jingrong 2004: 81; Zhang *et al.* 2005: 3, Xiao 2001: 95). Similarly, the CCP believes that the ideal model of society is an olive-shaped, harmonious and well-off society, with the majority of the population situated in the middle reaches.

There are hundreds of articles in the PRC's academic publications which expound the pivotal importance of the middle classes and the causes of their importance. It is customarily argued that

- members of the middle care are educated, cultured, civilised and creditable;
- the middle class, being the most secure and politically moderate, serves as a buffer zone and bridge between the rich and poor and maintains social stability;
- the size and characters of the middle class are critical for the establishment of democratic political institution;
- continued economic growth leads to demands for democratic reforms because the middle class naturally wants a say in government;
- the freedoms associated with liberal democracy are inseparable from the defence of property and profits by ordinary citizens;
- the middle class cherishes equality of opportunity and transparency in government decision making, and supports the expansion of civil rights and political liberty;
- the middle class has the political and organisational skills necessary to create political parties and other important democratic institutions, and it is best equipped to transmit, clarify, and endorse the people's demands.

The list goes on. Their inevitable conclusion is therefore that the middle classes should be expanded and regarded as role models. Whether the putative middle class qualities are acceptable or not is quite another question; most relevant here is whether the so-called middle classes are the actual bearers of these qualities. That is an empirical question, and yet the articles are mostly long on quotation and short on empirical evidence. They cite theorists such as Aristotle, Barrington Moore, Huntington and others who link political stability and democratisation to the presence of a large middle class, while the 'middle class' under discussion largely remains a phantom, as it either has no objective identity or there is no established link between the putative subjectivity of the so-called 'middle class' and any constructed schemes.

In other words, the discussion of the subjective dimension to the middle class is largely speculative, and extrinsic values and characteristics are imposed on objective social categories or projected onto imaginary groupings. This is better described as prescription rather than description, as political advocacy rather than scholarship. Its purpose is not to give one some idea about the size, composition or intrinsic characteristics of the middle class but to promote this class, together with its presumably attractive qualities, or advocate these values by riding on the wave of the fetishised middle class.

The middle class and the CCP

In sum, the current structure of Chinese society and its constituting classes can hardly be seen as phenomena independent of the analysts' volition and representation. Indeed, they are nothing but products of the very cognition, the very intellectual processes through which they are observed, classified, described and explained. An outstanding characteristic of these processes is the aversion to class struggle, which is translated into deliberate evasion of relations of conflict. On the one hand, Chinese analysts are keen to demolish the cornerstones of Marxian class theory; on the other, their description of non-conflictual, albeit unequal, social relations accords with the Party-state's emphasis on harmonious society. They are all too aware that relational class schemes almost inevitably lead to the identification of cleavage and conflict, whereas hierarchical and gradational schemes at worst reveal broad contours of inequality – inequality which can be easily managed and addressed.

A second prominent feature of the intellectual processes is the circumvention of class consciousness. The reason for this is not only the methodological complexity of investigating class consciousness but also the potential risk of capturing anything which may prove problematic politically. An additional advantage of this approach is that it enables analysts to impose presumed appropriate values and ideas on their favourite classes, so that the latter become models, to be embraced, emulated, nurtured, propagated, and elevated to central stage in Chinese society. In fact, adding values to the middle classes has been a major part of their construction.

The Party-state may not like the concept of 'middle class', but the 'middle class' by some other name is acceptable. In any case, the CCP's recent emphasis on social harmony encourages analytical methodologies which do not highlight social cleavage and antagonism and discourages those generating conflict-ridden class schemes and adding to the difficulty of constructing a harmonious society. Moreover, its vision of a harmonious *xiaokang* society requires the expansion of, and an increasing focus on, the middle reaches of society. The CCP's new focus on the middle legitimises the middle class in effect irrespective of lingering unease, and also means a shift away from the working class.

Promoting the middle classes in this way is designed to support the CCP's legitimacy, as the alleged aim is to expand middle China, enhance common prosperity, stimulate economic growth and ensure social stability. Taking advantage of the official discourse, intellectual elites have promoted the middle classes and putative middle class values which may differ from or even undermine Party-state values. Hence, the official social vision and the intellectuals' ideal society have actually converged on common ground in the middle reaches of society despite their differences. This new model of society, dominated by the middle classes – by whatever name – will necessarily differ dramatically from the Maoist two-class structure; so will the new status order as well as the nature and meaning of social life. But one thing has not changed; this society is still based on the 'doctrine of the mean' and suggests that the idea of age-old egalitarianism predominates.

Notes

1 According to official reports, the number of laid-off workers is only a dozen million. See Ministry of Labour and Social Security, National Bureau of Statistics 2001, p. 36. Estimates in internal reports and scholarly papers are much higher. Wang Depei's estimate is 60 million (Wang 2001: 25). Hu Angang stated that China had laid off 55 million people from 1995 to mid-2002 (*China News Digest* 9 July 2002). In a 1999 report, some government officials are cited as saying that the real number of unemployed, including those 'waiting for work', was as high as 100 million (William Overholt 1999). In 2006, there were 120 million rural migrant workers. About 20 percent had monthly salaries lower than 500 *yuan* (Research Office, State Council 2006).
2 The CCP's Department of United Front Work coordinates Party policies towards private entrepreneurs. It used to be the primary function of this department to liaise with non-communist allies (Ye 2007: 1).
3 The vision of a *xiaokang* society is one in which most people are moderately well off and middle class, and in which economic prosperity is sufficient to move most of the population in mainland China into comfortable means, but in which economic advancement is not the sole focus of society. Explicitly incorporated into the concept of a *xiaokang* society is the idea that economic growth needs to be balanced with sometimes conflicting goals of social equality and environmental protection (*Xinhua* 10 November 2002.)
4 Margaret Thatcher, cited in *Guardian*, 22 April 1992. In the words of a Chinese scholar, 'the Marxist theory of class may be an effective theory for wars and revolutions, but it is harmful during peaceful times, as it destroys national unity and hinders modernization.' (Tang 1989: 5).

3 Market transition, wealth, and status claims

Xiaowei Zang

Does wealth contribute positively to status claims in China? The Western literature on post-1978 market transition in China has not addressed this question directly. This is surprising since market reforms have provided scholars with a unique opportunity to study the changing mechanisms of status attainment in the post-1978 era. Indeed, Chinese social stratification and mobility has stood out as one of the most developed research fields in China Studies (Bian 2002; Li and Walder 2001; Nee 1989; Oi and Walder 1999; Walder 1995; Walder 1998; Walder, Li and Treiman 2000; Xueguang Zhou 2000; Xueguang Zhou 2004).

Much of this large and influential literature has focused on inequalities of earnings and political power in the People's Republic of China (PRC). It is clear that the reconfigurations of social and economic interests during market transition must have had a significant impact on the hierarchical orders of influence and esteem in China. But so far, few scholars have published on the topic. For example, only two journal articles on occupational prestige in China are listed in SSCI since 1976 (Bian 1996; Lin and Xie 1988) and there is not a single monograph on status hierarchies in China by scholars outside the PRC.

This does not mean that status acquisition is an unimportant research topic. On the contrary, status is a key aspect of social stratification and mediates many processes by which people are given access to rewards, evaluated, and directed toward or away from positions of power and wealth (Ridgeway 1998; Webster and Hysom 1998; Xueguang Zhou 2005; Berger and Zelditch 1998; Nan Lin 1990). Status is also seen as an intrinsic component of an individual's utility function that 'has important implications for social and economic systems because it can provide a powerful motivation to perform; it also can lead to unproductive competitions' such as the over-consumption of positional goods. Status acquisition is a widespread phenomenon as people 'in all cultures crave respect and recognition' (Huberman, Loch and Önçüler 2004:103–5). Given its social significance, there is an urgent need to examine the link between wealth creation and status claims in the PRC.

This chapter addresses that need through a study of entrepreneurship and status claims. Private entrepreneurs (those who own or control the means of production, and offer goods and services in a market for profits) are chosen for this study since they are a key component of the new rich in China. Field research shows that when people talked about the new rich, they invariably referred to private entrepreneurs. They remembered other components of the new rich only after being given a reminder. This is not surprising since private entrepreneurs have accumulated a large amount of wealth and have come to play a high profile role in the Chinese economy. They have also been intriguingly linked to powerful government officials and cadres of the Chinese Communist Party (CCP) (McGregor 2005; A Chen 2002; M W Peng 2001; K S Tsai 2005; Dali Yang 2006).

Nevertheless, it is still far from clear that private entrepreneurs enjoy a high level of influence and esteem in the PRC. Status acquisition is related to but distinct from economic resources or structural positions. Weber stressed that '"mere economic" power, and especially "naked" money power, is by no means a recognized basis of social honor' (Weber 1946:180). Are private entrepreneurs highly regarded by Chinese citizens? What role does their wealth play in the subjective evaluation of their social standing in China?

To answer these questions, this chapter first discusses how private entrepreneurs have been viewed by ordinary citizens in terms of their social worth in China. Next, it briefly reviews three existing explanations of their poor performance in status acquisition. It then proposes an additional explanation of the subjective evaluations of private entrepreneurs in the reform era. It argues that wealth has not formed an adequate basis for status claims in the PRC. For convenience, the following terms are used interchangeably: honor, prestige, respect, social distinctions, social standings, status, status ordering, status beliefs, status hierarchies, hierarchies of influence and esteem, and social worth.

To get rich is not that glorious

Communist ideology and the resultant political and economic campaigns of the CCP resulted in virtually no private businesses in urban China from the mid-1950s until market reforms were introduced in 1978. Twenty-nine years later, amazingly, the private sector is responsible for about three-quarters of economic output and employment in China. Private business people have amassed a vast amount of wealth in the post-1978 years. It is reported that 25% of global growth between 1993 and 2001 went to China, fuelling the emergence of the global middle-class. They and their family members probably do not exceed 4 percent of the total PRC population, approximately less than 45 million, or less than 0.74 percent of the world population of 6.1 billion in 2001 (A Chen 2002: 410; Edward 2006: 1677; Flannery 2006: 6).

The amount of wealth that the rich in China command can be seen from a different angle: in 2005, 29.1 percent of the rich (those with cash assets of US$1 million in addition to home-ownership) in the Asia-Pacific Region were from the PRC, and each had average cash reserves of some US$5 million (Yu Chunlai 2006). Twenty of the 946 billionaires cited by Forbes in 2007 are from the PRC, and the richest Chinese is Yan Cheung from the Nine Dragon Paper Company, ranking at number 390 in the Forbes's list (Kroll and Fass 2007).

On the other hand, unlike Sir Richard Bransom, Bill Gates, and Michael Dell, Chinese private entrepreneurs have not yet received the level of esteem and deference their wealth might be assumed to ensure. It is not always the case that 'To Get Rich Is Glorious' as Deng Xiaoping proclaimed. Findings from empirical studies are not very encouraging with regard to public evaluations of private entrepreneurs in terms of social worth. In a survey (n = 2,351) conducted in five major cities in 1993, for example, respondents rated private entrepreneurs the highest with regard to earnings but the lowest with regard to social standing. Private entrepreneurship ranked seventh out of the eleven career choices. As expected, in the survey, private entrepreneurs reported a stronger sense of deprivation in terms of political rights and social status than other social groups such as cadres, professionals, and state workers (Research Team 1993; Luo and Bai 1994).

As demonstrated in Table 3.1, the results from surveys on occupational prestige in China conducted in 1987, 1993, and 1999 showed that private entrepreneurs were rated higher in the prestige hierarchy than social groups such as junior cadres, technicians, office clerks, factory workers, and taxi drivers. They were then considered to be in the same league with entertainment stars, air hostesses, and middle or primary school teachers. They however received much lower prestige scores than social groups such as middle or high ranking cadres, scientists, and professors. (Xu 2000).

The new rich might have been expected to do a much better job of making status claims given that China has undeniably moved toward a market economy with strong consumerism and money fetishism (Croll 2006; Davis 2000c; Latham, Thompson and Klein 2006; Wu 1999; Li Qiang 2007; Zhao Xiao 2006). The size of their assets cannot be held accountable for their poor performance since, as already noted, these are large even by international standards. Yet popular money worship and the huge amount of wealth the private business people have accumulated since 1978 have apparently failed to attract esteem and respect from the masses.

These surveys were conducted at a time when ordinary citizens were still willing to learn anger management to put up with rising inequality (Ju 2005; Zhang Dajun 1997). China's new rich might well get an even lower prestige score today: instead of having become an esteemed social group for their economic performance, they have become the whipping boy of the mass media. They have been blamed for many of the social problems recently manifested, such as the massive lay-off of state workers, and the increase in unaffordable housing, and have been disgraced by contrast to philanthropists in Hong Kong and the West such as David Rockefeller, Bill Gates, and Warren Buffett. For example, Hong Kong tycoon Li Ka Shing was immediately compared favourably with China's new rich when he announced a donation of HK$50 billions to his charitable trust, the Li Ka Shing Foundation on 24 August 2006 (Li Ka Shing 2006). The mass media have also reported that the China Charity Federation received 75 percent of its cash donations from overseas contributors, as compared to 15 percent from domestic donors in the PRC. Media commentators have asked whether and when the rich in China will learn a better way of spending money other than conspicuous consumption and the sordid display of wealth (Nanfang Weekend 2003).

Since 2000, there have been heated discussions on 'wealth hatred' in the mass media and internet. This is a popular term used by ordinary citizens to reject the legitimacy of the claim to wealth by private entrepreneurs. The term reflects public anger at or public resentment toward the rich and has drawn an increasing level of attention from scholars in China and popularity among ordinary citizens (Hong Zhaohui 2004). In these discussions, the rich have been broadly labelled as the 'problematic rich' as their ways of making money have been portrayed as improper, unjust, or even illegal. A study undertaken at the end of 2004 found more than 6,000 entries if one searched on Google for the term 'the original sin of the rich' (*furen yuanzui*) and more than 20,000 entries if one searched for the phrase 'the mentality of wealth hatred (*jiufu xinli*) (Hong Zhaohui 2004). Replicating these searches on Google in May 2007 revealed increases in the entries for each to 235,000 and 304,000 respectively.

China's new rich have been condemned in articles with emotional and threatening titles such as 'I do not want to hate well-off people, but I cannot help since many of them are the problematic rich'; 'How can I possibly not hate rich people given the ways they make money?' and 'It is unbelievable that Professor Lin Yifu asks us not to hate rich people' (Professor Lin Yifu is a prominent economist and something of a celebrity in China) (Criticisms of wealth 2005–7). Public anger at the rich has been more than a threat: since the late 1990s there have been frequent reports and rumours of kidnappings, ransom demands, and murders of private entrepreneurs in China (Reports of violence 2004–6). The rich have taken the threat seriously: according to surveys undertaken by newspapers, many entrepreneurs believe that their wealth has brought them an acute sense of insecurity (Insecurity 2005–6).

Some scholars outside China suggest that private entrepreneurs have been constantly haunted by a nightmare of falling prey to seething popular discontent resulting from the 'unjustifiable' inequalities and suspect sources of their wealth. Public anger at the rich may in part explain why private entrepreneurs seem to have developed a profound sense of distrust in ordinary citizens and a general opposition to democracy if it means majority rule. They have sought protection from and close association with government officials and CCP cadres (A Chen 2003a; A Chen 2003b). Scholars in China have made similar comments in the mass media and written articles

Table 3.1 Prestige scales – Occupations in selected years

Occupation	1983 survey	1987 survey	1993 survey	1999 survey
Mayor		87.9	81.3	92.9
Government minister		82.8	87.0	91.4
Professor	83.8	88.6	87.6	90.1
Judge		80.6		88.3
Court prosecutor			78.4	87.6
Lawyer		84.2	70.8	86.6
Leading cadre in Party or government body	68.1	77.7	71.9	85.7
Natural scientist	83.8	84.5	75.5	85.3
Translator			67.1	84.9
Social scientist	82.7	83.5	79.2	83.9
Doctor	86.2	80.9	68.8	83.7
Writer	81.7	87.4	67.4	82.5
Reporter	81.1	83.2	66.2	81.6
Director or manager of a large or medium-size state enterprise		79.4	76.9	81.3
Industrial or commercial administrator/tax officer		68.3	63.0	81.1
Singer			55.1	80.1
Editor		83.0	65.2	79.7
Bank clerk		68.7		79.1
Private entrepreneur		67.6	58.6	78.6
Film or TV actor	57.7		60.0	78.2
Air hostess			56.9	78.0
Teacher in public middle or primary school	66.4	70.7	61.4	77.1
Policeman	43.8	65.7	66.5	76.2
Mechanical engineer			72.4	76.0
Director of small state enterprise		73.6		75.9
Sportsman	62.8		60.4	74.7
Accountant in large enterprise	66.4		60.4	73.4
Ordinary cadre in Party or government body	63.0	65.5		73.3
Car driver in Party or government body			59.8	70.1
Cultural self-employed worker			48.5	68.2
Political cadre in business unit or institution		63.9	67.6	66.8
Industrial or commercial self-employed worker		62.2	48.3	65.7
Nurse	55.3	66.7	50.2	64.1
Hotel cook		43.5	68.8	60.6
Taxi driver		66.5	50.4	59.5
Postman	46.3	63.0	42.3	59.1
Bus driver	63.2	67.5	50.4	58.5
Worker in an undertaker's		50.2	27.1	53.0
Shop assistant	42.1	59.9	33.4	50.8
Bus conductor	42.1	53.9	41.5	48.7

(continued on next page)

Table 3.1 (continued)

Occupation	1983 survey	1987 survey	1993 survey	1999 survey
Worker in large or medium-sized stated enterprise		64.8	52.4	47.4
Sanitary worker	25.9	54.6	28.5	45.5
Peasant	57.9	28.2		44.7
Worker in town or village enterprise		59.3	43.2	44.3
Restaurant waiter	39.0	58.0	33.2	43.5
Worker in small stated enterprise		61.4		43.5
Worker in collective enterprise		59.5	35.9	42.7
Employees of self-owned laborer			23.0	37.7
Housemaid	18.9	49.8	19.1	36.9
Sample size	1,632	753	3,012	2,599

Source: Xu 2000

on this issue. Some scholars such as Lin Yifu have argued that public anger at the rich is unwarranted and should be set aside. Many others however have insisted that the rich have only themselves to blame for their bad reputation (Xiu Yangfeng 2005; Chen Ziwu 2007).

Fieldwork conducted by the author in the past five years in China has also demonstrated the difficulties facing the new rich if they want to improve their public image. Many of those interviewed questioned the sources of wealth of the rich and rejected categorically any claim that they were rich because of their business acumen, risk-taking behaviour, hard-work, or sheer luck. The interviewees were completely convinced that most rich people never made money honestly. They also generally asserted that the rich were selfish, cheap, heartless, showy, contemptuous, sneering, and most of all, that they had amassed wealth at the expense of ordinary people and had no sense of social responsibility and citizenship (Jones 2007).

The magnitude and intensity of 'wealth hatred' have apparently alarmed PRC leaders and helped them see the urgent need for legal and administrative measures to protect the rich and their property, resulting in other things in the enactment of the law on property rights at the Fifth Session of the Tenth National People's Congress in March 2007. There have also been public campaigns to recruit private business people into the CCP. In addition, President Hu Jintao, Premier Wen Jiaobao, and other top leaders have repeatedly called for efforts to build a 'harmonious society' in the PRC (*Xinhua* 27 January 2006). The government efforts seem to have been partly motivated by the profound public sentiments against the new rich.

Public anger at the new rich

Why is there such intense public resentment about the new rich? Why have private entrepreneurs not earned the levels of respect and prestige that has been achieved by their counterparts in other countries? There would seem to be three main explanations of 'wealth hatred'. The first is an 'original sin' hypothesis, namely, private entrepreneurs are not held in high esteem because of the ways they first accumulated their wealth. The public believes that such individual private fortunes started through a process of primitive capital accumulation during the 1980s and 1990s based on smuggling, bribery, speculation, tax evasion, theft of state assets, and illegal business deals (Larry Hsien Ping Lang 2003; Sun Liping 2005; Wu Jixue 2006; He Qinglian 2007). How can the new rich be held in high esteem if their money is considered by the public to be 'dirty' and venally acquired?

The second explanation is an 'inequality' hypothesis, namely, rising income inequality is the root of public anger at the new rich in China. One study estimates that in 2005, the richest 10 percent of the urban population owned 45 percent of the assets in urban China, as compared with 1.4 percent owned by the poorest 10 percent (Inequality 2005). Another study reports that 'less than 1 percent of Chinese households control more than 60 percent of the country's wealth (by comparison, 5 percent of the households in the United States own 60 percent of the wealth)' (Pei 2006a). The perception of inequality has been heightened by the speed with which the income gap has widened. It took only twenty-seven years to turn China, an international example of egalitarianism in 1978, into one of the most unequal societies by 2005 (Wenren Jiang 2006; *Xinhua* 17 January 2007). Conceivably, the collective memory of an egalitarian society and nostalgia for the 'good old days' may have been an almost inexhaustible source of fuel to public anger at the widening gap between the rich and the poor in the reform era (Davies 2005; Misra 1998; Yang 2003). Many scholars have warned that rising inequality has the potential to cause jealousy and even hatred towards the new rich (A Chen 2002; Hong 2004; Tsai 2005; Yang 2006).

The third explanation is an 'unkindness' hypothesis, namely, that the new rich are not respected because they have not demonstrated their sense of compassion and social responsibility. In particular, there is concern that the new rich do not adequately contribute to charitable causes. This is seen to be unacceptable given the amount of wealth private entrepreneurs have accumulated in recent years. True, some entrepreneurs have made donations to charity organizations and sponsored some philanthropic activities, but these have only further undermined their public image since they are seen to have given in return for bank loans, fame, protection, and the like (Bai, Lu and Tao 2006; Ma and Parish 2006).

There is though an additional explanation of 'wealth hatred' that is derived from an examination of the interaction between entrepreneurs and ordinary citizens. Private entrepreneurs may be seen in some ways to have gained profits at the expense of state workers. This argument is examined further through considering the ideological and economic legacies of state socialism and how they have brought about a profound sense of injustice among ordinary people and an increasing level of public anger at the new rich in recent years.

Ideological and economic legacies of state socialism

After coming to power in 1949, the CCP undertook a series of campaigns to establish a system of state socialism. This effort reached a milestone during 1956–8 when the CCP built a centrally planned socialist economy with the nationalization of the private industrial and commercial sectors. Urban private entrepreneurship was basically wiped out as the state became the sole owner of all major assets such as plants, land, and banks. The public sector controlled the production and distribution of goods and services in urban China. It also allocated jobs and careers since there was no alternative labour market in urban areas. In addition, the government took care of issues related to welfare and the vast majority of urban people came to rely on the state sector for their livelihood (Brodsgaard 1983; Ip 1994; Schurmann 1968; Walder 1984; Walder 1986; Zang 1995).

At the same time, the CCP launched political campaigns to develop socialist citizenship. These campaigns were inspired by communist ideology, but also motivated by an economic rationale. China was a backward and impoverished country in 1949. It lost the major source of capital and technology for industrialization after the PRC broke off with the USSR in the late 1950s. The CCP thus came to stress 'politics in command' and harnessed human labour as the most important resource for economic growth (Gray 1974; Hearn 1978). It could not use coercion since it claimed to be the vanguard of the masses, and in any case coercion led to low productivity. The campaigns for socialist citizenship seemed to be an efficient option since they could create a belief among the masses that they were the masters of the PRC.

This may partly explain why before 1978 the CCP created a political underclass to manage public opinion. Capitalists and other politically undesirable elements such as landlords were used by the CCP as the negative example in its effort to model the masses into socialist citizens. The underclass was publicized as anti-socialist devils, parasites, and self-seeking (Mamo 1981; So 2002; Watson 1984). In contrast, the 'new socialist man' was honoured and exemplified by model citizens such as Lei Feng. State workers in particular were portrayed as the prototype of the 'new socialist man' (Braester 2005; Li, Lin and Zhang 2004; Reed 1995; Shirk 1982).

The campaign for socialist citizenship was supported by a new mobility regime that established political loyalty as the benchmark to determine rewards and life chances. Political loyalty was measured by the willingness to follow instructions from one's supervisor and through 'good class' backgrounds such as those derived from being a CCP cadre or manual worker. The mobility regime advanced the careers of the 'good' classes at the expense of others such as capitalists and landlords (Bian 1996; Goldman 2005; Lee 1978; MacFarquhar and Schoenhals 2006; Perry and Li 1997; Rosen 1982; White 1974). The campaign for socialist citizenship and the new mobility regime brought about a widely held belief among the masses that they were the masters of the PRC.

This belief system reinforced the workers' commitment to the socialist cause and was strengthened by various government policies. For example, there was a well-established 'replacement' (*dingti*) system in the state sector though it was not formally recognized until 1978. This bureaucratic procedure allowed a state worker to retire early from his or her work-unit in order for his or her child to be assigned a job in that same unit (Christiansen 1992; Davis-Friedmann 1985; Hung and Chiu 2003; McLaren 1979). This practice, together with other government policies, reinforced state workers' belief that they were the masters of the PRC. More concretely, they believed that they *de facto* owned their work-unit collectively.

These ideological and economic legacies of state socialism have led to unforeseen consequences for market reforms. As noted, the state sector controlled much of the urban economy after 1957. A few private businesses survived on the periphery of the socialist economy, such as hawking and small catering, but they were only a supplement to the state economy. Like the informal sector in other developing societies, peripheral economic activities were never going to generate a good profit margin due to low entry barriers and thus their intensely competitive nature. They are unlikely to account for the current success of private businesses. It is more likely that private businesses have expanded at the expense of the state sector since the latter controlled virtually all urban assets when market reforms started in 1978. In other words, the growth of private businesses has been partly based on their ability to turn state assets into private property.

The economic interests of the urban working class were rooted in the state sector, and these interests were reinforced by the widely held belief that state workers were the masters of the state and that as such they collectively owned units of state property, such as their workplace. If the assets of the public sector were encroached upon by private entrepreneurs, the urban working class might legitimately feel that they were losing out on a large scale. In addition to arguments about 'original sin,' inequality, and unkindness, it is then possible that public resentment of the new rich is also an example of working class interest articulation in a zero-sum game

Post-1978 wealth creation as a zero-sum game

The CCP changed its policy to permit private entrepreneurship in 1977, as a transitory arrangement to deal with urgent unemployment issues in urban areas. The state economy was greatly weakened during the Cultural Revolution of 1966–76 and was unable to continue to function effectively as an urban employment agency. This problem was compounded with the return to the cities of nearly 18 million 'educated youth' whom the CCP had sent to rural areas during the Cultural Revolution (Bernstein 1977; McLaren 1979). Urban unemployment threatened social stability and the political legitimacy of the CCP. The government thus modified its policy toward private businesses to create a new labour market for urban unemployed youth. While the CCP clearly defined them as the main beneficiary of the new labour market, lower status people such as ex-criminals, workers with a low-paid job, and rural peasants took advantage of this policy change since they could not otherwise find a better job elsewhere in the cities (Gold 1990; Szelenyi and Kostello 1996).

Individual businesses

Unexpectedly, in the early 1980s, these low status people became the backbone of a small or 'individual business' sector (*getihu*). By then the CCP had managed to place most unemployed urban youth in either the state or collective sectors. These individual business people were marginalized because of their humble origins and poor educational attainment. Many urban Chinese pointed out that only those without a better alternative would start an individual business of this kind. Starting an individual business was not a popular career choice because the small-scale enterprises operated outside the state sector. That meant that neither owners nor workers had career prospects, job security, medical insurance, subsidized housing, fringe benefits, or pensions. Nor were they entitled to welfare provisions such as grain and cloth rations, housing, pension schemes, and labour insurance since these were either non-existent at that time or controlled and distributed by the government to state workers. State workers might receive less cash income than those working in individual businesses, but the overall value of the compensation package in state employment greatly outweighed that for individual businesses and private entrepreneurship.

Individual businesses were also not respected because they often relied on trade speculation in making profits. They had no choices since the state monopolized all other urban economic activities, but historically speculation was not an accepted business behaviour. This Confucian belief was greatly reinforced by the CCP's communist ideology privileging production and labour. Under state socialism, redistribution allocated goods among the people and was not meant to be a means of profit making. It is thus not surprising that most people could not appreciate the potential for private entrepreneurship to make a meaningful contribution to society. Rather, it was widely regarded as a zero-sum game in which individual businesses parasitically made easy money at the expense of honest working people.

Equally important, individual businesses were not admired precisely because state workers enjoyed a higher status as masters of the PRC, as well as the fruits of the state monopoly over the urban economy. Individual businesses had to spend a far greater amount of time and energy than state workers to earn a living. They had to compete with one another in a labour-intensive market with low barriers to entry. They were not able to derive a large profit margin from their small-scale businesses. In most cases, the individual business was simply a hard way of earning a livelihood. This may explain why few if any of these individual business people have become part of the exceptionally rich in China today (Hong 2004). These businesses have been described as 'ventures that can never grow beyond 10,000 *yuan*'. This may also explain why during the first decade of reform, most accounts of individual businesses by non-PRC observers described how they lived and worked at the bottom of urban society, and how they suffered from low self-esteem and a lack of respect in China's cities (Chan and Unger 1982; Gold 1990; Hershkovitz 1985; Solinger 1984).

New opportunities

A new group of private entrepreneurs emerged after 1985. In that year, the central government encouraged state enterprises to increase their outputs after fulfilling the state production targets. They could sell surplus products in the market and keep the profits, though they had to find the raw materials for the increased production themselves. This policy aimed at boosting industrial production and quickening the pace of market growth. It quickly led to an imbalance between the demand and supply of some commodities and raw materials. State firms received regular quotas of raw materials at planned prices from the government to meet the state production targets. They paid higher prices in the market for additional raw materials with which they produced surplus products for revenue (Hare 1990; Qian 2000; Tsang and Cheng 1997; Wu 1987; Zhang Xiaoguang 1998).[1]

This brought about a dual-track price structure in which the same commodities were priced differently between the planned economy and the market. For example, in 1988, one ton of steel sold for 700 *yuan* in the state sector and 1,500 *yuan* in the market. In the same year, a ton of coal sold for 70 *yuan* in the state sector and 170–210 *yuan* in the market in Shanghai. Other examples of the price differences included the different interest rates for bank loans and exchange rates for foreign currencies.

Under the dual-track price structure, it was possible to earn profits by increasing production with high-priced raw materials. A more efficient way of profit making was to pocket the price differences between the state sector and the market. The key was the ability to obtain official quotas from the government. Many players were drawn into this market – it is estimated that nearly 41 million people (43 percent of the total labour force in the tertiary sector) participated in business activities related to the dual-track price structure by 1988. This was because participation in this market did not require capital or technology. The transactions dealt with official quotas rather than commodities. Business decisions did not entail substantial risks since the goods were in strong demand in the market.

The strong demand in the market determined hefty proceeds from the dual-track price structure. One study claims that the price differentials for commodities, bank loans, and foreign currencies between the planned and market sectors were worth 200 billion *yuan* in 1987, which was not a small amount since the total revenues the PRC Government collected in that year were 1,000 billion *yuan*. In 1988, the price differentials grew to 357 billion *yuan*. In a comparative perspective, this figure was worth almost 30 percent of the state revenues in that year. Another study claims that the total proceeds from the dual-track price structure were worth nearly 40 percent of the state revenues in 1988 (Wu Jixue 2006). Still, another study asserts that the total profits from profiteering in the 1980s were equal to 600 billion *yuan* (Private entrepreneurs 2007).

Who were the main beneficiaries of the dual-track price structure? Most players in this lucrative market were individual profiteers, although some state units also jumped on the bandwagon. Unlike individual business people, these profiteers were well-educated, worked in prestigious government offices and firms such as state trading companies, and were mostly children of high-ranking officials (Hu Xiaopeng 2004). In retrospect, this is not so surprising since the new market had a high barrier to entry, in contrast to the competitive nature of the small commodities market that characterized the operation of individual businesses. Only those who were connected to leading officials could have privileged access to valued goods controlled by the government.

In spite of their noble family origins, good education, and the large amounts they had earned from the dual-track price structure, these profiteers were referred to as *daoye*, a term of denigration that implied a negative image of hooligans. Their business activities were colloquially referred as 'official racketeering' (*guandao*): the unscrupulous combination of speculation and political power (People 2005). The profiteers were not respected since they were seen to have made money through illegal or more accurately improper connections to officials rather than through sound business decisions, private investment, and the exercise of business acumen.

Equally as important, the profiteers were seen as parasites since they made money by exploiting state assets, viewed as communal property by the citizenry. In their eyes, profits from the dual-track price structure should be part of state revenues rather than private wealth, or at least the profits should be shared more widely with the collective owners of public property in some way. In this sense, these profiteers were seen to be involved in a zero-sum game with the rest of society since their gains were balanced by everyone else's losses. The possibility that these profiteers would then be regarded as admirable was almost necessarily low.

Land developers

Starting in the late 1980s, another group of private entrepreneurs emerged from large-scale land speculation. The whole process started after the government gave a green light for the development of a real estate market in urban areas, using it as a major catalyst to quicken the pace of capital accumulation and market reforms (Yeh and Wu 1996; Lin and Ho 2005; Wu Fulong 1997; Wu Fulong 1999; Zhu Jieming 2005). Most players in the land market are private developers, who have reaped monopoly profits since the supply of land (especially land in good locations) has always been limited. It is difficult to discover the extent of their earnings. Indirect evidence suggests that on an annual basis, the government suffered nearly a 12 billion *yuan* loss of land taxes through speculation by private developers. The dual-track price structure produced some millionaires. In comparison, the real estate market produced all kinds of millionaires and also 'China's first billionaires and even a few trillionaires' (Hong 2004; Pei 2006a; Walker 2006).

As with the dual-track prices market, the real estate market has a very high barrier to entry since it is capital-intensive and requires access to land. Only those who are well connected to leading cadres are able to participate in the land market since the state owns all the banks and land. Local officials have sold lands to their family members, friends, and others related through various kinds of personal ties at give-away prices. They have also helped developers obtain low interest loans from state banks under their jurisdiction.

The twelve largest real estate developers in Guangdong Province are reported to be the children of high-ranking officials. In Shanghai, nine out of the ten largest real estate developers are said to be the children of high-ranking officials. Children of high-ranking officials also control thirteen out of the fifteen largest construction companies in the city (the other two are state firms). In neighbouring Jiangsu Province, all twenty-two of the largest real estate companies and the fifteen largest construction firms are owned by children of high-ranking officials. High-ranking officials in this context refers to those working as or retired from working as leading cadres in the central and provincial-level governments (Jones 2007; Children 2006).

Private developers have not earned a great deal of public esteem. They too are seen as having relied on illegal or improper connections with officials for their business success. They are not seen to have invested their own money, made sound business decisions, or borne any business risks. In the unlikely event that their business should fail, the wider expectation is that local officials would order the banks to write off the loans because of the developer's connections. Again, this is seen as a zero-sum game. The developers gain against everyone else, since the developers have mortgaged public assets (loans from state banks and state land) to their own benefit. Private gain is balanced by public loss since neither the state nor the broader citizenry have benefited from the land speculation. Ordinary people have in some sense borne the loss collectively.

Unlike the emergence of a dual-track price structure in manufacturing and processing that had a relatively minor impact on ordinary citizens, the development of the real estate market has victimized a large group of people. Land has been an essential source of income and a way of life for farmers. They have been a primary victim of land speculation as much of the land for real estate development has come from previous farmlands. According to the Research Center for Development under the State Council of the PRC, by 2004, farmers in China had lost 200 billion *yuan* in land expropriation (Cody 2004a; Hong 2004; Pei 2006a; Walker 2006). Residents in designated urban renewal areas who have often been forcefully removed from their neighbourhoods with inadequate compensation have also been victims of similar processes. Local officials seem not to be hesitant to use coercive measures to expropriate land in return for personal gains, or as a means to support the business goals of their family and friends (Tanner 2004; Li Fan 2006; Xia Yunfan 2004; Du 2005).

Land speculators have not only misappropriated public property for personal gain but also amassed wealth at the expense of individual citizens. It is reported that it has become harder for PRC homebuyers to buy a home than their counterparts in the rest of the world. The greed of private developers has been blamed for artificially high housing prices. The housing market has become one of the 'three new big mountains' (along with health care and college education) that have developed beyond the reach of ordinary people. Many citizens have asked why they have to pay high prices in the real estate market since they have housing rights and the land belongs to the state and the people (Shen 2006; Niu Dao 2006; Slaves 2007).

Former state managers

The rise of private developers has been accompanied by the growth of another group of private entrepreneurs, the former managers of state and collective enterprises. They may not have the support of powerful officials that private developers have enjoyed, but they are seen to have been equally aggressive, grasping, and vicious. More numerous than private developers, the harm they have inflicted on the urban citizenry is regarded as more widespread and personal.

The fortunes of these former managers started to develop in the late 1980s when the majority of state firms still operated on a non-profit making basis. Profitability was not a goal of these firms since they were part of the state sector and hence survived through government support. These firms had become a liability rather than an asset for the government. The government decided to transform most of these firms into 'shareholding' companies in the hope that once workers and managers became the shareholders of their firms, they would do their best to improve efficiency. The transformation was arranged in such a way that most workers received some shares and retained their jobs, while managers became the major shareholders of the firms (Hong 2004; Zang 1995).

The firms turned into shareholding enterprises in this way stayed within the state sector since the introduction of shares was meant to be a mechanism of income-distribution among employees and to encourage efficiency rather than a means of creating private ownership. The firms remained poor performers in the market since, unlike private firms, they still had to provide expensive health care, housing, and pensions to their employees. Moreover, the government was ultimately held responsible when they could not pay. Consequently, after 1998 the government moved toward further privatization. In a similar process to Russia's 'shock therapy' (Fish and Choudhry 2007; Holmstrom and Smith 2000) managers and some private business people bought the firms from local officials at a huge discount. The common view is that this was the result of their interconnectivedness and to their mutual benefit. The discount was justified by the fact that the firms were losing money. Managers used the same reasoning to buy shares owned by workers at a cheap price. Of course, once the firms became their private property it became possible for them to make workers redundant with a relatively small lump-sum payment (Hong 2004; Cai 2002; Cai 2005a; Chen Feng 2000; Chen Feng 2006; Giles, Park and Cai 2006; Solinger 2002).

The former state managers have taken full advantage of the existing equipment, land, and business networks of the firms they purchased. Land has been the major windfall, since many state firms were located in areas that have become the central business district in many cities.

These former state managers leading these new firms may have caused greater public outcry about the emergence of the new rich, more even than attends the individual business people, the profiteers, or private developers. Individual businesses supplemented the urban economy and provided urban residents services that were unavailable at that time. The economic activities of the profiteers did not directly bring them into contact with ordinary people, and their activities almost certainly increased industrial production. Private developers have been guilty of land expropriation, but they have improved living conditions in cities, and entry into the housing market has been largely voluntary. The gains from the zero-sum games they have been involved in have come from the redistribution of public property. Ordinary citizens have experienced the losses as a community rather than as individuals.

The former state managers now leading recently privatized firms have in contrast taken on the interests and livelihoods of urban people on an unprecedented scale. They have dispossessed state workers in ways that seem to threaten the vast majority of urban people. Their gains are balanced directly by the losses suffered by state workers. Unlike the outcomes of the previous rounds of primitive accumulation, many state workers have lost their jobs and been thrust into urban poverty through privatization. Ordinary people have experienced the losses as individuals rather than as a community, and the poor's hostility towards the rich has escalated steadily since 2000 (Hong 2004; Cai 2002; Cai 2005a; Chen Feng 2000; Chen Feng 2006; Giles, Park and Cai 2006; Solinger 2002).

There is considerable antipathy to the new rich, and particularly to the various categories of private entrepreneurs. At the same time, some individual business people have earned respect from ordinary people because of their entrepreneurship. In particular, some are regarded as 'intellectual businessmen' since they have derived their profits from the high-tech world (Kwaku, Li and De Luca 2006; Li Haiyang 2006; Watkins-Mathys and Foster 2006; Zhao and Aram 1995). They are admired also because

> The overall sense of social responsibility and business integrity are evidenced in this group's dutiful tax payments in 1998 that amounted to 2.25 times more than those rendered by all the other private enterprises combined. The government policy to support the development of high-tech industries in China ... have lessened the bureaucratic obstacles for this group to obtain administrative approval of their entrepreneuring undertakings, hence their limited need for engaging in rent-seeking.
>
> (Hong 2004: 30–1)

Wealth and status

Status acquisition is a key variable in research on the new rich since it is closely related to their lifestyles, cultural behaviour, and consumption patterns. It is also a key component of social stratification in any society. Yet little has been written on wealth creation and status acquisition in China by Western scholars. Through examining the status performance of private entrepreneurs, this chapter has sought to narrow this knowledge gap. It shows that wealth itself is inefficient as an explanation for status claims in post-1978 China. Instead, public resentment against the new rich seems to be widespread and pronounced.

Why has wealth not brought honour and respect for private entrepreneurs in China? The answer is clearly not the small size of their wealth since it is large even if measured by international standards. Nor are Chinese citizens the kind of people who do not care about material pursuits. A plausible answer is that money is only one of the determinants of esteem and influence. Indeed, social science research indicates that subjective assessments are mainly social influences (Martin 2002: 864). Public anger at the new rich in China can be best understood by reference to the fact that only social behaviours seen as appropriate or legitimate receive deference, prestige, or social status, and *vice versa* (Zhou 2005).

What then might be the social behaviour of the new rich that is unacceptable to ordinary people in China? Existing explanations have generally cited the 'original sin' of the new rich, rising inequality, and the reluctance of the rich to contribute to charitable causes in the PRC. While these explanations are certainly important, this chapter has offered an additional explanation to the pattern of public reaction towards the new rich in China. Private entrepreneurs and ordinary people were in a zero-sum game. The argument is that the state was the sole owner of major assets in the PRC before 1978. Through market transition public property has been gradually privatized. This process has been implemented by the controller of state assets, the CCP, which has thus brought to privatization a zero-sum nature: those who are connected to government officials and CCP cadres can amass wealth through privileged access to state assets, whereas those who are not are the losers.

The new rich have not then gained higher social standing for two reasons. First, many private entrepreneurs have accumulated wealth through large-scale appropriation of public property, or they would not be where they are today. But making private profits at the expense of state assets is unacceptable to the ordinary citizens in any country. This may be especially the case in the PRC since ordinary people have been socialized to take their (previous) status as masters of the PRC for granted. Public property is regarded as belonging to the state and 'the people' – the collective owners of state assets – by definition. The ideological legacy of state socialism has encouraged ordinary people to view the fortunes of the new rich as evidence of the theft of 'communal' property such as official quotas for valued goods, bank loans, and land.

Second, the economic interests of state workers were grounded in the state sector because of the state socialist system practiced before market reforms were introduced. Chinese workers were dependent on the state sector for employment, housing, health care, retirement, and welfare generally. The economic legacy of state socialism has determined that privatization of state assets is seen not only to have trespassed into public property, but also to have encroached on the very economic interests and livelihood of urban residents.

Both of these reasons would seem to explain why public anger at the new rich appears widespread and pronounced in the PRC and why ordinary people are so sensitive to the 'original sin' and the lack of generosity. There has been the primitive accumulation of capital in other societies, notably Hong Kong, Taiwan, and Mexico. However, in the PRC the zero-sum nature of primitive accumulation of capital is crystal clear. Unlike in non-socialist societies, the PRC state and 'the people' were the only owners of wealth before 1978. It is also clear that market transition has involved a process in which public property has been channelled into private hands. Ordinary people in the PRC have better reasons than their counterparts in non-socialist societies to believe that the rich are rich because they have taken from the state and the people. The ways private entrepreneurs encroach on the interests and livelihoods of ordinary people in non-socialist societies are far less direct and consequential than those of their counterparts in the PRC.

'Wealth hatred' in the PRC may nonetheless prove to be a temporary phenomenon since it has resulted through the transition from a state economy to a market economy. Privatization of state assets and thus the zero-sum game have more or less come to an end. With laid-off state workers being replaced by the next generation of urban workers, public anger at the rich may recede in the near future as the economy has grown and the livelihood of ordinary people has improved. Private enterprises may also provide more employment opportunities and become more involved in public affairs and charitable causes. As the PRC intensifies its efforts to develop a knowledge-based economy, the number of intellectual entrepreneurs may grow, and that too may improve the image of wealth and the new rich in general.

Note

1   The dual track price system was annulled in March 1997.

4 Richer than before – the cultivation of middle-class taste

Education choices in urban China[1]

Stephanie Hemelryk Donald and Zheng Yi

Many in the English-speaking world regard the middle classes as the drivers and guarantors for their vision of modernity, democracy, and freedom. This is especially the case when they view societies and polities in transition from authoritarianism, as is the case in China. However, the ready assumption that the middle classes are a universal phenomenon is almost necessarily challengeable and certainly requires greater interrogation of the concept in China.

Who are the Chinese middle classes? Whilst, it could be argued that the PRC has always had a leadership class in its cadre corps, and that China had a significant urban elite pre-1949: managers, state administrators, intellectuals, emergent media stars, and business people, our argument is rather different. Although it is the case that there are crossovers between those of wealth and leadership, between economic sectors of pre-1949 and post-1980, and indeed that the Asia New Rich phenomenon of the 1990s has both pre-figured and contributes to the current 'middle market' nonetheless we would suggest that it is important to note a break between those historical conditions and the present time. The group we are interested in includes some of the 'new rich,' some leadership cadres and some intellectuals, but it is neither defined nor limited by those categories. Defined in socio-economic terms as the 'middle market;'[2] the creative intellectuals, the entrepreneurs, and the managers of state and private enterprise may all be seen as members of this emergent class-grouping; but how are they defining themselves; through their tastes, their expectations, and their cultural credentials? How do these 'urban elites' seek to consolidate their position through the choices they make in their everyday lives? This question should ring through contemporary debates on the manifestations of China's transformation to a market economy; from the formal power it maintains as a regional leader, to its growing informal power as a source of young, talented professionals able to work across the Chinese-speaking and, increasingly, English-speaking worlds.

Our key question of how taste is asserted in China is premised on another fundamental but very complex question: how is class constructed in a post-socialist environment? Any answer requires a number of approaches from questions of politics to issues of culture. One also needs to acknowledge the presence of external influence and local habit, particularly where people and state are engaged in an accelerated process of internationalisation. In that process there is also strong national sentiment, exemplified in an emphasis on the fundamentals of Chinese 'cultural spirituality' (*jingshen wenming*) and 'civilisation work' (*wenming gongzuo*). In this chapter therefore, we examine the development of a self-conscious middle class aesthetic or 'taste structure', through discussions on education and lifestyle choices amongst people who may be rich, or may simply be, in an increasingly common phrase at least on the streets of metropolitan China, 'richer than before.'

Richer than before

China's economic revolution has induced profound changes over the past quarter of a century. Many of these changes are social and cultural in character. They are evident in massive re-organisations of everyday life: urbanisation and forced re-settlement, vast internal migrations, and the restructuring of industry, agriculture, and the military (for a snapshot of many of these phenomena see Donald and Benewick 2005). There are other signs of change, however, which suggest that, at least in the most affluent provinces, cities and population clusters, stability is possible. These signs include the rise of personal property (particularly in light of the National People's Congress's March 2004 and 2007 statements that certain sorts of personal land ownership are now permitted); increasing access to world media and advanced communication systems (Lee 2003); relaxation of rules for tourist visas for overseas travel; the development of Chinese cultural and creative industries and the luxury 'branded' goods market (J. Wang 1996, 2004); and an explosion of private schooling for privileged single children (Lin 1999).

The creation of wealth is now a major aspiration for individuals and families, and, whilst access to Party influence is still highly prized, it is often for reasons of business rather than for purely political advantage (Gore 2000, 135). Even small townships are eager to show that the 'quality' (*suzhi*) of their population is equal to the demands of international investors (Anagnost 1997, 76–80). Meanwhile, the new rich and middle-income earners are providing a stable market and population base for China's future development, and are doing so in step with Party-State priorities for speedy development within the frame of 'harmonious society'. At the same time, the pinch on those who are richer than before but not rich enough is reflected in the joke going round Beijing. China's policies are often promoted in numbers: 'the three represents' was a Jiang Zemin coinage to describe the productive, cultural and populist agenda of the CCP in 2000. Now, less officially, the 'three difficulties' are property, education and health, all drifting beyond the price range of many whose middle income cannot keep up with a cost structure that allows luxury before infrastructure.

In such an environment, it is not surprising that social structures are now very different from the categories employed in Maoist ideology (Brugger and Kelly 1990; Goodman 1994b), and even from the actual categories of privilege and power that obtained before 1976 (Walder 1994). The era of the bourgeoisie, the workers, the peasants, and the intellectuals, supplemented in practice by further divisions of cadre and urban privilege, has largely gone. Now, whilst urban residency and Party influence have retained, and even increased their socio-economic potency, new descriptive categories are required in order to understand how Chinese society works.

However, social re-classification in post-reform China would be mis-understood if it were conceived simply as a 'natural' process brought about by the market, by internationalisation, and domestic reform (Glassman 1991; Hsiao 1993). As Robison and Goodman have argued (1996b, 8–9) there is little evidence that the Chinese middle-market consumer will follow the paths of neo-liberalism and mediated civil society (Rodan 1998). Indeed, the historical contingencies of their emergence as a group suggest otherwise: the growth of the middle-income consumer class, or the 'new rich' (Fan 2000) in China is not historically equivalent to the emergence of a middle class as understood in a liberal political economy (Buckley 1999). Further-more, the average middle income professional and business player is far too dependent on the security of the state and on Party influence to have any interest in risking political activity or opinions that would jeopardise his/her financial and social futures (Goodman 1996; Rodan 1996).

Where there is dissent and organised opposition in China, it tends to arise either as religious populism (Perry 2002), or through the dissatisfaction of low-income workers (Lee 2003), the environmentally disadvantaged (Jing 2003), and the unemployed (Z. Wang 2003). Neo-liberal democratic aspirations are confined to relatively small groups of intellectuals (C H. Wang 2003) and in interrogations of popular culture (Link *et al.* 2002). There are, of course, individuals who protest land grabs, the environmental costs of development and the dangers of under regulated food production. These people are, like activists the world over, an extremely small percentage of the total population. However, as the 2005–2007 'nail-house' case illu-strated, they are drawn from those with property to protect as much as from those with nothing.[3] Perhaps the 'three difficulties' are a sign of the political consciousness of those who feel cheated by the promise of reform, but they are also indicative of the rising expectations of those who have profited by entrepreneurial opportunities. That said, the middle classes, or, rather, those that have an income, or sufficient intellectual capital, to match or gesture towards their aspirations, have not necessarily made the Habermasian con-nection between wealth, the costs of new living standards and democratic access to power assumed in European liberal philosophy.

For some, of course, the 'three difficulties' do not apply. More than 50 percent of the residents in the upmarket *Beijing Riviera* gated community are local Chinese. Residents admit that the Chinese population tends to be secretive about their business interests, and to pay in cash for very large properties with guaranteed security. Whilst *Beijing Riviera* contents itself with Singaporean trained guards, buyers of newer and even more prestigious developments nearby (one sited where the arms trading arm of the Chinese Government was formerly based) have UK security. This includes full handprint recognition on entry. This development is typical of several luxurious settlements off the Jingshun Road outside Beijing's centre. It is co-owned by a Singaporean management company, and boasts both local facilities: 'the club', 'the pool', 'the gardener' and imported brand names, the most prestigious of which is the k-12 Dulwich College which is situated on site and on a nearby campus. The children are bussed direct every morning and come home for homework, nannies, and swimming lessons. So, whilst some are content to be 'richer than before', others are in a different league altogether.

Theories of taste formation

We suggest therefore that the rise of the Chinese middle class(es) is a profoundly important example of new class formation and Utopian aspirations in a post-socialist society, but that its sustaining ambitions cannot be assumed from international versions of a similar relative income group. This 'middle class' is a catch-all phrase, that neatly sidesteps previous categorisations which are now of little practical advantage in China, rather than an indication of homogeneity. In our interviews with young professionals, students in elite universities, and creatives, it is those who are extremely well off who are usually referred to as the new rich or the middle classes. However, as conversations proceed, the interviewees themselves claim to have a middle class sensibility, even though they vehemently deny being 'rich enough'. This sensibility they suggest, consists of openness, understanding of international developments and a modern approach to education. Meanwhile, in interviews in a gated development outside Chengdu, with those who are indeed rich – and aware of that fact – the same 'sensibility' is demonstrated and referred to. In this set of conversations in Chengdu, the mainly thirty-something residents of *Luxehill* were unanimous on several points, not just with each other but also with students and young people elsewhere who denied being well off at all. Choice, lifestyle and differentiation were all available to these people in varying degrees, and schooling and an environmentally sound home for their family was the common way in which it found expression. Several were parents, and put their children's education at the forefront of their agenda. So, whilst in terms of both income and social behaviours, there are many strains and strands of the phenomenon of a 'middle market', nonetheless, whether underpaid public servants or business professionals in highly successful enterprises, their actual choices, and the reasoning behind those choices, were remarkably similar.

School is a central tenet of class formation and maintenance (Hunter 1988). Curriculum, values and pedagogy all combine to an image of how the child may be formed as an educated and acculturated subject within an emergent social formation. In the Experimental School for Foreign Languages in Chengdu, for example, children are enrolled as boarders in order to accelerate their English language learning and to develop their chances as 'culture champions' in national exams. The school is expensive although it is modelled on the local system, and so has acquired exclusivity. The Headmaster in 2006 felt however that this school was especially favoured by parents because it combined excellent education with an opportunity for children to network with future peers in the world of public service and business opportunity. In the same city, the Golden Apple kindergarten is alternately lauded as a model of international education (children tend to speak three languages before they leave for primary school) and reviled as a super-élite institution that separates children from the real world. The wife of one of our 'rich' interviewees at *Luxehills* was emphatic that, whilst she had decided to send her daughter to Chengdu's American international school, because it had a more relaxed approach to education and homework, she would never have submitted her to Golden Apple!

Siegfried Kracauer's critique of culture and class in 1933, when he saw in the 'pleasure barracks' of Berlin, the symptom of an 'ideological homelessness' of the salaried masses (Kracauer, 1998, 88–90), is useful here. His work and the observations inform the idea that, whilst new social formations may resemble equivalent groupings elsewhere, they are very unlikely to be more than superficially similar. Rather, what emerges is an amalgam of expectation, emulation and aspiration, of which the models and origins are diverse and contradictory For Kracauer, 'the deeper moral [of reading matter for the salaried masses in Berlin] ... is obviously to inculcate in the so-called middle class the conviction that even with a modest income they can maintain the appearance of belonging to bourgeois society, so they have every reason to be content as the middle class' (1998:90). Kracauer's observation of the transition to modernity in the Weimar Republic, helps us identify and analyse the structures of taste that induce contemporary postsocialist contentment and thereby sustain and deepen the category of the middle class in urban China without necessarily challenging a political status quo.

The groups in question are different in character and location, and income. Kracauer was less interested in the haute bourgeoisie (arguably on a par with at least the richer members of our target group here) than in the middle to low income salaried urbanites who were finding their way in the 'new' German city. But the focus of his inquiry is nonetheless related to our question of class and taste. He noted that people made cultural choices in order to establish themselves as a recognisable and compatible group. Likewise, we suggest that choices in education and lifestyle are an expression of class formation that may yet include a wide diversity of people and income levels, who are either not – or no longer – willing or able to accept the label of élites, leaders, or intellectuals. 'Middle-class' is then a catch-all self-identifier that serves an immediate social purpose. Yet its conditions for existence also require that the idea of this class alliance designs its own taste structures and opportunities, making reality from necessity.

In 1963, E. P. Thompson made his classic intervention in the discussion of class analysis when he defined class-formation as 'making' rather than a structural determination (Thompson 1966). For Thompson, 'class' as a historical phenomenon is not a 'structure' or 'category' that exists as an 'It' with ideal interest or consciousness, but something which happens in human relationships. However, Thompson's application of the historical *longue durée* still looks too much like an inevitable, if not simply 'natural' process. It is unable to provide a model for understanding class-formation as a Utopian project, the outcomes of which remain to be imagined and shaped rather than emerging as 'a result of common experiences' inherited or shared (Thompson 1966:9). Dror Wahrman usefully extends this notion of 'making' to a vision of a middle class-centred society-as-myth. He argues that the importance of the category of 'middle class' as a social and historical conceptualisation is not that it denotes a palpably distinct social stratum, but that it plays a central role in organising social and political experience (Wahrman 1995). Furthermore, in recent work on Euro-American history and society, especially that defined as new historical studies or cultural politics and poetics, there has been a steady increase in the attention paid to the 'shaping' and 'fashioning' of class and social identification through cultural practices (Kidd and Roberts 1985; Wolff and Seed 1988; Radway 1997; Harrison 1999).

Taking the lead from these (predominantly British) studies, and using the kernel of Thompson's notion of 'making' and Wahrmann's radicalisation of 'myth-making', we are building on Bourdieu's analysis of how socio-cultural relations are cultivated, lived and embodied, how they take on a particular form, which correlates with, but is not reducible to, economic capital (Bourdieu 1989). We suggest that, since both distinction and seduction of the mainstream are the very premises of this Chinese circumstance, transformational cultural consumption should be understood neither as social palliative (Latham 2002) nor heroic self-affirming expression. Rather it describes a very particular post-socialist Chinese 'situation' where social, cultural, political and economic forces, including the Party, the State and multinational capital, intersect and jostle for legitimacy and success.

We suggest therefore that seeing the limitations of the cultivation and range of middle class taste in China affords a necessary differentiation between political ambitions and social and economic aspirations. Schooling choice is both starkly new in the Chinese context and yet also working on a continuum from the longer tradition of Confucian education, emulation and 'person-making' (*xiusheng yangxing*) (Hall and Ames 1987: 229; Evans and Donald 1999).

Choosing a school

If we argue that the middle classes of modern China are both 'richer than before', but also in many cases not yet rich enough to avoid the 'three difficulties' or so rich as to be destroying the very taste structures offered as an aesthetic alternative to revolutionary purity or unrefined consumer display, what might we expect will train taste and tempt expenditure? One set of visual clues is offered in examples of the school prospectus. The particular prospectuses are for schools in metropolitan centres, whose very existence is contingent on the high incomes of a large enough, but still élite, group of consumers. Whereas the Experimental School in Chengdu was expensive, nonetheless we met ex-students whose parents were ex-academics, or relatively small-scale business people. The much glossier international schools are much more exclusive to the seriously rich. Nevertheless, the prospectuses collectively echo the symptoms of high-end modernity in a nation still oriented towards development and deep educational value; lifetime learning, and private education. Where Kracauer describes a disciplined pursuit of leisure as the key strategy for class-making in Weimar Germany, in China there is a stronger emphasis on access to special educational advantage. This is again not quite the same as the 'extra activities' fetish central to contemporary first world middle class society and cosmopolitan privilege, but the direction is similar.

Kracauer's trilogy of intent: conviction, contentment and the appearance of belonging; remakes itself in the school prospectuses, where the contemporary Chinese prioritisation of intellectual capital, the pursuit of taste, and the accession of class-through-(targeted) leisure is played out for parents. Conviction lies simply in the power of money and education combined to produce a 'classy' future for one's child. Contentment resides in the sense that one has done everything one can for that child, that the child's everyday experience is 'richer than before'. The appearance of belonging is more complicated however. Exclusive schools in metropolitan centres compete for the children of highly paid urban professionals, educators, private and state managers, and entrepreneurs. In order to do so effectively, they have become adept in selling an idea of distinction (*youwei*) and cultural caché (*wenhua qingqu*) along with the national priorities of comprehensive learning (*quanmian jiaoyu*) (Gu 2001) and social quality (*shehui suzhi*). In the private school prospectus, the value of education is no longer simply about helping your child to precious university places in a very demanding educational environment (Zhu and Hao 2001). It is also a ticket to participation in China's new status as an internationalising market (Keane 2003) especially when many of them will select education outside China at tertiary level. At the same time, the prospectus re-invents educated Chinese finesse as culturally discrete from the blandishments of global taste and MacDonaldisation (Ritzer 2004).

The peculiar genre of the school prospectus combines images of class embodied in well-dressed and uniformed children (different uniforms for numerous occasions in some cases), homilies on the values of comprehensive education with an emphasis on English and technology, and a fetishisation of classroom spaces and infrastructure. It does not take much imagination to see a decided link between these forced landscapes of achievement with the posters of the revolutionary era, where children were similarly posed as the successors to a perfected modern future. The uniforms are often modelled on English public school or French Lycée styles, with kilts and tartans in abundance. Where the school is part owned by an existing élite institution (such as Dulwich College) in London, the colours in their publications are muted. Bottle greens and navy blues seem to emphasise quality and tradition. The crest is much in evidence. Where the school is 'borrowing' (one assumes) the class clout of an international brand a crest is deployed, although its provenance is highly dubious. The 'Eton Montessori Kindergarten' is an example of this interface between the 'idea of class' and class itself. As one British expatriate parent ruefully noted: 'Eton would expect us to come to them, surely?'

This semiotic surface of internationalisation hints at the very deep expectation that all such schools will produce internationalised (that is English speaking) graduates for the international business job market. This is of course quite different from the political posters of the 1960s and 1970s, where children are primed for the long revolution, although one could draw a connection with the tendency at that time to show children in formation with other international revolutionary cultures and aspirants, specifically those of Africa and South America. Again, the representation was frankly unconvincing, but the political intent and underlying convictions were in earnest. Belonging is thus a multi-faceted value, in which the child belongs to the international regime of executive business opportunities (Devine 2004), to a local rubric of national development and culture, and to an imagined world of class betterment and global status.

In these publications the answer to the leading question, 'who are the Chinese middle class at a crucial point in China's post-socialist development?' thus revolves around capability and the job market, culture and national pride. This Chinese middle class, an educated élite, represents a powerful regional grouping in terms of trade, cultural influence, and indeed the prevailing national imagination of China itself. This is in part a planned outcome. The activities of 'choice', and 'education', especially in the Chinese context, are not simply functions of individual behaviour, but are also matters of planning and implementation as well as cultivation at the level of Party policy and involving direct intervention by the State. The emphasis on 'harmonious society', in Party pronouncements since 2004, is also an emphasis on 'contentment'. Or, as Kracauer reminded us from a failing republic, the deeper morals served in the soothing of 'ideological homelessness', are those of a state in the throes of chronic transition.

Ian Hunter's thoughts on the teaching of distinction (1988) are a reminder that the socialisation of the adult follows on from the education of the child. Hunter's grave estimates of the planned pedagogies in the governance of cultural character underline the real political constraints inherent in middle class aesthetics and taste, and the ways in which 'education' and 'choosing' encourage, elaborate and cultivate a Utopian set of social distinctions which support a national agenda.

There is coincidence here with Bourdieu's distinction of the three different forms of taste dynamics (Pinches 1999:34) and his assertion that the culture of the middle-class (or petit-bourgeoisie) is by necessity an 'intermediary' between the 'legitimate' taste or 'high culture' and the 'popular' aesthetics of the working class (Bourdieu 1989: 247). The historical vision and aesthetic underpinning of the project of contemporary Chinese cultural class transformation, as tested by the new 'middle-brow' reading materials (in this instance by the promises of selective and élite private schools) is the contesting ground for the 'high' and the 'low,' or, more accurately, for a transformation of both to something unknown.[4]

China class – global class

Globally, there is significant and renewed interest in contemporary class formations, as dramatic economic, social and cultural changes arise from globalisation and from upheavals in post-socialist societies, and in the so-called 'late-developing' regions (Hann 2002; Chua 2000). This interest is particularly evident in post-colonial scholarship, and in Chinese Studies. From India to Peru, scholars have joined the search for adequate models for understanding and representing social and cultural history. They have conducted empirical and theoretical investigations into the creation of class structures in a fractured modernity (Joshi 2001), the vision of middle class centred society (Torri 1991), and the 'idea' of the middle class (Parker 1998). Over the last decade, scholars of China have also increasingly rehearsed the significance of social classification and political differentiation. They have offered critical evaluations of recent Chinese political and intellectual debates (H Wang 2003; CH Wang 2003; Zhang 2001; Huters 2003; Davies 2001); and have mapped out the political economy of social structural change and the emergence of new social forces in reform and post-reform China (Goodman 1994b; Unger 1994; Hendrischke 1994; Gu and Kelly 1994). They have commented upon the historical legacy and the global situation of post-socialist Chinese nationalism in relation to social classification (Zhang 2001; Zheng 2003), and the formation of post-reform China as a consumer society (Robison and Goodman 1996b; Fan 2000). In a closely related field, researchers of the Asia-Pacific region have provided illuminating theoretical elaboration as well as empirical studies of the cultural configurations, consumer behaviours, economic success and social status of the Asian new rich (Young 1999; Chua and Tan 1999). Most of these studies are anthropological, sociological and politically oriented, although cultural studies researchers are also paying attention to contemporary Chinese popular culture (Tang 2000; Liu 2004; Dai, 1999) and have elaborated the complicated relationship between the new Chinese cultural industries and what might be called the emerging 'society' or 'public sphere' (Dirlik 1994; Dutton 1998; Donald 2000).

Despite this volume of work, it remains a significant challenge facing the field of contemporary Chinese cultural studies to understand how the intersection between, on the one hand, the social and cultural spheres and, on the other hand, areas of political and economic development and power, creates contemporary transformations in social structure. By noting school promotional materials, we can see hints of the sometimes rather aggressive, construction of a select readership which is thereby offered a stake in the 'mainstream of world civilization' (Sun Liping 1996: 19). The theoretical ground is not steady however. Bourdieu's theorisation on 'cultural capital', on 'class tastes and life-styles', as well as his notion of 'habitus' (Bourdieu and Passeron 1979; Bourdieu 1989) are indispensable to our current understanding of cultural practice and class-formation, although we must re-formulate cultural capital to take note of the actual circumstances of a Chinese middle market, of Chinese culture and aesthetics, and of Chinese priorities and experience. Similarly, when we use Kracauer's ethnographic techniques in elucidating how people are experiencing class, 'spiritual homelessness' and a paradigm of self-education through 'choosing', we do so recognising that Weimar Berlin, and urban China in the twenty-first century, are not one and the same place. Or indeed, modern Britain: would for instance a Chinese parent recognise the crest, the brand-name 'Dulwich' 'Harrow' 'Eton', or the colour 'bottle green' as the best semiotic evidence of educational quality? How reliant are they on international league tables – as clearly is the case for top Universities across the world market of higher education, where one of the league tables comes out of Shanghai – or word of mouth about what constitutes 'a class education'? And, why does a British education constitute class in the first place? Certainly, many well-off parents in Chengdu were uncertain. They trusted the Chinese system and felt that it was tried and tested for quality. International schools were new, market interventions with no track record in China. Therefore, if they did choose them for their children, it was because of their more relaxed approach to education not for their traditions in European class privilege.

The cultivation of class is variously understood as a political project, as an economic reaction to changing circumstance, and as an unmanaged historical trajectory determined by the rise of capital. We are arguing here for a theory of the formation of class as an aesthetic intervention; one which is characterised by activity and performance – what we might term 'a *contingent* identity', but which is also dependent on a series of gate-keeping economic and political activities at the level of the state, what we term, 'a *necessary* identity'. In this sense, the management of identity is canvassed through the deployment of taste structures, which return a bounded middle class sensibility that refuses the vertical bleeding of class and experience from the immediate past to the aspirational present. This refusal is necessary to the overriding political project that underpins and is formed through Chinese economic reform, a project of conservative social development and barely regulated capital production. These bounded and quite unadventurous taste structures are concerned in the instance of education just considered both with the reproduction of a tasteful self (through the choosing of élite education for one's children). What is sought here is a nationally acceptable version of internationalised experience, mediated through more or a version of educational design and textual form, and yet good enough to constitute a sensation of belonging to the realms of ordered and careful adventure, so clearly introduced in Kracauer's work: 'one works-council member defends rowing because it brings people into contact with Nature' (104).

Questions of choice and taste

The critical reflections, which we have put forward in this chapter include the ever-necessary determination on the transferability of international (in this case, European) categories of descriptive judgement to Chinese social and cultural conditions and contingencies. Should we, for example, pursue micro-studies of class formation as entirely separate from over-weaning Eurocentric and Anglo-American assumptions of how middle classes access and maintain their status and habitus? Or, might we expect that an analysis of the level and nature of state support for class stability, based on the production of an aesthetic sensibility amongst middle-income earners, will tell us as much about global trends towards selective gentrification as it does about the changing nature of Chinese social capital? Our argument is that the making of class is itself a transferable notion, but one which does not carry any necessary political outcomes, conditions or formative stages. That is, in order to attain nuanced understandings of the socio-cultural ambitions of an aspirational, commercially productive, and property-driven group, glossed as the Chinese 'middle-class', we must be both locally intuitive whilst open to clues gleaned from the post-modernity of early capital. This is therefore to suggest an anti-Marxist materialism that challenges the inherence of democracy, autocracy or even apathy in the achieved contentment of middle class experience.

The significance of this hypothesis is both theoretical and pragmatic. Current socio-economic usages of the term 'middle class' in reference to China are somewhat misleading, and an approach foregrounding socio-cultural *choice* and the cultivation of *taste* will greatly improve our capability to understand China's present and future society. This is particularly important given the impact of Chinese professionals, students and business people in global societies, and particularly within Asian and Pacific populations. This chapter has offered a brief sketch of our working conception of the appropriation of international theories to contemporary Chinese conditions, noting that the application is inspirational and referential, rather than exact. The contingency of time, location, and cultural histories make any absolute rendition of experience untenable. Nonetheless, we would contend that the rise of the salaried masses, contemporary semiotic manifestations of the Englishness, and the emergence of a modern Chinese middle class are comparable cases of class formation, seen in the context of a national history and nationalism in a moment of chronic transition.

Notes

1   This research is supported by the ARC Discovery grant: DP0665537, The Cultivation of Middle Class Taste: reading, Tourism and Education Choices in Middle Class China.
2   In addition to the concept of the 'middle classes' (*zhongchan jieji*) (as discussed in Ch.2) state publications also refer to 'affluent society' (*xiaocang shehui*) and 'the salaried classes' (*gongxin jieceng*).
3   The nail house was a property in Chongqing which was targeted for demolition having been in a family's possession and occupation for over forty-five years. The owners refused and mounted a two year campaign to resist. A compensation deal was reached only after adverse publicity for the developers in the wake of the property law debate in the 2007 National People's Congress.
4   To fully understand these contentions and their implications, we also refer to the scholarship (Johnson *et al.* 1985) on the traffic between the 'elite' (*ya*) and 'popular' (*su*) cultures in Ming-Qing China, when social mobility, reclassification and cultural re-orientation were similarly cast as the signs of the times.

Part II

Entrepreneurs, managers and professionals

5 Corporate CEOs as cultural promoters

Colin Hawes

The CEOs and other senior executives of large corporations, both state-controlled and privately-managed, are an influential group among the new rich in China. However, the majority of these corporate executives are not content to be seen merely as materially rich: they also wish to become culturally rich too, and to raise the cultural level of their employees and even of their customers. Culture in this context refers primarily to high culture activities such as literature, art, architecture and philosophy, but also to more popular cultural forms such as television dramas if they have a didactic purpose beyond mere entertainment.

This chapter examines the phenomenon of senior corporate executives as cultural promoters from three aspects. First, it considers the frequent attempts by corporate executives to represent themselves as cultural connoisseurs, through composing poetry, practising Chinese calligraphy, sponsoring literary and artistic publications and exhibitions, and through quoting traditional Chinese philosophy. Second, it describes the cultural activities that many large corporations organize for their employees, which are aimed at promoting 'spiritual civilization' among those employees and creating a 'harmonious' environment within the workplace. Third, it shows how some corporate executives, particularly in the real estate development business, are attempting to educate their newly rich customers in how to adopt a cultured lifestyle, or working with local governments to promote cultural ideals through the popular media. The chapter concludes by examining the various reasons for this fixation of corporate executives on culture, which range from political pressures to business factors and traditional Chinese concepts of the 'scholar merchant' (*rushang*).

Corporate CEOs practising culture

In the early 1990s, the PRC government withdrew much of its funding from state-sponsored literary journals. There were hundreds of these journals throughout the country, many connected with provincial Chinese Writers Associations, and many were extremely popular among educated readers. But with the growth of competing forms of popular entertainment in the

1980s such as television and commercial films, these literary journals lost most of their subscribers, and the government decided they were no longer effective as a way to reach the hearts and minds of the Chinese people. So the government set these literary journals loose and required virtually all of them to become self-supporting. Desperate for money to keep their journals going, many editors turned to business corporations. In return for receiving generous funding from these corporations, prestigious journals like *Beijing Literature* ran advertisements, and more surprisingly, they even agreed to publish poetry by the CEOs of their corporate sponsors. To give just one example, on the back cover of the January 1994 issue of *Beijing Literature*, one finds an advertisement for the Beijing Badaling Tourism Corporation, and inside the back cover is a classical-style regulated verse poem by Qiao Yu, General Manager of the Corporation (Kong 2002: 111–22).

The enthusiasm among corporate executives for writing and publishing their poetry at first sight seems to have little connection with their business concerns. But it is quite a common practice even today. So much so that in 2005 the Beijing Six Classics Arts and Culture Institute and the World Chinese Poetic Association announced the publication of a *Chinese Entrepreneurs Poetry Anthology* (Chinese Entrepreneurs 2005). Corporate executives with poetic tendencies have also banded together to form their own societies. In June 2007, in the industrial heartland city of Changchun, in Jilin Province, an Entrepreneurs Poetry Society held its inaugural meeting with several dozen local businesspeople in attendance. The Society's stated mission is to 'promote creative exchanges and explorations among entrepreneurs and poets, and to raise the creative level of entrepreneurs who love to write poetry' (Jilin Daily 2007). Clearly, these CEOs and businesspeople want to be viewed by the world not just as generous patrons of the arts or good corporate citizens, but as expert cultural practitioners themselves.

Not all Chinese CEOs are proficient at writing poetry (although a surprising number like to recite classical-style poems whenever one gives them half a chance). Instead, they may prefer to practice brush calligraphy. Many Chinese companies publish corporate magazines, and the titles of these are often written in flourishing calligraphic strokes by their CEO. For example, the masthead of the *China Metallurgical Group Weekly News* was written in fluent running script by the firm's CEO and Party Secretary Yang Changgheng. The practice of asking an authority figure to inscribe the name of a newspaper or magazine with a brush, and then using the calligraphy as the masthead, is a well-established cultural tradition in the PRC. The characters for the PRC's leading official newspaper, *The People's Daily*, were originally written by Mao Zedong, and other Communist leaders have written the mastheads for numerous newspapers and magazines over the past few decades (Kraus 1991: 11–13). An inscription by an authority figure is a sure sign that the contents of the publication have been endorsed by that person, and that the author may be protected by that person. At the same time, being able to write well with a brush is also evidence that one is cultivated and self-disciplined, and therefore worthy of being a leader (Kraus 1991: 72–4). Corporate CEOs are clearly emulating these aspects of Chinese leadership tradition by writing out the titles of their company magazines in traditional-style calligraphy.

Corporations also ask visiting Chinese political leaders to write calligraphic inscriptions to show their support for the firm's work, and these inscriptions are often posted up in the corporate headquarters and even on the corporate website. See, for example, the series of calligraphic inscriptions by various visiting dignitaries such as Wen Jiabao and Jiang Zemin on the website of China Unicom, a major telecommunications service provider (China Unicom). Some CEOs adopt a similar practice when visiting the different divisions of their own companies. Liu Suisheng, Chair and Party Secretary of the Datong Coal Mining Group, regularly writes calligraphic inscriptions to commemorate various company events, and some of these are posted under Liu's profile on the China Enterprise Confederation website (China Enterprise Confederation (n.d.)). As with poetry, CEOs have also formed calligraphy societies to share their work with likeminded businesspeople. One example is the Shenzhen Entrepreneurs Society for the Study of Calligraphy and Painting, established in 2006. The Society's website displays a generous selection of traditional-style artworks and calligraphy by its forty-two members, most of whom are high-level executives in Shenzhen's major business corporations (Shenzhen Entrepreneurs).

Even CEOs who do not have the time or inclination to master traditional arts like poetry and calligraphy may display their cultural awareness by portraying themselves as philosophers, using ancient Chinese wisdom to guide their business and life choices. When Zhang Ruimin, CEO of the Hai'er Group, one of China's most successful white goods manufacturers, was asked by a reporter what was the most important thing for CEOs to understand, his answer was: 'I'd say philosophy.' He then quoted two phrases from the *Daodejing*, an ancient Daoist text, and applied them to contemporary management situations (Hai'er Group (n.d.)). Clearly, Zhang wants to be seen not just as a highly successful business manager but also as a deep thinker.

One would not expect to come across such CEO-philosophers in the ruthless and cutthroat world of Chinese real estate developers. But Pan Shiyi, Chair of the high-profile and enormously profitable SOHO China Corporation, also claims to be an enthusiastic reader of Daoist and Buddhist texts. According to an article in the online magazine *China Today*:

> In recent years Pan Shiyi has been doing two things: continually building houses, and reading [ancient texts] such as *The Book of Changes*, *Diamond Sutra*, and Laozi's *Daodejing*. They contain thousands of years' accumulation of wisdom and profundity. When talking about reading these works, his face lights up, 'When creating anything one needs inspiration, and the real estate industry is no exception. I get

inspiration from reading ancient books, especially *The Book of Changes*. I get new ideas each time I read it.' Pan says that as he is busy dealing with the temporal all day, he can get spiritual sustenance from reading these texts in the evening

(Zhan 2003).[1]

Pan almost goes as far as suggesting that his money-making real estate deals are a sideline to his real ambition in life, which is to be an enlightened sage:

> Since 1990 I have made new friends, under whose influence I became interested in Buddhism and Zen. For a time I was obsessed with these philosophies, and there were books on Zen everywhere at home and in my office. One night I had a dream. In it a voice told me that enlightenment could be attained simply by being happy and maintaining a good humor. This had great impact on my character. I now believe that wisdom can come naturally in the course of being happy and humorous
>
> (Zhan 2003)

Some CEOs prefer to create their own pithy sayings distilling the essence of management, whose style is reminiscent of the *Analects* of Confucius. Zheng Jianjiang is the CEO of the AUX Group, one of China's largest privately managed electrical goods manufacturers. He has a page on the Group's website entitled 'The Way of the CEO' (*Zongcai zhi dao*), which includes wisdom such as the following:

> The character *qi* [in *qiye* (business enterprise) is made up of the elements *ren* (people) and *zhi* (stop)]. So if you take away the 'people' everything will 'stop'. People are the crucial link that allows the enterprise to survive and grow.
> On Fresh Flowers: There has never been a flower that did not wither. Growth and decay, change and substitution are historical laws. The only way to attain success is by using rational reflection to extend one's life cycle
>
> (Zheng Jianjiang)

Some CEOs have reacted against this philosophical and cultural posing by their peers, arguing that it serves no useful purpose and it merely obscures the actual performance of the company's business. Ning Gaoning, CEO of the COFCO Group, decries what he calls the harmful 'literary tendency' of Chinese corporate executives: 'When describing their companies ... they like to tell a lot of "stories" that have nothing to do with the company's management, and turn business operations into "literature"' (Ning 2006). Instead, Ning declares, companies should present plain facts and figures about their strategies, market segments, research, and development just like 'international corporations' so that investors and other stakeholders can gain a clearer idea of whether the company is performing well or badly.

Of course, in a different socio-political environment such as Australia or the United States, Ning's criticisms would be perfectly reasonable. But as I will argue in the concluding section of this chapter, there are rational and utilitarian explanations to justify the very literary and cultural preoccupations of CEOs that Ning attacks so roundly. Before doing so, however, I will examine two other ways in which CEOs promote culture.

Promoting culture among corporate employees

The CEOs of China's largest corporations do not just practise culture themselves; they also enthusiastically promote cultural activities among their employees. This occurs in three major ways.

First, CEOs encourage employees to contribute to in-house corporate e-magazines or cultural forums on corporate websites.[2] Some magazines even offer annual prizes for the best employee contributions. These are not limited to creative writing, but may also include employees' paintings, calligraphy and photography too. The first issue of *Tengen People*, the e-magazine of the Tengen Group, a privately managed electrical instrument manufacturer, explains the function of these magazines in flowery language:

> Tengen People ... brings variety to our work lives. It is a spiritual harbour, a fragrant meadow of ideas, and a stage to display our talents and wisdom
>
> (Tengen Group 2005)

Few Australian or Anglo-American companies would describe their in-house magazines in such lofty and culturally-imbued terms.

The second way that large Chinese corporations cultivate their employees is through formal educational programmes – sometimes called 'universities'. Not content with merely providing practical skills training and business administration classes, these programmes also generally include cultural classes to help employees grow into rounded human beings. One report on such a cultural class held by Huawei Technologies in 2005–6 lists the following eclectic selection of texts studied over the past year: The *Analects* of Confucius; a video entitled *Europe and the Modern Age*; Sun Tzu's *Art of War*; selections from the Bible; and *Zen: The Chinese Transformation of Buddhism*, by Peking University Professor Tang Yijie. (Huawei Technologies 2006). Employees found studying these texts worthwhile because they 'opened up new perspectives, helped them control their impulsive tendencies, gave them ideas to apply in their work, and allowed them to have spiritual exchanges with their workmates' (Huawei Technologies 2006).

Some employee interpretations of Tang Yijie's text on Zen Buddhism are also given in the report. They display an interesting mix of practical and spiritual concerns. For instance, employees interpreted the Zen practice of sitting meditation as follows:

> Normally we face a lot of work pressures, but if we take a bit of time to sit and meditate when we get up in the morning or before we sleep at night, ... it will greatly help to relax our bodies and minds, and allow us to maintain a happy mood ... Even though our understanding of Buddhist principles may be limited, couldn't we treat our work as a form of spiritual cultivation? ... No matter how busy and tiring our work becomes, we should do our very best to maintain a peaceful heart and try to seek out beauty in our lives and work
>
> (Huawei Technologies 2006)

The third way that Chinese companies attempt to raise employees' cultural awareness and build their characters is through getting them to repeat corporate mission statements and songs, and to engage in various group activities and contests organized within the corporation. The words of the mission statements and songs generally praise the company's values, its wonderful family atmosphere, and the joys and privileges of working there. Often they have very moralistic content: one must not only be an efficient and reliable employee but a good person too and a patriotic Chinese citizen. For example, the Company mission statement, or 'declaration' of the Tengen Group must be recited every day by all its employees. Some of the phrases in this declaration include:

> Each new day is full of hope.
> Our lives must have purpose,
> And our work must be well planned.
> Today's work must be finished today:
> We must not waste any precious time in our lives.
> Let us use our determined will to conquer difficulties and correct bad
>   habits,
> And let us use our industrious sweat to create a glorious future.
> As self-improving and self-confident Tengen employees,
> The ideals in our hearts will certainly be realized!
>
> (Tengen Group)[3]

The constant repetition of such slogans is clearly designed to drum these positive sentiments into employees' heads. The company songs have a similar effect. They are often set to revolutionary tunes and sung by massed corporate choirs, to get the employees whipped up into a frenzy of enthusiasm. The company song of Guanghui Group, a privately managed conglomerate based in the Western province of Xinjiang, is based on a tune entitled 'March of the Chinese People's Liberation Army'.[4] It contains uplifting phrases such as:

> Guanghui is our stage:
> On which we can display our youthful talents.
> With our singing we tell the world about our miracles,
> And with our wisdom we create the future ...
> Fearlessly we mold the spirit of Guanghui's employees;
> We are the generation that will build a new century
>
> (Guanghui Group 2005a).

While corporate mission statements do not strictly belong to cultural activities in the elite sense, they share with corporate songs the aim of encouraging employees to feel an emotional connection with the firm and a sense that their work has a broader social meaning. Other cultural activities organized by corporations clearly have a similar purpose. For example, among the activities put on by Guanghui Group during 2006 were the 'I belong to Guanghui' speech contest; the Healthy Seniors Variety Show (in which retired employees were the performers); and the Annual Guanghui Talent Show (Guanghui Group 2005b).

One important point to note is that while corporate CEOs doubtless have a strong influence on the kinds of employee cultural activities that take place, the Communist Party branches that are established within the vast majority of corporations frequently take a central role in organizing and promoting such activities. I will discuss the significance of this Communist Party involvement further in the concluding section below. Before doing so, however, I will describe one more area where Chinese CEOs have acted as cultural promoters.

CEOs promoting culture among customers and the wider community

Some high-profile CEOs are not content with merely developing and displaying their own cultural prowess, or even with promoting the cultural betterment of their employees. They wish to have a broader impact on their customers and the Chinese public. Therefore, they transform the launches of their new products into cultural events, and claim that customers who buy these products will miraculously create a whole new cultured lifestyle for themselves.

Obviously, certain kinds of products and corporations are more suited than others to this form of cultural packaging. Chemical fertilizer producers or industrial power-tool manufacturers may be hard-pressed to persuade their customers that they are buying into a whole new cultured lifestyle. But this technique seems especially suited to real estate developers, and it is one way that they can distinguish themselves from their competitors. Here is a description of the cultural approach adopted by Pan Shiyi to market his company's SOHO New Town development in Beijing:

> Pan Shiyi's success lies more in his concepts than his actual housing. His avant-garde housing theories always draw attention, favorable or otherwise. He says, 'I am looking at lifestyles of the future. In an industrial era, everything is distinctly pigeonholed. Activity space is divided into work, leisure, shopping, and recreational. The partitions in the apartments of my SOHO New Town are movable; they can be dismantled and installed at will. Various intelligent networks are incorporated into the apartments, so their occupants can work at home, thus combining the home and the workplace. This represents the lifestyle of the future'.
>
> Every new project taken on by Pan Shiyi in recent years has been preceded by a completely new architectural concept ... He says, 'The charm of the projects ... is that they represent not only a new design theory, but also a new lifestyle.' Many people buy houses developed by Pan Shiyi's company specifically because they like their avant-garde ambience
>
> (Zhan 2003)

The SOHO New Town development even includes an Art Gallery with installations by contemporary Chinese artists, which is profiled on the company's website (SOHO China.[a]).

The report on the SOHO New Town focuses only on Pan Shiyi, the Chair of SOHO China, but Pan's wife, Zhang Xin, who is actually the CEO of the company, also plays a central role in promoting this cultural approach. The company's website introduces her in the following glowing way:

> Zhang Xin loves art: she loves to lose herself in any activity in which she can display her creativity, and she is full of enthusiasm for the art of architecture. As an investor in some of China's most avant-garde buildings and as an entrepreneur with a highly innovative spirit, she has won numerous internationally-recognized awards. The creative impulse for all of SOHO China's development projects comes from Zhang Xin
>
> (SOHO China [b])

Rather than merely building and selling houses, corporate executives like Pan and Zhang want to be seen as cultural arbiters or gurus, helping a new generation of affluent, upwardly-mobile consumers to refine their tastes and spend their money in a discerning way – or in their own words, to become part of the cultural 'avant-garde'.

It is not just through building projects that Pan and Zhang spread their avant-garde ideas. They have also published books on contemporary

Chinese architecture, in which their own company's projects have a prominent but not exclusive place, and on other cultural themes (SOHO China [b]). And their company sponsors a free monthly magazine called SOHO Journal, which contains essays on various cultural topics, lyrical prose and contemporary fiction (SOHO Journal Editorial Board). The Journal can be distinguished from the corporate e-magazines already mentioned, in that it invites well-known writers and intellectuals to contribute articles, and these articles can be on any subject, not necessarily connected to the company's business. As the introduction to one edited collection of articles from the Journal puts it: 'SOHO Journal adopts its own unique perspective and opinions to describe and analyze the city in which we live and the lifestyles that we lead' (SOHO Journal Editorial Board 2005, inside front cover). Finally, like several other newly-rich Chinese CEOs of privately-managed corporations, Pan has set up his own blog, where he regularly posts his pronouncements on business, culture, philosophy, and the meaning of life to what appears to be a wide audience of admiring and envious 'netizens' (Pan).

The behaviour of Pan Shiyi and Zhang Xin is not unique among Chinese CEOs. Wang Shi, CEO of the Vanke Group, another real estate conglomerate, has also published a book on his life and business philosophy (Wang 2006). He is especially keen on mountain climbing, which seems at first sight far removed from elite culture, but in its more traditional guise of 'climbing high and looking into the distance' (*deng gao wang yuan*) has been a pursuit of Chinese poets and cultural officials for over two thousand years. Of course, Wang gives a contemporary slant to this activity by attempting such gruelling peaks as Mount Everest and Mount Kilimanjaro, and by foregoing the use of a sedan chair.[5] The Vanke Group publishes an online business, culture and contemporary art magazine called *Vanke Weekly* with the slogan 'Corporate perspectives, humanistic feelings' (Vanke Group). And the *Vanke Weekly* site hosts dozens of blogs on various lifestyle and cultural topics such as book-reading, poetry, hiking, and eating and drinking.

Through his company, Wang Shi has also invested heavily in the Chinese culture industry. In 1999, with profits from his real estate business, Wang established a subsidiary called Vanke Cultural Broadcasting Corporation (since renamed Vanke Film and Television Corporation). Yet rather than focus only on love stories, crime dramas and other popular genres, this subsidiary has collaborated with China Central TV and the Propaganda Department of the Shenzhen Party Committee to produce remakes of classic Communist novels such as 'The Tempering of Steel' (Yu 2000: 193–4). When observers commented that it was strange for a ruthless privately managed enterprise like the Vanke Group from the wheeling and dealing metropolis of Shenzhen to be producing an archetypal mainstream Communist television drama, an official from the Shenzhen Propaganda Department sprang to Vanke's defence:

Once the socialist economy with Chinese characteristics has developed to a certain degree, it inevitably leads to demands for a superior culture. Shenzhen does not merely want to make first-rate economic products; it also wants to make first-rate cultural products

(Yu 2000: 194, n.1)

This response leads naturally into a discussion of why Chinese CEOs are so transfixed by culture: why do they so conspicuously display their own cultural knowledge and talents? And why do they promote cultural activities so enthusiastically among their employees and (in some cases) among the wider Chinese public?

Reasons for CEOs and corporations to promote culture

Several reasons combine to make it almost inevitable that CEOs will take a keen interest in cultural promotion. First, there is the ambivalent attitude that the Chinese government displays towards business enterprises in general, and rich CEOs in particular. On the one hand, the Communist Party wants to encourage corporations to be profitable and create more employment, so China can become rich and Chinese people can raise their standard of living. But on the other hand, the Party still becomes concerned when it sees large groups of people organizing themselves, especially when they have enough power and money to challenge the Party's authority. So it also expects corporations to actively promote the government's policies, and this includes establishing an 'excellent corporate culture', being 'socially responsible', and helping to spread 'spiritual civilization'.[6] Even privately managed corporations cannot avoid these obligations, as they too have to set up Communist Party branches within their enterprises just like state-controlled corporations. In fact, they have to promote the Party's policies even more enthusiastically to show that they are above suspicion.[7]

When they educate their employees and encourage them to engage in cultural activities to 'improve themselves'; or produce cultural magazines and television dramas on Party-approved topics, CEOs clearly have one eye firmly fixed on the Party. They realize that they must balance the economic value of their business with its social value, in order to stay on the good side of the government. As Zong Qinghou, CEO of the Chinese drinks company Wahaha Group, put it: 'If the government doesn't support you, you can hardly move one step. Your company has to help solve the country's problems' (McGregor 2005: 288).

Viewed from a slightly different perspective, one could also argue that the more canny CEOs are using culture as a way to maximize their profits in the unique Chinese marketplace. This is most obvious in the case of companies like Vanke Group that have diversified into the culture business and produced television dramas on revolutionary themes. There is a huge market for revolutionary nostalgia in China, especially among the older generation of consumers, and any product that can capitalize on this nostalgia is likely to be hugely profitable. Vanke made so much money out of selling advertising and distribution rights for 'The Tempering of Steel' that it recently invested in another remake of a foreign Communist classic, 'The Gadfly,' in collaboration with the Shenzhen Propaganda Office and two other television production companies (Vanke Film and TV Corporation).

Likewise, in the case of Pan Shiyi's and Zhang Xin's promotion of an avant-garde lifestyle, their various SOHO developments have appealed so strongly to 'trend-conscious Beijingers' that they have generally sold out within days, netting the company hundreds of millions of yuan in profits (Zhan 2003).

A similar economic argument could be made for CEOs promoting the cultural development of their employees. Many successful Chinese companies have grown from virtually nothing in a couple of decades. They have recruited thousands of new employees, most of them are young and come from other parts of the country, and they live in company dormitories or apartments. So the company becomes their new home, and they expect the company to arrange various social and cultural activities so they can get to know their colleagues and feel they are more than just production-line robots. Many employees are not well educated either, and may have left school early for various reasons. A corporation that spends some of its resources encouraging its employees to develop their potential as rounded human beings, and that rewards employee creativity with public praise and financial incentives, is likely to retain those employees for longer. This will then save the much greater expense of constantly recruiting and training new employees.

As for CEOs who practice cultural activities themselves – and publicly draw attention to it – this appears to serve a number of related purposes beyond mere aesthetic enjoyment. It was noted earlier that traditional arts like calligraphy and poetry have long been practised by Chinese elites, and that a good leader is expected to display excellent writing talents. For those without the time to master these difficult traditional arts, an interest in ancient Chinese philosophy and values – such as Pan Shiyi drawing inspiration from the *Book of Changes* – suggests that these CEOs are more than just money-grubbing capitalists. When combined with their generous patronage of the contemporary cultural scene through magazines and sponsorship of artists, such activities allow them to join the ranks of the cultural elite and gain broader support and positive publicity for their commercial activities. In other words, practicing and promoting culture becomes a way of deflecting negative attention away from their capital accumulation within what is still nominally a socialist society.

There may even be a traditional Chinese influence at work here, which is that merely doing business, or making money, is not a worthy thing to do. If one must be a CEO, one should at least also be a cultivated person and a moral example to others. This distaste for business has deep roots in

Confucianism, and in the past led to the compromise ideal of the 'scholar-merchant' (*Rushang*): in other words, one can engage in business but must not lose sight of the higher virtues attainable through self-cultivation (Zurndorfer 2004).

Of course, since the Communist government gained control in 1949, this Confucian distaste for business has been reinforced by the Communist suspicion of capitalist exploitation. This provides an even stronger reason for CEOs to make themselves out to be cultural leaders rather than greedy salesmen of the meanest ilk (Zurndorfer 2004: 2–3). Indeed, CEOs can gain the active support of the PRC Government for any efforts that they make to develop their own cultural attainments and those of their peers. The home page of the Shenzhen Entrepreneurs Society for the Study of Calligraphy and Painting clearly demonstrates the local government's close interest in improving the cultural level of business leaders:

> As part of the strategic plan of the municipal government and municipal Party Committee to build the city [of Shenzhen] into a centre of culture, and with the support and encouragement of ... the municipal government ... the Shenzhen Entrepreneurs Society for the Study of Calligraphy and Painting held its first meeting in the ceremonial hall of the Municipal Investment Tower. ... [The Society] will display the artistic talents of entrepreneurs, ... it will raise the spiritual and cultural level of entrepreneurs, and create a positive image of entrepreneurs within society. It will also promote exchanges, co-operation, and friendship among entrepreneurs and among corporations, and will provide an excellent platform for spreading progressive corporate culture.
>
> (Shenzhen Entrepreneur)

A final reason for CEOs promoting culture within their corporations relates to a point raised earlier: CEOs must share the governance of their corporations with in-house branches of the Communist Party. Indeed, many of the employee cultural activities that take place within corporations are organized by the firm's Communist Party Committee or by affiliated sub-groups such as Corporate Culture or Spiritual Civilization Committees. So another explanation for the burst of cultural activities taking place within corporations is that these Party organizations are searching for ways to make themselves useful and relevant to the firm's operations, as opposed to being superfluous appendages left over from a past political era. One influential text on corporate culture expresses this point quite clearly:

> Corporate culture and corporate ideological and political work are both targeted at the whole body of corporate employees ... and both advocate understanding, care, love, and respect for other people. ... It goes without saying that ... company chairs and CEOs, with their central

status within the company's operations, should naturally become leaders in establishing its corporate culture. But the company's Party organizations, who are responsible for ideological and political work within the company ... should be the driving force in nurturing the corporation's spirit and building its corporate culture. And the broad mass of Party members should also become core leaders and model workers in building this corporate culture

(Zhang 2003: 282)

Thus, Party Committees are trying to carve out a place for themselves within the contemporary corporate structure, and to justify their role by referring to Western concepts of corporate culture and employee morale building, mixed up with traditional Chinese ideas of culture as a way to improve moral character. By encouraging the cultural development of employees and CEOs, the Party can therefore claim that it is helping to balance the economic benefits of business enterprises with a healthy dose of social benefits.

Some corporate executives, like COFCO's Ning Gaoning, might complain that all this focus on culture by CEOs and corporations detracts from their performance and leads to poorer returns for shareholders. Yet it is unlikely that Chinese CEOs – especially in the highly competitive world of privately managed real estate developers – would engage in any such activities unless they believed there was a benefit for the bottom line. Rather, just as large Western corporations must put resources into numerous external activities such as lobbying, cultural sponsorship, and community relations, in order to ensure that their businesses run as smoothly as possible, so successful Chinese CEOs realize that they must display their own cultural talents and promote cultural awareness among their employees and the wider community. In the current Chinese social environment, this is one crucial way to gain the support of the government, to deflect criticism from their massive accumulation of capital, and to prove that they are worthy members of China's new social and political elite. In other words, it is profit-maximization, Chinese-style.

Notes

1 On Pan Shiyi's blog, he also describes how he was invited to speak about the *Daodejing* at a Hong Kong conference on Daoism, and he posts his speech on the blog for viewers to offer their comments and suggestions for improvement (Pan 2007).
2 Review of 125 websites of the largest Chinese corporations found that 52 of these sites included corporate e-magazines, and the vast majority of these magazines encouraged employees to contribute their creative writing or other creative artworks for publication.
3 Besides giving the words of the company's declaration, Tengen's website also includes a video of the employees reciting the declaration in a suitably solemn fashion.

4   This is actually one of two songs used by the Guanghui Group, both of which can be viewed and listened to at the company website (Guanghui Group 2005a). The Group's broad range of businesses includes liquefied natural gas, car servicing, and real estate, amongst others.

5   Mountain climbing appears in several chapters of Wang's autobiography, such as chapter four, on his ascent of Mount Everest (Wang 2006); and his blog contains plenty of pictures of his most recent mountain climbing tours (Wang).

6   The duty to be socially responsible is contained in article 5 of the amended PRC *Company Law* (which came into force on 1 January 2006). The requirements to promote spiritual civilization and excellent corporate culture appear in a Chinese Communist Party document issued at the Third Plenum of the Fourteenth CCP Central Committee in 1993 (Chinese Communist Party 1993: section 1.7).

7   Article 19 of the PRC *Company Law* states that a branch of the Communist Party shall be established in all companies, with no distinction made between state-controlled and privately-managed companies.

6 From coal black to hospital white

New welfare entrepreneurs and the pursuit of a cleaner status[1]

Beatriz Carrillo

Since the start of the reform period private entrepreneurs have struggled against public prejudice which portrayed them as uneducated greedy individuals, and sometimes even as criminals. Popular images of these entrepreneurs, however, have changed dramatically over the past twenty years, as socially-upwardly-mobile private entrepreneurs constitute themselves into a new wealthy class. Their newly gained status has been aided by an ideological shift within the CCP, by which private entrepreneurs are recognized to be an important pillar of China's economic and social development. Social status is usually as much a result of wealth display (through conspicuous consumption) (Veblen 1939), as it is of other more subtle forms of capital, such as cultural values and knowledge of specific taste cultures (Ollivier and Friedman 2004). In China, another dynamic is added to the equation; that is, the use of population quality (*renkou suzhi*) discourses, which serve as another marker of social distinction. These discourses have been used to differentiate between small-scale and often of rural origin individual business people (*getihu*) and more substantial business people (*qiyejia*), the latter regarded as educated entrepreneurs developing highly sophisticated enterprises (Hsu 2006).

Private entrepreneurs have also sought to overcome social and political favour by engaging in charity donations, and by investing in the education and the health care sectors. These business activities are seen as benefiting society, and thus provide them with social prestige. Yet, while this new welfare entrepreneurialism is winning private business people social legitimation, it has also proven to be a remarkably good business. As has been the case around the world, health and education have become increasingly commoditized in China, and people have become more willing to pay in order to get better services. While public service provision continues to fall short of demand, more client-oriented private providers are profiting from a growing demand for educational and medical services.

This drift towards welfare entrepreneurialism has been particularly pronounced in Shanxi Province, not least because of the contrast with the coal industry that dominates almost all of the industrial landscape (Goodman 1999b). Coal mining dominates Shanxi Province's economic life despite its low social standing and low cultural value. The antipathy to coal mining is not only related to its low social prestige, but also the sense that it is dangerous work. It is common knowledge that working in the coalmines is akin to going into a slaughterhouse.[2] In Shanxi Province rising coal prices – the result of rapidly growing domestic energy demand[3] – has nonetheless lured increasing numbers of people to look for coal even in the most remote corners of this province crossed by mountains. In Shanxi – China's largest coal producer – the landscape is dotted with millions of coke chimneys, and only a few counties are not endowed with coal reserves. There, coal mining is responsible for many 'rags-to-riches' stories.[4] The majority of entrepreneurs in Shanxi Province have links with the coal industry, which has become the foundation of Shanxi's thriving private economy. Interestingly though, as a case study of Hongtong County exemplifies, some of those to have made their wealth from coal mining have gone on to become welfare entrepreneurs, not least in a search for greater respectability.

The status of entrepreneurship

Private entrepreneurs, in general, have gone a long way to gain recognition in China's post-socialist society. Whereas nowadays successful entrepreneurs have become role models for the younger generations, the first petty entrepreneurs to start small private businesses throughout the 1980s were often described as criminals, illiterate, and uncultured (Goodman 1996; Wu 2006; Chen, Li and Matlay 2006; Hsu 2006). These prejudices were partly a reflection of a social reality. In the early stage of reform, within a context of weak institutions and a lack of property rights, participation in the market was a risky endeavour. According to Krug and Polos, in transition economies, weak institutions, competitive and process uncertainty – termed the 'liability of newness' – define the threshold of entrepreneurship, limiting (or facilitating) the number of private firms (Krug and Polos 2004: 73). Given the lack of security and legitimacy of market activities often only those with little to risk and limited opportunities for socio-economic mobility were the ones to resort to 'plunging into the sea' of business.

During the 1980s and until the early 1990s the majority of private entrepreneurs had indeed originated from the lower social classes. They were for the most part based in the countryside, where the communes were quickly being disbanded. As power (control over resources) moved towards marketization (from political goals) the distribution of rewards shifted to those who held market rather than redistributive power (Nee 1996: 910). Often those who opened their own private business had few skills and limited understanding of the workings of market mechanisms, but were able to negotiate their position and activities through informal mechanisms that gradually brought about institutional change (Tsai 2006).

As early as 1988, the official media and the press were talking about the special role entrepreneurs could play as agents of change (Goodman 1996:

227). Earlier on, in 1984, Deng Xiaoping had legalized the existence of individual businesses (*getihu*) in the small-scale private economy stating that it was a necessary complement to the public sector of the economy, although he stressed the fact that it should operate 'within certain pre-scribed limits and under state control' (Quoted in Hsu 2006: 7). By the early 1990s, as private economic activities became legalized and hence legitimized by the government (Kong 2003: 539–540) and as market competition became more sophisticated, people with more human and political capital took to entrepreneurship (Xu 2006: 391).

Private entrepreneurs, however, remained a highly diverse group; their social categorization reflected not only the size and financial power of their firms, but was also related to the type of economic activity they carried out. In Chinese there is no one single equivalent for the term 'entrepreneur' as is understood in the English language. Rather, business people are classified according to various quantifiable and non-quantifiable variables that deal with the size of their business, their social origins, and their consumption patterns, among other variables. Often those referred to as the 'real' entre-preneurs (*qiyejia*) or 'good business people' (Hsu 2006) are those who head large firms, usually engaged in developing technologically sophisticated products or that have in place modern modes of production. Hsu's field research carried out during the early 2000s in Harbin in Northeastern China, found that the capitalist heroes were 'intellectual' entrepreneurs with college degrees, who had made their money through their knowledge (*zhishi*) in the 'high technology' (*gao keji*) industries, such as computing, software and automobiles (Hsu 2006: 16).

This more nuanced social categorization is also closely linked to the entrepreneur's actual or supposed 'human quality'. During the reform era the term *renkou suzhi*, roughly translated as 'population quality', became part of the official rhetoric designed to encourage improvement in the qua-lities of the population,[5] and was gradually adopted as a popular discourse and marker of social distinction (Anagnost 2004; Kipnis 2006, 2007). Given that the concept of *suzhi* includes embodied qualities that result from both nature and nurture (Kipnis 2007: 388), the term also implies the possibility of improvement of one's quality. Nonetheless, as Kipnis explains, the pop-ular use of the term – especially by those living in urban areas – implies that there are certain social groups – such as peasants and migrant workers – that would never be able to raise their *suzhi* (Kipnis 2007: 389–340). The discourses of *suzhi* have developed into a complex and sophisticated mechanism of distinction used by urban residents, who feel the need to differentiate themselves from the growing number of migrants, some of whom have become substantially wealthy. As Kipnis points out:

> Very few urbanities would suggest that the 'peasants' do not try hard enough or do not work hard enough. Rather, the implications are that no matter how hard enough they try, no matter how much effort they

put into wearing the right clothes (Pun 2003), getting a better education, speaking with the proper diction, or behaving politely, they will never overcome their lack of quality.

(Kipnis 2007: 389)

Petty entrepreneurs or individual business people – many of whom are rural migrants – thus continue to be viewed as peddlers with low education and little or no culture or taste, irregardless of their economic success (Zhang 2001; Lei 2003; Hsu 2006). This is the same social stigma many coal entrepreneurs face, even long after they surpassed the size of individual businesses.

Private entrepreneurs: the new 'role model' class

Throughout the reform period private entrepreneurs' economic weight has been their main safeguard and legitimation mechanism.[6] Yet, no other social group in China has faced more pressure – domestically and internationally – to become role models, entrusted with the goal of building a democratic system (Chen 2002; Dickson 2003b; Tsai 2007), creating new jobs, upholding the right moral values, while dictating fashion trends (Goodman 1996; Donald and Yi 2008). Juggling these often-contradictory goals has been no easy task. Stories abound of the humble rural origins and 'frugal' lifestyles of China's new super rich (York 2007) alongside stories of waste and their conspicuous consumption (*Business Week* 6 February 2006; *CRI* June 11, 2007). However, private entrepreneurs are far from constituting a coherent social stratum, nor are they all members of the so-called middle class who share common values and practices (Heberer 2003: 62).

As the private sector continues to expand and as control over the economic means of production, information flows and individuals by the Party-State diminishes, and with state and society becoming more clearly differentiated, the state itself has had to change its own view of the relationship between state and society (Goodman 2008). To maintain its hold on power the Chinese Communist Party (CCP) has thus co-opted technical and economic elites (Dickson 2003b: 28; Dickson 2003a; Pei 2006b: 92–95), in the process establishing itself as guardian of the entrepreneurial and middle classes against the threat of the lower classes (Chen 2002: 421). Narrowly classified by disposable income, the middle classes and the massively affluent in China constitute a minority (around 6 percent of the urban population in 2007) (*Xinhua* 18 June 2007), who might perceive that they face a potential threat from the poor in China's increasingly unequal society. Thus, as was the case in countries like South Korea, the middle classes and the new rich tend to be more interested in good governance (understood as legal security and efficient and transparent administration) rather than on bringing in a democratic system, (Ruland 1997 cited in Heberer 2003: 63). Or, as more cynically put by Pei China's new capitalists support the CCP on the condition that it provides them with favours and that it protects their privileges and property (Pei 2006b: 94).

The Party-State's protecting role over the private entrepreneurial class represents a relatively new strategy. Up to the early 1990s, the Chinese government had run various campaigns against the development of private businesses (Li *et al.* 2006: 561). Constitutional reforms beginning in the late 1980s gradually provided the legal basis for the private sector to legitimize and secure its operations (Tsai 2006: 25). Finally in 2001 the then President Jiang Zemin introduced the slogan of the 'three represents', which committed the ruling party to work with and protect the interests of everyone seen to be acting on the nation's behalf, including necessarily entrepreneurs, and in the process creating an opening for them to be part of China's political process (Huang 2002). Private entrepreneurs were recruited into the CCP, alongside growing numbers of former managers of state owned enterprises (SOE) who had become private entrepreneurs through 'insider' privatization (Pei 2006b: 93). As to the protection of private property, only after five years of debate in the National People's Congress (NPC) was a new property law covering individuals' right to own private assets implemented on 16 March 2007 (*People's Daily* 16 March 2007).

Private entrepreneurs themselves did not remain passive observers of changing political attitudes and changing legislation regarding their economic activities. Working within a framework of weak institutions they adopted a series of formal and informal strategies that not only protected their businesses, but which also secured them access to land, financial resources and tax holidays.[7] Through what Kellee Tsai (2006) refers to as 'adaptive informal institutions' private entrepreneurs managed to influence institutional change, despite their lack of political power. Weak institutions and imperfect markets also pushed some entrepreneurs to influence policy formation by entering into local politics. According to one set of research findings, private entrepreneurs whose business is located in a province where market-supporting institutions are underdeveloped are more likely to participate in politics, through membership in local People's Congresses or in the Chinese People's Political Consultative Conference (Li *et al.* 2006).

One of the main reasons for private entrepreneurs to become members of local councils was to be able to limit additional tax and fees imposed by cash-strapped local government departments (Ma and Parish 2006: 948). Likewise, political participation allowed them to cultivate formal and informal ties with important government and Party cadres who could help them secure resources not accessible through markets (Li *et al.* 2006: 560). Yet, as Pei stresses, private entrepreneurs, though willing to be co-opted as individuals, firmly refused CCP efforts to establish Party cells inside their firms (Pei 2006b: 94–95). Political access, however, has been non-gratuitous. In order to gain political capital, government favours, and social recognition the newly emerging business class has also had to provide substantial charitable contributions to government and quasi-government agencies

(Shue 1998; Ma and Parish 2006). Using the 1995 national survey of private entrepreneurs Ma and Parish found that contribution levels by private firms was relatively high[8] and that all but 13 percent of the firms in the survey sample had made some charitable contributions during the lifetime of the firm (Ma and Parish 2006: 956). The increasing activism of private entrepreneurs branching into the 'welfare market' develops within the framework of this ambivalent relationship between private entrepreneurs and the ruling party.

Public service provision and welfare entrepreneurialism

Despite the enthusiasm in the media at the advent of social entrepreneurs and the important role they will play in closing the gaps in welfare and social services provision (*Xinhua* 20 May 2005; Young 2002; *CDB* 19 April 2007) most welfare entrepreneurs have entered the realm of health and education provision because it is good business. There are, of course, other structural and economic reasons for entering these two markets. As in the case of coal entrepreneurs, there is generally the need to diversify to reduce the risk of focusing on one line of business in a still uncertain market environment (Gregory and Tenev 2001). Another reason is that health and education have only recently been officially opened to private investment.

Before 1978, both health care and education had been described in the Chinese Constitution as non-profit sectors, providing services through the state's public service units (PSU) in the urban areas, and through the communes in the countryside. Over the reform period the state has allowed for increased participation of *social forces* in these two sectors. Yet, despite this more permissive stance, government policy toward private providers and public-private cooperation in the provision of these public goods has remained characterized by its ambiguity (Meng *et al.* 2000). In general, the education sector has been a bigger recipient of private investment (Lin 1999; Wang and Secombe 2004; Mok 2005), which was consolidated with the passing of the law on private education in 2002. No such law exists in the health care sector (Burriss and Shen 2005) even though – as is the case in the education sector – medical services have largely become commoditized.

In fact, the number of private providers in the health care sector may be larger than in education, given that a large part of rural health care facilities have been privatized. Private health care providers overall, however, remain small scale, and even in the big cities private hospitals are in the minority.[9] According to statistics from 2003, public hospitals accounted for 96 percent of all hospitals in the country, and private hospitals only 4 percent (China. org.cn 30 November 2005). Moreover, by 2005, only 10.8 percent of China's 8,703 major hospitals were privately run (*China Daily* 22 March 2007). In contrast, private education institutions have become widespread in urban areas, thus targeting a so far much more profitable market. By the end of 2003 there were over 70,000 private schools (around 11 percent of all educational facilities) hosting 14.16 million students, or just over 3 percent of student enrolment in the country (*The People's Daily* 26 March 2004). Private education providers are present at all educational levels, from kindergartens and boarding schools, to secondary schools and institutions of tertiary education. Some of these institutions have franchises around the country, while others have been able to recruit a large number of students in a single location (Walfish 2001). According to one report, by 2006 of the 1,250 private higher education institutions, 50 had over 10,000 enrolled students each (Lin 2006 cited in Mok and Lo 2007).

Private participation in health care and education has continued to thrive due to rapidly increasing demand, and to the failing of public provision (Liu *et al.* 1994; Mok 2005). Nonetheless, although public provision continues to fall short of demand, PSUs – which include all public schools, universities, clinics and hospitals – continue to dominate health care and education sectors. In 2004, over 1.3 million PSUs employed nearly 30 million people, managed around 300 billion *yuan* of state assets, and were recipients of more than 30 percent of total government expenditure (*The People's Daily* 24 March 2004). That same year over 95 percent of teachers and doctors throughout the country worked in those PSUs (Lan 2004). It is this particular role as employer that had delayed government attempts to reform public service units.

Furthermore, existing policy incentives, decentralization and changing funding mechanism have pushed PSUs' personnel to operate these public institutions as mostly for-profit enterprises (Bloom *et al.* 2000; *CDB* 2006). At the same time, governments at various administrative levels have encouraged social groups and institutions to establish schools, clinics and hospitals, implicitly admitting public funds and efforts are not sufficient to address the growing demand for educational and medical services. Meantime, people's expectations over the 'right amount' of government intervention both in economic and social areas are also gradually changing (Wong and Lee 2000) and most are increasingly viewing health and education as both public and private goods.

In an interview in June 2006, Ding Zuyi – president of Xi'An Fanyi (Translators) University – talked about his battle with local authorities back in the late 1990s, who required him to pay a business tax for running a private university (China.org.cn 20 June 2006). He claimed his was not a for-profit business but rather a public welfare undertaking. Nonetheless, later in the interview he admitted that private education had great economic potential, and that Xi'An Fanyi University's annual revenue of over 300 million *yuan* was clear proof of this. Health and education are no longer considered solely as non-profit sectors, and are being allowed to make a profit. The 2002 Private Education Law, which allowed private education institutions to become legal entities for the first time, differentiated between for-profit and non-profit institutions.[10] Those registered as non-profit organizations – which is the majority of private education institutions – are largely tax exempt, and are allowed (under article 51) to make a reasonable economic return (Yan and Levy 2003). The Law describes this economic return as a governmental reward rather than as a profit, but does not establish what exactly a 'reasonable' economic return is (Yan and Levy 2003).

Private medical practice has been allowed since 1982 and by 1987 health workers in the public sector were allowed to practice privately (through dual practice) though private hospitals continued to be restricted (Liu *et al.* 2006: 214). For-profit hospitals were allowed to operate under government regulations implemented in 2000. Yet, contrary to the case of education, most private hospitals are registered as for-profit entities. Moreover, as noted previously, private medical providers tend to be small-scale and to provide only ambulatory health services, while large private hospitals remain in the minority. Also contrary to education, hospitals usually require a larger initial investment than schools, particularly if they are to provide more sophisticated – and hence more profitable – in-patient services. Nonetheless, a rapidly growing demand for health care services – the result of population ageing, epidemiological transition, growing pollution-related disease, changing lifestyles, and the increase of food-borne disease, among many other health problems – will attract more private investment to tackle the demand for more expensive medical treatments.

Hongtong County's welfare entrepreneurs

Hongtong County, located within Linfen City, is part of one of the most economically dynamic prefectures in Shanxi Province and presents some good examples of emergent welfare entrepreneurialism. Hongtong's economy is the 8th largest in the province, with agricultural and coal-related industries being the most economically significant. Two large state-owned coal by-products enterprises are important employers, as well as being large contributors to the county's coffers. Non-state coalmines have also played an important economic role, becoming the main source of private wealth in the county. Apart from the larger state owned enterprises, a sizeable part of the state-owned sector has been restructured. In half a decade, from the mid to the end of the 1990s, around 95 percent of the state owned enterprises in Hongtong County had changed or were in the process of changing their ownership structure.[11] The majority of those enterprises became shareholding enterprises, while smaller enterprises or those experiencing bankruptcy were privatized. From the late 1990s, and particularly since 2002, coal and coke prices have kept an upward trajectory, which has meant that many in the coal-mining sector in this county have made sizable fortunes.

Mr Qin is a young entrepreneur who ventured into education in 2003, and was interviewed in Hongtong shortly after (in October 2003). By the mid-1990s, at only 25 years of age, he already owned two coalmines and an auto-repair workshop in the county town. He graduated from a local technical school, was married at 23, and became a member of the CCP in 1996.

By the late 1990s, Mr Qin had become substantially wealthy. In 1999 he bought a house, expanded and renovated it, spending altogether over half a million *yuan*. Besides being very young, Mr Qin had little political capital and connections with county leaders. As his wealth grew, Mr Qin started to more actively pursue his contacts with various county and town cadres.

Through a friendship with a county cadre, he was able to get a position in the local Public Security Department (PSD), which was intended more as an honorary position than as a real job. The appointment also turned him into a government employee, thus rendering him an insider for many purposes. In Mr Qin's opinion, 'special relations' (*guanxi*) were the single most important factor in finding a job or starting a business; education came only second, while registration status (*hukou*) – he thought – was no longer relevant. Socially, his position at the Public Security Department also conferred him a degree of social status, which he had not previously enjoyed as a private entrepreneur. Meanwhile, Mr Qin preferred to refer to himself as an entrepreneur in education, and during the interview he was reluctant to talk about his coal mining business. Yet, it was precisely the profits from coal mining that allowed him to invest heavily in his private English school.

Mr Qin had observed that many private schools were being opened in the outskirts of the county town (mainly because land was not available within the town). He knew that these schools were being run like any other business and that they were mostly financially successful. The idea to open an English school, however, came from the son of a county cadre. At the time this cadre's son was a postgraduate student of English at Shanxi University in Taiyuan – the provincial capital. He was the one who pointed out to Mr Qin that English teaching was the business of the future. Mr Qin provided the investment and this student became the manager of the English school. The school was opened in rented premises in a building next to Shanxi University, and was registered as a non-profit organization. Mr Qin hoped to be able to make a profit after two years of opening the school, but after the first year it was already turning a profit.

Only six months after starting operations the school had over 100 enrolled students and by 2006 that number had more than doubled. The school continued to be a successful and profitable business, even though a number of copy-cat schools had sprung up around the university but because the school had built its reputation through its links to the English department at Shanxi University, it was keeping ahead of the game. Its links to the university also meant that the school would get a first pick at the few foreign English teachers who came to work for the university. Back in the county town, Mr Qin had become a usual guest at various county officials' homes and various public security vehicles were at his disposal. He was proud of being able to contribute to so many children's education and future success, and was planning to open an English school in the county town. Meanwhile, Mr Qin kept himself busy running his real business: the coalmines.

Many local coal entrepreneurs have contributed to education by donating money to fund the construction and repair of rural school buildings around the county. Those donations are usually acknowledged during the annual celebration of Teacher's Day on 10 September. In 2005, 124 private individuals donated over 40 million *yuan* for that purpose (*Huaixiang Education Park* 10 September 2005). The County Education Department ran a story in its departmental newspaper under the heading: 'In 2005 a hundred dangerous classrooms are repaired by a group of highly commended people'. All the names and amounts contributed by each individual were published in the news article. Other than serving as a note of gratitude, this sort of article gives face to participants and encourages others to donate (Carrillo 2008).

In 2002, Doctor Liu retired from his job as director of the Hongtong County No. 1 People's Hospital, after fifteen years working in the public health care sector. Soon after, however, he was sought out by Mr Huo – a local coal entrepreneur – who offered him the directorship of the first private hospital in the county. Mr Huo had already invested in a small hospital in a nearby city, and was keen to continue investing in the health sector, as he had become aware of the growing demand for cheap medical services. Given low insurance coverage rates in both small urban centres and in the rural areas, a large number of people are seeking a variety of medical services, which tend to be costly in public hospitals, but which are not available in small private clinics. Mr Huo thus tapped into a demand for non-critical in-patient services (various medical treatments and minor surgical operations) not yet available in private clinics.

Opening the hospital required the exercise of some influence. Mr Huo's social and political capital was quite vast; he used his contacts with local county cadres, who introduced him to Doctor Liu. By early 2003, Mr Huo had secured land in the county town and had begun construction of the hospital building. Dr Liu was then put in charge of using his networks in the public health care system to recruit personnel for the hospital. Huimin Hospital was opened in early 2004; when Dr Liu was interviewed in November it already had 23 permanent staff members (11 of whom were medical personnel) and 20 hospital beds. The hospital had only been in operation for ten months, yet Dr Liu already described it as a promising business. However, given that private hospitals are registered as for profit organizations, Dr Liu complained of the harsh imposition of regulations, particularly on compliance with medical services price benchmarks. In his experience from working in the public health care sector, public hospitals had more leeway to set their own prices and fees, and often compelled patients to buy medicines in the hospital's pharmacies.[12]

Studies on the public perceptions of private health care providers (Meng *et al.* 2000; Lim *et al.* 2004; Liu *et al.* 2006) have found that survey respondents who visited private clinics showed higher overall satisfaction levels than those who had gone through public medical institutions.

Nonetheless, the majority of respondents thought doctors in the public sector had better skills than those in the private sector. Therefore, people tend to visit private clinics for minor illnesses and to go to a public hospital for a major illness (Lim *et al.* 2004: 228). Although there are certainly a large number of unqualified doctors, an increasing number of doctors from the public sector are choosing to practice privately. At Huimin Hospital all medical staff had worked for or were working in one of the public hospitals in the county town. According to Dr Liu, patients were more satisfied with their services (compared to those provided in the public sector) because they had a better services attitude, they provided cheaper services, and they offered more flexible payment methods (Carrillo 2008). Private hospitals, in general, compete with public ones on services differentiation and price.

Mr Huo had instilled his business practices into the new hospital. Patients were able to negotiate the price of the treatment once a medical examination had been carried out, and payment methods were also negotiable. Prices for services need to be kept at competitive levels in order to attract costumers, but also to comply with price regulations. Mr Huo had also struck a deal with the insurance company China Life (*Zhongguo Renshou*) to treat those covered by their insurance schemes (Carrillo 2008). Although the majority of the hospital clients came from the countryside, Mr Huo hoped that through their strong advertisement campaign in both local TV and radio, they would be able to attract more local residents.

Moreover, as noted previously, many doctors from the public sector have turned themselves into entrepreneurs by opening small clinics where they practise privately, and from which they make most of their income. Furthermore, in Hongtong County Catholic groups have been active in opening up non-profit private clinics and nursing homes. Hongtong County is one of six Catholic dioceses in Shanxi Province, and one of the largest centres for Catholicism in the province.[13] Health and education have traditionally been sectors through which those better off give back to society. Being involved in those two sectors, both directly and through charity, hence confer certain social prestige. For this purpose, Mr Qin and Mr Huo prefer to be known through their business enterprises in those sectors, rather than being identified solely as coal entrepreneurs. While many have been able to make small fortunes from coal mining, fewer have endeavoured to open schools and hospitals. Welfare entrepreneurs' human capital may not be greater than that of other entrepreneurs; nonetheless, their economic, social and political capital has certainly been increasing through their involvement in welfare entrepreneurialism.

Welfare entrepreneurialism and social status

China's widening income inequality and consequent social stratification of the last two decades has heightened social frictions, and has made the general populace increasingly suspicious of the means by which the new rich class has accumulated so much wealth. A survey carried out by the China Youth Daily in early September 2007 found that 70 percent of respondents believed the well-off were immoral and not worthy of respect, and questioned how those people had become rich in the first place (Wang Zhuoqiong 2007). According to respondents, for the rich to become respectable they needed to have a sense of social responsibility, be self-disciplined and have a caring heart. This moral responsibility to give back to society is also expected from private entrepreneurs, who are perceived to be the biggest winners of the last decade of reform. By opening schools and hospitals, private entrepreneurs are offering services that are perceived to directly benefit society. Yet, paradoxically, given increased commoditization of both medical and educational services, these two sectors have at the same time become very profitable businesses. By investing in health and education, private entrepreneurs can thus potentially reap both social and economic gains. So far, private providers of education and medical services have shown a better response to the demands of those markets. Not only are they tackling both the higher and lower ends of the market, but they have also in particular circumstances offered a more equitable provision of services than the public sector (Meng *et al.* 2000; Liu *et al.* 2006; Carrillo 2008).

In Shanxi Province, where the coal industry has dominated and boosted the local economy, many private entrepreneurs are venturing into health and education seeking to gain a cleaner status. Although profits from coal and its by-products remain the main source of finance to invest in building and staffing their private schools and hospitals, they prefer to de-link their image from the negative reputation of China's coal mining industry. Instead, they prefer to describe themselves as welfare entrepreneurs, in charge of more civilized and sophisticated organizations, that are perceived to be giving back to society.

Incursion into welfare entrepreneurship is not a direct path to social recognition. At the same time, as pointed out earlier, most welfare entrepreneurs treat education and health as any other business, and not necessarily as a philanthropist endeavour. Furthermore, given the growing number of former government officials and former SOE managers who have become private entrepreneurs (Wang Jun 2007), public concerns over practices of nepotism and corrupt use of connections may tarnish the reputation even of those in the 'cleaner' sectors of the economy. As a result, the construction of hierarchical popular terms to describe different types of private entrepreneurs, not only in relationship to their rural or urban background, but also according to their previous or existing relationship with the Party-state is likely to remain. Participation in health and education activities *per se*, particularly when carried out for profit, will gradually cease to be a marker of social status. Increasingly private entrepreneurs will have to more openly engage in charities and other philanthropic activities to gain social status not only as individuals, but also as a social group, if social recognition is to improve.

Notes

1 This paper was first presented at the biennial conference of the China Studies Association of Australia (27–29 June, 2007) as part of a panel on China's middle class, the result of an Australian Research Council Discovery Grant on 'The Cultivation of Middle-Class Taste: Reading, Tourism and Education Choices in Urban China'. The author was senior research associate of the project.

2 Eighty percent of the deaths in coal mining around the world take place in China. Coal mining has been described as the deadliest job in China (Zhao and Jiang 2004). Official figures put the total number of deaths in coal mines throughout China at 5,986 in 2005 and 4,560 in 2006. Independent research estimates the fatalities are about double the official figures. Underreporting of accidents and the fact that under Chinese Law coal mine owners are not obliged to report incidents involving less than three deaths means this claim is not unreasonable (Kolo 2007).

3 Coal is the source of two-thirds of China's total power and 79 percent of its electricity. China is also the world's top coal producer and consumer (coal production is twice that of the US) using about 42 percent of the world's thermal coal for generating power and 48 percent of its metallurgical or coking coal for making steel. It uses more coal than the United States, Europe, and Japan combined. Nine out of ten of China's new power plants run on coal, and it is claimed that a new coal-fired power station is built every seven to ten days (Callick 2007).

4 As well as many grim stories of villages where most of the male population has died in coal mining accidents.

5 Initially introduced at the time of population control policies.

6 By 2001 China's private sector had 38 million registered firms employing over 160 million people and producing more than one third of the total industrial output (Li *et. al.* 2006: 561).

7 During the 1980s and the early 1990s an important strategy adopted by private entrepreneurs to gain these benefits was to register their business as a collective enterprise (a practice referred to as 'wearing a red hat') thus allowing local governments to have a degree of involvement in the firm. In March 1998, however, the Central government issued a directive requiring all red hat firms to 'take off the hat' and register as private enterprises by November of that same year (Gregory and Tenev 2001).

8 1.2 percent of pre-tax annual profit, compared to 0.9 percent of US corporations (Ma and Parish 2006: 956).

9 Around the country there are only around 200 joint-venture and cooperative venture hospitals with foreign business partners (Young 2006).

10 The Regulation on Education Run by Social Forces (State Council Decree No. 266) signed in 1997 by then Premier Li Peng was an attempt at regulating an already extensive private education sector, but also a signal of government recognition of their legitimacy.

11 Interview, Vice-Director of the County Labour and Social Security Department. Dahuaishu Town, Hongtong County. (31 October 2004).

12 One study on hospital price regulation found that although the Price Regulation Bureau conducted frequent audits on public hospitals, price violations were a common occurrence. In most cases public hospitals negotiated a fine with the department after the annual audit (Liu *et al.* 2000: 160).

13 The first Catholic mission to come to Shanxi Province – lead by an Italian priest – in 1620 during the Ming Dynasty was based in the area of Hongtong County (Beijing University 1987). The county was not established as an apostolic prefecture until 1932 and was promoted to diocese in 1950. By the late 1980s there were around 12,000 Catholics in the diocese. There are currently one Archdiocese (Taiyuan) and six Catholic dioceses in Shanxi Province (Giga-Catholic Information (n.d.)).

7 Entrepreneurial women

Personal wealth, local politics and tradition

Minglu Chen

During the last three decades, China has seen the rapid development and emerging prosperity of the private economy. Previously, in the mid-1950s, the Central Government had managed to all but eliminate the private sector of the economy. Over the next 20 years or so, the economy remained dominated by the state sector. The collective sector became the non-planned (outside the state plan) state sector and the existence of the private sector remained exceedingly small with only occupations such as ice-cream sellers, tinkers and itinerant barbers left (Goodman 1995: 12–32). With reform, the state sector has decreased in scale and scope; and both the collective and private sectors have boomed. According to the first economic census survey conducted by the National Statistics Bureau, by the end of 2004, China had altogether 179,000 state-owned enterprises accounting for 5.5 percent of the country's total; 343,000 collective enterprises (10.5 percent); and 1,982,000 private enterprises (61 percent) (Zhongguo Guojia Tongjiju 2005). The All-China Federation of Industry and Commerce forecast in 2005 that by 2010 the private economy will contribute more than 75 percent of the country's GDP (Liu Jing 2005). Moreover, the private sector has also become a major source of employment for workers laid-off from state-owned enterprises and the country's increasing surplus labour force.

The Party-state has attached great importance to the private sector, not least because of the decline of its state-owned economy. The government has to depend on the private sector for ensuring employment and generating revenue. Furthermore, private enterprises are also a major source of funds for social welfare (Qin Yan 2000). The Party is paying attention to the private sector, so as not to 'shut itself off from the best supply of human resources' in China (Dickson 2003a: 38). The private sector has become so important to economic development that some local governments and officials regard the growth of the private sector as a central agenda item in their political activities. For example, the Henan Provincial Government has stated that the development of its non-state sector – of which the private sector constitutes a substantial part – would be regarded as a significant goal for the development of its departments and institutions (Henan Renmin Zhengfu 2005).

The prosperity of the private sector has created a group of new rich in China – owner-operators and managers of these enterprises (Goodman 1996: 225–42; Li Peilin 2004; Lu Xueyi 2002; Qin Yan 1999; Zheng and Li 2004; Zheng 2004b). These people have taken advantage of the country's economic reforms to ensure the accumulation of capital in less than three decades. Most obviously, the new rich have been portrayed in scholarship in terms of their lifestyle, including but not confined to their clothes and personal appearance. As personal wealth increases, the new rich in China have invested in houses and cars, especially luxury cars; and they also tend to follow trends that are more specific to the time and place. For instance, in the early to mid-1990s the ownership of a mobile phone became a potent status symbol, and was worn or carried accordingly. During the mid-1990s, China's new rich were also prepared to go to McDonalds restaurants to 'pay much more than most Chinese will earn in a fortnight for a hamburger' (*China Daily* 21 July 1992, p. 2).

Economic reform has not only created wealth for China's new entrepreneurs, but also changed their status in local politics. These new rich are now regarded by the local government as partners, rather than 'class enemies' in the project of increasing local income, local employment and local taxation. They themselves, on the other hand, also seek to establish special relationships with local government to make better use of capital, resources and information controlled by the government, as well as to ensure their political security (Tsang 1996). As a result, reform has created 'a system of increasing dual dependency, with entrepreneurs depending on administrators for favours, and administrators depending on entrepreneurs for income' (Michelson and Parish 2000: 134–56).

Reform has created opportunities for women to be involved in social and economic activities. Many women turned to the private sector to seek employment or simply to start their own business. However, existing scholarship has largely ignored the role of women, and particularly women entrepreneurs as part of the study of the new rich in China. There are a number of lines of inquiry that are particularly interesting. Under the continued influence of a tradition that values men more highly than women, does these women's accumulation of wealth bring them increased status both inside and outside their family? Similarly, do these new rich women now have more access to political power and less commitment to traditional domestic responsibilities than women in earlier periods?

From 2003 to 2005, three series of interviews were conducted in different localities in China, each with different economic features and at different administrative levels. One was Jiaocheng County, Shanxi Province in North China, an area of low foreign economic involvement but nonetheless considerable non-state economic development. Another was Qiongshan District of Haikou City in Hainan Province, an area of considerable migration and external investment. The third was Mianyang City in Sichuan Province, a former heavy industry centre that is now one of China's major light industrial bases, particularly for white goods and televisions. Altogether 171 women were interviewed. These women were running businesses either on their own or in collaboration with their husbands, or taking leadership management positions in the enterprises. Most of the interviewees were engaged in tertiary industries, such as retail activities, advertising, the theatre, dispensaries, welfare services, education, hotel and restaurant businesses, as well as insurance, though in some cases they were operating in the traditionally male-dominated manufacturing sector. During fieldwork, the interviewees were asked questioned about their economic and social involvement, as well as their family and personal life.

Research revealed that compared to the general population of the country, these women as a whole appeared to have extremely strong connections with the Party-state. Their political participation was realized in terms of their obtaining of CCP membership, holding leadership positions in the local Party-state, and in the award of various titles and honours from the Party-state system which led to a process of incorporation and political socialisation. A comparison of the interviewees across the three localities suggests that wealth usually precedes political involvement, but also that later wealth also increases that involvement. As their wealth increases, these new rich women have more voluntarily sought closer relations with the Party-state and at the same time, they have attracted more attention from their local government.

Despite their significant personal wealth, the roles these new rich women play in their enterprises still appear to be determined by the traditional gendered division of labour with 'men outside, women inside' (of the family). In the domestic sphere these women still, to large extent, have to bear the burden of household responsibilities. However, as the evidence from of the interviews made clear, the wealth of these new rich women has had an effect in lessening their domestic roles.

Personal wealth

Generally speaking, the interviewees clearly fall into the category of China's new rich. The interviews found it difficult (for understandable reasons about disclosure) to provide a direct indication of their wealth in many cases, such as their income. At the same time it is fairly clear from the scale of their economic activities, their apparent life-styles, and individual behaviour that these are the economically well off, even in Qiongshan where the scale of economic activity was smallest and the nature of enterprises was largely confined to the small-scale in the retail and service sectors.

Table 7.1 provides data on the size of the enterprises in which these women operated. The interviewees' businesses have been classified according to the standards adopted by a survey conducted by the United Front Work Department of CCP, All-China Federation of Industry and Commerce and Private Business Institute of China in 2005. ('2005 Zhongguo

Table 7.1 Research localities: Enterprise assets (yuan)

	Below 999,999	1 million – 9.99 million	10 million – 99.99 million	Above 100 million	Information not available	Total
Jiaocheng	30 (48.4%)	20 (32.3%)	5 (8.1%)	2 (3.2%)	5 (8.1%)	62
Qiongshan	34 (64.2%)	3 (5.7%)	1 (1.9%)	1 (1.9%)	14 (26.4%)	53
Mianyang	16 (28.6%)	15 (26.8%)	7 (12.5%)	11 (19.6%)	7 (12.5%)	56
Total	80 (46.8%)	38 (22.2%)	13 (7.6%)	14 (8.2%)	26 (15.2%)	171

siying qiye diaocha baogao') According to the 2005 survey, enterprises with a capital of less than 1 million *yuan* are labelled as small-sized, those with a capital of 1 million to 10 million *yuan* are medium-sized, those with a capital of 10 million to 100 million *yuan* are large-sized and those with a capital of more than 100 million yuan are extra large-sized. As Table 7.1 details, the majority of these women were operating business with capital of 1 million *yuan* or more. On a close look, interviewees in Qiongshan appear to be involved in smaller business (with the most in small-sized and the least in large and extra-large enterprises), while those in Mianyang were operating bigger business (with least in small-sized and most in large and extra-large enterprises). The Shanxi interviewees were ranked somewhere in between.

In his research on the new rich in China published in 1996 Goodman said, 'One of the first investments made as personal wealth increases is to buy a house, although the costs vary greatly as between rural and urban areas' (Goodman 1996: 239). After more than a decade, this remains the case. In Mianyang those interviewed had all bought at least one house. A majority (50 out of 56) of the interviewees' households had a living space of more than 100m. According to the statistics of the housing conditions of urban households in Sichuan Province in 2004 (Sichuansheng Tongjiju 2005: 172), the average per capita living space of the province was 27.31m, while the figure of middle income households was 25.96m, that of upper middle income households was 30.31m and that of high income households 36.12m. Supposing each interviewee's household had three people,[1] a great many of these women entrepreneurs would have better housing conditions than the provincial average and most would have even bigger per capita living space than the average of upper middle income households in the province.

In the pre-reform era, China's urban residents relied upon their work-units for the distribution of housing. The more politically important people such as bureaucrats were privileged to have better living conditions. Since the early 1980s, housing reforms based on market principles have been introduced to the urban areas. As the reforms progressed, houses have been turned into private property at market-based prices. However, privileges still exist. For example, government officials and employees of some wealthy state-owned or public enterprises have access to favourable housing loans, a subsidy for buying a house, houses built by the work-units sold at a favourable price or houses from their work-unit with a favourable rental as a part of their remuneration (Li Bin 2002: issue 2). Quite a few of those interviewed in Mianyang belonged to such privileged groups, as 19 of the 56 interviewed reported that they had bought houses from either their own or their husband's previous or current work-unit at a much lower price than that the market might have determined.

The interviewees also provided interesting details of car ownership, a clear status marker in a transitional economy such as the PRC. Certainly, the prices of different types of cars vary widely. In the big cities of Beijing and Shanghai, lower- or medium-priced cars are increasingly regarded as a necessity of daily life, and only luxury foreign cars remain a symbol of wealth. However, the situation is different in a small city such as Mianyang, where the urban area is 50 km and the urban residents' average annual income in 2005 was 12,898 *yuan* (Mianyang Tongjiju 2005). While it costs one *yuan* by bus, three *yuan* by pedicab and five *yuan* by taxi to get around the city's downtown area, to have a car is undoubtedly something extravagant. Notably, except for two interviewees where the relevant information was not available, an impressive majority (45 out of 56) of those interviewed had their own cars. Moreover, for these women most of their cars were foreign brands costing more than 100,000 *yuan* each.

Entertainment and leisure time activities, or at least those undertaken by the new rich women interviewed in China, cost money. Travel, for example, is an important pastime. 42 out of the 56 interviewees in Mianyang said that they travelled at least once a year. Those who did not travel frequently claimed that they did not have time, their health conditions did not allow them to travel, or that they did not like to travel. Noticeably none of them said they were not able to afford the cost of travelling. While this could certainly be a matter of 'saving face', it is also possible that the cost is not a concern for these new rich women anymore. Most of these women reported that they had been to most of the provinces and municipalities of China. Interestingly, many of them said they disliked the common practice of travelling in organized tourist groups, although that way is clearly much more economic. They chose to travel individually.

Yang, the wife of the owner of a big private enterprise with a capital of 500 million *yuan*, said 'I like travelling very much, but not in a tourist group. I don't like my trips to be planned by others. I prefer to travel alone, so that I can have more freedom and flexibility.' Overseas trips (and trips to Hong Kong and Macau) symbolize higher status and greater wealth in China, not least because of the much higher costs and the difficulties and troubles involved in obtaining visas and permissions. 25 of the interviewees said that they had made at least one overseas trip. The most common overseas destinations for these women were the Southeast Asian Countries, Hong Kong and Macau, while the wealthier ones had also travelled to Europe, Australia, New Zealand and America. One of the interviewees, Gao, was wife of the owner of a private electronic enterprise. Gao's husband was a racing car fan. He was member of a local car racing club and one of the first people to have a car-racing license in China. The couple travelled twice a year. They had been to Vietnam, Mongolia, Myanmar and Russia driving their Chevrolet jeep. Another interviewee, He, was the general manager of an enterprise with a capital of 80 million *yuan*. She was also a shareholder and had a 20 percent share in the enterprise. She said, 'I don't like travelling very much, but travel once a year anyway.' Besides the many trips to other provinces in China, He had travelled to New Zealand once and Europe three times.

At the same time, most of those interviewed in Mianyang went camping and swimming, did exercise at the gym or played ball games at the stadium regularly. Some had even hired private coaches. Moreover, these new rich women were also frequent customers of beauty salons and cafes. Considering the average income of local people, these are all expensive pastimes. This pattern of wealth and leisure time activities was repeated in the interviews conducted in Jiaocheng and Qiongshan, though the scale of operations and of wealth was generally less in Jiaocheng and much less in Qiongshan.

Political participation

Table 7.2 provides data on the CCP membership of the interviewees and the Party-state leadership positions they had ever held. Calculated from the figures provided by the Party-state, by the end of 2005, some 2.1 percent of China's female population were CCP members.[2] In contrast, almost one quarter of the new rich women interviewed in Jiaocheng, Qiongshan and Mianyang were members of the CCP: 12.9 percent of the Jiaocheng interviewees; 15.1 percent of the Qiongshan interviewees; and 41.1 percent of the Mianyang interviewees reported that they had obtained Party membership. Compared with women in general, new rich women seem to be more politically involved, and may be assumed to have stronger Party connections.

The leadership positions the interviewees had held include leadership in villages and neighbourhoods, leadership at various levels of government and CCP committee, as well as leadership in the People's Liberation Army, the People's Congress, the People's Political Consultative Conference, the All-China Federation of Industry and Commerce, the All-China Women's Federation, the All-China Labour Union and the People's Court. These positions are

Table 7.2 Interviewees: CCP membership (including candidates) and Party-state leadership positions

Locality	*CCP Membership*	*Leadership*
Jiaocheng	8 (12.9%)	6 (9.7%)
Qiongshan	8 (15.1%)	3 (5.7%)
Mianyang	23 (41.1%)	5 (8.9%)
Total	*39 (22.8%)*	*14 (8.2%)*

those that ensure access to resources, loans, and raw materials as well as information and business contacts. At least one such position of leadership had been held by 8.2 percent of the interviewees: 9.7 percent in Jiaocheng; 5.7 percent in Qiongshan; and 8.9 percent in Mianyang. These figures also suggest that those interviewed were more politically active than the general population.

While the CCP membership and Party-state leadership positions of those interviewed do indicate that these women have a close affiliation with the Party-state, they also seem to be an indication of the effect of the accumulation of personal wealth on the improvement of political status, which can be illustrated when comparing the situation of Mianyang interviewees with that of those from Jiaocheng and Qiongshan. In terms of CCP membership, although all the three groups of interviewees had a high percentage of CCP participation (in comparison with the average population) all the Jiaocheng and Qiongshan CCP interviewees reported that they had joined the Party as government officials, factory workers, teachers, PLA soldiers and so on. None had obtained their Party membership as private enterprise owners and operators. In other words, none of the Jiaocheng and Qiongshan interviewees joined the Party after they came into the private economic sector. On the other hand, the better-off Mianyang women were the only group that had shown initiative in joining the Party as private enterprise owners or managers. Two of those interviewed obtained their Party membership after establishing their own businesses. Another two interviewees became Party members after making it to senior management positions in private enterprises.

Jiang was the owner of a restaurant chain with a capital of 'several million *yuan* without doubt'. She joined the Party in 2002, 15 years after the start of her business. Jiang also revealed that a Party branch and a labour union had been established in her company.

Shen used to be a staff member of a state-owned factory. After being laid-off in 1999, she set up her own business. At the time of the interviews, she was the owner of a funeral and interment chain with branches all over the province and in Beijing. Shen did not apply for CCP membership when she was still employed in the state-owned enterprise. But as her business success expanded and her personal wealth grew, she decided to pursue a closer Party connection. Shen submitted her CCP membership application in 2005 and at the time when the interview was conducted, she was on probation as a candidate for membership.

Yang used to be staff member of a public vocational school. In 1995, she quit her job to seek business opportunities. Like Shen, Yang did not want to join the Party until she had achieved success in the private sector. In 2000, she became a Party member when working as the executive manager of a private enterprise. When the interview was conducted, Yang owned a high-tech industry company with a capital of some 8 million *yuan*.

In a similar case, Xie used to be a staff member of a collective factory. In 1991, she left the factory to join in a private company where she started as a manual worker. In 1999, Xie joined the Party as the general manager of the company.

When it comes to Party-state leadership positions, although interviewees from all the three localities appeared to be closely connected to the local Party-state through their leadership experiences, again difference could be detected between the less-wealthy Jiaocheng and Qiongshan interviewees and their better-off Mianyang counterparts. In the cases of the Jiaocheng and Qiongshan interviewees with Party-state leadership experiences, all of these women invariably worked as CCP or government officials before they became private entrepreneurs. In other words, their leadership experiences were obtained before their current entrepreneurial roles. However, interviews conducted in Mianyang presented a different story. Some of the Mianyang interviewees were appointed to leadership positions in the Party-state system after they became private entrepreneurs. Interestingly, these women had all achieved significant success in business. This seems to indicate that political recognition comes through business success and wealth.

Shang was the *de facto* owner and general manager of a trading company, while her husband acted as the board chairman. Shang's business started in 1991, with an investment of 9,000 *yuan*. In fourteen years it had grown into a large company with capital of some 100 million *yuan*. As a result of her business success, Shang was offered a position as an executive member of Mianyang Federation of Industry and Commerce.

Another interviewee, Deng owned a vocational school. The business started in 1994 with an investment of 40,000 *yuan* and six employees. In 2005 when the fieldwork was undertaken, the school had a capital of 600,000 *yuan* – more than ten times the initial investment. Moreover, the number of staff had increased more than five times. Considering Deng's entrepreneurial achievement, as well as her close personal relationship with local cadres,[3] it is not really that surprising that she also became an executive member of the city's Federation of Industry and Commerce.

So the logic seems to be that the accumulation of personal wealth comes hand in hand with political participation. In other words, the new rich women's enthusiasm to join the Party-state seems to increase with their wealth. Moreover, these women's high profile business success has also bought them political titles from the Party-state. The second point is further proved by examination of the interviewees' other Party-state connections, in terms of membership of the People's Congress, membership of the People's Political Consultative Conference, membership of the Federation of Industry and Commerce, membership of the Women Entrepreneurs' Association and various other mass organization congresses and activities. All these political roles can be regarded as indicators of the interviewees' political and social status for several reasons: first, these new rich were co-opted to the political associations because of their professional excellence, their possession of wealth and their social reputation (Li Guoping and Huang Qing 2003); on the other hand, these roles added to their social reputation and presumably their possession of wealth later. Moreover, such roles are commonly regarded as a kind of social recognition (Qin Yan 1999: 138).

Those interviewed in Mianyang were more politically active than their counterparts in Jiaocheng and Qiongshan. One explanation of this distinction could well be related to the greater business success of the former. Four of the Jiaocheng interviewees reported themselves to be members of the local People's Congress, the People's Political Consultative Conference, and the Federation of Industry and Commerce. Two interviewees were members of the provincial Women Entrepreneurs' Association. And another two were leaders of the county's Association of Date Processing Industry. In Qiongshan, where the business scale was the smallest and business sector was mainly retail and service, only one interviewee reported that she was appointed as member of the provincial Youth Association because of her entrepreneurial success.

In contrast, among the better-off Mianyang interviewees such co-option was fairly common. In one case, the interviewee was a representative to the county-level People's Congress, and five others reported themselves to be representatives to Mianyang People's Congress. Moreover, one interviewee was a representative to the local district Political Consultative Conference and another to the higher-level Mianyang Political Consultative Conference. Two of the Mianyang interviewees reported that they were members of the Federation of Industry and Commerce, two were members of the Self-Employed Labourers Association and three were members of the committee of the Women's Federation at district or city level. Two Mianyang interviewees reported that they were representatives to the district and city Party Congress. One was a member of the local district labour union. Another interviewee was a member of the provincial Association of Women Entrepreneurs (AWE). Although the AWE is a nongovernmental organization, it is subordinate to the Women's Federation. Moreover, it claims to be the organization for 'successful women entrepreneurs, outstanding management personnel, as well as directors and managers of famous enterprises' (AWE website). It seems reasonable to regard membership in the AWE as another point of connection to the Party-state, as well as a sought-after honour.

The leash of tradition

Despite the claim of government and in particular the All-China Women's Federation (ACWF) that women's status has improved in the reform era and that women are enjoying equality with men in the fields of politics, economy, culture, society, and the family (The General Office of The State Council of The People's Republic of China 1994; The All-China Women's Federation 2005) the existing scholarship points to the opposite. It indicates that reform, though creating more opportunities for women in China, has not lifted Chinese women's status higher than before. Instead gender disparities still exist in terms of education (Judd 2002; Jacka 1997; Croll 1995; Gallagher 2001; Korabik 1994; Fang *et al.* 2005), employment (Korabik 1994; Gallagher 2001; Rosen 1994; Honig and Hershatter 1988; Entwisle and Henderson 2000), political participation (Howell 2002; Rosen 1995: 315; Fang *et al.* 2005; Edwards 2004; Korabik 1994; Blecher 1989) and family (Wolf 1985; Diamond 1975; Korabik 1994; Jacka 1997). In general, scholars examining the status of women in post-reform China suggest that women remain poorly represented in China's economic development.

The interviewees' reflections on the roles they play at the enterprises and in their families suggests that gender inequality can be seen in these new rich women's lives, but that the situation might not be as bad as described for the general female population in China in the existing scholarship. Although the interviewees still had to face gender inequality, the interview results show that the situation was improving. Firstly, these women were able to take the initiative in the establishment of the business. Most of the women interviewed were playing an equal role with their husband in developing the ideas on which their enterprises were built. Secondly, the interviewees were actively engaged in the business operation and strategic planning. Often in comparison to their husbands, these women were playing a more substantial part in the management and daily operation of the enterprises. When encountering difficulties, they sought advice from their husbands, family members, friends and colleagues, but in many cases they made the final executive decisions. In general, these women were the *de facto* bosses of their business. However, the interviewees' reflections on the roles they play at the enterprises and in their families suggests that traditional gender stereotype can still be seen in the articulation of these entrepreneurial women's lives, although wealth seems to be able to dissipate its effects to a certain extent.

Although economic development has greatly changed women's status in China, many traditional stereotypes about gender roles have persisted. One of these values is the 'men outside, women inside' stereotype of the traditional Chinese agricultural economy, in which men went out to work in the fields and were responsible for affairs that occurred outside their households, while women were limited to the 'inside' sphere to look after the family (Jacka 1997; Entwisle and Henderson 2000). Economic development and the 'opening up' of China have to some extent dissolved this stereotype. Nowadays it is not uncommon to see a group of women sitting in an expensive restaurant drinking alcohol, enjoying themselves at a karaoke centre or even relaxing at a health and fitness centre – venues formerly dominated by male clientele. However, the 'man outside, woman inside' cliché still affects the division of labour in economic production, although understandings of 'outside' and 'inside' have altered. To till in the fields, for example, is no longer considered an 'outside' activity in rural China, as people start to seek employment outside their home village and those left 'inside' the village have to take care of agricultural production. There is a sense in which 'inside' the family has extended to include the family's economic enterprises.

Some of those interviewed in Jiaocheng, Qiongshan and Mianyang were still affected by the traditional practice of having the husband represent the family to the outside world. When asked who had developed the original idea for their business, in some cases the interviewees revealed that the enterprises were established on the basis of an idea developed by themselves or through joint efforts with their husbands, but the companies were still registered under their husband's name alone. The interviewees rationalised this variously as: 'man has the priority (in business)', 'it doesn't matter (who runs the business), as we are a family', 'it is the tradition of China to have a man at the front', 'a man should decide on the big issues', or just simply 'it should be (registered under) a man's name'. These kinds of responses were found in all the three research localities.

Chang, a woman who ran a restaurant in Jiaocheng County, talked about her role in establishing the business. Coming from a poor family, she chose to enter the restaurant business in 1995 to improve her family's financial situation. The restaurant was set up with a loan of 40,000 *yuan*. To save money, she designed the building, drew up the blueprint and bought building materials all by herself. As she explained, 'I didn't even discuss it with my husband. He didn't care about it anyway and always responded to my questions by saying "I don't know."' During the interview, Chang's husband was on the side carefully cleaning the floor of the restaurant, which was the job assigned to him by his wife. Though Chang played a dominant role in both the business and the family, the restaurant is registered under her husband's name. That was because, she said, 'women in business are likely to be negatively judged by society. Older people would say I overpower my husband'.

Su, one of the Qiongshan interviewees, had leased a counter in a shopping centre together with her husband. Before the start of the business, Su wanted to sell clothes and house appliance. Her idea was turned down by the husband, who planned to sell cosmetics. So the business was established according to the husband's plan and registered under the husband's name, while Su is the operator, selling cosmetics.

Shang was wife of the owner of a trading company in Mianyang. The business started in 1996, based on an idea developed by Shang alone. She was in charge of business operations as well, while her husband 'is not responsible for anything but money'. But she still preferred to have her husband represent the enterprise to the outside world. The company was registered under Shang's husband's name from the beginning, despite Shang admitting that 'many people only know me (as the owner of the business), so it is not very convenient to have him as the legal owner'.

Certainly, the sexual division of labour with 'men outside, women inside' exists in these women's business operation. Some of the Jiaocheng interviewees mentioned the 'outside' and 'inside' notion when talking about their work.

These women regard activities such as management, production, personnel, and basic administrative duties as 'inside' work suitable for women; and consider entertaining clients, establishing business connections, dealing with government administrative units, demanding payments for debts and purchasing as 'outside' work: the rightful province of men. In keeping with tradition' the tasks labelled as 'inside' work tend to be taken care of by the women themselves whereas the 'outside' jobs tend to be allocated to their husbands. Although the entrepreneurial women in Qiongshan and Mianyang did not explicitly mention the 'inside' and 'outside' notion, they reflected that they found it hard to entertain customers, business partners and cadres outside their offices, as it was 'inconvenient' (to be read as inappropriate) for women to go to entertainment centres (which were popular places for businessmen to entertain their business partners), and they did not drink and smoke, and could not joke as freely as men. Moreover, socialization with males might cause gossip and innuendo about their behaviour. Even worse, it might as well cause jealousy from male customers, business partners and cadres' wives.

The interviews also indicated that domestic work is still regarded as remaining the responsibility of these women. A large proportion of the interviewees reported that they had to shoulder the responsibilities of cooking, cleaning, washing clothes, shopping and childcare at home. This is commonly regarded by these women as the downside of being businesswomen.

In Jiaocheng, 24 of the 62 interviewees reported that they had obtained help from their family members with housework, with the greatest source of help being their husbands. Twelve (19.4 percent) of the Jiaocheng women's husbands shared domestic responsibilities with them and three (4.8 percent) of the husbands were solely responsible for housework. Family-in-law were also reported as sources of help with housework, though the percentage is not high. Altogether 43 (69.3 percent) of the Jiaocheng interviewees had to shoulder household responsibilities either by themselves or with help from others. Three of the Jiaocheng women reported that they had hired maids to assist with housework.

The Qiongshan interviewees – the group with the least business success – reported that they had the fewest sources of help with domestic tasks. Nine of these women had family members such as adult children, sisters, parents and parents-in-law to do housework for them. These women's husbands, on the other hand, had not provided much help in this aspect either. Only four of these women's husbands were reported as sharing the burden of housework with their wives and none of them took responsibility alone at home. Eight out of the 53 interviewees in Qiongshan had employed maids to take care of the household for them.

The Mianyang interviewees, on the other hand, were the group with the least burdens of household tasks. A large proportion (42.9 percent, 24 out of 56) of these women reported they had at least one family member helping with housework tasks. Their husbands were a considerable source of help. Sixteen out of the 56 interviewees reported that their husbands undertook house-work at home. Compared with their Jiaocheng and Qiongshan counterparts, it was much more common for these women to hire one or several maids to do the housework (19 out of 56 – 41.1 percent, as opposed to 4.8 percent and 15.1 percent respectively).

The wealth of these new rich women would clearly seem to have an impact on their traditional domestic roles. Those in Mianyang, with the greatest business success, had the least burden from their family – only 41.1 percent of these women reported they were involved in household tasks, while the percentage of their counterparts in Jiaocheng and Qiongshan was 69.3 percent and 52.8 percent respectively. Presumably, as the major bread-winner of the family, these new rich women found it easier to get help from their family members for housework, seen as 'trivial' perhaps or of less importance. These wealthy interviewees had a considerably higher status in the community, a position reinforced by the usual practice of hiring a maid to do the housework.

New rich women and social change

Women who are enterprise owners and operators are a particular sub-group of the new rich in China, not least because they are partly masked by reason of their gender. There is a complex series of relations between their accumulation of personal wealth, their role in local politics, and their con-tinued commitment to certain 'traditional roles'. There can be little doubt that as a result of accumulating significant personal wealth new rich women begin to increase their participation in local politics. While signifying a new degree of participation in the public domain, the increased personal wealth of these women has not freed them from traditional gendered expectations. The interviews in Jiaocheng, Qiongshan, and Mianyang reveal that women entrepreneurs in China still feel that they should keep to the private domain and take primary responsibility for domestic duties. However, the more successful of these new rich women seem to be able to set aside their domestic responsibilities to some extent, with various sources of help including both family members and hired maids.

A comparison of the situation of interviewees of the three research localities helps to better illustrate the power of wealth. The wealthier Mia-nyang women were more substantially involved in local politics. On the one hand, they appeared to be more actively seeking connections with the Party-state to reinforce their entrepreneurship. On the other hand, these women's significant business success had certainly attracted more political appoint-ments from the local government as an effort to co-opt and motivate the development of the private sector. Comparatively, Qiongshan interviewees, who on the whole were running smaller scale businesses and engaged in the less significant sectors of retail and service, reported that they had the least political involvement. In Jiaocheng, where the interviewees were wealthier than those in Qiongshan but poorer than those in Mianyang, the new rich women were similarly of a middling level of political activity.

Wealth definitely seems to have been the element that releases women from the leash of household tasks. The Mianyang interviewees – those with the greatest entrepreneurial success – were more able to obtain help from their family members and to afford to hire maids to assist with housework. The comparatively less successful Jiaocheng and Qiongshan interviewees had to carry more domestic responsibilities on their own shoulders.

Notes

1   With the introduction of China's One-Child Policy in 1979, most China's urban families have only one child.
2   According to the Central Government, by the end of 2005, China's female populatioin was 633.81 million ('Zhongguo Renkou Xianzhuang' 2005).
3   Deng's school cooperated with Mianyang Women's Federation to provide domestic service courses for girls seeking employment as maids. As a result many local officials asked for her help to find capable and reliable maids. When Deng Xiaoping's family asked the provincial governors of Sichuan to find them local maids who could cook authentic Sichuan dishes, they came to Deng's school. The one-hour interview with Deng was interrupted many times by calls from local officials. Deng talked with them over the phone as a friend.

8 The professional middle classes
Management and politics

Ivan Cucco

Building an endogenous system of innovation has been one of China's top priorities since the outset of reforms. Particularly since 1986, China has embarked on an far-reaching attempt to modernize its national Science and Technology (S&T) system through landmark national-level projects like the High-Tech Research and Development Program (the 863 Program), the National Plan for Long-Term Science and Technology Development, and the 'Torch' Program – to name but a few. Alongside the growth of national high-tech industries, the technological upgrading of existing industries, and the increase in domestic technology absorption capacity, one of the key aims of the policies implemented in the last two decades is the creation of closer linkages between reformed research institutions and commercial enterprises (Chen and Chen 2005; Li and Hitt 2006; Segal 2003). Progress in this direction, though far from being complete, is undeniable. Gross Domestic Expenditure in Research and Development (R&D) as a ratio to GDP has more than doubled in ten years, rising from 0.57 percent of GDP in 1995 to 1.34 percent of GDP in 2005. The share of total R&D expenditures financed by industry topped 67 percent in 2005, thus signalling a shrinking role for direct government financing of R&D activities (OECD 2007). National high-tech industries are being incubated in innovation districts characterized by a wide array of (local level) state – university – private sector partnerships akin to those found in technopoles around the world (Castells and Hall 1994; Walcott, 2003).

These achievements have not gone unnoticed, and clinging to the view of China as simply the 'factory of the world' is becoming harder. Finally, overcoming deep-set fears related to the loose protection of intellectual property rights, and rejecting the cliché of China as a place not conducive to innovation, a growing number of multinational corporations (MNCs) is setting up or expanding R&D activities in China. In 2005, around 750 foreign-invested R&D centres have been estimated to be operating in China (Walsh 2007), their number undoubtedly growing since then. These include global giants such as IBM, Intel, Nokia, Microsoft, Motorola – as well as companies which have made creativity and innovation a crucial part of their brand identity like Google or Dyson. Apart from the sheer numbers, the quality and nature of foreign-invested R&D operations is changing, with a growing number of companies being involved in medium-term projects which are expected to lead to commercial applications in a timeframe of five to ten years (Walsh 2007). While it is still unclear whether increased foreign R&D presence is effectively contributing to the upgrading of the Chinese S&T system through spill over effects and technological transfers (Sun *et al.* 2007; and the works reviewed therein) it certainly signals an evolving role for China in the global geography of industrial location.

The increased concentration of foreign-invested R&D activities is in itself a not so surprising consequence of the growing middle-class consumer space, since China is perceived as a mature and receptive market for high-end products. And a market which, at least in its most affluent part, is calling for increased flexibility and continuous, innovative product adaptation. However, this is only half the story, particularly for that segment of the middle class which is after all the raw material of innovation: highly skilled professionals in fields like IT, advanced engineering, biotechnology – as well as for those professionals who, combining technical knowledge with good managerial skills, are able to perform the hybrid functions required to coordinate an innovation-driven production system.

As a key component of the 'soft' infrastructure required to sustain an innovative milieu, professionals have become a valuable and increasingly scarce resource. Consequently, professional labour markets are becoming extremely competitive. In Shanghai for example, entry-level salaries for young graduates from good universities in subjects like IT, engineering or biotechnology are around 6,000 *yuan* per month.[1] In 2006, professionals' voluntary turnover rates have been estimated at around 16 percent, compared to an overall turnover rate of 13 percent (Hewitt 2006). While significant by any standard, these figures are not able to fully convey the extent of pressures converging on the professional labour markets. Late entrants in established markets, or companies setting up green-field operations, pursue extremely aggressive recruitment strategies aimed at getting hold of professionals with good technical skills and relevant job experience. Quite often, this means luring skilled professionals away from their competitors through offers which can easily reach a doubling of their current wage. The chances for someone to get that lucky are of course not too high. However, the consciousness of being part of a particularly heated segment of the labour market in which things like this may and indeed *do* happen (maybe to someone you personally know) helps to fuel high expectations.

In terms of income therefore, professionals can easily fit the profile of an affluent segment of the middle class. The more so, as in most cases salaries are only one component of a professionals' income. In the face of relatively high turnover rates, companies have to devise ways to capitalize on the often costly and lengthy training provided to their employees – while at the same time making sure that proprietary knowledge does not leave the firm. Compensation packages in the private sector are therefore being designed to encourage long-term appointments within the company. Among such measures, the provision of housing funds, or of company housing with ownership rights passing over to the employee after a certain number of years of continued work with the company play an important role. Through such mechanisms, professionals in the private sector are being offered a privileged path to homeownership, a path which until recently tended to be one of the prerogatives of public sector employees (Tomba 2004). Similarly, the offer of healthcare and retirement schemes is also seen as an effective way for companies to reduce turnover rates. If productivity bonuses, various forms of allowances, and sponsored training are also included, the lifestyle enjoyed by professionals and their disposable incomes have to be considered as set at a much higher level than would be suggested by their base salary alone.

An analysis of the income structure of professionals is however not the main focus of this chapter. Rather, the aim is to identify some of the economic and institutional forces which are shaping the emergence of a professional middle class. The view proposed here is that professionals are located in a bridging position between the local levels of the state, the private business sector and the various hybrid organizations which participate with different functions in the implementation of local development policies. The evolving logic driving the interaction between local, quasi-state and non-state actors offers professionals the chance of moving with relative ease between these sectors during the course of their careers, thus building networks of relationships spanning different sectors of the public and the private sphere. In at least some cases, professionals can choose to directly mobilize these networks for their own advantage at a later stage of their careers – for example to start their own business, to take on senior positions in state-invested companies, or to join the ranks of the public administration.

Being in a liminal position not only gives professionals a structural advantage; it is also becoming one of the layers through which their identity is articulated. Even when mobilizing networks of support or building genuine business partnerships with people located in structurally different positions, professionals tend to perceive themselves as different from the other groups with which they interact in terms of both competence and motivation. Being in a bridging position also implies that professionals recombine opportunities from different realms – from the state as well as from the corporate world – in ways that can be quite distant from the simple sum of the original blueprints.[2] Whether this ongoing process of recombination will eventually lead to the formulation of common stances able to catalyse forms of professionals' collective action – or at least forms of concerted bargaining aimed at improving their positions vis-à-vis the state and employers – is at this stage still far from clear.

The analysis in this chapter is based on data and information collected by the author during six months of fieldwork in Nanjing, Jiangsu province (March–August 2007). During this period, 51 semi-structured interviews were completed.[3] Documentary evidence was collected from companies and from development zone administrations. Unless otherwise specified, the observations reported are based on evidence collected during fieldwork.[4]

Between management and politics

The crucial role played by professionals in the process of techno-economic transformation occurring in China locates them at the intersection of several interrelated fields spanning multiple and complexly interacting scales – from the global, to the national, to the local, and further down to the urban and sub-urban levels.[5] Professionals are at the same time one of the forces that the central government is trying to mobilize to the service of its ongoing modernizing project; a key resource in the strategies implemented by localities attempting to upgrade their position in the global production system; and a precious asset for individual companies (foreign and domestic, private and non-private) which need to build or maintain a competitive edge in process and product innovation.

At a wider level, the rising demand for professionals is one of the results of the modernist vision to introduce advanced technology – an integral part of the message delivered by the central leadership since the beginning of the reform era (Gabriel 2006: 8–9). The formulation of technology employed here includes not only the 'hard' technology embodied in advanced equipment or innovative engineering processes, but also 'soft' technology, a concept which includes the social relations of production (Gabriel 2006: 123). Professionals are functional to the national modernization project in at least two regards. On the one hand, they are expected to actively contribute to the production of innovative, endogenously generated 'hard' technology. On the other hand, they operate within an industrial system which in its most technologically advanced sectors is undoubtedly moving towards a new techno-economic paradigm which, though still in an experimental stage and surely not simply mimicking foreign forms of organization, appears to share many of the traits identified in other economies by post-Fordist analyses.

Professionals are also one of the vehicles through which the 'soft' technology at the core of the new techno-economic paradigm – including new standards of efficiency and new managerial models (Perez 1985), as well as evolving forms of labour relationships – can be disseminated outside the borders of the firm. A further channel is opened for 'soft' technology to reach those spheres of the public administration which are operating as an interface between state and non-state actors in the Science and Technology system. This is through the increased mobility of professionals between the private and the public sector, favoured among other things by converging wage levels (Tomba 2004) and the diffusion of hybrid ownership forms in the high-tech sector (Segal 2003). The influx of advanced 'soft' technology in the S&T system contributes to upgrading its absorption capacity, to facilitating its interaction with global players, and to promoting its assertiveness on global markets.

Initiatives emanating from the central leadership signal a growing willingness to gradually shift China's development strategy towards selective support to high-tech industries and to other industries of strategic relevance.[6] Pressures in this direction are obviously felt at the local level, where sub-national development strategies have to take into account the set of incentives posed by the central state. Competition between firms (foreign as well as national) to recruit and retain professionals overlaps therefore with competition between localities – as the capacity to nurture, attract and territorialize inherently mobile skilled human resources proves to be crucial in attracting investment in the high-tech industries favoured by central policies. The convergence of central government efforts to upgrade the S&T system with the global business discovery of China as a potential future high-tech powerhouse has in fact opened up a novel space for localities, as the opportunity to raise their position in the global urban hierarchy from low-end manufacturing bases to regional hubs of innovation appears to be within reach. While it is true that most of the internal technological capacity as well as foreign R&D centres tend to congregate in the well-established high-tech districts of Beijing, Shanghai and Shenzhen (von Zedtwitz 2004), so called second-tier cities are emerging as an attractive alternative, given lower wage levels and a relatively less severe degree of competition (hence of turnover) in professional labour markets. Nokia Siemens Networks for example has recently announced plans to develop its R&D centre in Chengdu into one of its largest R&D centre worldwide (*SinoCast China Business Daily News* 23 August 2007).[7]

The ways in which localities compete is however changing; particularly so, if their aim is to attract investment in high-tech and advanced industries. Conventional localized investment attraction strategies based on a combination of tax incentives and cheap land prices appear to be not only less viable – due to more restrictive central policies[8] – but also inadequate by themselves to start the upgrading of the local industrial base. The repertoire of strategies and the range of alliances enacted by local governments in China appear to be expanding along the lines of the 'entrepreneurial local state' (Mayer 1994: 327). The use of indigenous skills and entrepreneurship; the emphasis on innovation and new technology; the involvement of non-state actors in the organization of conditions for local development are the tools used to build a climate responsive to the needs of new business models. Seen from the local perspective, professionals are again a crucial building block in this strategy. Mobilizing endogenous skills and innovation capacity requires in the first place having an adequate concentration of localized human resources. Therefore, as much as localities need to present themselves as attractive production sites to corporate entities, they also have to (re)shape themselves as desirable living and working environments for skilled professionals. Attempts at building an innovative milieu are consequently leading to intentional interventions in urban areas, articulated again on multiple and not always coordinated scales – as individual districts within the same city try to assert their position in the local economy.

Furthermore, professionals are starting to play an important bridging role at the local level. The range of actors involved in implementing local development policies in different degrees of partnership and interaction with the local levels of the state has expanded to include private producer services companies; national and foreign chambers of commerce; private or quasi-private training and educational institutions; private employment services; quasi-private or private development corporations. Skilled professionals with relevant experience in the private sector are placed in a better position to act as an interface between local state agencies and their various partners, and in such a capacity they are often entering the ranks of the public administration. This osmotic process holds true also in the opposite direction: as the interactions between the local levels of the state and other organizations is in no way limited to the unidirectional provision of political and administrative support but often requires a certain degree of real coordination between the parts, professionals with experience in the public administration are also actively sought after; among others, by foreign firms.

The competition between state and non-state actors is leading to a convergence in the levels and forms of compensation offered to professionals. For the state, this means bringing salaries in line with the levels offered on the market. It also means being able to offer state-employed professionals access to continued training and to opportunities for career development, elements on which private companies put a great emphasis and which professionals themselves perceive as an important component of their remuneration packages. State agencies (and particularly development zones) are setting up training centres, which are used to train their own employees as well as to offer training services to companies in their jurisdiction. Usually these centres are set up in partnership with private entities or universities, with the local state agency being one of the shareholders.

For the companies, the process of remuneration convergence implies – as already noted – the use of benefit packages which are very similar to those traditionally offered by the state. Through this mechanism of institutional isomorphism (Di Maggio and Powell 1983) in HR and remuneration policies, privileged access to specific benefits is being expanded outside the ranks of the public sector. Housing is a good point in case. Young professionals are highly mobile not only across companies but also across localities; housing is seen as an important way to territorialize them. Knowing that a range of accommodation solutions is available for its employees is therefore an important determinant of a company's decision to invest in a district or a development zone. Local governments at the district level and development zones administrations build housings complexes in their area (by themselves or through the involvement of private and quasi-private developers) catering to different categories of workers: basic dormitories for unskilled workers; smaller apartments for skilled workers; higher standard apartments for professionals; luxury villas for senior managers or foreign experts. Some of these will be on offer at commercial prices; some at subsidized prices (Tomba 2004). Apart from ensuring that an adequate housing stock is available, the local government can also provide access to subsidized housing to the companies as part of the incentives offered in an investment deal. In this way, the company can in turn pass these on to its employees, who will be given the chance of becoming homeowners at a price which can be as low as fifty percent of the current market price. This, as already said, is usually conditional upon the employee remaining with the company for a specific period.

In localities trying to promote the creation of new high-tech industry and the upgrading of the existing ones, the space in which professionals operate appears therefore to be marked by an increased interaction between state and non-state actors. Nanjing is a city in the midst of such transformation. Being a relatively late starter when compared to major cities like Beijing or Shanghai, and facing strong competition from the dynamic smaller centres of the Yangtze (Changjiang) River Delta, Nanjing offers the possibility to observe how professionals are being perceived as a crucial asset in the development strategy of a locality trying to design a new role for itself in China's urban hierarchy.

The case of Nanjing

Nanjing is the capital of Jiangsu province in the Changjiang River Delta sub-region; it is the main inland port along the Changjiang River. Its position as an important fluvial hub located at a short distance from Shanghai (around 300 km) and linked via the river to the central and western provinces (particularly to the far inland cities of Chongqing and Chengdu) offers Nanjing good advantages in terms of logistics and infrastructure. Nanjing is also a city with a long and often tragic history. The former capital of six dynasties, Nanjing has been somehow respectful of its heritage. Of course, much of the urban transformations occurring elsewhere can be observed in Nanjing as well, with the usual combination of high-rise building, newly built gated communities and old quarters undergoing rapid development dotting the urban landscape. However, the central part of the city retains wide tree-lined boulevards, long segments of the city wall system, places of historical significance and a number of pleasant parks and green spaces.

The geography of industrial development in Nanjing follows the line of post-socialist urban transformation (Ma and Wu 2005b). Industrial activities have been progressively moved out of the centre through the establishment of a number of industrial development zones on the fringe of the city (Figure 8.1)[9] While some of the industrial districts and development zones are host to a varied mix of industries (like Jiangning Development Zone in

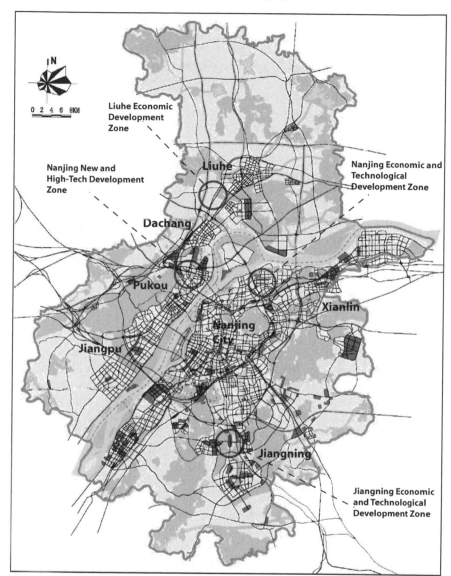

Figure 8.1 Nanjing and development zones

the south), others show a more specialized character. For example, the chemical industry concentrates in Liuhe district and in the Nanjing Chemical Industrial Park – both located north of the Changjiang River. Clustering is partly motivated by location economies, partly by the local government willingness to confine industrial activities with more adverse environmental externalities to some specific areas. The trajectory of urban growth has been following the axes of industrial development. Urban growth has showed a cyclical path, with moments of edge-expansion followed by periods of in-fill growth (Xu *et al.* 2007). As a result, the originally separated suburban districts are becoming increasingly linked to the city centre. This is mainly true for the southern districts, and particularly for the Jiangning area. For the northern districts, the Changjiang River still acts as a powerful barrier hindering their full integration with the centre. Notwithstanding the presence of three bridges across the river, transportation is not easy and the traffic is often heavy.[10] The municipal government is placing high priority on improving linkages with the area north of the Changjiang, with nine additional transportation lines planned to be in operation by 2012. These include tunnels under the Changjiang and the extension of the metro system to the north of the river. However, the population remains heavily concentrated in the city centre (Luo and Wei 2006).

In terms of economic activities, the city centre is taking on the specialized functions of a CBD. It is here that the bulk of the financial and service industries, and particularly a growing number of national and foreign-invested producer services companies, are located. Traditional working class districts in the central areas are undergoing processes of fragmented gentrification centred on gated communities. While in some cases original occupants have been given the chance of going back after redevelopment, this is usually associated with lower quality development projects (Wu and He 2005). Cases of functional transformation are also evident, with some of the quarters retaining traditional architectural features being converted into upmarket leisure and shopping areas. Such is for example the case of the 'Nanjing 1912' area, similar in intent and nature to Xintiandi in Shanghai. Global luxury brands have their outlets in the various shopping malls in the city centre, and efforts to improve the quality of urban architecture are evident in landmark projects like the new Nanjing Library building and the Nanjing Olympic Center. Nanjing shows therefore all the sign of having achieved its transformation from a producer to a consumer city. As such, it posits itself as the core of a megapolitan area spanning across central Jiangsu and Anhui provinces, which includes the cities of Zhenjiang, Yangzhou, Ma'anshan, Wuhu, Chuzhou and Chaohu (van Dijk 2005). In order to fully attest its new status, Nanjing is placing great emphasis on the transformation of its industrial base, through the upgrading of existing industries and the concurrent creation of new strengths in innovative and high-tech industries, particularly in the ITC sector. In the midst of such structural transformation, Nanjing offers an interesting case study for the analysis of the emergent professional middle class.

Competition between urban districts

Nanjing inherited an industrial structure centred on the automotive and the chemical sectors from its period as capital of the Nationalist government (1927–37); these industries were further developed following the establishment of the People's Republic. After the beginning of the reform era, the presence of important state owned groups like Nanjing Auto Co. (automotive) and Yangzi Petrochemical Corporation (YPC, a subsidiary of SINOPEC)[11] worked to attract foreign investment in both sectors.[12] Foreign investment has also been relevant to related industries like automotive components, robotics and automation, chemical fibres, and metallurgy. The electronics and consumer durables industries have also been developed, and have attracted a good share of international activity. However, the presence of a strong SOE sector meant that Nanjing had to go through a period of hard restructuring, with massive workers layoffs hitting the city after the acceleration of SOE reforms in the middle of the 1990s (Wu and He 2005).

Until the recent past, Nanjing was perceived as a quite conservative city in terms of its industrial development strategies. Levels of FDI as well as overall growth rates lagged behind the more dynamic growth poles concentrated in the southern part of Jiangsu province and in neighbouring Zhejiang province (for example the Suzhou–Wuxi–Changzhou area). Nanjing has however a significant advantage over its neighbours: together with Beijing and Shanghai, it is one of the main centres of higher education in China.[13] It seems only natural that the local government would try to leverage this strength of the Nanjing educational system. The city is marketing itself as a favourable place for investment particularly because it offers access to a wide pool of trained professionals. In fact, the availability of skilled human resources has been often quoted by the interviewed companies as one of the main reasons for locating their activities in Nanjing. Furthermore, since Nanjing is a major research base, many national companies have been set up here to grant access to research facilities as well as to specific technologies they are developing in cooperation with local universities. National level policies like the 'Torch' and the 863 Plans have provided the institutional framework within which to favour a closer integration between industry and research institutions. During the 1990s, a number of universities traditionally based in the central city area have been asked or encouraged to set up new campuses within the existing industrial development zones. New 'university cities' have sprung up in districts like Jiangning and Pukou. The task of promoting integration between industries and research institutions has been delegated to hybrid organizations based on a variety of institutional arrangements involving local administrations, universities and private enterprises. The Nanjing High-tech Industrial Development Zone (NHTDZ) offers a good illustration of these processes.

The NHTDZ is one of the fifty-three national level high-tech development zones created by the 'Torch' Plan. It is located in Pukou district, north of the Changjiang. It was jointly established by the Jiangsu Provincial Government and Nanjing Municipal Government in 1988, and recognized by the State Council in 1992.[14] Six universities have set up new campuses within the NHTDZ area (see Figure 8.2); among them, leading universities such as Nanjing University and Southeast University. Four more universities are

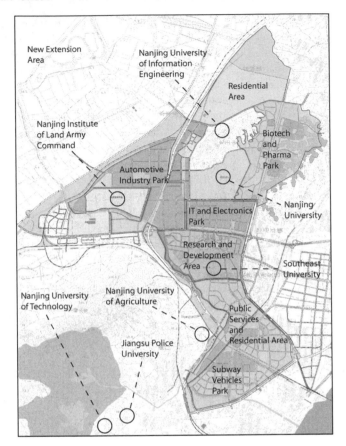

Figure 8.2 Nanjing New and High Technology Development Zone, Pukou District
Source: Nanjing New and High Technology Economic Development Corporation, 2007.

located within 2 km of the zone. These universities are involved in a number
of projects driven by what could be called 'innovation district' logic. One of
these is the Nanjing Software Park, a 'Torch' Plan National Software
Industry Base.

The Park was jointly established by the NHTDZ and Nanjing University,
with the aim of developing innovative applications for the power and communication industries. The Nanjing Software Park operates in close cooperation with domestic and foreign enterprises. It performs research projects
for companies like IBM, Intel and Motorola, which outsource to the centre
part of the research activities coordinated by their R&D centres located
elsewhere in China. At a lower level, a number of software development and
training centres have been set up as joint-stock corporations between the
NHTDZ and various private enterprises. The NHTDZ is also home to a
number of incubation centres offering facilities and support for innovative
start-up enterprises, like the Nanjing Pharmaceutical and Biological

Engineering Park, the Jinling Enterprise Park for Returned Overseas Students, the Nanjing Technology Industry Incubation Centre.

While the national level status and the direct involvement of the municipal government offer the NHTDZ an advantage in terms of visibility and access to higher-level support, they have also somehow hindered its development in the past. The NHTDZ has to comply with central and local regulations, particularly with regard to the kind of industries it can host, as well as in terms of stricter environmental impact constraints. Therefore, it faces strong competition from other industrial districts in Nanjing which, due to their more independent status, have enjoyed greater leeway in implementing their investment attraction strategies. The once suburban industrial development zones like Jiangning target the same kind of high-tech industries the NHTDZ is trying to attract. Moreover, central city districts are also becoming involved in similar activities since they are trying to capitalize on the high concentration of universities and research institutes by establishing new urban high-tech development corporations like the Gulou Science and Technology Park or the Zhujiang Road High-Tech Development District. The level of coordination between the initiatives of individual districts is low and, rather than configuring a citywide high-tech innovation system, the creation of new high-tech poles is taking on the features of intra-city competition for the same potential investors (van Dijk 2005).

One of the main points of competition is the ability of each district to attract and retain professionals within its area. The NHTDZ is disadvantaged in this regard by being located to the north of the Changjiang. As already noted, transportation problems can be severe and few people are willing to commute from the city centre to Pukou on a daily basis.[15] The NHTDZ consequently needs to present itself as an attractive living area for professionals, thus eliminating the need for them to commute. At the same time, it has to show that the presence of universities and research centres in its area can really be leveraged in favour of potential investors. As part of the attempts to achieve these objectives, the administrative structure of the NHTDZ has undergone a wide restructuring process which has led to a greater level of interaction with non-state actors – in terms of both institutional linkages as well as of personnel exchanges. Part of the former administrative structure was given independent status in 2006, when it was renamed the New and High-Technology Economic Development Corporation. While still operating within the policy directives set by the NHTDZ administration, it operates according to a profit-driven logic. It has an independent budget, has been given residual claims on the income derived from new investments and has a greater independence in terms of hiring and management policies. Among the approximately 80 staff of the Development Corporation many are people with a professional or technical background who have only recently entered the corporation coming from a private sector experience, often in foreign-invested enterprises.[16] The

Corporation is also employing returned overseas students with good technical training, and is planning to send some of its staff abroad to receive further education. In order to better manage the transition to a quasi-private corporation, a US-based management consultancy firm has been called in to design and implement an employee performance evaluation system based on Key Performance Indicators (KPI). The Corporation is also a shareholder in a number of training centres set up in cooperation with domestic and foreign private companies.

The newly employed professionals participate in the development of strategies aimed at creating a better living environment for those working within the zone. The binding idea behind these projects is the creation of a stimulating environment conducive to innovation. Among the recently undertaken initiatives is the organization of weekly seminars for professionals living within the zone, with guest speakers from the academic and the corporate world lecturing on managerial and technical issues. These seminars are also seen as a networking opportunity, and it is hoped that they will promote the cross-fertilization of ideas. Similar monthly breakfast seminars are being offered to senior managers. The Corporation has also entered into negotiations with a number of foreign partners to set up a new international school within the NHTDZ, to offer professionals living in the area access to advanced educational facilities for their offspring. Apart from these initiatives, the improvement of the housing stock catering to professionals through the construction of additional living quarters is of course seen as of paramount importance, and private sector developers are being involved as well.[17]

Competition between companies

As already noted, competition between companies for skilled human resources is fierce, and professional labour markets are characterized by relatively high turnover rates. In the case of Nanjing professional labour markets seems to be based on a system of credentialism, with personal connections losing their importance as a means to accessing highly rewarded segments of the labour market. Among the interviewed companies, the majority exclusively relied on impersonal channels for recruiting professionals: the internet, newspaper advertisement, and job fairs.[18] Paradoxically enough, many of the companies have expressed concern that the predominance of impersonal channels means HR departments are often flooded by a large number of resumes not relevant to the position being advertised. It is therefore extremely costly to process the information and to spot promising applicants. Some of the companies are actively trying to promote the use of a referral system; three of the interviewed companies also offer monetary incentives to their employees, if they are able to introduce valid candidates for open positions;[19] however, the use of referral remains very marginal. Other companies are trying to place at least a minimal barrier by not accepting applications sent via their websites or via e-mail. Applications can only be posted by hand mail, as this at least requires some greater effort by the applicant.

Credentialism is not only mediated by public educational institutions. Having graduated with good grades from a reputed university is of course an important achievement. However, within a corporate world characterized by deep transformations in management and organizational practices, increasing importance is also being given to adherence to a system of values and work attitudes, to leadership skills, to personal motivation, to the ability to communicate and propose new ideas. No trust is placed on the capacity of the university system (nor of other public or social institutions) to train people in this range of 'soft' skill.[20] As a result, candidates for appointment who have worked in companies known to provide good leadership and management training, and which promote a corporate culture favouring the active involvement of employees, are undoubtedly advantaged. The places for the construction of credentials are therefore extending beyond the reach of the state, and in many cases, these tend to be located within the corporate world itself.

Access to these corporate forms of credentialism is perceived by professionals to be of the outmost importance for the development of their careers. All of the interviewed companies concurred in noting that one of the main reasons for professionals to leave the company is, apart from salaries, the lack of continued training opportunities and spaces for professional development. There is therefore a huge effort by companies to provide access to a range of training opportunities for their employees, both internally and through the services of external providers. Technical training usually takes place through a combination of on-the-job training and lectures from senior professionals or from university staff. However, even more emphasis is being given to training on 'soft' skills: from management, to leadership, to foreign languages, to career planning. These forms of training are provided through a combination of means, often implying the establishment of online training platforms on the company HR department website. The relevance of soft skills is also aimed at addressing one of the main issues faced by companies operating in China: the lack of an adequate pool of professionals able to take on hybrid managerial functions at the middle level. Middle managers are in fact required to ensure an adequate succession within the company internal promotion system, and no external actors are entrusted with this task. Knowing that a combination of 'hard' and 'soft' skills is a key to success, professionals for their part tend to prefer working for companies that offer better training and career development opportunities. Working for a company (particularly a foreign company) with a well-established brand name is seen as boosting chances for future career advancement. Companies and MNCs which do not produce consumer goods (and have therefore not become household names in China) are making strong efforts to build a recognizable brand identity amongst other things to access professional labour markets.[21]

Professional labour markets in China seem therefore to obey strict market logic. A further indication of this comes from the observation that even companies set up in close cooperation with local universities (and therefore directly involved in the training of their future employees while they are still undergoing graduate studies) have to face similar pressures in terms of high turnover rates. Four such companies were interviewed during the course of research.[22] The only company declaring that high turnover was not a problem ascribed this to the fact that its technology was extremely specific, and that no other competitors were operating in the same field in the Nanjing area. Conversely, the case of computer animation companies shows how market pressures overcome even work relationships that are originally established through internalized channels. Nanjing has become host to more than 30 computer animation companies, most of them set up by Taiwanese investors. Since trained experts in computer graphics were scarce, one of the interviewed companies set up a shared graduate programme with one of the Nanjing universities. Students would spend two years in the university, two years in the company; after graduation, they would be automatically employed by the company. However, of the around 300 graduates to complete the programme, the company has been able to retain only 80. Most of the people leaving the company have been employed as lecturers by other universities setting up similar programmes. Working in an academic environment is seen as offering high social prestige and a good salary, apart from leaving enough free time to work as a freelancer for private companies.

The case of HR managers: individual motivation and collective interests

As most of the interviewees were human resource managers, some observations regarding the set of motivations driving professionals in choosing their career paths based on their specific case would seem in order.[23] It was extremely common for the interviewed managers to have moved during the course of their careers between the state and the private sector. Employment in the state sector included working for SOEs, as well as for the public administration. For example, four of the interviewed managers had at a certain point worked for the NHTDZ administration. Geographic mobility was also high, with six of the interviewees having moved to Nanjing within the three years before interview from places like Guangzhou and Beijing, as well as from neighbouring Zhejiang Province. With few exceptions, employment in a company did not last much beyond three years.[24]

When asked about their future career plans, respondents were equally distributed between those who would have liked to continue working in the private sector; those who would be willing to move to the state sector at a later stage; and those thinking to set up their own business in the future (a consultancy firm, or a private HR services company for example). For the first group, the motivations provided revolved around the idea of working in a competitive environment in which personal skills are rewarded. Working in the private sector is also seen as a continued challenge to self-improvement, as opposed to a state sector in which personal connections and automatic career advancement are the norm. As one of the interviewees said (the HR manager of a Sino-foreign joint venture) people entering the state sector are after signs of social prestige, like obtaining free VIP cards for clubs or golf courses, or being invited as special guests to dinners and social events. On the other hand, 'by staying in the private sector you are continuously exploring your limits and trying to overcome them'. A similar position was expressed by another of the interviewees (HR manager of a wholly-owned foreign company) who said that he would change jobs every time he felt he had learned enough. In the past, he worked for a large SOE; and had been able to gain the trust of the General Manager who eventually appointed him as his deputy. This, he said, clearly implied that he would be trained for succession. But he felt there was nothing else he could learn in the company. When he was offered the opportunity to take up a low-level job in a foreign company, he accepted even if this meant starting from the shop floor again, because in this way he could learn new skills and show himself that he was able to climb the ladder of success (once again). The manager of a university-private joint company who used to be in the army expressed a similar attitude. He used to say to his employees:

> You are now in your late twenties. If you were in the army, by this time you would be commanding several men. If you worked for as SOE, you would be workshop directors. But in this company, there is no good in waiting. The only way for you to be promoted is to work well and to work hard.

At the same time, even when willing to enter the state sector, professionals set themselves aside from employees in public administration or in state-owned enterprises, as they feel they are driven by completely different sets of motivations. The idea of entering the state sector is in fact mostly seen as an opportunity to be used at a later stage of their careers – when they have achieved further skills and competence – as a way to put in practice what they have learned by working in the private sector. In particular, this option is advanced by employees of foreign companies, who often feel that senior level positions are still mostly reserved to foreigners. The idea of entering the public sector is therefore driven by the desire to overcome a barrier in their career development, and it is conditional on entering an organization where their potentialities can be fully expressed. Similarly, professionals perceive themselves as different from the rampant entrepreneurs who are seen as profiting more from their social connections than from their real business acumen. As already said, by moving between the state and the private sector professionals can build a more differentiated network of relationships. They can at a certain point decide to mobilize these networks (some of the interviewees have actually done so) to enter into new business activities, usually related to their field of competence. However, they tend to describe themselves as exponents of what could be called a 'knowledge-based' entrepreneurship, as opposed to the 'social-based' entrepreneurship in which success is exclusively achieved through connections with the political establishment.

In articulating their collective interests, HR managers are again mediating between the corporate and the societal levels. Initiatives aimed at forming adequately trained and 'responsible' employees are seen as not only contributing to the success of their companies, but also to China's modernization effort. At the organizational level, they are often active proponents of social responsibility programmes. Advancing corporate responsibility is perceived as an effective way to raise awareness and to promote 'new' values among individual employees. At the wider level, some common themes emerge from the interviews; particularly the environmental concern and the worries about an increasingly individualistic social structure. Many expressed a willingness to actively participate in the reform of the educational system, if they were given the chance; and some are making use of the (reportedly limited) volunteering opportunities to lecture or otherwise act in public spaces. However, no forms of collective action aimed at advancing such stances vis-à-vis the state have been observed in Nanjing. This lack of coordination has been lamented by some of the interviewees, who regret that most of the efforts in this sense are still based on individual initiatives.

Where forms of collective action can be observed, they are articulated at the occupational level and directed at affirming a greater role for HR management within the companies. The institutional spaces in which these collective interest articulations take place can be surprising, as they originate from the corporate world. One such case is the Human Resource Working Group organized by the European Chamber of Commerce in China. The working group holds monthly meetings, in which issues related to human resource management are discussed. Guest speakers are often invited, and company representatives give presentations on specific topics in order to share experiences and practices with their peers. The vast majority of the attendees are managers of foreign-invested companies; however often guests from government departments and bureaus are invited to attend as well. Apart from the official meetings, the group has led to the development of informal advice relationships between the participants. Among the common perspectives is the recognition that HR management is not simply an administrative function, but rather an important component of corporate strategies. In addition, a private training company organizes a set of regular networking and training events for HR managers in Nanjing, which have a high attendance rate. Through these spaces of interaction, a wide circulation of ideas is favoured, and a specific occupational identity is being built for a profession which, until a few years ago was not even taught as a major in Chinese universities.

Convergence and specificity

The evidence presented in this chapter is based on a limited number of interviews conducted in only a single and specific location. Generalization about the emergence of the professional middle classes is necessarily difficult. Fieldwork in Nanjing seems to suggest that caution should be used in locating professionals in the middle of a polarized view of the world that juxtaposes state and market. Since China's reforms are of a formerly planned economy, and in a historical moment characterized by the demise of the welfare state in the name of neo-liberalist modes of regulation, many of the conditions which characterized the emergence of the professional middle class in the West are being eroded. There is therefore little doubt that the equation between the professional middle strata in Chinese society and the professional classes that emerged in the modern North American and European nation-states in the first part of the Twentieth Century, or the white-collar classes of the mass production system, is hard to sustain. A more relevant question seems to be whether China's opening up will necessarily lead to a convergence with patterns of class stratification similar to those that emerged in the industrialized world after the crisis (or transformation) of the Fordist system. Focusing on professionals offers an interesting vantage point to observe how evolving forms of global economic organization interact with local specificities, and it may provide insights whose relevance goes far beyond the borders of China itself.

Notes

1 In Nanjing, where fieldwork for this chapter has been conduced, entry-level salaries are about 20 percent lower than in Shanghai. Unless otherwise indicated, detailed information is drawn from author's interviews in Nanjing, 2007.

2 The combination of individual career development goals with national projects is related to the concept of 'patriotic professionalism' proposed by Hoffman (2006).

3 There were two groups of interviews. The first group included 33 interviews with representatives from 24 companies differentiated by ownership, sector and scale. For each company, the human resource manager was asked a set of questions regarding the strategies adopted by the company in recruiting, training and retaining professionals. For six of the companies, additional interviews have been conduced with one or more managers from other departments. Information on the personal, educational and professional background of the 33 interviewed managers has also been collected. The second group includes 18 interviews with Chinese professionals; officials of development zones and development corporations; representatives of business associations; managers of agencies providing training, recruitment and other employment services. At the request of the interviewees, no material is provided in the text which allows the identification of a specific company.

4 For this study professionals are defined as people engaged in a range of occupations which require a high degree of technical competence, achieved through the completion of at least college-level education. The category of professionals also includes people performing hybrid managerial functions in fields where technical competence as well as managerial skills are required. For example, production

managers, directors of engineering departments, supply and purchasing managers, and human resource managers are also included.

5 On the relevance of scale theory for China (Ma and Wu 2005a; Cartier 2005).

6 A clear example is the new Enterprise Income Tax Law, adopted by the National People's Assembly on 16 March 2007 and due to become effective on 1 January 2008. The new law stipulates a unified income tax regime for foreign-invested and domestic enterprises, thus ending the preferential tax treatment conceded in the past to foreign-invested and export-oriented enterprises. The preferential tax treatment for foreign-invested enterprises typically consisted in the exemption from the corporate income tax for a period of two years (starting from the first year of profitability) followed by a 50 percent reduction of the corporate income tax for the following three years. Foreign-invested enterprises set up before the promulgation of the law continue to enjoy preferential tax treatment for five years (Art. 57). With the new Corporate Income Tax Law, the new tax rate is set at 25 percent for both foreign and domestic enterprises. However, the tax rate is lowered to 15 percent for high-tech industries (Art. 28). Preferential treatment, in the form of reduction or exemption from the corporate income tax, can also be conceded on income generated through the transfer of technology (Art. 27), as well as for enterprises involved in agriculture, environmental protection and the construction of public infrastructure (*Beijing Review* 14 June 2007).

7 The distribution of high-tech industry and R&D capacity shows however a strong clustering effect, with sub-regions like the Changjiang Delta (the Suzhou-Wuxi-Changzhou area, Nanjing, Hangzhou); the Pearl River Delta (Guangzhou, Shenzhen); and Tianjin remaining natural attractors (Chen and Chen 2005). China is characterized by huge degrees of internal variations, and the experience of the professional middle classes in urban high-growth poles of the Eastern seaboard cannot easily be generalized to China as a whole. On the other hand, the uneven geographical distribution of R&D and high-tech activities is also consistent with the idea of a 'perforated sovereignty' (Mayer 1994), whereby local forces actively design and implement localised policy strategies aimed at building direct linkages with global markets and production forces.

8 Starting January 2007, for example, foreign-invested firms are not exempted anymore from paying land-use taxes (*People's Daily Online* 3 January 2007). Authors' interviews in Nanjing show that, starting from 2007, new regulations regarding industrial land prices and fees are being strictly implemented, thus leaving little leeway to industrial districts to offer direct preferential treatment to investors in this regard.

9 As part of a widespread process of urban annexation characterizing Jiangsu province, Nanjing municipality also took over three formerly independent county-level cities: Jiangning in December 2000; Liuhe and Jiangpu in April 2002. The three annexed district were all well-established poles of industrial growth. These have now become urban districts, thus bringing their number from the original ten to thirteen. The annexations have more than quadrupled the municipal area, from 1026 square kilometers to 4728 square kilometres (Zhang and Wu 2006).

10 In July 2005, the daily flux of vehicles on the First Changjiang Bridge had already reached a peak of 66,000 (*Jiangsu Xinhua Ne*, 8 July 2005).

11 The names provided here are the names currently in use, after various waves of restructuring and privatization in the SOE sector.

12 Particularly after the 1990s a number of important Sino-foreign joint ventures were established in the automotive and petrochemical sectors, including Nanjing IVECO Motor Co (established in 1996); Nanjing Fiat Auto Co (1995); BASF-YPC (2000) and many others.

13 Nanjing is home to 33 universities and some 80 national-level research institutes. Among them, Nanjing University is consistently ranked among the top five universities in China, while six more appear in the top 50. At the end of 2006, Nanjing's university system was host to 557,100 graduate students (about 300,000 of them in technical subjects and engineering) and 63,700 postgraduates, in a total population of 6,400,000. Data provided to the author by Nanjing New and High Technology Development Corporation, 2007.

14 While the other development zones are usually placed under the district level jurisdiction, the NHTDZ is directly placed under the authority of the municipal government. The developed industrial area is 17.5 sq km, and further 54.8 sq km are currently being developed for Phase Two. More than 1700 enterprises are registered in the zone, 320 of which are foreign-invested. Among them Eastman, Honeywell, Siemens, Fujitsu, Ericsson, DSM, Twentsche and Dyson. Samsung has established an R&D centre within the zone. More than 200 enterprises have recognized high-tech status, and are therefore eligible for the new preferential corporate income tax policies. Around 50 enterprises have been listed as innovative enterprises in the state level 863 or 'Torch' plans.

15 Even when professionals are trained within the framework of initiatives originating in the NHTDZ it proves particularly hard to retain them. For example, among the 170 IT professionals who graduated in 2006 from the Nanjing Software Park, the overwhelming majority is currently employed outside the NHTDZ. Their places of employment convey a clear idea of the extent of competition for highly skilled human resources, which extends far beyond the border of the city and of the Changjiang Delta itself. About 15 percent of the graduates are currently working for MNCs in Beijing, Shanghai, and Dalian. 74 are employed in the Changjiang Delta. Of the remaining graduates, only 23 have decided to remain in Nanjing.

16 The new General Manager of the corporation used to be a senior manager in an important high-tech foreign enterprise. Similar career paths can be found among middle-level managers. For example, the Corporation has a Human Resources department which, apart from managing internal human resources issues, is also providing support and consultancies to companies investing in the NHTDZ. Apart from administrative matters and advice on labour issues, the kind of support provided includes staffing services (either through internal channels or through a network of established relationships with external staffing and recruitment providers) and training services (particularly in demand from small domestic companies which cannot afford the services of private training providers). The current manager worked for ten years with Japanese and Korean companies. Similarly, other middle-level managers in charge of investment attraction policies used to work for foreign institutes of commerce and trade promotion bureaus.

17 The housing stock in the NHTDZ is mixed, with accommodation ranging from workers' dormitoriess, to basic houses for relocated farmers, up to luxury villa complexes for senior managers and foreign experts. Apartments catering to professionals cost about 2,500 *yuan* per square metre. Just outside the NHTDZ, housing in private developments currently sells for 4,500 *yuan* per square metre. This compares with prices which, in the central city area around Nanjing University main campus in Gulou district, can easily reach a range between 13,000 to 16,000 *yuan* per square metre.

18 In some cases, companies manage the recruitment process internally. In most of the cases however, they use the services of specialized recruitment and human resource service providers. These can be either state-owned (for example, FESCO) local government agencies, or private companies.

19 The incentive usually takes the form of the equivalent of one month's salary of the referred employee being offered to the referrer, given that the new employee remains with the company for at least one year.

20 During the course of the interviews, the inability of the university system to produce graduates able to combine good technical skills with the 'soft' skills required to operate within a 'modern' corporate environment has emerged as a constant complaint from both domestic and foreign firms. The importance given to marks and grades during the course of the academic career is seen as promoting an attitude of being afraid to give the 'wrong' answer when faced with an unfamiliar situation. This attitude goes against the requirements of companies working in innovative fields, where the ability of the employees to actively propose new ideas to their seniors even if they turn out to be wrong is seen as an important asset. The overly protective attitude showed by families (particularly as a consequence of the one child policy) is also seen as a hindrance to young graduates' integration with the corporate environment. HR managers have quoted cases of their young employees who when faced with problems as simple as using a fax machine or a water dispenser prefer to phone their parents to ask for instructions rather than asking their senior colleagues. This can of course be as much a cliché as a really diffused problem. However, even as an urban myth it surely hints at a clearly perceived cleavage between the values put forth by the state and by society at large, on the one hand, and the requirements of the corporate sector, on the other. HR managers in particular feel they have an important role to play in forming a class of people able to move beyond the limits posed by the state education system, by diffusing new values and attitudes through corporate training programs and through the implementation of new managerial and organizational models.

21 On the other hand, companies with a very recognizable brand name have declared that high turnover is not a serious problem for them. When asked to explain the reasons, they said that it was exactly because of their brand name that people would never think about leaving. Working for a famous company is seen as bringing higher social prestige, and also implies that the employee has been trained to work in an environment characterized by superior organizational and managerial practices.

22 For the interviewed companies, the range of institutional arrangements linking them to universities was quite varied. In one case, the company had purchased the right to develop a proprietary technology from the university for a period of five years. In two other cases, the university was directly involved as a shareholder in the company. In the last case, there was a partnership corporation jointly set up by the university and a development zone. In all cases, university senior staff were directly involved in the management of the company; in one, university staff were also involved as private investors. Students at either the graduate or post-graduate levels were involved in developing or researching the technologies applied by the companies, providing the pool of labour from whom key professional employees are chosen.

23 A total of 24 human resource managers were interviewed. Of these, all but one were Chinese. The majority of the interviewed HR managers were females (21) generally in their thirties. This reflects the general gender distribution observed in HR management in Nanjing. The reasons behind this skewed gender distribution are rather unclear. Interviewees usually ascribed the predominance of females in HR management to their being better academic achievers in fields like sociology and psychology, as well as to their generally higher English language competence. It can also be hypothesized that, since HR management in China was until recently seen more as an ancillary administrative that a strategic managerial function, male professionals if given the choice would prefer to enter more tech-

nical roles (engineering departments, sourcing departments, finance department). However, the gender distribution appears to be shifting towards a more balanced structure, possibly as a consequence of the growing importance given to HR management within enterprise strategic development. Among the younger generation of HR managers, the percentage of males appears to be rising. Also, the path to entry seems to be shifting towards more specific training. While for the older generation the usual path was the completion of a degree in social sciences or humanities later complemented by a master in business administration or management, the new generation can count on academic qualifications that finally includes (since the mid-1990s) specialized graduate programmes in Human Resource Management.

24 However, many of those interviewed worked in companies that had only recently been established.

9   Professors, doctors, and lawyers

The variable wealth of the professional classes

Jingqing Yang

Professionals such as doctors, lawyers and university professors are usually regarded as central elements of the middle classes. While the People's Republic of China (PRC) certainly has substantial numbers of doctors and university professors, and growing numbers of lawyers, these professional classes are not certainly part of that country's new rich. In the first place in relative terms professionals such as doctors, university professors and those engaged in legal affairs are more automatically to be sited as part of the established middle class between the establishment of the PRC in 1949 and the start of the reform era in the late 1970s. In the second place, though it is clear that certain professionals, and even some doctors, lawyers and university professors have benefited disproportionately from reform policies and the marketization of the economy in general, change has proved to be more variable, even in large numbers of cases leaving professionals as less comfortably off than previously if not quite the 'new poor'.

This chapter explores the institutional and policy changes that have affected the economic conditions of professionals in the reform era, drawing on the experience of doctors, lawyers, and university teachers – the three best established groups of professionals. It first discusses the economic conditions of intellectuals and professionals in the pre-reform era, suggesting that they were the effective 'middle classes' of the earlier PRC located between the more privileged government officials on the one hand and the worker-peasant classes on the other. Then it considers the general decline of the economic status of professionals in the reform era and the opportunities that economic reform has presented. The last part of the chapter focuses on each of the three professions in turn, identifying the paths that lead most usually to individual wealth.

Professionals before 1980

The PRC had substantial numbers of professionals after 1949 and even before the changes of the late 1970s. The Chinese government, in its pursuit of modernization that started in the 1950s committed considerable resources to the education and training of professionals. The Chinese Communist

Party (CCP) itself relied heavily on educated cadres with specialist knowledge and skills in the administration and operation of the country's bureaucratic, service and industrial systems. Ironically, these professionals and other educated intellectuals were economically better off and enjoyed more privileged social status than other less educated social strata, such as workers and peasants, who the CCP always regarded as its natural constituency.

While professionals were often regarded with political suspicion by the CCP before 1978, not least because of Mao Zedong's ambivalent attitude to intellectuals, on the whole they were materially well-looked after by the regime. For a start, the majority of professionals were salaried state employees. In addition to their state salary, each professional received fringe benefits through their work-unit, according to policy and the availability of resources, differentiated by activity and location.

In the early 1950s, the CCP implemented several institutional changes which greatly influenced the social and economic life of professionals (Davis 2000a). Firstly, all the educated, especially the highly educated, were nationalized. The state became the sole employer of intellectuals. University teachers, engineers, doctors, artists and writers became salaried state-employees. Secondly, the private sector was rapidly reduced and then disappeared. With the demise of the private sector, the market where intellectuals could sell their expertise all disappeared. Thirdly, education, especially tertiary education which is the dominant producer of professionals in a modern society, was also nationalized. The Party-state not only took over the administration and financing of all universities and colleges, but also allocated jobs for graduates. After 1953, all graduates were assigned to public sector work-units. Fourthly, salaried intellectuals were isolated by the work-unit system. They were not able to establish linkages with their peers located in other work-units, and there was no professional association.

The results of these policy settings left professionals powerless organizationally and politically. In face of the Party-state, they had virtually no bargaining power and were on the receiving end of any economic terms that the Party-state decided to impose on them. As salaried state employees, accumulation of personal wealth became impossible. According to a survey conducted by the Central Government in 1955, the average salary of senior intellectuals (mainly well-known professors, writers, scientists and doctors) was only about 16.8 percent of that in 1937, just before Japan's invasion (Chen, Mingyuan 2006). In comparison with other social strata, however, their salaries left them as the 'middle class', between the more powerful political cadres employed in the administrative work-units on the one hand, and workers and peasants, on the other.

The Communist government implemented its first significant across-the-board wage reform in 1956 (State Council 1956). A major achievement of this reform was the establishment of a general wage scale. New occupational categories were also established with wage ranks delineated within each category.

There were 30 grades on the general wage scale, corresponding to 30 grades of administrative responsibility. The highest salary grade for the Beijing region was 579.50 *yuan*, and lowest was 23 *yuan* per month. Different occupational categories (including administrative positions) occupied different spectra on the scale. Each occupational category was further divided into hierarchical ranks. For example, the category of state cadres had 26 ranks on the wage scale, occupying grades 1 to 26. Judges and court personnel had 25 ranks, occupying grade 2 to grade 26 (Korzec and Whyte 1981). University teaching positions were broken down into four professional levels – professor, associate professor, lecturer, and assistant professor – and 12 wage ranks, covering grades 6 to 21 on the scale. The monthly salary for a rank 1 Professor was 345 *yuan*, and for a rank 12 Assistant Professor 62 *yuan*. Medical technicians (including doctors and nurses) had 6 professional levels and 21 wage ranks, covering grades 6 to 26 (Korzec and Whyte 1981; Chen, Mingyuan 2006). For a rank 1 Chief Doctor, the monthly salary was 333.5 *yuan*, while for a rank 4 (lowest rank for a doctor) Assistant Doctor, the monthly salary was 62 *yuan*.

In comparison, technical workers were divided into 10 ranks, covering grades 19 (99 *yuan* per month) to 28 (27.5 *yuan* per month) on the scale. Industrial workers had 8 ranks, covering grades 19 (99 *yuan* per month) to 26 (33 *yuan* per month). Service personnel in state organs had 6 ranks, covering grades 25 (37.5 *yuan* per month) to 30 (23 *yuan*) (Korzec and Whyte 1981). Intellectuals had higher salaries than urban workers and considerably higher incomes than peasants. For example, in 1956, the average net income per peasant in Shandong Province was 86.72 *yuan* for the whole year, about 11.6 percent of the lowest level of salary for a university graduate (62 *yuan* per month) (Shandong People's Government n.d.).

These disparities became a concern to the government. Li Yi observes that the 1956 wage reform produced differentials that were even larger than in the Republican Era (1912–49), in which generally the highest salary was about 15 times the lowest (Li Yi 2005: 60–62). To remedy these differentials the government took action in 1956 and then later again in 1960 to reduce the upper levels of salaries and to increase wages at the lower end. In December 1956, a resolution was enacted to reduced the salary rates of grade 10 and above on the 1956 salary scale (Li Yi 2005: 64).

These changes affected remuneration rates for professionals. In 1957, the salaries of technicians and engineers of level 1 to 3 decreased. Probation for four-year university graduates was extended from six months to twelve months. After probation, the starting administrative and salary grade was downgraded from 21 to 22 (to 56 *yuan* per month) (State Council, Personnel Bureau 1957). Furthermore, the State Council called a halt to all wage increases and promotions in 1957 (State Council 1957). These practices were maintained for two decades so that from 1957 to 1978 wages for cadres and professionals declined. For professionals in universities, research institutions and hospitals, as well as technicians and engineers in the industry and other state agencies, promotion was non-existent between 1966 and 1978. After 1957, university graduates' salaries were frozen at 56 *yuan* per month for twenty years without a pay rise (Chen, Mingyuan 2006).

Nonetheless, before the 1980s, educated state-employees enjoyed a higher income than ordinary workers and peasants. Moreover, professional personnel also had access to a wide range of fringe benefits through their work-units. These included highly subsidized housing; nearly free healthcare, and heavily subsidized healthcare for non-working family members; and the provision of food, household goods and clothing rations that were not otherwise available. The relatively higher wages and access to fringe benefits made tertiary education one of the major channels of upward social mobility even during the Cultural Revolution when education, graduates and intellectuals were generally viewed with extreme political suspicion.

Xu Weiguo's story is illuminating. Xu was a worker-peasant-soldier student and graduated in 1976 from Central China Normal College. Before entering the college, he had been a peasant in Hubei Province with only junior middle school education but with a politically trustworthy background. Upon graduation, he was duly employed by a government agency in a big city and earned a salary of 52 *yuan* a month. The appointment brought with it status and benefits, as well as a stable income. He was not required to return to his home village to work the land; his wife and children were given urban household registration and lived with him in a big city; his parents could live with his family and enjoy the urban lifestyle. Xu notes, 'For people like me [that is, worker-peasant-soldier students] going to university was an unexpected gift presented by the time. It was a blessing from heaven that allowed us to leave the poor countryside, to eat state [provided] rice, and to earn a stable income!' (Yao 2004).

Walder shows that in the pre-reform era, education was a prerequisite for aspirant individuals to attain privileged administrative positions and professional positions, although administrative posts usually brought more material privileges to individuals than professional positions. Generally speaking, in a period of austerity in which the state was almost the sole source of individual income and fringe benefits, and private wealth were non-existent, individuals with tertiary education were apparently 'richer' than workers and peasants who were allegedly the natural allies of the CCP (Walder 1995). Between the 1950s and the 1970s, university graduates were truly high earners, regardless of wage rates (Yao 2004). However, their relatively well-off standard of living did not continue automatically into the reform era.

Professionals in the reform era

On the surface the beginnings of 'reform and openness' in the late 1970s and early 1980s appeared to have been good news for intellectuals in general and professionals in particular. In 1977, one year before reforms were adopted, intellectuals started to feel the change. The restoration of the national unified university entrance examination indicated re-emphasis on the academic quality of tertiary education and revival of the meritocracy that had been abandoned during the Cultural Revolution. In various well-publicized talks during 1977, Deng Xiaoping signalled a sea change in the regime's hostility to intellectuals and made commitments to ensure the development of conditions for professionals. (Deng 1995: 6; 54; 63–64; 69).

While the politics of state attitudes to professionals certainly changed, with the introduction of the reform era, the economic reality was more depressing. The wages of state employed professionals in the major sectors of research, education, culture and health have declined steadily since the late 1970s. In the late 1970s and early 1980s, wage readjustments were targeted at low wage employees and those whose wages had been frozen since the 1960s. The 1956 wage scales were not altered and individuals with low incomes were simply promoted. Incomes for those at the upper ends of the professional scales were not affected (State Council 1982).

In 1985, the 1956 wage system was abandoned. In future, the wage rates of different occupations and positions were not to be linked to specific administrative grades. The unified wage system was broken up into two major schemes: one in the for-profit state-owned enterprises and organizations, and the other in not-for-profit institutions (CCP Central Committee and State Council 1985; State Council 1985). For the majority of professionals employed in the public sector, the new wage scheme in not-for-profit institutions provided the new standards for their salaries.

In the new scheme, a professional's salary was structured to have four components: a base wage, a position wage, a standing stipend and provisions for bonus. The base wage was the same for all professionals: 40 *yuan* per month. The standing stipend was 0.5 *yuan* per month for each year of service. Salaries were differentiated mostly by position wages, while the bonus was highly contingent and not usually calculable in advance.

The results were harsh. For a newly promoted professor, the highest rate of wage he or she could earn was only 255 *yuan* a month plus the standing stipend, which was no more than 20 *yuan* per month providing he or she had worked for 40 years. The bonus was not guaranteed. It depended on how much the work-unit could save from the state budget. In other words, while in 1957 a Level One professor could receive 345 *yuan* in salary per month, his or her colleagues in 1985 could only make 275 *yuan* at most (providing he or she had 40 years service in the university), a 20 percent decrease. In 1957, the wage for a top-level lecturer was 149.5 *yuan* per month, while in 1985, it had dropped to 140 *yuan* (base plus position wage). For professionals of middle level and above, there is an apparent decrease in nominal wages. In the new scheme, only the rate for a commencing position, such as the beginning level of Assistant Professor, Intern Researcher or Doctor, those who were newly graduated from universities, were raised from 56 to 70 *yuan*.

In terms of real wages, incomes for professionals dropped even further. In the 1950s, the top-level monthly wage of a professor (345 *yuan*) could buy 575 kg lamb. In 1985, the wage for the same level of professor, namely 255 *yuan*, could only buy 32 kg lamb (Lin 1999: 132). As Deng Xiaoping observed at the time: 'I am told that an old professor at Beijing University said recently, "My salary has remained the same as it was when the People's Republic was founded. But with the way prices have gone up, my standard of living has dropped by two thirds"' (Deng 1994: 270).

In comparison, workers seemed to benefit more from the reforms of the 1980s and early 1990s. With the reinstatement of performance wages and piece-rates, their income rose faster than professionals. According to a 1982 survey of eleven work-units in Beijing, state employees with tertiary education who were under the age of 49 had lower incomes than those with only primary and secondary education. (Li Qiang 1996; Zheng 2004: 147–148). The outcomes of this survey were widely cited as evidence of the existence of reverse wage disparity between professionals and workers: a disparity that did not improve in favour of professionals throughout the 1980s (Li Qiang 1996).

This disparity ran counter to the widespread belief among all Chinese intellectuals, including professionals, that they were entitled to earn more than workers, because of their greater investment of time and effort in knowledge acquisition, and because their work contributed more to the development of the country (Pang 1989; Yang 1989). With all the political rhetoric, intellectuals had a reason to believe that they held the key to China's modernization and should be better off than other social classes. Many writings published in the 1980s and the early 1990s claimed that the educated earned more than workers in all developed and many developing countries (Wei and Huang 1993). Some even warned that a reverse wage disparity could lead to social unrest (Yang 1989).

The warning was not as far-fetched as might first appear. The participation of professionals alongside other intellectuals in the events culminating in 4 June 1989 in Beijing was to some extent motivated by their economic treatment. They protested for example on 15 May 1989 in support of students on hunger strike under banners that read: 'Professors, Professors. The longer they teach the thinner they become', 'Poor professor', 'poor PhD', and 'no money in research' (Zhang Liang 2001: 403–404). The clearing of Tiananmen Square was followed in October 1989 by moderate pay rises for intellectuals. The highest rate for a professor, for instance, was increased to 420 *yuan* per month, but the commencing rate for a professor at 180 *yuan* per month was still lower than it had been in the 1950s (Lin 1999: 132). A more substantial pay rise for university teachers, medical doctors and other knowledge workers came in 1993, though it was not particularly well received. The problem was that their support staff in the state sector received even larger pay rises (Lin 1999: 133).

The dual wage system was blamed for the wage disparity between educated professionals and the less educated (Xie and Chen 1989; Li and Li 1991).

Under conditions of economic reform, enterprises were allowed a management and fiscal autonomy denied to the public sector work-units where most professionals work. Employees in public sector work-units depended almost entirely on the government allocation for their salaries, while enterprise workers had their incomes linked to individual and company performance (Ministry of Personnel 1983; State Council 1985). Moreover, these disparities were exacerbated by the development of the private sector.

While the relativities have not been totally or systematically restored, there has been improvement in the economic returns available to professionals through a series of pay reforms and institutional changes introduced since the mid-1990s (Li 1998; Liu and Cai 1998; Lin 1999). Between 1993 and 2003, a series of six wage adjustments more than doubled the fixed salaries of university teachers and doctors. The pay rises came with a revamp of the wage structure established in 1985. A professional's salary was re-designed as consisting of two parts: a fixed position wage and a flexible stipend. The position wage is usually guaranteed, while the rates and purposes of flexible stipend are determined within work-units according to the performance of the individual and the work-unit. This component cannot exceed 30 percent of the entire salary for a full-budget work-unit employee (for example, university teachers) and 40 percent for a marginal budget work-unit employee (for example, medical professionals) (State Council 1993).

In 2006, another round of wage reform was implemented, featuring a further substantial change to the wage structure and providing increases (Ministry of Personnel and Ministry of Finance 2006). The new system introduced wages calculated by position grades, wage levels, performance wages and stipends. Position grades and wage levels determine the basic wage of an appointment. Specialized technical positions such as university teachers and medical doctors are classified by 13 grades and 65 levels. Grade 1 appointments have to be approved by the Ministry of Personnel, and thus have only limited applicability in reality. Normally senior specialized technical positions fall between the second and seventh grade, including Professors and Associate Professors in universities, as well as Chief Doctors and Associate Chief Doctors in hospitals. Salaries range from 1247 *yuan* per month (Grade 7, Level 16) to 4500 *yuan* (Grade 2, Level 65). Middle level positions (Lecturer, Responsible Doctor) are listed at the eight to tenth grades with salary rates ranging from 861 *yuan* per month (Grade 10, Level 9) to 3380 *yuan* per month (Grade 8, Level 65). The eleventh and twelfth grades are reserved for junior professionals (Assistant Professor, Doctor). Salaries for these positions range from 715 *yuan* per month (Grade 12, Level 5) to 3220 *yuan* per month (Grade 11, Level 65) (Ministry of Personnel and Ministry of Finance 2006).

Pay rises since the mid-1990s have meant that overall professionals may be regarded as earning middle-ranked incomes. The highest possible base income for a state employee is 5,400 *yuan* per month, or 64,800 *yuan* per annum (Grade 1, Level 65 in the 2006 wage scheme). Clearly, it is unlikely that on the basis of their state provided income a professor or senior doctor will make it into the ranks of the high-earners, still less the majority of middle rank and junior teachers, doctors and other professionals. The opportunity for some professionals to create substantial personal wealth has come from the introduction of the market and the commercialization of tertiary education, healthcare and other services (including legal services).

New rich professionals

When economic reform started the government encouraged university teachers, doctors, engineers, lawyers, and other professionals to trade their specialist knowledge and advanced skills for extra income in the newly emerging market. In 1978, for example, the Ministry of Education, Ministry of Finance and National Bureau of Labour promulgated a provisional regulation on remuneration for concurrent activities by university teachers working outside their host institution (Ministry of Education, Ministry of Finance and the National Bureau of Labour 1978). In 1982, personnel in the fields of science and technology were permitted to take up second jobs in other work-units (State Council, Bureau of Technical Cadres 1982).

In practice, few people took up second jobs, despite apparent official encouragement. In the 1980s, state-employed specialists who provided services for fees outside of their host work-units found that they could easily be charged with engaging in illegal economic activities, such as soliciting bribes, or engaging in illicit speculation, resulting in their incomes being confiscated (Xiao *et al.* 1986: 107–111; Ding and Yao 1987: 30–32; Zhu *et al.* 1989: 147–151). Access to the market was highly restricted by the work-unit system, professionals' disciplines and the immaturity of the market. Employees had long been regarded as 'owned' by their work-unit and mobility between work-units was restricted. Many work-units implicitly opposed the government's policies and discouraged their staff from taking second jobs through concerns about loyalty and complaints about uneven incomes. Moreover, until the mid-1990s the market demand for advanced knowledge and skills was more than somewhat limited.

Dramatic change came in the late 1990s when the government started to reform the institutional work-unit personnel system. This policy change promoted management of professionals as professionals, loosened administrative control over them and provided more freedom for them to use their professional knowledge and skills in non-state organized economic activities (Ministry of Personnel 2000).

University professors

Throughout the 1980s and 1990s, the economic condition of university teachers was a main indicator of the Party-state's treatment of intellectuals.

Between 1978 and 1998, university teachers were not happy about how they were treated for two fundamental reasons. The first was the slow growth in their nominal salaries; and the second was the scarcity of subsidized housing due to insufficient government investment in tertiary education (Lin 1999: 53).

Market reforms created opportunities for university teachers. At first, the demand for specialist knowledge was limited to only a few disciplines, among which foreign language teaching was most popular. The opening-up policy had encouraged enthusiasm for major foreign languages, mainly European languages and Japanese. Demand surged hugely above the provision from the centrally planned tertiary education system. This allowed foreign language departments in universities to organize extracurricular short-term non-award courses to generate income and to pay bonuses to staff. In 1981, the Ministry of Education required all university teachers' workload to be quantified and all extra work above the formal workload to be paid (Ministry of Education 1981). Often these activities were organized departmentally, but university teachers and professors could also organize their own extra-workload fee-paying activities. Numerous language schools emerged in Shanghai in the 1990s and language teachers, especially those teaching English, were in high demand. As a result, language teachers from Shanghai Foreign Language University were the first among Shanghai's university teachers to pay income tax. It is estimated that they could make an additional 7,000 to 10,000 *yuan* per month (Lin 1999: 60).

In recent years, the market demand for specialist knowledge has diversified. The payment for university teachers working outside their main employment is determined by the market in light of their specialty and seniority, as well as the reputation of their university and themselves. Teachers of other disciplines, such as information technology, law and business administration started to be in considerable market demand towards the end of the 1990s. A first class professor in a field related to economics and business management can make 20,000 to 30,000 *yuan* for a one-day lecture; a second-class professor 10,000 to 20,000 *yuan;* while a third class 5,000 to 8,000 *yuan*. The most famous in the field can receive up to 80,000 *yuan* for a lecture (*Jiangnan shibao* 21 September 2005).

Increasingly in the PRC companies have become publicly listed. In 2001, the China Securities Regulatory Commission required all publicly listed companies to hire independent directors. Some of the posts for independent directors are earmarked for experts, such as those with specialist knowledge in business administration, accounting and finance. Professor Na's story is illustrative. He is the head of a research institute of finance in a university in southwest China, and sits on the board of directors of four publicly listed companies. Each company pays him 40,000 to 50,000 *yuan* per year for acting as an independent director. That alone brings in around 200,000 *yuan* each year, in addition to his salary, stipends from the university and research funding (Personal interview 14 June 2007).

Universities contain more than just languages, IT and business administration departments and professors – the areas for which there is most demand. There has been pressure on the university administration from those disciplines without much market demand to assist in the generation of income. Since the early 1990s, university-run enterprises have been widely adopted as a legitimate way to ensure additional funds. In 1993, Beijing University dismantled the wall along the southern end of its campus and built instead a string of small retail shops. Beijing University claimed that this represented a changed view towards education, though it provoked heated debate among intellectuals even whilst widely copied by other universities (Wang Jianbing 2001).

Drastic structural reform was introduced for university teachers in 1999 (Ministry of Education 1999). The government no longer assigned university teachers to their teaching posts, nor is their employment protected. Rather, universities need to establish the number and categories of academic posts that are required, and then advertise these posts internally or externally. Teachers have to compete for these posts. This has led to the emergence of a labour market for tertiary teachers. There has been a decrease in job security, and an increase in remuneration. The salary for a university teaching post is now composed of the basic salary prescribed and supposedly paid by the state, a position stipend, and a performance award. Universities need to raise the funds themselves to meet position stipends and performance awards.

The pressure on university funds has consequently increased at a time when state funding has also become limited. Universities have managed to afford higher payment for their teachers thanks to the deregulation of fees and the commercialization of tertiary education activities. Fees are an important component of funding. Tertiary education had remained substantially free for students up to 1989. In 1989, the state sanctioned a change to tertiary tuition fees. A universal 200 *yuan* per annum was introduced and since then tuition fees have risen repeatedly to 610 *yuan* per annum in 1993, 700–800 *yuan* per annum in 1995, 3000 yuan in 1999, 4200 *yuan* in 2000, and 5000 *yuan* in 2001 (Chen, Mingyuan 2006).

The commercialization of tertiary education and increasing financial autonomy of the institutions has meant that universities are able to increase payments for their academic staff. The expansion of admissions has also meant that universities have been under pressure to employ increasingly more teachers. One result is that university teachers have gained increased bargaining power, not least because of the reform to the personnel system that effectively encouraged job mobility. There has often been an intense competition for professors, associate professors and those with doctoral degrees. Universities have formulated favourable policies and enticing packages to attract qualified academics both within China and from overseas. For example, the North China University of Technology in 2002 offered a 90 square meters apartment; 50,000 to 100,000 *yuan* start-up funds; and a 70,000 *yuan* one-off settlement fee to attract graduates with doctoral degrees (North China University of Technology 2002). In 2003, Shanghai University offered favourable benefits to attract members of the Chinese Academies, doctoral degree supervisors under the age of 55, professors under 50, and associate professors with doctoral degrees under 30. The offer for a professor included 100,000 to 200,000 *yuan* housing subsidy, as well as special or university position stipends (Shanghai University 2003). In 2004, Guangzhou University promoted additional benefits, on top of normal remuneration, for reputable and award-winning academics. For instance, it offered an additional 300,000 *yuan* settlement fee for professors supported by the 'Cheung Kong Scholars Program', jointly funded by the Li Ka Shing Foundation (founded by Hong Kong tycoon Li Ka Shing) and the Ministry of Education in 1998 (Lin 2004).

While elite academics have benefited greatly from these changes, other university teachers have also managed to improve their living standards. The expansion of tertiary education and the emergence of private colleges have resulted in fierce competition for university teachers. Higher remuneration and improved housing conditions have become prerequisites for retaining staff. The scale of costs is indicated by the case of Jilin University, which through the amalgamation of five colleges between 2000 and 2004 grew into the biggest university in China. To prevent loss of teachers to other universities, it has doubled its stipendiary payments to staff (to 100.6 million *yuan* a year) (Wang Lei 2007) and added 220,000 square meters of new residential housing to provide accommodation to its staff (He Zhongzhou 2007).

The emergence of a labour market, the expansion of universities and the demands of a mature market for advanced knowledge have given many university teachers, and especially the more senior and qualified, a better market position. Since 2001, university professors have been one of eight professional categories that have been monitored by taxation offices as 'high' income earners (Li He 2001). In 2005, the State Taxation Administration established a new system to monitor nine professional categories of high-income earners, including university professors, despite the latter's complaints (Li Lihui 2005).

Medical Doctors

All the wage and personnel system reforms that have applied to the university sector have been almost simultaneously applied to health professionals. However, fiscal policies for the two sectors have followed different paths since the early stages of reform. The differences result from the legitimacy of income-generation patterns in the two sectors and government regulation of profit pursuing activities. In particular, the difference is related to the timing of commercialization in the two sectors. Commercialization of healthcare was introduced earlier than that of tertiary education, which means that the healthcare sector started to rely on user fees for finance much earlier than higher education.

Hospitals have been classified as marginal budget work-units in the state financial system since the early years of the People's Republic. This means that they have long needed to generate part of their revenue from user fees, with government finances meeting the balance. In the reform era, with the decline of state budgets, hospitals have been forced to rely increasingly on user fees. With the collapse of the health insurance system in the rural areas and the drastically reduced healthcare coverage for the urban population, patients have been required to meet costs out of their own pockets.

Health professionals are able to obtain extra income in two different ways. As with their colleagues in universities, medical professionals are also able to organize themselves to sell their specialist knowledge and expertise. In addition, it is more prevalent for hospitals and clinics to organize additional for-profit activities in which healthcare professionals participate. The major form of state-sanctioned individual income-generation practice has been providing after-hour services.

Since 1985, health professionals, including doctors, nurses and midwifes, were encouraged to provide local after-hour services. These activities could be organized by professionals themselves or by their work-units (Ministry of Health 1985). Individual professionals were permitted to provide diagnostic services or surgery for other medical work-units in return for fees. The policy of encouraging after-hour services was reaffirmed in 1989 (Ministry of Health, Ministry of Finance, Ministry of Personnel, State Prices Administration, and State Taxation Administration 1989). The expectation was apparently that activities would be organized collectively by appropriate work-units for the purpose of easier supervision, and income generated from these collectively organized after-hour services were required to be redistributed by those work-units. The policy stipulated that individuals participating in after-hour services should be limited to an additional income of no more than 60 *yuan* per month (Ministry of Health, Ministry of Finance, and Ministry of Personnel 1986).

Health professionals, especially senior staff, have proved themselves resistant to these attempts at regulation. They are not very keen on collectively organized after-hour services. The commercialization of healthcare and the collapse of health insurance schemes in both urban and rural areas have led to a situation where patients effectively choose where they go providing they can afford the services. Hospitals, especially those non-state-owned facilities that usually do not have reputable specialists on the staff, tend to employ specialists from major hospitals in major cities as consultants who operate or conduct surgeries during weekends and public holidays. In recent years, moonlighting among doctors has become a major source of hidden income for senior specialists who are monopolized by major hospitals in major cities (Yang 2006). It is apparently possible for a specialist to earn 1000 *yuan* in a weekend in this way. Surgeons may make even more. For example, the payment for a cataract extraction is between 400 and 500 *yuan* per operation. A specialist can perform seven to eight operations a day (Zhi 2002).

Moonlighting is privately organized. Work-units employing the moonlighters are usually not aware (at least in any formal sense) of the concerned specialists' activities. The secrecy of moonlighting also means that the income is not reported for taxation. It is understandable that the health authorities expect more transparency and accountability of practice. The Ministry of Health spells out clearly that it does not support moonlighting, but encourages doctors to take up officially arranged secondary jobs (Zhu 2002). While moonlighting remains controversial it is recognized as a necessary evil. On the other hand, some other privately arranged income-generating activities are completely illegal. In the past decade, the health authorities have been targeting drug kickbacks, as well as 'red packet' taking among health professionals.

Public hospitals control over 80 percent of drug sales in China (Chen Wenling 2005). In 2006, on average, 41 percent of hospital revenue came from drug sales (Ministry of Health 2007) and it is reported that drug sales provide up to 70 or 80 percent of revenue in some hospitals (Wang Lei 2004). A mark-up of 15 percent on drug prices has long been endorsed by health authorities to compensate the deficit generated from the delivery of healthcare (Gao 2005). With the liberalization of the pharmaceutical industry, competition has been fierce. To boost the sales of pharmaceuticals in hospitals, the major market for the pharmaceutical industry, drug representatives pay secret kickbacks to individual doctors for prescribing the drugs they sell (Wu 2000; Fang 2004). Some senior doctors can collect up to 100,000 *yuan* per month from prescribing drugs (*People's Daily* 21 December 2005). In 2004, 56 doctors from the Ruian People's Hospital in Zhejiang Province were found to have taken drug kickbacks worth 1.1 million *yuan* (Zhao Anping 2004).

The practice of 'red packets' refers to the informal payments patients give to doctors for services. They form another source of income for medical doctors, surgeons in particular. The popularity of red packets is partly attributable to the state's regulation of medical services pricing. The prices of medical services have always been determined by the government. To increase healthcare accessibility, the government has deliberately marked down the value of medical services, keeping prices low. A survey of 32 hospitals in Zhejiang Province in 2003 revealed that the rates for 92.9 percent of surgical procedures could not cover the costs (Gu 2003). Payment for the technical component of surgeries is very low, accounting for 10 percent of the total payment for a surgical procedure (Duan 2007).

Patients find that they have to motivate doctors with extra payments out of their pocket if they wish to obtain quality services. The size of red packets is determined by many elements, including the complexity of the operation, the professional rank and reputation of the surgeon, the length of the waiting list, and the strength of the local economy. The Government has had taking red packets in its anti-corruption spotlight since 1992, but campaigns targeting this practice have failed to root it out (Li Gang and Zhao Xinpei 2004). On the contrary, it has become the norm in the public healthcare system. In 2004, 1135 doctors from hospitals in Beijing handed in red packets worth 830,000 *yuan* (Li and Zhao 2004). In 2005, 32,000 red packets worth 5.286 million *yuan* were declined or handed over to authorities in Guangdong Province (Liao and Gan 2005). In 2006, 4062 red packets were handed to the authorities in Heilongjiang Province, with a total value of nearly 1.9 million *yuan* (Lin 2007). It seems likely that the red packets doctors are publicized for having handed over or declined are only the tip of the iceberg. Even the authorities admit that in spite of their past regulatory efforts, it is very difficult to investigate red packet transactions. 99 percent of red packet givers would not report their doctors as long as they are satisfied with the outcome of surgery (Li and Zhao 2004).

According to the Minister of Health in 2005, the government budget accounted for 30 percent of hospital revenue in the 1970s and 1980s, but only 7.7 percent in 2000 (Gao 2005). As a result, hospitals have to rely on user fees for operational expenses, development, payroll, and updating infrastructure. A widely adopted measure to increase doctors' incomes within work-units is to link the performance part of a doctor's wage package, in some cases even the whole wage, to their 'performance', namely, the quantity of drugs prescribed, provision of diagnostic tests, and the use of other fee-paying services.

For example, Shenyang Traditional Chinese Medicine (TCM) Hospital enacted a new wage scheme in 2003. It features a 'redistribution according to second performance assessment' procedure. All the doctors and nurses are only guaranteed 30 percent of their wages (most probably referring to their position wage), and are required to find 'ways' in their own work to earn the remaining 70 percent, and indeed anything else. A position with a normal monthly wage of 1,700 *yuan* is only paid around 700 *yuan*, including 500 *yuan* of the fixed wage. The rest of the salary has to be made through the prescription of drugs, tests and other services. There is also a system detailing the kickback rates for prescriptions. For instance, doctors will get 11 percent for prescribing herbal medicine, 10 percent for pathology tests and 13 percent for injections and bandage change. Consequently, doctors in some popular departments could pocket up to 10,000 *yuan* extra per month as a reward for prescribing drugs and services, while others from the least popular department would only receive about 100 to 200 *yuan* kickback from the hospital (Cong 2004).

Although the Ministry of Health has prohibited health facilities from linking staff wages to prescriptions since 2004 (Ministry of Health 2004), wage schemes like the one implemented in Shenyang TCM Hospital have been widely adopted to motivate doctors and as a means to increase revenues for the hospital (Tang 2004). Township and village clinics, which have not usually received any government funding since the start of the reform era particularly favour 'performance' wages as the basic remuneration system for their staff (Min and Wang 2007). Apparently, this model has led to over-prescription and over-provision of services.

As the prices for medical services are determined by the government and are usually kept low, hospitals have needed to resort to charging illegal fees or overcharging patients to raise funds. Revenues from these sources are partly used to fund bonus or other incentives for staff. According to media reports, illegal charges seem widespread in hospitals. In 2004, the National Audit Office found over 11.89 million yuan of overcharges in all ten major hospitals in Beijing that it selected for audit (Zhang Xuemei 2005).

Lawyers

Lawyers have been around in the PRC for a relatively short time, only having been resurrected as a profession as a direct result of the changes introduced during the late 1970s. The number of lawyers remains limited and is no match for the establishments of doctors and university professors. By mid-2006, there were only 156,000 practicing lawyers and 12,000 law firms in China. At the same time, the legal profession is considerably more marketized and enjoys more autonomy in its organization and business. For this reason alone lawyers are more clearly and unambiguously regarded as part of China's new rich.

Apart from a brief appearance in the mid-1950s, there was no profession of lawyers in the PRC during the decades before 1978. With the promulgation of the Criminal Procedure Law in 1979, defendants of criminal cases were allowed to have lawyers to defend them. The legal profession was re-established from scratch in that year. The reestablishment of the legal service profession was not designed as an independent function of the judicial system representing the interest of clients, but a minor appendix of the public security-prosecution-court system, representing the government interests rather than clients' interests. Understandably, they were initially public employees of work-units, and each lawyer had the status of cadre (Fung 1987). The Provisional Regulations on Lawyers drafted in 1980 and enacted in 1982 stated expressly that lawyers were state legal workers and their workplace, called legal advisory offices, were institutional work-units (NPC Standing Committee 1980). All lawyers were on the state payroll. The government determined staffing quotas and set budgets for each legal advisory office, which was subordinate to the local judicial department (Zhang Na 2006).

As state employees, lawyers were supposed to put the state interests above their clients' interests. For instance, during the 1983 'campaign to strike hard on crime' lawyers had the job of persuading convicted criminals who received a capital sentence to appeal their verdict. If the convicted chose not to appeal, they would have ten days before execution. If they appealed, their appeal could be rejected immediately and they can be executed within five days (Zhang Na 2006).

Within a few years, the legal profession was reformed. In a ministerial circular enacted in 1984, the Ministry of Justice granted more staffing and financial autonomy to legal advisory offices. State-budgeted offices could use the surplus from their business income to hire lawyers on a contract basis. The government also encouraged the development of legal offices completely without a state budget and state-set employee quotas. These offices were to be staffed by specially appointed lawyers, part-time lawyers and contract-based supportive staff (Ministry of Justice 1984). For offices which did have a revenue surplus, the rules of 'self-determined business income and expenses and retaining or redistributing the surplus' applied. The staff of those offices could have higher bonus rates than their colleagues whose revenue left them dependent of a state allocation. For those offices operating at a deficit, the government continued to subsidize the balance. The ministerial circular of 1984 also clarified that lawyers were intellectuals and should be treated as professors, associate professors, lecturer and assistant professors politically and economically. All the policies relative to intellectuals were regarded as equally applicable to lawyers.

In a report submitted to the State Council in 1986, the Ministry of Justice requested additional budget for more staff in the next five years, but it also proposed its retreat from government funding and staff control of legal offices. Offices should be allowed to recruit lawyers outside the state-imposed staffing quota. They were paid through office revenues generated outside a state allocation (State Council, General Office 1986). Furthermore, it was proposed that the government's full control of staffing, budget and administration should be changed. To solve the problem caused by a budget shortage, the Ministry suggested in the report that some legal offices in good financial shape should be allowed more financial autonomy. It suggested that greater autonomy be possible for independent accounting; assuming responsibility for profits and losses; self-control of revenue and expenditure; and retaining the revenue surplus.

The 1986 report reaffirmed that lawyers were intellectuals and should be treated equally with those in other specializations. In 1988, the Ministry of Personnel approved the wage rates of lawyers proposed by the Ministry of Justice. The positions of lawyers were divided into five hierarchical ranks, Grades One to Four for lawyers, and a fifth grade for Assistant Lawyers. As with other wage grades, Grade One was the highest rank. The salary rates for Grade One to Four were exactly the same as those for university teachers of equivalent ranks formulated in 1985 (Ministry of Personnel 1988).

The state employment of lawyers and state ownership of law offices impeded the development of the legal profession. In a proposal made to

Tianjin Municipal Government in 1988, the Tianjin Bureau of Justice complained that the current lawyer system no longer met the needs of social development and the construction of the profession. In the first place, the state-imposed staff quota prevented the expansion of the profession to meet the needs of the society. Secondly, a lack of competition meant that the system failed to motivate lawyers. Thirdly, as cadres serving the interests of the state, lawyers were not trusted by their clients, especially foreign clients. This had an adverse impact on the opening-up policy. A major reform that the Bureau proposed was to trial cooperative law firms in the city (Tianjin Municipal Government 1988).

After a few months, the Ministry of Justice proposed the trial of cooperative law firms throughout the country. A cooperative law firm is designed not to receive any state funds and to have at least three full-time lawyers not on the state payroll. Lawyers who willingly join the cooperative law firm have to resign from public positions, or keep their positions without pay. Cooperative law firms are outside the state accounting system and assume complete responsibility for their own profits or losses. Lawyers do not receive fixed wages, but are paid in accordance with their performance. In return, law firms enjoy autonomy in the management of their business, staffing and the use of their revenue (Ministry of Justice 1988).

The privatization of law firms gained momentum in 1993 with the promulgation of the Ministry of Justice's 'Plan to deepen the reform of lawyers' work'. The 'Plan' encouraged lawyers to team up voluntarily, assume responsibility for their firm's income and expenditures, take control of their own development and discipline, and to set up firms that did not require state appointed staff or financial support. The marketization of legal services has been central to this reform, transforming law firms from state-financed institutional work-units into non-state-budget self-disciplined legal service organizations, and lawyers from state cadres into professionals. The Ministry further required lawyers who applied to set up law firms to produce evidence of resignation from public positions or disconnection with previous public sector work-units, and to specify in their application the firm's financial management system, revenue distribution patterns and the responsibility for liabilities. The 1993 reform is hailed as the 'most profound, most thorough, and most open-minded' reform of the legal system (Gong 2005).

The promulgation of the Lawyers Law in 1996 was a further milestone in the professionalization of lawyers. Lawyers are defined as 'personnel who have obtained a business license for setting up a lawyer's practice in accordance with the law and who are providing legal services for the public' (NPC Standing Committee 1996). They are no longer viewed as state workers serving the interests of the state. Lawyers may practice in three types of law firms: state-owned, cooperative, and partnerships. The latter two types of firm do not receive any financial support from the state.

However, even state-owned firms do not necessarily receive a state allocation. In the mid-1990s, nearly half of the law firms established with state funds stopped relying on the state for funding. In 1998, state-funded law firms accounted for 59 percent of the 8,946 law firms. 27 percent were partnerships and 11 percent were cooperatives (Peerenboom 2002: 353). By 2007, 70 percent of the more than 13,000 law firms had become partnerships (Zhang 2007).

In spite of the state regulation of pricing for services, lawyers have enjoyed much higher autonomy in determining the rates they charge. While the government sets the guiding rates for lawyers representing clients in civil, criminal, administrative and state compensation cases, they can negotiate with their clients about the rates of fees for other services, such as acting as legal advisors and providing non-litigious services.

Economic autonomy has contributed greatly to the emergence of rich lawyers, but the regional differentiation is striking. As of the year-end 2003, about two-thirds of the more than 10,000 law firms were located in big cities, while the poorer regions and China's West had shortages of lawyers. In 2003, two Beijing law firms generated over 200 million *yuan* in business each, while in 2002, there were 16 provinces whose lawyers were unable to generate more than 200 million *yuan* gross income in a single province (Gong 2005). Table 9.1 compares average business turnover for lawyers in Beijing, Shanghai and China as a whole between 2001 and 2002.

The grand total of lawyers' business reached 15 billion *yuan* in 2004, more than one-third of which was generated in Beijing. The average business turnover of Beijing lawyers was about a half million *yuan* in 2004 (Yu 2005; Zhang Lijing 2005). Shenzhen had 3100 lawyers with an annual turnover of 1.06 billion *yuan* in 2004, or nearly 350,000 *yuan* per lawyer on average (Su and Wu 2005). The 6000 odd Shanghai lawyers made 1.6 billion *yuan*, or 300,000 *yuan* per lawyer (Wei 2004). In other cities, the figures are much lower. For example, the average business turnover of Chongqing lawyers was only 50,000 *yuan* for 2005 (Chongqing Daily 31 March 2006). The 371 lawyers of Guilin, a medium-sized city in south China, generated only 12.19 million *yuan* in 2005, or 32,800 *yuan* per lawyer (Xu 2006).

Table 9.1 Legal business turnover 2001–2002

Location	Number of lawyers 2001/2002	Turnover (billion yuan) 2001/2002	Turnover/person (yuan) 2001/2002
Beijing	6,000/7,500	1.8/2.7	300,000/360,000
Shanghai	4,500/5,000	1.2/1.5	250,000/300,000
All China	100,000/120,000	8/12	80,000/100,000

Source: Gong 2005

Income disparities amongst lawyers are severe (Peerenboom 2002: 366). There are four major employment models in the legal profession: intern lawyers, full salaried lawyers, commissioned lawyers and partners. Senior partners and directors of major law firms are usually the highest income earners. Their annual income can reach over one million *yuan*. The number of such lawyers, however, is very limited. Annual incomes of ordinary lawyers in major cities can be anywhere between 10,000 to 400,000 *yuan,* depending on their experience and competence, reputation, and source of business (Gong 2005; Wei 2004; Zhang Lijing 2005).

In Beijing, a full salaried lawyer is paid 3000 to 5000 *yuan* basic salary per month plus bonus, but he or she does not need to seek new businesses. Commission based lawyers have two wage patterns. For fully commission-based lawyers, they have to give 30 percent of the revenues generated from businesses to their law firms. Lawyers can also receive a basic salary ranging from 800 to 2000 *yuan* per month, plus 20 to 50 percent of the revenues of the businesses they service. The lowest income earners are the intern lawyers, who, according to the law, have to spend a one-year internship in law firms before they can be granted a practising license. Their monthly income is between 1000 and 2000 *yuan* (Zhang Lijing 2005). In general, an established lawyer in a major city can expect an income of 100,000 *yuan* a year.

The income of lawyers is also determined by their specializations. It is reported that those who are not involved in litigation receive the highest incomes. These lawyers include those with licenses to provide legal services related to securities, stock exchanges and listing of companies on stock markets; as well as in the privatization of state-owned enterprises or conveyancing (Yu 2005).

The variability of wealth

It is clear that in recent years some university professors and doctors, and most lawyers have benefited from changes in the economic environment to achieve significant individual wealth. Nonetheless, it is also clear that different professions have different patterns of wealth generation and accumulation. University teachers and doctors remain public sector employees, however much their immediate environment has become commercialized. For those who are high earners in these professions, the major sources of both their wealth and their income do not seem sustainable and are highly susceptible to government changes in both budget and regulation. The public sector salary rates for university teachers and doctors remain limited. For doctors, even the state salary rates are not guaranteed. Professionals from both sectors have had to resort to individually organized activities to generate extra income that may sometimes put their total income in the ranks of the highest income earners. The extent of their success though is very contingent on both the individual's ability and their specialization. Not everyone has the capacity to build on such opportunities. Moreover, in the healthcare sector, many of these opportunities are illegal.

In contrast, the legal profession has undergone a major privatization. Lawyers' incomes are now all but completely determined by the market. Their sources of incomes are more reliable and their wealth more sustainable than professionals in tertiary education and the healthcare sector. While the excess wealth of very rich university professors and medical doctors depends on government policies and actions, their equivalent colleagues in the legal profession have an independence that draws on the market.

Economic success has only come to specific individuals within the professions, and only then under particular conditions. The majority of professionals are not particularly better off as a result of the changes wrought by the reform era. In spite of the Party-state's promotion of commercialization, the markets for professional services remain subject to various but nonetheless strict control by government. The Party-state is indecisive about its policies on professionalization. On the one hand, it has introduced market elements to the professions in the hope of reducing its financial burden and motivating individuals to provide quality service. On the other hand, bound by its ideological commitment to socialism and the poor, the CCP has employed strict regulation on the pricing of professional services. The regulation of prices has kept the average income of professionals low. Professional services are thus made seemingly more accessible to the poor so that government can claim political merit. The Party-state has used low-wages, even for professionals, as a major competition strategy to boost China-made in the international market. The lack of political, economic and organizational autonomy and power has prevented professionals from monopolizing their markets and further impeded their attainment of higher percentile incomes. Only a small number of elite professionals have been able to take advantage of their specific environments to achieve a measure of excess wealth.

Part III

Lifestyles

10 The Forest City

Homeownership and new wealth in Shenyang

Luigi Tomba and Beibei Tang

On 18 June 2007 the government of Shenyang's old industrial district, Tiexi, inaugurated a permanent exhibition on the lifestyles of the industrial workers who had been living in a neighbourhood known as the 'workers' village' for the last five decades. The exhibition is located in one of seven buildings singled out for preservation in this Soviet-style residential area that, built in 1952, originally included 143 large three-storey constructions and a total area of over 700,000 square metres. The exhibition featured reproductions of the one-room apartments with shared basic facilities and kitchens, and displayed the evolution of daily life in the neighbourhood since the 1950s. Young university graduates wearing wireless microphones told the curious visitors the pioneeristic adventures of China's working class and paid tribute to their struggle to build the glory of the socialist state.

Next door, in a twin building on the same day, an art management company was holding the vernissage for a new art space. Ironically, it was a photo exhibition on the ailing industrial sites of China's rustbelt, abandoned and mostly demolished in the last decade. The remaining five buildings under renovation, we were told by one of the young long haired art managers, will host cafes, restaurants and art ateliers.

In front of one of the workers' village's old buildings, still standing but bearing the unmistakeable marks of imminent demolition, an old lady stood up from her Majiang table to ask us, the very occasional out-of-towners, whether we were willing to buy her apartment. '250,000 *yuan* would be enough' she said 'at least I could buy an apartment in this area. It is becoming so expensive now.' She was still waiting for a good offer of compensation for the small apartment she had obtained in the 1960s from the Shenyang Electric Cables Company, one of the city's socialist behemoths that recently stopped production, letting go of 20,000 employees.

These three images, adjacent and related to one another, prompted an observation. In urban settings, the functional relationship between a demobilising working class and the new rich is much closer than one sometimes expects and the balance of this relationship is often decided by the heavy hand of the city planners. The unemployed may still live in housing built for them when they were working in state-owned factories, but they occupy land that the local state wants to re-allocate to more profitable use. The social landscapes created by urban 'renewal' (read demolition and reconstruction) are therefore not decided uniquely by capital flows and price gaps but also, by the lifestyle choices of a growing class of homeowners and by the powerful intermediation, planning and decisions of the state.

Disparities in wealth distribution, segregation and stratification have often accompanied processes of industrialisation and urbanisation (O'Loughlin and Friedrichs 1996; Smith 1996). In no other setting has the impact of China's new rich in re-shaping urban life appeared more comprehensively and clearly than here, in the heartland of China's socialist industry, at a time when the traditional urban suburbs are experiencing a process of industrial decline.

On 18 June, the district government was celebrating the fifth anniversary of the establishment of the 'New Tiexi' and the beginning of a systematic rebuilding of the area that included the almost complete annihilation of its industrial side. Tiexi's world famous Soviet-style heavy industrial plants were either closed or relocated outside town in a new 'development zone', in which workers are mainly rural migrants. While the traditional socialist working class is rapidly losing its long-held entitlements, a new home-owning middle class and their promoters (local authorities and real-estate developers) are claiming a de-industrialising Tiexi as the next frontier of urban living and investment. This is happening on the back of the state's mammoth effort to rebuild the city's decaying housing stock, infrastructure, environment and reputation. The re-branding of Shenyang from China's industrial base to a 'Forest City' (with the hosting of the World Horticultural Exhibition in 2006 and green policies for the fast-paced reconstruction of inner city suburbs) is just one sign of the city's fundamental shift to a post-industrial metropolis (see also Cucco in this volume).

This chapter deals with both how housing reform has affected China's patterns of urban social stratification (by providing opportunities to some and denying others); and the 'transformative' power of the new rich, something that could be defined as their ability to produce value through their practices of consumption. It contends that the state has two roles as social engineer: as *co-funder* of the new wealth and umpire of individual enrichment (policies have shaped patterns of access to housing); and as a *social manager*, as social, political and financial capital (in the form of rights and entitlements but also of land and resources) is redistributed from the traditional working class to new, white-collar, professional and entrepreneurial urban elites (see also Guo in this volume).

Research through long periods of fieldwork and participant observation in Shenyang[1] asked two empirical questions. One is structural, about the relationship between the individuals' position *in the system* (type of employment, family background, relationship to the state and residence) and their ability to gain access to quality housing for the first two decades of the housing reform. Housing is an important element of the state's *funding* of the new rich and a determinant of the different paths to wealth experienced by different groups (entrepreneurial, professional and public servants). The ability of certain households to profit from state policies and get ahead in the housing market is largely dependent on their position within or without the system, although the structure of incentives is changing rapidly (to the disadvantage of the younger generation). This chapter is mainly concerned with the opportunities for upward social mobility provided by housing reform. It focuses on those who, while not properly rich, have experienced a significant enhancement of their status and consumption ability.

The second question concerns the role played by the new wealthy in changing the cities, especially by providing an alternative source of value-making and embodying the aspiration to a competitive, clean, modern and efficient city that is replacing the traditional image of the dirty and conflict-ridden industrial site. While industrial production moves to new anonymous peri-urban areas crowded by a transient population, traditional city districts are reconfiguring themselves and competing with one another for a slice of the commercial, service and residential economy. The different levels of the government play a major role in promoting this transition, one in which there is a clear role for the wealthier groups.

Housing reform: creating a middle class

Housing provision has been fundamentally reformed in the last twenty years. A wealth of academic analysis has been produced on the changing housing policies (Ma 2002; Wu 1998 and 2002; Wu *et al.* 2007; Yeh 1995; Gaubatz 1995b; Wang and Murie 1999; Hu and Kaplan 2001; Li 2000; Li and Fung 2001) so only a brief summary is necessary to help set the context for more recent changes. Until the late 1980s, urban residents employed in State-Owned Enterprises (SOEs) had access to housing through their employer. Housing was generally built by the work-units or by the local state. In both case registered urbanites (but not migrants, who do not have access to urban welfare) had access to almost-free housing.

The reform of housing entitlements began in 1988 when SOEs took advantage of a provision that allowed them to get rid of some of their expensive and unproductive housing stocks by selling partial or full property rights to their employee-tenants. The practice was, initially, not very popular as, in the absence of a real estate market, residents could not see the advantage of homeownership and were unwilling to pay relatively large amounts of money for the same apartments they had always occupied for free. Work-units therefore often slashed the prices to a fraction of the market value and discounts were granted on a number of different bases, including seniority, family composition and age. This practice continued for more than a decade and by the year 2001, for example, 58 percent of Beijing families had purchased their first apartment from the work-unit in which they were working (Tomba 2004). This practice also 'froze' the existing unequal housing situation that had characterised the 1970s and 1980s. Those who had been entitled to a better quality or larger apartment due to their position in the enterprise, their age and family composition or their political performance were able to buy more valuable assets. In 1988, at the beginning of the housing reform, cadres had average living spaces 30 per-cent higher than workers, Party members had bigger homes than non-party members and workers in state enterprises did better than those in collective enterprises (Li 2002).

By the mid-1990s, with the rapid development of a market for residential housing, the initially ignored advantages of early ownership became very significant indeed. With the construction of whole new neighbourhoods and commercial housing estates (*shangpin fang* – privately owned housing) to meet growing demand, the emergence of a mortgage industry among the state banks, and a market characterised by rapidly rising prices, those who had entered the market early and at a low price enjoyed significant advan-tages as they could use the property as collateral or as an extra source of income through the rental market. A 2003 nationwide survey found that 78 percent of urban residents have partial or total ownership rights over at least one apartment, and that about 13 percent also own more than one.[2]

Despite the emergence of specialised development companies and the consequent declining role of work-units in the construction of housing (since 1998 SOEs are no longer allowed, in theory, to assign apartments to their employees[3]), employees in the public sector continued to enjoy a wide range of privileges in their access to housing. Some companies purchased apartments to be sold to their managers or highly skilled professionals for a fraction of the price; successful SOEs managed to provide in-kind subsidies or to establish a 'housing provident fund' from which employees could borrow at low interest rates; local authorities, who controlled the allocation of land-use rights were also able to manipulate the housing market: land releases at lower prices were granted, for example, to developers who were prepared to sell part of the built housing at below-market prices (often at 25–30 percent discount).[4]

The implementation of housing policies, which remained in the hands of local authorities, was characterised by a significant variation across different localities. In a similar way to that which occurred in cities elsewhere in Asia (Groves *et al.* 2007), housing policies privileged the subsidisation of owner-ship (even among the lower middle income families) over the provision of inexpensive rental housing.

Gated city, gated people: a toponymy of gated communities

Our short answer to the question about the relationship between state policies and access to housing is, therefore, that despite increasing dereg-ulation and privatisation, those 'within the system' – even at comparatively low salaries[5] – have done better than those outside the system in obtaining access to quality housing and, in turn, higher social status. Those who have enjoyed stable occupations within the public system of employment generally find themselves in a better housing situation than others. This is because better work-units were able to distribute better housing in the socialist period. During the reform period, policies further favoured employees who wished to buy the houses that they were occupying, while a number of subsidy schemes were provided by either the government or the employer to urban residents.

Since the beginning of housing reform, the government has encouraged ownership as an effective way of maintaining economic growth and development and of stimulating consumption. In Shenyang, the dream of homeownership is now ubiquitous: it fills newspapers and glossy magazines, TV commercials and street advertising boards, as well as the internet, where homeowners now account for a large proportion. Ironically, in this former bastion of the revolutionary working class such slogans as: 'Ideal for White Collar Elites!', or 'Become a neighbour to nobility!' or again 'Living here will change your life!', linking housing and lifestyle with the pursuit of status and 'quality' are a common sight today.

But who can afford to live the high life in a private gated community?[6] The continuous growth of privately owned housing compounds offering a wide variety of properties, suggests that the common sense answer (those who make a lot of money), is not enough to explain increasing rates of homeownership among urban residents and the continuous hunger for better quality dwellings that accompanies the re-making of the built environment.

The housing careers of our interviewees in Shenyang reveal the importance of a family's position within the public system as a determinant of successful ownership. Ninety percent of the families interviewed in different types of middle-class residential compounds were at some point receivers of welfare housing (*fuli fen fang*) in the 1980s or 1990s. The quality of the original welfare housing was in general poor and apartments were not larger than 50–60 square metres. Residents reported spending between 10,000 and 30,000 *yuan* (between 1,000 and 3,500 USD) to buy their first apartment and many were able to resell at a significant profit within a few years, when the same apartment had become worth up to ten times more.

There are different types of gated residential communities in which the new rich make their nests, and a toponymy of Shenyang's middle-class compounds assists in understanding the distinctive paths to homeownership.

The first type comprises the so-called 'Commercial Housing Estates' (*Shangpin fang xiaoqu*). Despite a relatively slow growth in average housing prices in Shenyang,[7] the market prices of better quality apartments in commercial housing easily surpasses 6,000 *yuan* per square metre. A typical 80 square metre apartment at this price would cost 480,000 *yuan*, equivalent to more than 29 years of an average Shenyang salary in 2005 (16,393 *yuan*) (SYNJ 2006: table 2–5)

Commercial estates house residents from different occupational backgrounds. Private business owners without access to subsidised housing often buy in these areas, but public servants and professionals are also widely represented. These communities are generally large (from several hundred to a few thousand families in high-rise buildings) and are managed by private companies chosen either by the developer or by the residents themselves through their 'owners' committee' (Read 2003; Tomba 2004 and 2005). Residents pay monthly management fees of up to 2 *yuan* per month per square metre (a lower rate than in Beijing or Shanghai but still a significant amount) for such services as security, maintenance of public spaces, environmental services, and facilities such as public parks and sometimes swimming pools and gymnasiums. The visibility of state institutions is very limited, although in some communities the Party-controlled neighbourhood committees and the management companies have been merged into one organisation.

While this type of private community is now very common, in Shenyang despite 20 years of housing reform, work-units and government departments still control large amounts of housing and contribute to building and redistributing apartments to some of their employees. Work-unit managed compounds still constitute a surprisingly large component of post-reform available housing in urban China. One nationwide survey revealed that in 2003 more than 40 percent of urban residents lived in this type of housing, although most had become owners (see note 2).

During the 1990s employers often bought apartments in private developments or, when they had land available, built their own compounds. In many cases these compounds were comparable in quality to the private ones, and had similar market value (see also Cucco in this volume). They also often enjoyed a better reputation among homebuyers than private compounds, as their residents, who were generally either public servants or public professionals are believed to be of a 'higher quality'.[8]

In Shenyang, government departments still fund the upgrading of housing conditions for specific categories of public servants. For example, a first-grade cadre (the lowest level) married and with one child, is entitled in Shenyang to an apartment of at least 100 square metres. Minimum floor limits still apply to public employees in government departments and universities, and vary depending on the position employees occupy within the organisation. If housing is not adequate, the employer can intervene by either providing an extra discount or offering monetary compensation for the purchase of a new apartment. Higher-level cadres also get better deals when they buy from or through their departments. Some communities built by government departments, and generally of higher quality and in prime locations, are exclusively for cadres above a certain administrative ranking and are not accessible to other members of the same administration. Ownership rights are, nonetheless, in the private hands of individuals.

Some of these communities are developed by different government offices or by some particularly well off large enterprises and then sold to their employees at a discount.[9] Although the residents living in these compounds might come from different work-units they generally belong to the same supervisory department, or to the same 'administrative system' (*xitong*).[10] For example the so-called 'Public Servant communities' (*gongwuyuan shequ*) are often built by the district government, and then redistributed to different work-units under the supervisory offices according to a quota. Work-units then proceed to allocate the apartments to their employees who pay only a fraction of the price but acquire close to full ownership.

The case of the 'Scientists Garden' in Shenyang is emblematic. This community features high quality, large apartments and is inhabited by well-regarded scientists occupying important positions in large hospitals, universities and research centres in Shenyang who paid only 2,000 *yuan* per square metre out of their own pockets (about a third of the market price). The remaining cost was subsidised by their work-units.

Some units may attach clauses that prevent employees from leaving the enterprise or from selling the apartment for a prescribed period. Some, for example only allow apartments to be sold to employees under the same supervisory department. These clauses however do not prevent residents from taking full advantage of the property and many reported their ability to rent out or sell the apartments despite the formal restrictions.

In addition to cheap housing prices, residents in work-unit sponsored communities also enjoy all sorts of other benefits, such as free heating (a major household expenditure in a city of freezing winters) or, significantly, cheaper management fees. In these housing communities, managers are hired by the work-unit or the supervisory department and provide better quality services at lower fees. Residents in these compounds reported paying management fees that were 50 to 70 percent lower than the standard fee in comparable commercial estates.

A third category is one in which commercial housing and work-unit sponsored dwellings coexist. Work-units that build their own compounds often strike deals with developers. In exchange for high-quality, low-price apartments, to be sold to employees, the developer is assigned land-use rights for a number of commercial buildings to be sold at market prices. Often identical in quality, subsidised and commercial housing are built next to one another, producing a mix of different types of owners who pay different prices for the same apartment and different management fees for the same service. Interestingly, coexistence of cadres or employees and private buyers often determine rivalries and resentment over the different conditions with the former labelling the latter 'low quality' new rich.

Generational distinction

This positional advantage enjoyed by employees within the system that has produced very high rates of homeownership among residents in the main cities and is among the main reasons for the growth of China's middle class, might be fading. Shenyang, where the impact of de-industrialisation and economic reform has had devastating effects on the consolidated social structures, shows a peculiar pattern of housing distribution and access among different generations.

The younger generation of employees within the system, in particular, appears less advantaged. For those who entered the workforce after the formal end of housing allocation in the late 1990s, access to housing is becoming increasingly difficult, as it relies mainly on a stable income and limited public subsidies. The advantage of long-term employment in the public service or large enterprises is still great, especially in places like Shenyang where the state used to dominate the local economy and the incentive structure still favours public employees.

Generational disadvantage produces a reverse dependency of the younger generation on the older generation. Parents, especially those who worked in positions of authority in the public service or in large state-owned enterprises, and who retired before industrial restructuring took place, find themselves having to contribute to their children's livelihood. For families affected by layoffs in the industrial sector this often results in the unemployed 35–45 year old relying on their parents' pensions to send their children to school. In better-off families, the older generation's stable income and access to housing is essential to fund the younger generation's access to their first apartment. A good home, for example, is commonly considered essential to a 'good marriage' and the difficulties experienced by the younger generation are an important reason for late marriages. Also, while earlier generations who had access to subsidised housing from their work-units were able to cash in the housing price hikes of the last decade, those who tried to enter the market late find themselves struggling in a rising price environment.

Homeownership remains a very important element in the strategies of upward mobility. At the same time, the structure of incentives appears to be changing and evolving. The result is that families are forced to implement new strategies to cope with the pressure of the housing market.

Post-industrial Shenyang

The boom in homeownership is also associated with the city's transition away from its industrial tradition. A construction and residential economy has become central to Shenyang inner districts' re-orientation as a competitive, global and post-industrial city, and the new rich, with their consumption habits and their hunger for quality lifestyles are an essential factor in the city's re-branding. In 2005, Shenyang was, to the surprise of many, awarded the title of 'Forest City', only the second in the country after Guiyang. This was in recognition of the exceptional efforts made by the city to produce 'urban forests', improve the environment and increase the per capita green areas from 3.5 to over 12 square metres between 2000 and

2005. In 2005, the mayor, Chen Zhenggao, described the transition as one necessary to improve the city's competitiveness:

> If we don't pursue the transformation of Shenyang into a forest city, we won't be able to improve our condition; with no improvement we won't be competitive, and with no competitiveness we won't be able to develop and flourish.

(Chen 2005)

It is no coincidence that the greening of Shenyang had to be 'built' and that the forest city reputation now flagged by the city government relied heavily on the demolition, reconstruction and gentrification that has happened in the last five to seven years. Forest 'building' occurred to such a degree that in 2005, 38.9 percent of all urban green area was located inside almost inaccessible private residential compounds.

When asked about the most important consideration prior to buying an apartment in these communities, informants generally mentioned good management and a green environment as essential for maintaining the value of their investment. They also, however, associate efficient management and the green environment with the need for 'quality neighbours'. 'Choosing where to live' said one, 'means to choose a good living environment. This community is much better than where we used to live. The old community was dirty and filled with all sorts of people.' Another continued, 'We have to think about the living environment, a good management and a green community. We have to consider the quality of our fellow residents too. We are not going to live with those people at sixes and sevens. But I don't think that kind of people could afford to live here anyway.'

The planning of a 'forest city' therefore goes hand in hand with improving the quality of the population, by providing a better living environment, and matches the move away from the city's dirty industrial image and working class tradition. With the loss of the working class, urban districts are, increasingly, gentrified.

Gentrification in Shenyang is not happening as a result of revitalisation of the existing neighbourhoods. Gentrification involves a thoroughly planned demolition and re-construction of residential spaces, and a redefinition of land use (mainly from productive to residential or from public to private) with the precise intent of making both available to a different section of the population and to obtain a better return on land usage.

This process is one that involves the new rich both as subjects of policies to increase homeownership rates (as seen earlier) and as factors in the re-valuation of the urban territory. The middle-class quest for a better lifestyle is more valuable to the production of a post-industrial Shenyang than a conflict-prone working class. 'Value' here refers to both the commercial value of the land, or of the housing estates built on it; and the human and moral values (better quality people) that become attached to specific areas and that make certain areas more desirable than others. Changing the designation of a block of land increases the value of the land but, as in all processes of gentrification, it is the middle-class aspiration to live in a new place that changes the overall value of the area. In other words, the re-making of certain spaces changes not only the monetary value of that space but also the original moral geography of the city (Pow 2007). Specifically, higher quality humans produce more valuable communities (Tomba 2008).

As argued elsewhere, the rhetoric of quality and of a civilised city do not stop at setting standards inspired by the 'civilised' behaviour of the middle class. They also prescribe a performative role for the bodies of those who are civilised. The intrinsic quality of civilised middle-class bodies is portrayed as a contagious force, to the point that they can create value by re-inventing physical and social spaces, often for the simple reason of inhabiting them (Tomba 2008) (the effects of quality discourses on status formation in China are also analyzed in other chapters of this volume; see Zang, Carrillo and Sun).

Observation of such processes of value-making in Shenyang confirms this picture. In one gated community we investigated in Tiexi residents admitted their original scepticism about buying an apartment in an expensive compound in a 'low quality' district. The developer (a company from Hangzhou) started with a small development on the dilapidated site of a glass factory that had been recently closed. The first development was intended to showcase the potential for the area to become a convenient and attractive living environment for middle-class residents and was then expanded to about eight times the original size after the success of the first phase (at more than double the price).

The developer's main problem was to transform the perception of the place, and improve the potential for the area to become attractive to middle-income homebuyers from other districts. The developer's marketing philosophy therefore, beyond building houses, was to 'create an environment, a culture and a spirit'. A slogan reproduced several times was:

> Real estate is not only a market for land, building materials and services, it is also the product of its time, of cultural and spiritual change. A building is not only steel and concrete, it is also cast around the culture and spirits it requires.

The marketing of these compounds is therefore based on the idea of a spiritual and cultural recreation and valorisation of the dilapidated industrial area that is not only a task for the developer but also for the residents. 'Who could even imagine that such a lush and modern new city stands on the ground of what were the ruins of an old factory!'

The discourse applied here to the promotion and valorisation of the area also reproduces the government's rhetoric of 'harmonious communities' (Hu 2005) with its implications for community governance (Tomba 2008; Feng 2005; Zhao 2005; Tao 2005). The 'creation of a spirit' is explained on the developer's website in terms of planning that 'places humans at the centre' (*yi ren wei ben* – a slogan often used also by local government to describe the nature of community services) and that aims to achieve 'harmony between residents and the built environment'. A harmonious community of high quality people can also only be achieved by 'building a beautiful space for spiritual and material life' where 'the highest value is obtained only when it is shared with others' (www.sinhoo.net).

Planned gentrification in Tiexi

While developers market Tiexi and its new gated communities by mimicking the government's slogans, the government itself has been busy providing an overhaul of the district's infrastructure. During the celebrations of the fifth anniversary of New Tiexi speakers repeatedly proclaimed the grand progress of the district that now features large parks, wide roads and high buildings, and where everyone can now buy good quality meat conveniently at the next door Carrefour superstore.

Once a traditional centre of Japanese industrialisation and early socialist Soviet-funded heavy industrial development projects (here were located a large number of the 156 Soviet funded heavy industrial plants built in the 1950s) Tiexi appears today as yet another new dormitory city with an increasing commercial flavour. The old industrial heritage (together with hundreds of thousand of jobs once held by the socialist workers' aristocracy) has been completely wiped out. The factory and traditional neighbourhood life are all but gone and there is no visible trace of industrial production in the whole district.[11] The planning strategy for the district has been 'demolition and relocation'. Most of the old workers who lived in small and unsafe single story houses were forcibly moved into high-rise crowded residential communities where they no longer live with their old workmates. At the same time, the land that had been occupied by industrial sites was targeted by residential developers for new and expensive gated communities of the three types described earlier. The result is a high level of segregation within the district with gated communities on one side, and low quality housing built with a substantial injection of public investment, on the other. In Tiexi the district government plans to invest, in 2007, 2.26 billion *yuan* (US$250 million) or 65 percent of its budget in 35 subsidised new housing compounds to relocate about 480,000 people, or almost a third of the district's entire population (SYNJ 2006). The new apartments will then be sold at a price comparable to the average compensation that the inhabitants received for their old houses (2,400 *yuan* per square metre is the average). In addition, the local government is also investing 300 million *yuan* in infrastructure and 127 million *yuan* to improve the living environment of the district.

These investments are only made possible by the generous injection of funds in the last few years, from the central coffers into the cities of the

Northeast, struggling to cope with industrial restructuring. The ability of the local levels of the state to fund these projects is significantly effected by the fact that large portions of Tiexi's now valuable land-use-rights are sold to private and public developers for the construction of new privately managed gated communities that sell for two to three times the price of the subsidised housing. In the first four months of 2007 alone, 3.2 million square metres of private commercial housing were sold in Shenyang for over 10 billion *yuan*.

At the same time, the local government is investing heavily in administrative personnel at the community level. Tiexi's residential areas are divided into 10 subdistricts (*jiedao*) and each district contains an average of 10 to 13 residential communities (each with 2,000 to 4,000 families). The 126 community offices (the lowest level of urban administration) employ about 2,500 people: cadres, employees and 'volunteers'. These community offices have an important role in maintaining order, providing subsidies, containing social conflicts and managing relocations in the poorer neighbourhood. In the private gated communities (served by a management company), however, they are virtually irrelevant or work in strict collaboration with the management company.

Tiexi's gentrification process, therefore, not only has the displacement of old residents, the improvement of the housing stock and the change in character of the neighbourhood (the three characteristics of a 'classic' gentrification process) (Atkinson and Bridge 2005; Smith 1996; Huang 2006), but also two original characteristics: the direct involvement of the state, as land owner and economic planner, in designing the transition; and an increasing segregation and privatisation of residential life, with high rates of home-ownership and gated communities becoming the new dominant form of urban revitalisation.

After analysing processes of gentrification in European and North American inner-city neighbourhoods Neil Smith concluded that the movement of the middle classes into dilapidated working class areas that originates gentrification and value creation was 'a back-to-the-city movement all right, but a back-to-the-city movement of capital rather than people' (Smith, 1996). Similarly, in the case of Tiexi, it is hard to imagine gentrification without a substantial decision by the state to facilitate or attract the capital necessary for revitalisation.

The transformation of this 1.2 million strong district into what was called New Tiexi in 2002 therefore also corresponded to a dramatic re-organisation of its geography and of its inhabitants. During the 1980s and 1990s, Tiexi was believed to be a dirty, polluted and uncomfortable worker area, physically separated by the rail tracks from the more civilised and liveable centre and commercial areas of Heping and Shenhe. Still today it is not uncommon to hear demeaning comments about the 'quality' (*suzhi*) of Tiexi from residents in other districts of Shenyang. But in the short span of five years, under pressure to find resources to fund the ailing social services for the mostly unemployed population, the city and district government have refashioned the image of the district into that of an appealing and affordable middle-class residential paradise. This has been achieved by moving all industries to the new development zone, pulling down any reference to the dirty industrial past, selling land use rights to private and public developers; and finally mummifying and gentrifying the few remaining spaces that remain today reminiscent of that past (as described at the beginning of this chapter).

To be sure, to talk about Tiexi as a well-established middle-class paradise is nothing short of an exaggeration. While this remains the probable ultimate aspiration of the local government, in fact large numbers of disgruntled workers and unemployed living on subsidies or on informal employment opportunities still make up the largest part of Tiexi's population. Moreover, the transformation of this area is in fact also serving the purpose of reducing conflicts among the poorest communities of former workers now living off subsidies and occasional employment, as it has deprived the workers of all the elements of their identity, by demolishing the factories that were the focal point of the numerous conflicts of the late 1990s.

In a recent book, Lee Ching-kwan argues, based on research in the late 1990s and early 2000s, that the unemployed in the Northeast would be able to sustain their conflicts for a longer time because their work-unit-based communities will maintain a certain level of collective identity (Lee 2007). Today, this possibility seems less likely locally after the physical transformation of Tiexi. The destruction of any potential reference to industrial production, the increased direct control over community life, and the progressive disintegration of the social texture of these communities has drastically reduced the ability of these workers to organise around either industrial disputes or residential proximity.

In contemporary China, the state's policies to favour the emergence of a new middle class are often justified with the accepted argument that such a 'responsible' social group will reinforce social and political stability (Lu 2002; also Guo in this volume). But advanced and educated elites have become more than just a factor in maintaining social stability. The promotion of the middle class as 'exemplary' (Bakken 2000) occurs at various levels – in official state campaigns, the media, and neighbourhood institutions, through the interest and policies of local governments, and with the support of marketing strategies of real estate developers, commercial property managers, and among middle-class communities themselves. Academic discourse also often reinforces this understanding of the central role of these groups in China's contemporary developmental path. One author, for example, goes as far as saying:

> Our country needs the middle stratum (*zhongchan jieceng*), because it is the political force necessary for stability, it is a regenerative force of production, it is the scientific force behind creative production, it is the

moral force behind civilised manners, it is the force necessary to eliminate privilege and curb poverty, it is everything

(Zhu 2005: 148)

New Tiexi's gentrification, therefore serves different purposes. On one
side, it contributes to the prevention and dispersal of the conflicts that the
final years of de-industrialisation have inevitably created. On the other, it
uses the rhetoric and practices of middle-class creation to reposition the
district within the city's new moral geography.

The new rich and the city

The analysis of housing patterns in a late de-industrialising Chinese city
reveals continuity in the role of the state as a planner of urban space and
substantial discontinuity in the aims and the priorities of this planning.

Among the continuities, the Shenyang case confirms that the privatisation
of housing was not driven by market forces alone and that the system
worked to the substantial advantage of at least one generation of public
employees and public servants who now make up the most visible component of the new homeowners in the city. Employers and public departments
maintained an important role in determining access to resources, to the
point that subsidised private properties de facto replaced earlier forms of
welfare housing for those lucky enough to maintain employment in a city
with over a million layoffs. This had consequences for the composition of
the new home-owning groups that appear, today, stratified along the lines of
their relationship to the state rather than along those of income. This might
change in the future, with increasing competition for resources and a less
advantaged younger generation who missed out on housing redistribution.

The experience of Shenyang also reveals how the housing economy and
the consumer-oriented new rich are becoming a dominant force that shapes
the processes of urbanisation and the attitude of the government towards it.
Shenyang's traditional industrial districts are now open building sites and
the construction industry seems to have become the only productive activity
in the traditional urban districts. Under pressure to find resources for a city
burdened by immense social problems, the local state has discovered that
the most useful asset in their hands is the availability of land and the
eagerness of the new rich to achieve better lifestyles and social status. The
control over land and the ability to determine prices and allocation was
only the first part of the equation. The government also needed a way to
turn such areas as Tiexi into attractive and valuable opportunities for
investors. The extensive reconceptualisations of Shenyang into a 'Forest
City' and of Tiexi into a land of opportunities for the middle class are
strategies central to the building of a post-industrial city.

While local authorities maintain control over value-making in the post-
industrial city, there is the bigger question of what this transition means for

China's urbanisation and for Chinese society. Has the 'potential for autonomy and community' that researchers started observing in the early 1990s (Davis *et al.* 1995) materialised? Has the 'relaxation' of state control over individual lives envisaged long ago led to the emergence of more autonomous lives, autonomous forms of consumption and opportunities for free choice? Chinese cities today are more open, their societies more complex and the opportunities they present much greater than twenty years ago. Large cities have mostly lost their traditional vocation as industrial centres and are establishing themselves as 'global' centres (Sassen 2001; Rohlen 2002; Amen *et al.* 2006) whose development depends on their ability to compete in the national and international markets by providing the necessary conditions, infrastructures, environment, and concentration of human resources. In this process of catching-up (Li 2006) new social groups (the professionals, the educated, but also the politically reliable, in one phrase 'the people with quality') become central to the city's strategic re-positioning. The professional and political elites merge to produce a model of modern, consuming, clean, green and orderly city whose wealth and future depends greatly on the ability to maintain stability and to marginalise and segregate social discontent.

Notes

1 Research for this chapter is funded by an Australian Research Council Discovery Grant 2006–2008 (DP662894). The authors spent a total of 12 months in Shenyang between 2006 and 2007, visited over 20 communities, and conducted over 200 one-to-one qualitative interviews with residents, local cadres, community officials and managers.
2 Total ownership rights are held by 66.6 percent, while 11.4 percent have limited ownership rights. This information was collected by the research project *China General Social Survey* (CGSS) sponsored by the China Social Science Foundation and carried out by the Department of Sociology, Renmin University of China & Social Science Division, Hong Kong Science and Technology University. The project is directed by Li Lulu and Bian Yanjie. The authors appreciate the assistance in providing data from these institutions and individuals (China General Social Survey 2003).
3 Factories or administrative units with availability of land use rights (and the ability to afford it) engaged in what has become known as the 'last meal' and built subsidised compounds for their employees even after 1998 (Unger and Chan 2004).
4 Many different schemes were put in place by local governments. Research both in China and outside shows that subsidised housing has only partially benefited low income residents, and has contributed to the accumulation of housing patrimony in the hands of the wealthy or of the stable-income professional middle class and public employees (Li 2002; Tomba 2004; Wu 2002). A similar point has been made by Li and Niu who define this group as a 'middle class within the system' (*tizhinei zhongchan jieji*) (Li and Niu 2003).
5 Monetary salaries in the Shenyang public administration are still very low. The monetary salary of a departmental director in the local district government (*juzhang* – a mid-level cadre in an administration with responsibility over more

than 1 million people) is making around 3,000 yuan a month (or about 300 USD), but this amounts to a fraction of its potential income once all perks are included. The average salary of formally employed Shenyang residents was 1366 yuan per month in 2005.

6 The gated community has become the dominant feature of the contemporary urban built environment. In this context this term refers to those communities housing middle to high income residents (Tomba 2008).

7 The average price per square metre rose from 2686 *yuan* in 2000 to 3110 *yuan* in 2005, or slightly more than 15 percent. Prices of higher quality housing have, however, been growing much faster (SYNJ 2006).

8 Several authors have commented on the importance of the discourse of quality (Anagnost 2004; Kipnis 2006; Yan 2003; Jacka 2006; Tomba 2008).

9 Discounts can vary and are based on different criteria (age, family composition or employment). They sometimes reach 50 percent of the market price.

10 The 'administrative system' (*xitong*) is central to China's institutional landscape (Lieberthal 1995).

11 Beijing documentarist Wang Bing's 9-hour film *Tiexiqu* (West of the tracks), shot between 1999 and 2001 is possibly the only remaining document of the industrial aspect of the district and of the struggle of the workers and residents to retain some of the traditional entitlements and lifestyles that had characterised the harsh life of industrial workers (Wang 2004).

11 The Shanghai-Hong Kong Connection

Fine jewelry consumption and the demand for diamonds[1]

Carolyn Cartier

For the new rich and aspiring middle classes in the People's Republic of China (PRC), fine jewelry has become the third most important item of acquisition after a house or flat and a personal automobile. *The People's Daily* (for example: 23 December 2004; 13 January 2005) periodically repeats this ranking as if it is a national fact and so propels into media circulation the notion that precious metals and diamonds are among the most highly desired things in contemporary life. In this list, fine jewelry has displaced the personal computer, which commonly held third position in a list of the 'three major items' (*san da jian*) of consumer interest in the late 1990s. Jewelry industry data supports the claim while the realities of jewelry consumption are highly uneven and associated with the consumption practices of the new rich in major cities. It also suggests just how quickly consumers have acquired a full complement of personal goods and household furnishings, appliances and electronics. Now the things that drive consumer passions are more often items with luxury characteristics and investment potential. Young professionals are especially showing increasing interest in luxury goods, whether they are following new rich consumption practices for fine jewelry or participating in the 'democratization of diamonds.'

Rather than focusing on the purchasing power of the new rich, this chapter provides a contextual assessment of jewelry and precious metals in the consumer economy through interrelated conditions of consumption and production. First, it introduces the idea of 'maximalism,' or the conditions and representations of spectacular production and consumption, as a basis for generating popular perspectives on style, desire and demand and for understanding some particular characteristics of evolving consumerism in the PRC. Next, the focus shifts to 'Golden Week,' or the three week long Chinese holidays, to contextualize the realities and experiences of luxury shopping, and how the market for jewelry has grown and in relation to decreasing demand for traditional 24-carat gold or *chuk kam*, 99 percent pure gold jewelry and ornaments. The transformation is explained through the new mobility of the affluent and middle classes and their evolving sites of leisure consumption, which necessarily incorporates travel to Hong Kong as the PRC consumer's primary 'overseas' shopping destination. Finally, the widespread consumption of diamond jewelry could not be taking place without the 'democratization of diamonds,' the proliferation of diamond jewelry with small stones and related expansion of jewelry manufacturing and retail firms. In this process, the role of the financially independent professional woman and the young female consumer in purchasing their own diamond jewelry is contributing to market expansion.

These explanations—finding the rising demand for diamonds in replacement goods for traditional gold purchases and the regionalization of consumerism and jewelry brands—contrast with global industry claims that De Beers International diamond group developed the diamond market in the PRC through advertising and retail promotion (Harris and Cai 2002). The central state and municipal governments are also involved in supporting the long-term growth of the industry through the establishment of preferential economic policies, including an international diamond-trading center and proposed diamond and gold jewelry shopping districts in Shanghai.

'Maximalism' and the demand for diamonds

A stylistic exuberance has characterized consumption among the new rich in the mid-2000s, especially in Shanghai: a man orders a bouquet of 999 roses for a Valentine's Day gift at a cost of 35,000 *yuan*, while a Shanghai luxury goods fair promotes a diamond-encrusted mobile phone for 3.5 million *yuan*. The Shanghai-based online company www.Gem21.com highlights its auctions with advertisements for extraordinarily large and colorful diamonds, while the mainstream press makes a representational spectacle of its events: 'A 19.305-carat natural diamond 'Siam Star' will debut at an auction in Shanghai ... with a price estimated at over ten million *yuan* (about 1.25 million U.S. dollars), the most "precious" natural diamond in the Shanghai auction history' (*Xinhua* 12 January 2006).

The Pudong Shangri-la Hotel widely advertises a luxury Valentine's Day package at a cost of 388,000 *yuan*, which includes dinner, a deluxe suite, diamond jewelry, Cartier watches, massage-for-two and a fireworks display. Stanley Ho Hung-sun, the casino mogul of Macau, acquires a 218-carat diamond to be placed on display in his new casino-hotel, the Grand Lisboa. When asked about the value or cost of the stone, Mr. Ho allows: 'It's a matter of hundreds of millions. Just think of it – some one-carat diamonds are worth over US$100,000 and their prices keep rising' (Ho in Hu 2007). Because of its size and significance – the second largest flawless D-colored diamond in the world – Mr. Ho can officially name the diamond as a matter of record with the Gemological Institute of America: The Star of Stanley Ho.

While most diamond and precious metal jewelry purchases in the PRC are small, a trend toward what may be called 'maximalism' – in which size reflects not only the product or thing consumed but also symbolizes the competitiveness and achievements of institutions (as the person, firm, city and nation) and their cultural economic characteristics (economic success, high-style and global competitiveness) – has swept the media economy around contemporary consumption.[2] Some reality drives the hyperbole: large, flawless diamonds appreciated in the early 2000s, and are more contemporary and highly concentrated forms of wealth than traditional purchases of *chuk kam*, which have long characterized individual and household-based precious metal consumption. Indeed, increased demand for large flawless diamonds in Asia is driving up prices for the best stones (Forden 2006; Interviews 2007). Such trends are likely not so much what is 'Chinese' about consumption (Latham 2006) but rather expressions of economic power in an era of rapid economic growth. Neither is maximalism a set of sustained practices, since open flaunting of wealth has periodically become a contentious issue and hotly debated in the PRC press (Rosen 2004: 159–60). As 'large' purchases, fine jewelry is typically not publicly flaunted but worn in private circumstances and as one investment choice for the new rich.

The significance and value of extraordinary gems is constructed and conferred in diverse local and global sites. Shanghai and Hong Kong are China's major centers of fine jewelry consumption, while they are also connected through networks of production and historic and contemporary circulations of leisure culture and industry capital. In the arena of maximalism – spheres of production and consumption of the best, brightest, largest and most valuable gems – one of these sites is the auction house. Not the online activities of 21 Gem, but the one with elite pedigree and global reach. In this arena, Christie's and Sotheby's both serve China through Hong Kong where Christie's especially handles fine jewelry. In 2005, a Christie's auction at the Hong Kong Convention and Exhibition Centre contributed to a new annual high in the firm's jewelry sales (Blauer 2007). The outstanding lot was a 42.21-carat yellow diamond, which received a high bid of $2.62 million from a Hong Kong buyer, while Mainland Chinese bidders acquired seven of the ten most expensive lots. More than a new high in jewelry prices, the press reported the event in cultural economic terms of fine art. Indeed, it was a 'rare art market event. ... Jewelry is now looked at as an art form, not just an accumulation of precious stones' (Melikian 2005). The idea of fine craftsmanship in precious metal working and jewelry-as-art is not new, while intensification of interest in internationally significant gems from buyers in the PRC is significant.

Events featuring spectacular gems, jewelry and art coalesced in Shanghai in the early 2000s. In 2004, 'The Art of Cartier' appeared at the Shanghai Museum – the distinctive building in the shape of a Shang dynasty *ding*, a legged ritual vessel, in People's Square in central Shanghai whose permanent exhibits include a range of Chinese antiquities. This show of jewelry-as-art media, which toured to Tokyo and Singapore in addition to several European and North American world cities, featured historic gems and large named stones such as The Star of Africa and commissioned pieces for members of the European aristocracy. 'The Art of Cartier' preceded by a few months the spectacular ceremonial opening of Cartier's flagship PRC store at Bund 18, the renovated neoclassical building originally designed by Palmer & Turner for the Chartered Bank of Australia, India and China in the 1920s. The opening event, attended by a vice-mayor of Shanghai and stars of the Chinese film and fashion industries, was heralded across the city by a blimp that rode above the Huangpu River blazing 'Cartier' in lights, while the Australian large format projection specialists, The Electric Canvas (2004), transformed the building façade into a night-time light sculpture in Cartier motifs. The conservation of Bund 18, designed by the Italian architect Fillipo Gabbiani and Kokaistudios, led to a UNESCO Asia-Pacific Heritage Award of Distinction and international recognition for adaptive reuse of a historic building. A mixed-use commercial development, the project includes Bund 18 Creative Center, a noncommercial contemporary art space directed by a professional curatorial staff whose opening exhibit in 2005, 'Frozen Feelings – An Emotional Market,' showed a multi-media installation by French artist Maurice Benayoun, which was one of many events of the 'Year of France in China' official international exchange (*China Daily* 9 October 2004).

Sponsorship of cultural events and the promotion of luxury goods in association with cultural sites is becoming a high-profile strategy for luxury goods firms in China's world cities. The positioning of luxury goods brands in such commercial-cultural spaces seeks to re-differentiate the luxury object from the so-called democratization of designer brands, which has characterized world city consumerism since the late twentieth century (Thomas 2007). In a world of designer names on t-shirts, and fake watches and copy-bags, the luxury goods firm is seeking to recover its distinction and reinstantiate the exceptional qualities of its products in the eyes of elite and aspirational consumers. Such strategies are taking place in prominent sites of historic authenticity and leisure experience, places where visitors encounter the luxury brand in association with unquestionable sites of world-class significance. In 2004, 'Watches and Wonders,' an exhibit of ten European luxury brands, including Cartier, appeared inside the Forbidden City's fifteenth century Tai Miao (Imperial Ancestral Temple), while 'the last descendent of the imperial family, the brother of Pu Yi, the last Chinese emperor, was entrusted with the calligraphy for the exhibition' (Mailliard 2004). Industry and Beijing government officials prevailed at the opening, where *métiers d'art* demonstrated watch-making, precious metal craft and diamond setting. The exhibit presented hundreds of historic mechanical watches, which resonated with the Forbidden City's own Watches and Clocks Museum in the Feng Xian Tian (Chamber of Serving the Ancestors) and the Qing imperial court's known interest in European timepieces, followed by an area for 'brands to receive visitors and guests in a more private setting' (Mailliard 2004). Thus the exhibit mixed commercial and historical genres of encounter, placing the visitor in the symbolic position of reception at the imperial court to consider acquisition of a fabulous object, as if a unique opportunity and singular experience, where the material resonance of hundreds of years of Sino-Western exchange might be purchased for mere thousands of *yuan*.

Through news media, business advertising and public exhibitions, the circulation of information about these events brings to common knowledge the rise of demand for fine jewelry and diamonds among the new rich and aspirational consumers. Exposure to such information arguably develops more general demand for such 'positional goods' (Hirsch 1976) through 'demonstration effects' (Frank 1985) and their reverberations in different arenas of society. However, actual purchases of such European brand name luxury goods grew slowly in the early 2000s (Croll 2006: 317–22); while recent reports suggest that a luxury goods market is growing among 20- and 30-something year olds new rich in major cities (*Beijing Youth Daily* 19 July 2005), an age group that is younger than luxury goods consumers in developed regions.

Ultimately, what is important to luxury goods industry interests is that while the PRC consumed 13 percent of the world's luxury goods in 2004, compared to 40 percent in Japan, Japan's share is dropping and within a decade the two countries are expected to become relatively even in their total consumption share (Brown-Humes 2005). These figures, from Goldman Sachs' equity research division, and presented at the 'Financial Times 'Business of Luxury' Summit' in Shanghai in 2005, predict that by 2015 the PRC will rank first among countries in luxury goods consumption. However, the figures do not represent that over 80 percent of what is counted as the PRC's luxury goods consumption is from non-domestic purchases, which includes Hong Kong – and thus the role of places at a distance in the evolution of cultural economies of consumption (James 1987).

'Golden Week'

European designer shops fill Hong Kong's major malls and line several streets in the city's Central District, yet shoppers encounter the city's famous jewelry stores in greatest concentration along Nathan Road in Mongkok – a streetscape where gold and diamonds glitter through the windows and the Mandarin dialect or national language (*putonghua*) is an increasingly common language of exchange. 'Golden Week' is an economic opportunity for the retail sector in Hong Kong while its official origins are in Beijing, in the government policy to promote consumerism and development of a national market based on household consumption. Citizens of the PRC have historically saved too much to generate a consumption-driven economy, and the government wants them to go out and spend (Croll 2006,: 269–70). In 2000, the State Council and the National Tourism Administration announced three week-long holidays – commencing with Chinese New Year, the May 1 Labor Day holiday, and October 1 National Day, which have become prime times for domestic leisure and overseas tourism.[3] As a survey in five PRC cities (Beijing, Shanghai, Guangzhou, Chengdu and Dalian) by the Hong Kong Trade Development Council (HKTDC 2002: 1–2) confirmed, 'consumers have the habit of visiting jewelry shops, especially on holidays. The peak seasons occur at the three "golden weeks"' in both the PRC and Hong Kong, while 'consumers are interested in buying jewelry products in Hong Kong because of their wider selection of designs, reasonable prices and guaranteed quality.'

Outside the Mainland, Hong Kong is the most common destination for business and leisure travelers, and it is also the first city that most have sought to experience. 'Hong Kong and Macao are ... incubators for ... newly globe-trotting Chinese travelers. It is where the Chinese are taking their first tentative steps outside the mainland' (Greenlees 2005). In the late 1990s, when PRC elites began to hold passports and before leisure travel took-off, travel was primarily for business and Hong Kong was the primary destination (Croll 2006: 92–3). In the mid-2000s, three-quarters of PRC outbound travel was to Hong Kong and Macau, while Hong Kong's 40 percent of the national total accounts for just over half of the city's 23–25 million annual visitors (HKTB 2007c, 2007d). Under the 'one country, two systems' formula, the Hong Kong-Guangdong border remains controlled; but in July 2003, in the aftermath of the SARS crisis and in the wake of the 1997–99 financial downturn, Hong Kong and Beijing agreed to implement the Closer Economic Partnership Agreement (CEPA), which, among other products, allowed Hong Kong-made jewelry to enter the Mainland duty-free, and loosened up individual travel by creating the Individual Visit Scheme (IVS). Not unlike the geographical trajectory of reform itself, the IVS scheme was first available only to residents of the wealthy coastal cities in the Pearl River Delta, followed by Beijing and Shanghai. By 2007, the scheme included all 21 cities in Guangdong province, 3 cities each in Jiangsu, Zhejiang and Fujian provinces, 2 cities in Liaoning and 13 inland provincial capitals. Partly as a consequence, Hong Kong has become a relatively regular business and leisure destination for Pearl River Delta residents, while the Hong Kong Tourism Bureau (HKTB) (HKTB 2007a, 33) calls such multiple short journeys 'consumption visits.'

As Golden Week draws near, as many as 300,000 Mainland visitors enter Hong Kong on the preceding Friday, crushing the land border at Luohu (for example *Xinhua* 3 October 2004). Those who are on leisure journeys prefer to shop and spend little time in or money on hotels. While companies do not maintain sales data on individual customer place of origin, general figures for the mid-2000s hold that Mainland visitor expenditures on jewelry accounted for up to 50 percent of a firm's total sales during Golden Week (*Xinhua* 30 September. 2005; Horscroft 2007).

In Mongkok, Hong Kong jewelry stores Chow Tai Fook and Chow Sang Sang predominate and, among Mainland consumers, are the most popular and highly regarded, even by comparison to international and domestic brands (HKTDC 2002: 14), in part because of their strong regional lineage. Chow Tai Fook, which has two branches on Queen's Road Central, otherwise maintains six shops on Nathan Road in Mongkok. As Hong Kong's oldest and largest manufacturing and retail jewelry firm, having begun in Guangzhou in 1929, followed by a shop in Macau before locating in Hong Kong in 1939, it historically specialized in selling *chuk kam* and gained a leading reputation by establishing the 999.9 pure form of yellow gold that has become a standard. Chow Sang Sang, with four stores in Mongkok, also has roots in Guangzhou and moved to Hong Kong in 1948. In the late 1980s, these firms began shifting standardized design manufacturing into the Pearl River Delta, and now about 75–90 percent of a Hong Kong firms' productive capacity takes place in Panyu, Shunde and Shenzhen. In 1998 Chow Tai Fook opened its first PRC branch in Beijing (Chow Tai Fook 2006) and by mid-2007 the company had 500 jewelry stores, including at least one in each province, more than any other retail jewelry firm in the larger Greater China region.

Even as Hong Kong jewelry stores have been expanding in the PRC, its consumers have had many reasons for buying jewelry in Hong Kong. The port's tax-free status on import of precious metals and stones combined with local and regional production means that the cost of fine jewelry is lower than elsewhere in the region, while the city's regulated and service-oriented consumption environment provides assurance for expensive purchases. Its history as one of the few world gold commodity exchanges means that 24-carat gold is readily bought and sold even by individuals, so that a piece of jewelry or ornament may be sold back to rejuvenate discretionary and investment income. Hong Kong is also a major jewelry design center, and it is an industry strategy to differentiate stores and locations by limiting design availability, keeping the newest styles in Hong Kong and apportioning stock so that each shop shows about one-third unique merchandise. The discerning consumer knows this. In one group interview, a 30-year old professional woman from Shanghai explained that when she learned her father was going on business to Hong Kong, in 2002, she dispatched him with cash to purchase her diamond wedding ring. What mattered most to her was that the quality would be excellent and that the design would be up-to-date, and probably not available in the PRC. She had no primary interest in whether her fiancé purchased the ring or made a ritual presentation of it. Her story prompted an elderly woman originally from a small town in the Yangzi River Delta to recall how Shanghai served a similar function in the consumer's mental map in the pre-war era: if an uncle was making a journey to Shanghai your mother might ask him to buy a dress – from a distance what mattered most was that it came from Shanghai, that era's pinnacle of fashion.

The new rich have particular reasons for shopping in Hong Kong. Not unlike high technology production, the jewelry industry's latest designs and highest value products are still manufactured in the city by family-owned firms, including workshops in the high-rise Central District where stagger-ing rents are less consequential than maintaining proximate control and security over the largest stones. Even though this production environment is relatively small, it is a world where customers arrive on referral and they know that the best jewelry has always been crafted in platinum. While transactions involving rare stones, such as those auctioned through Chris-tie's, and The Star of Stanley Ho, are typically managed by intermediaries, the world of unique diamonds and custom-diamond jewelry is one in which the new rich often consume individually and directly. Another social milieu comes to light in this context: the so-called mistress culture of the Hong Kong-Shenzhen city-region, in the form of significant 'presents' for wives, which have little to do with normative gifting but rather the economic bar-gain in which a wife gains assets as if compensation for loss of a husband's fulltime presence in the form of spectacular jewelry. Principals of fine jew-elry firms insist that such social relations underpin a significant part of consumer demand for large stones among women from wealthy households, and across Asia (Interviews 2007).

Of course, gold has long had a particular resonance in Chinese society among all classes, and the importance of 24-carat gold jewelry among traditional household assets and in dowry wealth is well known, though practices concerning the use and transfer of jewelry-as-wealth are less well documented. Gates (1985: 263) notes that gifts of gold jewelry, especially the older forms made from softer gold, were 'the real money' and were not to be worn except on special occasions. It was possible for individual consumers to buy 24-carat gold jewelry in China as early as 1982, and later during the reform period, about 80 percent of the gold consumed in the PRC was in the form of jewelry (rather than gold bars and coins). Yet the People's Bank of China regulated the trade and only a few state-owned enterprises were permitted to manufacture, which yielded common designs – unappealing to the new rich. Deregulation of the gold market was projected to take place in association with continuing economic reforms and the PRC's membership in the World Trade Organization, but before the Shanghai Gold Exchange opened in 2002, and most barriers to gold trade were removed in 2003, gold jewelry in the PRC was subject to a VAT and a consumption tax that made local prices more than 20 percent higher than in Hong Kong (O'Connell 2003).

By comparison to the gold market, the trade in platinum was relatively unregulated in the PRC (Lee 2004; O'Connell 2003), and while the price of platinum is traditionally higher than gold, its perceived value alone makes it an investment target for the new rich. In the context of this shift, yellow gold color quickly came to be viewed as not only old fashioned, but also less precious. In 1992, the International Platinum Association introduced platinum products to the PRC (Courage 2004). By the late 1990s, branches of Hong Kong jewelry stores began appearing in major cities; and, in the context of the rising trend for platinum, white gold came to be accepted as a lower cost visual substitute. From a position of unremarkable consumption in the early 1990s, the PRC became the world number one consumer of platinum in 2002, displacing Japan (Han 2002). Considering the influence on Asian styles from Japan, where platinum and white gold have long been the preferred jewelry metals, it is reasonable to conjecture that Japan's role as a regional center of taste-making also influences jewelry consumption. Indeed, the HKTB (2002: 12) survey on jewelry consumption in Chinese cities shows how respondents in Shanghai, Beijing and Dalian, cities with relatively strong Japan connections, preferred platinum more than consumers in Guangzhou and Chengdu. Allowing for multiple responses, 68 percent of respondents overall chose platinum as the most highly desirable jewelry material, while only 30 percent chose *chuk kam* and 21 percent chose carat gold. In market research conducted by the London Bullion Market Association in 17 PRC cities in 2002, 26 percent of women interviewed responded that they already owned a piece of platinum jewelry (Courage 2004).

While consumer tastes and preferences for precious metals and fine jewelry have been shifting away from yellow gold toward silver-colored metals and with stones, especially diamonds, it would be wrong to suggest that the consumption of gold in the PRC is declining; rather it is declining in the form of consumption of yellow gold jewelry and by comparison to preference for consumption of platinum. In the mid-2000s the PRC was the third largest consumer of gold, after India and the US, and, after deregulation of the gold market, became the third largest producer in 2006 behind South Africa and the US, displacing Australia (*China Daily* 20 July 2007). In the mid-2000s the PRC consumed over 200 tons of gold and produced somewhat less, while gold industry analysts project its gold consumption to increase to as much as 600 tons by 2012 (*China Daily* 6 September 2004). Such increased gold consumption will be positive for the economy, according to the Bank of China (*China Daily* 25 September 2003), because significantly increased demand should increase gold imports, thereby cutting the foreign trade surplus, decreasing foreign exchange reserves and easing geopolitical pressure to let the *yuan* appreciate. Before the end of the third quarter 2007, the PRC's gold production had increased so much that analysts predicted it would become the largest producer in the world, displacing even South Africa (*Shanghai Daily* 17 September 2007).

The 'democratization of diamonds'

Several factors in the transformation of production and consumption of diamonds are combining to make diamond jewelry accessible to and desired by consumer groups who are not typically considered to share purchasing positions with the new rich and aspiring middle classes. This penultimate section considers changes that are turning the Chinese jewelry industry into an industrial regime with some mass production characteristics, and focuses on general trends in diamond consumption and especially the role of women in purchasing their own diamonds – a longstanding regional trend that is emerging in China and in association with leisure and discretionary consumption in Hong Kong.

On the production side, in addition to the conditions raised above, including the shift of Hong Kong-based firms to the PRC and the deregulation of markets in precious metals, key suppliers in the world diamond trade are partnering with manufacturing firms in China. In addition to the entry of the Diamond Trading Company (DTC), the distribution subsidiary of De Beers Group, diamond trading and manufacturing firms from Belgium, India and Israel – traditional centers of diamond cutting and polishing – have been locating in the PRC, where they find the production environment less bureaucratic and the market for diamonds growing faster than in India (Arole 1999; Hasan 2006). In addition to Chow Tai Fook and Chow Sang Sang, some of these firms are DTC Sightholders (the highly restricted number of firms to which the De Beers cartel sells rough diamonds), and all fall under the Kimberly Process Certification Scheme, the international agreement established in 2002 that seeks to prevent conflict diamonds from entering the regulated trade. The PRC established the Shanghai Diamond Exchange in 2000, became a member of the Kimberly Scheme in 2003, and is seeking to increase diamond import and processing. On 1 July 2006, under power of the Ministry of Finance, the State Administration of Taxation and the General Administration of Customs, the value added tax on imported uncut diamonds was abolished and the tax rate on imported refined diamonds was lowered from 17 to 4 percent, in a move reported to address 'widespread smuggling;' in the first quarter of 2007, the PRC's import of diamonds increased 170 percent over first quarter of 2006 (*Xinhua* 28 April 2007). Thus, the development of more favorable conditions for the production and consumption of diamonds and fine jewelry has central state coordination and provincial-level management oversight, with Shanghai as the international trading center. In 2007, the Shanghai Gold Exchange began to allow individual consumers to purchase, keep and trade gold bullion (*Shanghai Daily* 26 June 2007).

The role of Shanghai as a center of trade in diamonds and precious metals is also evident in the planning and development of the consumer landscape. In 2006, the local government of Huangpu District, the area behind the Bund whose major axis is Nanjing Road, announced a '5–3' plan for a redevelopment of retail shopping with a focus on fine jewelry and diamonds (*Shanghai Morning Post* 17 June 2006). The '5' stands for five gold consumption areas, while '3' refers to three jewelry design and production zones. The plan for retail development names five concentrated areas of jewelry shopping, including parts of the Nanjing Road pedestrian street, the Jiangan Temple area and the old West Gate neighborhood. The three design areas would encompass existing municipal facilities, namely the

Shanghai Urban Industrial Design Center and the Shanghai Tourist Souvenirs and Handicrafts Design Center, and develop a new tourist exhibition site dedicated to demonstration of stone processing and jewelry manufacture for the new diamond consumer. In 2002, the Huangpu District government was already working with the Shanghai office of the US consulting firm McKinsey to plan the revitalization of Nanjing Road by 'bringing in international brands while phasing out the outmoded businesses' (Woetzel in Thorne 2002). This integrated production-consumption environment for diamond jewelry is also evident in coordinated advertising campaigns in Hong Kong and Shanghai by Chow Tai Fook and the Hong Kong Tourism Board.

On a construction wall hemming the sidewalk along People's Avenue, where it cuts across People's Square in central Shanghai, Karen Mok gazes out from an end-on-end row of advertisements. Large format ads from the same 2006–07 advertising campaign could be found in any one of a number of MTR or subway stations in Hong Kong, as well as along Nathan Road in Mongkok. Karen Mok is an acclaimed Hong Kong-born actress and a pop star in Greater China, as well as being Karen Joy Morris, her birth name, in Hollywood film. She embodies a certain cosmopolitan iconicity of global possibilities for young women: successful and unmarried in her late 30s (while looking 20-something in the ad copy), she appears thoroughly self-possessed, in charge, sexy and solo – indeed, possibly man-free. She is the celebrity representative of Chow Tai Fook's Achievement Collection and its 'Love Yourself, Buy It for Yourself' tagline. As considerable market

Advertisement, Nathan Road, Mongkok (photograph by the author)

research by the diamond and jewelry industry confirms (HKTDC 2002; Hudson 2007), women in Asia commonly buy their own fine jewelry and so the industry markets directly to their independent decision-making.

The basic profile of the average PRC visitor (either business or leisure) to Hong Kong in 2006 was clear. *She* (57 percent of Mainland visitors in 2006 were women) was in her mid-thirties, married, college educated and employed (HKTB 2007b). She was on a single-destination repeat vacation to Hong Kong, came with friends or family members and did not join a tour group. Her primary activity was shopping, and her primary items of purchase were clothing, shoes and fine jewelry. She was from Guangdong, most likely Guangzhou or Shenzhen, and otherwise from Shanghai or Beijing. Indeed, the HKTB's consumption tourism growth strategy focuses on 'young offices ladies' from the Pearl River and Yangzi River deltas (HKTB 2007c). The HKTB also promotes Hong Kong as a consumer destination for women through a celebrity television series, featuring Karen Mok, Jacky Chan, Andy Lau, Fu Mingxia and Ding Lei, which has shown in Mainland cities that are party to the IVS scheme (HKTB 2007a: 36). During 2005–07, one campaign featured Karen Mok for the Shopper of the Year Contest and the annual Hong Kong Shopping Festival, which target women through images of latest-trend shopping and cosmopolitan lifestyle. Theses events are also advertised through China UnionPay, (the bank card network established in China in 2002, launched in Shanghai), so consumers receive direct marketing information about Hong Kong shopping through ATM or bank account use in the Mainland.

Chow Tai Fook's Achievement Collection represents an aspirational luxury for young women because it features larger diamonds (minimum 0.3 carats) than typical purchases, which are 0.01 – 0.15 carats. Indeed, the average price of most diamond jewelry sold in the Mainland during the early and mid-2000s was under 1,000 *yuan* (2000 *yuan* in Shanghai), including gifts purchased for Valentine's Day (HKTDC 2002: 15; Yuan 2005). Thus with growth rates for fine jewelry consumption in China at 15–20 percent per year (*China Daily* 30 January 2007; Hasan 2006) most consumption will be for small diamonds. Diamond jewelry manufacturers in the Pearl River Delta set mostly small stones and, whether in Hong Kong or in Mainland cities, women are the primary consumers for these relatively affordable pieces. Industry origins of this low-cost diamond jewelry market are in the early 1990s in Hong Kong, where MaBelle, one of the city's more ubiquitous fine jewelry brands, explicitly sought to overcome the historic view that diamonds are 'luxurious and unreachable' by popularizing the 'everyday life diamond' and the HK$1,000 diamond ring (MaBelle 2005). Wearing diamond jewelry on an everyday basis has not yet spread widely to Mainland cities, but the trend is alive; and such democratization of diamonds will also evolve in the context of increased demand for diamond wedding rings. Survey research on diamond wedding ring acquisition by DTC China for De Beers Group shows that four out of ten Chinese brides received a diamond ring in 2006, while numbers are significantly higher in Shanghai and Beijing (Hudson 2007). However, use habits suggest that diamond wedding rings tend to be viewed as a form of wedding equity not unlike dowry gifts (*China Daily* 30 January 2007). When asked directly about wearing jewelry, several women interviewed for this project in Shanghai said that they had diamond wedding rings but wore them only on special occasions; they kept them stored at home, in a manner that reflects historic habits of keeping *chuk kam*. Nevertheless, when asked what is their most highly desired luxury item, 48 percent of women in China ranked diamond jewelry number one, apparently second in the world only to Hong Kong, at 61 percent (Hudson 2007).

A tale of two cities

In setting forth some basic contextual conditions of the production and consumption of fine jewelry in China, we can see how the role of particular cities and their cultural and economic connections underpin the growth and transformation of the jewelry industry and its rise as a focus of consumption interest among the new rich. Hong Kong's position as the capital of jewelry design and manufacturing in Asia in the second half of the twentieth century, combined with its firms' manufacturing base in the Pearl River Delta and the proliferation of Hong Kong jewelry brands across PRC cities, demonstrates regional origins of the jewelry industry and its development across the country at large. Rising consumer interest in fine jewelry has also grown in the context of the Hong Kong shopping trip and especially in association with the experiences of millions of women, and their demonstration effects, who hone their tastes in the latest styles through multiple leisure trips to trend-setting destinations. While multinational corporate marketing analysis credits De Beers Groups with building a market for diamond jewelry in the PRC, the reality is that what the industry calls the self-purchase market, especially purchases by women for themselves, was already strong in Asia. When the question of what is 'Chinese' about consumption is considered, the contemporary demand for the highest quality metals and the best stones suggests that contemporary consumption of fine jewelry reflects historic practices of keeping *chuk kam*, including as dowry gifts.

Shanghai under reform has reclaimed its role as a center of consumer culture and business leadership, no less so in the fine jewelry industry. The city now serves as a base for internationalized metals trade and diamond trading, and while it is premature to suggest the larger trajectory of jewelry production and consumption growth in China, it is clear that the industry base in Shanghai will assume greater significance. The focus of European luxury goods brands on urban China and the Shanghai market particularly reflects a certain excitement about the city's potential consumer culture, rather than realities of contemporary consumption practices. Yet, based on surveys of travel destination interest, Europe is the number one region that

PRC travelers desire to experience. So European brands such as Cartier are seeking to tap this interest domestically while reinstantiating the meaning of 'true' luxury goods in the collective mind of the new rich and in the face of the proliferation of low-cost fine jewelry. It is also premature to draw conclusions about the impact of China's rising demand for precious metals and diamonds on world markets, yet it is clear that industry analysts already interpret rising prices in relation to increased demand from the PRC.

Notes

1   Information in this chapter includes data from interviews carried out in Hong Kong and Shanghai in 2006 and 2007, which were supported in part by a US CIES-Fulbright Fellowship, held in the Department of Geography at Hong Kong Baptist University. Normal protocols of informant anonymity are maintained. Hong Kong Baptist University student Joanne Yuen-yi Lo conducted preliminary research for the project.
2   This strategy is also reflected in the contemporary PRC trend especially in smaller cities to generate recognition and publicity by staging a mass activity that will gain a place in the *Guinness Book of World Records* (*Southern Weekend* 17 August 2007).
3   At the end of 2007, the State Council designated additional national holidays and shortened the May Day Golden Week to three days.

12 Issue-based politics

Feminism with Chinese characteristics or the return of bourgeois feminism?

Louise Edwards

The emergence of the new rich in the PRC was no accident of the liberal-ising economic system. Rather, it was a conscious consequence of CCP design. The CCP has been instrumental in providing the economic and social structures required for the creation of this wealth, and as well-schooled Marxists, the Party leadership no doubt realised that such a fundamental change in the economic substructure would produce equivalent dramatic shifts in the superstructure of culture, ideology and politics. Scholars and commentators expended considerable energies during the 1990s exploring whether the emergence of this would indeed generate demand for liberal democracy. It quickly became apparent through cross-national studies that the new rich have had no difficulty cooperating with a full range of government structures: from democratic through to author-itarian (Robison and Goodman 1996b: 2–3). However, research findings also showed that while the economic reforms propelling wealth creation did not always produce a USA-style political system, they have produced change in the relationship between the ordinary people and the state (Saich 2000).

In the case of China, recent scholarship has explained this new relation-ship as being one typified by the Party-state's greater flexibility (Gries and Rosen 2004), increased tolerance of dissent (Wright 2004) and more dex-terous cooption of disparate interests groups (Dickson 2004). A central question emerging from this work has been to explore the mechanisms buttressing the CCP's claims to legitimacy as the sole ruling group for the nation. Vivienne Shue suggests that the CCP's central legitimatising plat-form is their perceived ability to maintain order and stability while produ-cing economic growth (Shue 2004). Perry and Goldman (2007) argue that the need for the CCP to curb official corruption and enhance accountability is central to upholding both the appearance and reality of this social stability.

For the CCP, legitimacy is routinely supported by explicitly theorised political philosophy that is disseminated not only to Party members but also to the broad mass of the population. The CCP has retreated from explicit direct control of the economy since 1978 but it has not resiled from its self-appointed position as ideological guide for the nation. Dickson (2004: 142)

has noted that in the reform period the CCP still constructs and dis-
seminates ideological rationales for policy decisions as they have since the
PRC state was founded in 1949. Thus, the desired social order with economic growth and the emergence of the new rich is presented as being
embedded within an overarching philosophy of grand CCP-design. The raft
of legitimising maxims accompanying the reform campaign such as 'The
Four Modernizations', 'Socialism with Chinese Characteristics' and 'The
Three Represents' stands as evidence of this imperative.[1] This process of
establishing philosophical rationales for policy shifts provides historical
and intellectual weight to the CCP's increasingly technocratic pragmatism
while still allowing ideological change. They are designed to reduce challenges
to the fundamental principle underpinning governance in China – the
continuation of the CCP's sole rule.

The new rich have emerged as significant new political forces within this
context of a CCP-led philosophy of rational design that has produced
radical economic change and increasing flexibility in state-society interaction. Apart from their direct involvement in elite provincial and national
government systems as well as CCP politics, the new rich appear within a
dynamic sector of the Chinese political scene, loosely called 'issue politics'.
Through a case study of the politics of the women's movement since the late
1970s, this chapter argues that issue politics are emerging as an important
new feature of the twenty-first century Chinese political scene as a direct
result of the emergence of the new rich. Individuals and organisations are
cooperating and mobilising to effect change in CCP policy on matters of
local or sectoral concern without seeking the overthrow of the Party's
monopoly on power. The new rich promote stability for the political and
economic status quo (since it produces the very wealth they presently enjoy)
and simultaneously avoid the unwelcome punitive attention of the
authoritarian Party-state.

The CCP is far from threatened by these issue politics. The very segmentation of the problems addressed in issue politics implies the authority and
legitimacy of the overarching moral, social and political order. The fragmentation of campaigns into bite-size problems not only makes them
appear solvable but also confirms the need for a strong political structure to
implement any required changes. Just as contesting Provincial interests in
China confirm and invigorate awareness of the PRC as a Nation rather than
fragmenting it, activism around issues of sexual or domestic violence or sex-
based exploitation confirms the need for more Law and Order, more structure and ultimately more government. Therese Wright shows that the activism on labour issues reflects a similar trend towards fragmenting social
problems and presenting them as isolated incidents rather than symptoms
of broad systemic inequities. For example, discrete cases of worker exploitation (unpaid wages, dangerous work conditions) can be raised within the
broad context of recognition of the Party-state's role in correcting these
deviations from official policy. Wright presents this phenomenon as a

'pressure release valve' (2004: 136) that helps keep social order by reducing the potential for mass revolt by millions of oppressed workers. However, it is also a far deeper feature of the political structure of the Communist Party-state – incumbency provides the Party-state with scope for encouraging multiple sites for enhancing popular engagement with and ultimately a sense of ownership of the current system. The publicity given 'isolated incidents' of worker exploitation or the execution of 'individual' corrupt cadres, function like the maxim that runs 'the exception proves the rule'. They are essentially presented as isolated cases that confirm the status quo.

To explore the phenomenon of newly emergent issue-based politics, this chapter examines the transformation in the Chinese women's movement during the reform period. The evolution of the movement is an excellent example of the shift in relationships between the Party-state, various government and non-governmental organisations and individual PRC citizens (Howell 2003). But most importantly, as a major social campaign that has been sustained over a number of decades, the efforts to enhance the status of women in the PRC provides a case study of the way issue politics are emerging as significant forces within the Chinese body politic. China's women activists are not seeking fundamental change in CCP-control of China, but they are seeking to influence the way their society functions. Inequality between men and women is presented as a series of loosely linked issues rather than as part of the broader problem of the resilience of patriarchal structures under socialism or the inadequacy of CCP leadership.

Communist women versus bourgeois feminists

Political activism advancing women's rights relative to men's has a lengthy history in China. This feature makes the women's movement a particularly useful case study for monitoring the pulse of Chinese politics. In addition, because privileged women – largely urban-based and educated – have dominated the Chinese women's movement from its inception in the last decades of the nineteenth century through to the present, it provides scope for the exploration of the changes in the connection between privilege and politics. And the new rich are nothing if not privileged.

The first decades of the Chinese women's movement focussed on inequities that privileged women faced in comparison to their brothers, such as equal access to political rights, inheritance and education (Edwards 2008a). Winning equality with men in marriage, divorce and adultery laws also featured significantly. Like vanguard movements seeking fundamental social change, they also fought on behalf of their less privileged sisters for parity with men in work and wages. The membership base of the women's movement broadened over the course of the first three decades of the twentieth century to include a wider cross section of the urban population. But with the formation of the CCP in 1921, feminist politics were seen increasingly through the lens of European Marxism's deep suspicion and disdain of 'bourgeois feminists'.

The dismissal of women's activism for women's equal rights as 'bourgeois feminism' was imported to China directly from Europe along with the core of Marxist philosophy. Boxer has explored the origins and impact of 'bourgeois feminism' as a concept within an international and historical context. She notes that it emerged first with Clara Zetkin in 1889 with her promotion of the idea that the 'woman question' would only be solved by a Communist revolution. Such a revolution would change the relationship between labour and capital in ways that a bourgeois women's movement could never achieve. This position soon became a foundational principle for Socialist and Communist parties and persists up to the present day (Boxer 2007). The CCP's adoption of this policy promised myriad benefits for their then-small political party. The bulk of publicly politically active women in China in the 1910s and 1920s were located and organised within the women's rights movement. The CCP sought to attract these women, with their extensive organisational and networking skills, to the communist movement. CCP advocates publicly denounced non-CCP women activism as a waste of effort and a diversion of talents (Xiang Jingyu 1923). At the same time, they sought to invite these same bourgeois women to participate in CCP-led activities in order to harness their skills (Goodman 2000; Gilmartin 1995).

While many active feminists in China joined the Communist cause and allied their interests to the goal of achieving a class-based revolution those that prioritised the campaign for women's rights had to contend with the dismissive accusation that they were 'bourgeois feminists' seeking a limited and elitist political change. Moreover, women that sought to promote greater sex equality within the CCP structures and operations frequently faced the stern criticism that they were lapsing into 'bourgeois feminism'. Some women, such as the writer Ding Ling, who was severely criticised for this stance in 1942 (Ding Ling 1942: 317–21) suffered repeatedly over the ensuing decades for their ideological 'deviation'.

To achieve the goal of drawing women activists to their cause, the CCP established a central Women's Bureau and Women's Associations in every locality under their control to specifically address the special problems of women. The cadres allocated work within these spheres were undertaking CCP sanctioned 'woman's work' (Edwards 2004). The duties of this portfolio included mobilising women for the CCP agenda as well as raising literacy and knowledge of equal rights principles among women. However, the disdain with which feminist advocacy was held among the CCP camp cast a pall over the entire project of 'women's work'. Women communists frequently complained that they were 'relegated to' or 'trapped in' women's work ('Funü yingdang' 1939). The Ding Ling example noted above shows that the CCP's contradictory policies of inviting feminists into their cause and then corralling women's activism within the 'women's work' rubric constrained both feminism and socialism.

The CCP's suspicion of and active disdain for non-CCP led women's movements continued for the remainder of the twentieth century. After the establishment of the PRC in 1949, the Party transformed its Women's Bureau into the All China Women's Federation (ACWF). The existence of the ACWF was regarded as obviating the need for any independent or antagonistic feminist movements since the ACWF was deemed to address all significant special problems for women and girls. Wang Zheng (2006) describes the ACWF members as 'state feminists'. Jude Howell writes: 'The ACWF became the sole officially recognized organization for representing women's interests ... [with] the dual role of transmitting Party policy, interests and perspectives downwards to women, while simultaneously reflecting the needs and interest of women upwards' (Howell 2003: 192–93). In effect, between 1949 and the mid-1980s, the ACWF was primarily a conduit for disseminating CCP policy to the women masses, rather than an advocate for women.[2] China's 'state feminists' of the PRC drew a clear line between themselves and their 'bourgeois' predecessors throughout the decades of engagement with the Party-state.

The economic and political reforms that have occurred since 1978 have produced scope for novel roles for China's 'state feminists' and significantly they have also created space for women's activism outside of ACWF control. The ACWF commenced energetic lobbying on behalf of women in the post reform years and new groups also emerged to promote social change on specific aspects of women's interest. Much of the style and scope of these groups would in earlier periods have been dismissed as a dead-end, dangerously distracting bourgeois feminism. The new rich would have been titled China's new bourgeoisie and their version of feminism regarded as 'bourgeois' and therefore threatening to the overall CCP discourse of legitimate governance. However, the emergence of a political space for issue-based politics since the middle of the 1990s has enabled China's women's movement to maintain and even extend its credibility and effectiveness within broader Chinese political and social spheres. They have achieved this new position while simultaneously avoiding the political problems of being labelled 'bourgeois feminists'.

The women's movement in post-reform China

Issue-based political activism emerged in the 1990s with the government-sponsored movement to encourage the growth of 'social organizations' that would serve to take on the community welfare tasks the state was no longer performing and also as a response to the intrusion of international NGOs into China's development policy mix. These social organisations addressed specific social problems or dealt with localised issues. Accordingly, the special problems of women in the transformation to market-socialism became a focus of widespread attention from international aid agencies, new social organisations and the ACWF. The 1990s was a period of rapid growth in the phenomenon of 'women organizing' for women's issues (Hsiung, Jaschok *et al.*, 2001; Milwertz 2002).

Some of the issues these groups highlighted were clearly results of the economic shifts: extensive rural-urban migration; unemployment caused by the closure of state owned enterprises; exploitation caused by unregulated private ownership of workplaces; and the need for increasingly technology-based skills from a previously largely rural workforce. All of these problems affected men as well as women but the ACWF and associated agencies targeted the specific problems women faced in this environment. For example, they ran training courses for unemployed or rural women and provided advice on establishing small businesses specifically aimed at women. The overarching goal was to enable women to engage more fully with the new economy and to gain personal benefits that otherwise might not accrue. The major groups within this sphere, dominated as it is by the ACWF, are welfare agencies and self-help groups. For example, the 'Working Sisters' Club' in Beijing provides support for rural women working in Beijing and emerged from the activities of journalist-activists producing the magazine *Rural Women Knowing All* (Nongjianü baishitong) (Jacka 2000). The magazine is sponsored by the ACWF and is dedicated to enhancing skills, knowledge and opportunities for rural migrants to China's urban areas. Women active in this sphere are by no means restricted to the urban new rich. Rural women are an integral part of this aspect of the women's movement, albeit often with considerable support and organisational leadership from the urban elites, like those in the ACWF.

However, China's women's groups also addressed a number of problems that did not have direct links to economic liberalisation policies: domestic violence; sexual assault; the kidnapping of women and girls; female infanticide; the buying and selling of women and girls; commercialised sex; and sexual harassment. These problems are not new to the post-reform period and have deep historical roots. But the novel feature in the post-reform period is that they are now publicly discussed rather than remaining burdens of private grief or shame and conceptualised as 'remnants of feudalism' that would be remedied as socialism progressed. In response to the greater willingness to discuss these sex-related problems domestic violence hotlines, women's legal and health services and research groups emerged. The ACWF has become a sponsor or supervisory organisation for many of these newly formed groups and is sometimes directly involved as well. Prime among semi-autonomous or autonomous bodies are groups like the DV-Net (Domestic Violence Network) that aims to bring diverse professional groups together to improve service delivery on issues of family disputes and violence. Other groups within this category include the Maple Women's Psychological Counseling Centre, Women's Media Watch Network, and the Legal Advice Centre. The membership of this segment of the women's movement is more clearly privileged with education, wealth and status. They routinely have professional training, and strong links to international and national bodies.

A further development in the sphere of women's activism has been the emergence of women and gender studies courses within the Higher Education sector. Since the mid-1980s China has rapidly developed its Higher Education sector (Walder 2006: 16–17). Accompanying this broad sectoral growth there has been a proliferation of research institutes and courses on women's studies and gender issues established around the country. Beginning in 1985 with the establishment of Zhengzhou University's Women's Studies Institute, many major universities in China now offer courses relating to women and gender (Li Xiaojiang and Zhang Xiaodan 1994: 141; Wang Zheng 1997).[3] These courses and the publicity they generated across campuses and in the media provided China's educated classes with access to fresh visions of the connection between women and the state, and women and men that extend beyond the orthodox Marxist notion that the problems of women would be solved by class struggle or transformations in the relationship between labour and capital.[4]

The areas that have become fashionable in this feminism are sex and sexuality studies, and identity politics. A dynamic and fluid group of new activists has emerged from around these institutional structures – younger women who adopt public campaigns to address controversial and sensational issues such as sexual violence and deep-seated discrimination against women and girls. Ad hoc groups such as the V-day activists that mobilise around the performance of Eve Ensler's *Vagina Monologues* (1998) and its anti-Violence against Women message are typical of this type of activism. They link themselves directly to global, high profile and glamorous campaigns on topics of a risqué nature (Bu Wei and Mi Xiaolan 2005; Edwards 2008a). Theirs is not a feminism of the ACWF welfare-style; rather it is antagonistic, confrontational and demanding of public and peer attention. The membership of this group lies primarily within the demographic cohort that can be labelled the new rich. The young women featuring in this grassroots level activism are students privileged with time, space, money and intellectual energies to risk potential displeasure of their peers, parents and teachers.

Political significance of the new style women's movement

The increasing number of the organisations mobilised around women's issues and the wider nature of the problems addressed by these women's groups in the post-reform years has broad political significance for understanding the PRC. Often, the phenomenon is regarded as evidence of increasing democratisation or the emergence of an expanding civil society. Jude Howell asserts that the evolution of women's activism provides a 'useful barometer for gauging the shifting power relations between Party-state and non-governmental actors' (Howell 2003: 208). She notes that they reveal an increasing intellectual and organisational space for political actors outside of the Party-state, but also the increasingly sophisticated reflection on gender issues beyond the straight Marxian paradigm.

Going beyond Howell's observations though, it would seem that the particular space being created rests primarily around issue-based politics, for example around such matters of sexual violence or trafficking in women and girls, and that addressing these issues fundamentally buttress the political and economic status quo. They are challenging patriarchal privilege but they are not challenging the CCP's control of China or the CCP's vision for economic reform. Activism on women's issues of rape or female infanticide is framed within the rubric of either redressing injustices or correcting abnormal phenomenon or illegal acts. The underlying moral code is one of consolidation with the status quo and restoring a putative 'lost' law and order. Similarly, in regards to the women's various efforts to address economic problems such as women's unemployment and lack of training; women's support; and mobilisation to increase women's personal wealth and skills base all fundamentally aim to consolidate the economic reform policies not undermine them. These initiatives aim to further integrate women into the CCP-led economic miracle and ensure their support for the system by creating a sense of investment in and a sharing of the benefit from its success.

The new rich, with their purchasing power, education skills, demands for diversion, aspirations to be internationally integrated and in self-appointed positions of superiority within China are fundamental to creating this wider popular engagement with the status quo. The new rich produce the structures (for example: glossy magazines, theatre houses and galleries) of dissemination. They create the content for these structures (essays, art-works, plays, photographs and documentaries). They enthusiastically embrace the notion of cultured civility through widespread discourses of 'quality' (*suzhi*) and use this discourse to justify their current privileged status. The embracing of social problems, such as the issue of rape, sexual harassment or female infanticide mitigates against self-congratulation or self-satisfaction. It speaks of an enlightened and socially responsible section of the population with a philanthropic consciousness and not of a revolutionary class dedicated to the overthrow of oppressive structures.

'Feminism with Chinese characteristics' or 'bourgeois feminism'?

The impact of the longstanding CCP dismissal of 'bourgeois feminism' is still evident today but a new perspective has emerged in the post reform years that has hampered the adoption of the word 'feminist' even among groups that could easily adopt the description themselves. While the term 'feminism' was problematic historically because of its link to the 'bourgeoisie', more recently it has been rejected because of its assumed link with 'western' values. The combination of the two ideological problems has generated a problem of determining appropriate labels for the women actively lobbying on behalf of women in China.

Howell's research tells us that of the women's groups active now 'Very few describe themselves as "feminist" organisations seeking to undermine male domination' (Howell 2003: 198). Even among that small group of scholars and activists that call themselves 'feminists' Dorothy Ko and Wang Zheng have explained that there is preference for the term 'feminine-ism' (*nüxing zhuyi*) rather than 'women's rights-ism' (*nüquan zhuyi*) since the former 'is often taken to mean an ideology promoting femininity and thus reinforcing gender distinctions' rather than the latter 'which connoted the stereotype of a man-hating he-woman hungry for power' (Ko and Wang 2006: 463). This behaviour is regarded as un-Chinese and not productive to a more collaborative approach to improving the whole of society. Accordingly, the ACWF has embraced the role of promoting 'the rights of women' (*funü quanli*) thereby neatly avoiding links with any existing form of '-ism' that may undermine its public connection to the super '-ism' of communism.

In the post-reform period, the discursive potency of terms like 'feudal', 'capitalist' and 'bourgeois' has become rather confused and their frequent use is likely to identify the speaker as being out of step with the reform rhetoric encapsulated by the phrase 'to get rich is glorious'. This shift suggests that the old link between 'bourgeois' values and 'feminism' may not entirely explain the broad-based resistance to the use of 'feminism' or 'feminist' as self-descriptors. Instead, the answer may be found within the matrix of nationalism that has become a cornerstone principle of the reform period. Chinese scholars explaining their reluctance to embrace the f-word usually frame their discussions around the importance of resisting hegemonic 'western' concepts and of the need to create an indigenous Chinese understanding of the women's movement. Feminism is often described as being inappropriate for Chinese conditions or extreme (Wang Zheng 1997). Li Xiaojiang and Zhang Xiaodong write that:

> For scholars in unofficial women's studies groups, however, avoiding the term *feminism* or not identifying their work as 'feminist' is a deliberate and voluntary choice rather than a political consideration. Such scholars respect Western-based feminist theory, and yet they still believe that Chinese women's studies has its own background and circumstances unique to Chinese history and social reality
>
> (Li Xiaojiang and Zhang Xiaodong 1994: 148)

The internationalism inherent in feminism from its inception, and China's early participation in that global movement from the late 1890s, is diminished and replaced with defensive calls for a 'national' voice or an indigenised movement that is distinguishable from a homogenised and derided 'western feminism'. Embedded within this desire for a Chinese-style woman's movement is the increasingly common demand that the value of socialism to women's progress be recognised more broadly. There is strong abhorrence of the 'deficit model' which posits Chinese women's consciousness as having been retarded until the Open-Door policy allowed the light of true feminism to shine through (Lin Chun 2001: 1282). The fragmentation of the political category of 'women' as an international constituency into myriad national or ethnic movements produces such phenomenon as 'feminine-ism'. Nationalism could stymie productive outcomes for feminism just as Boxer noted had occurred in the unhappy connection between European Marxism and feminism a century earlier (Boxer 2007). At the same time, the adoption of an issues-based 'Chinese' approach to effecting positive change in women's lives enables women active in organised movements to engage with the international feminist movement and gain energy, efficacy and prestige from that global exchange (Edwards 2008a).

One international trend that has flowed through into the PRC has been the adoption of the self-descriptor 'feminist' from among a small group of young, well-heeled urbanites with aspirations to appear fashionably cosmopolitan. Their spokespeople include a set of younger women working within the cultural sphere, such as writers and artists (Zhong Xueping 2006: 636). In their enthusiastic embracing of the label 'feminist', they display an aspiration for non-conformity. Exemplified by Wei Hui, the author of the sensational 'sex and shopping' novel, *Shanghai Baby*, this group thrive on being identified with precisely those aspects of the term their elders have averred. Within this form of female empowerment, female sexuality, sexual power and sexual appetites prevail and women's independence is determined by purchasing power and the consumption of European labelled luxury products and European men. Ko and Wang comment that feminism for this group 'appears to be a fashionable cause in popular discourse, embraced by writers and readers seemingly oblivious to its charged historical meanings' (Ko and Wang 2006: 471). *Shanghai Baby* feminism carries the same problems as 'raunch culture' circulating among youth in Europe, Australia and the USA (Levy 2006). It has co-opted the concept of women's power to present sexual and financial promiscuity as a form of empowerment. China's young new rich dominate this group of 'feminists'. This notion of feminism trumpets consumerism ('I will spend my money as I please'), risk-taking ('I'm independent enough to make my own decisions') and sexual availability ('I am in charge of my own body and its pleasure'). There is no space for philanthropic welfare-like activism of the ACWF's 'the rights of women' within this triumphal individualism. The term 'feminism' is a fashion label rather than a political concept to this group and serves as an extreme example of the tendency for newly rich individuals to co-opt political concepts as lifestyle accessories and indulgent accoutrements. But most importantly, those political ideas require appropriate editing in order to ensure that they are unlikely to upset the system that produced the new rich's current comfortable position.

Interest articulation and change

Despite their self-identification as feminist, the well-heeled youth of the urban 'raunch culture' crowd act with an individualistic flare that suggests the appellation is little more than a fashion accessory invoking daring cosmopolitanism. Few of these 'sex and shopping' feminists are part of an organised political movement aimed at provoking fundamental social change. However, they demonstrate that 'individualism' is no longer a dangerous political position within twenty-first century China. Un-organised individuals remain politically impotent while economic growth continues and are no threat to the Party-state in these conditions. The fragmentation of political energy reflected in increasing individualism is mirrored by the rise of issue-based politics that has enabled their 'sisters' in the women's movement, both inside and outside of the ACWF, to make considerable gains in promoting the legitimacy of women's rights and interests. The fragmentation of women's myriad concerns into distinct, albeit related causes has ensured their continued presence in the public sphere. The new rich, complete with their diverse technical, financial and cultural skills, are active in producing and consuming these 'good causes' as 'issues of social concern'.

This situation coexists with the commonly expressed concern that the state's retreat from direct intervention in society would negatively influence women's position by removing protective measures guaranteed by the state (Hooper 1984; Cartier and Rothenberg-Aalami 1999; Fan 2004a). However, the state's retreat has had evident positive benefits in the realm of the increasingly diverse nature of and increased numbers of people involved in women's issues. No longer are women's concerns isolated to the ACWF and no longer are they restricted by dismissive (and sometimes dangerous) accusations of deviationist 'bourgeois feminism'. There has been a reorientation in the depiction and perception of key issues towards highlighting their sex-specific nature. Patriarchy becomes more explicitly identified within the post-reform political frame. For example, in earlier years problems such as domestic violence, female infanticide and discrimination against girls in access to education were conflated within the broad problem of 'remnants of feudalism'. Equally, the rare discussion of rape or trafficking in women was dismissed as criminal deviance. Sexual harassment or the trade in sex for services was largely ignored since it would have challenged the integrity of the power holding CCP cadre (Jeffreys 2006). In contrast, in the last two decades it has become possible for these issues to be presented as having emerged from fundamental differences in the power relations between the sexes and not purely as a result of feudal remnants or echoes of incomplete class-based revolution. Identifying women's special concerns is no longer a major political or moral problem. Sex-based problems for women and girls now feature routinely in the media and China's new rich are instrumental in creating this space and filling it with content. The Communist Party-state is affirmed and legitimised by this phenomenon.

Notes

1 The 'Four Modernizations' were announced as policy goals in 1978 and were designed to improve development in agriculture, industry, technology and defence. 'Socialism with Chinese Characteristics' emerged in a 1984 speech by then-President Deng Xiaoping and was designed to theorise a connection between the market and state controls that would enhance wealth and wellbeing for China's population. 'The Three Represents' announced in 2002 were President Jiang Zemin's contribution to CCP ideology. The Party declared that it must represent the development of the most advanced productive forces, the most advanced cultural forces and the fundamental interests of the overwhelming majority of the population.

2 In part, this mono-directional information flow resulted from the precarious position of the ACWF within the Party-state apparatus of these years. In the 1950s the ACWF faced the very real threat of closure because some prominent Party leaders were of the opinion that with the advent of the socialist state, special pleading on behalf of women was redundant (Wang Zheng 2006). During the Cultural Revolution (1966–76) the ACWF was indeed closed, but this was not a direct result of the CCP's rejection of the relevance of women's special status. Indeed, the Cultural Revolution years are often seen as being a period of increasing strength of women under the leadership of Mao Zedong's wife, Jiang Qing. The closure of the ACWF during these years was part of the broader movement to revolutionise and energise the CCP's structures and membership.

3 The ACWF had established Institutes of Women's Studies from 1979 onwards and through their various branches conducted foundational local history research (Gilmartin 1984: 57–66).

4 I have argued elsewhere that the link between labour, capital and women's subordination is being challenged even at the level of the ACWF (Edwards 2007).

13 Men, women and the maid

At home with the new rich[1]

Wanning Sun

Mr Shen, in his mid-40s, was a public relations consultant working for an American software company in Beijing. He spoke good English and had lived overseas numerous times in his life, including a few stints as a visiting fellow at universities in the US. Still single and considering himself an infinitely eligible bachelor, he owned an up-market car and an expensive spacious 150 square metre apartment in a new gated community in Chaoyang District Beijing. When he found out my research interest in domestic workers, he offered the information that he had a local *baomu* (maid) who came once a week for half a day to clean his apartment, do his laundry and iron his shirts. Shen also mentioned that he did not know his maid that well, as he was never home while she came to work in his apartment. 'I am not particularly interested in her private life'. Shen intended to get married, although he still had not found the right woman – to his mother's disappointment. He said that he was 'easy and relaxed' about his future – and imaginary – wife's option to work or stay at home, but he was firmly of the view that his wife should not engage in any dirty menial housework.

> A beautiful woman should not be involved in dirty work. I can't put the two things together. If she wants to work, she can do some charity work or community work. Or she can work out in the gym and keep herself beautiful. The only exception is cooking, as it is more personal, and one's wife knows one's taste better. What is more, one needs to know proper nutrition and hygiene.[2]

What I find instructive is Shen's projection of the domestic arrangement of his future home, and the indispensable role of a maid both for his current bachelor's life and for his future married life. Indeed, he has a current practical material need to have his apartment cleaned and his shirts ironed; equally importantly, he also has a symbolic need to be able to carve out a social identity suitable for himself and his future imaginary wife. And indeed, in his case, it seems that both levels of need can be conceivably met by having a maid. A highly 'successful' man working in a foreign company in Beijing and with an annual income which could be astronomical to most people, Shen obviously considered himself a 'success', a judgement made in professional, economic terms. This perceived personal success permitted him to occupy a certain subject position as a man and also to carve out for himself a designated gender role in relation to his future wife. To Mr Shen and the like, the need to outsource domestic work is a given.

Both Shen's anticipation of the need for a maid in his future married life and his current engagement of domestic help is indicative of a distinctive middle-class projection of the ideal family life, in which having a maid is essential. After all, the connection between a middle-class family life and the presence of a maid is *de rigeur*, be it middle-class families in colonial India (Banerjee 2004), or middle class homes in Victorian England (McClintock 1995), or middle-class families in modern Malaysia (Chin 1998) or Brazil (Owensby 1999). The possession of one or more servants became an often-used shorthand measure for Victorian middle class status (Young 2003: 54). A study of the servant class in England and France in the nineteenth century in fact states that the 'most distinctive expenditure of the middle-class budget was the employment of a servant' (McBride 1976). Shen's projection of his future wife's role in his home and his determination not to let her do 'dirty' housework also betrays a structure of feelings typical of the middle class. Unlike the American middle-class in their mid-twentieth century homes, where the wife of middle-class men were expected to do housework, thus creating a 'classlike difference between the middle-class men and women' (Ehrenreich 1990: 39), the role of Shen's wife, imaginary as she is, is already inscribed with both the middle-class's 'hope of rising' and the 'fear of 'falling' (Owensby 1999: 99). Shen's future wife must not undertake dirty housework which is suitable to rural migrants or laid-off factory workers – women and girls who are, in Betty Friedan's words, 'feeble-minded' and lacking the intelligence and education of middle class women (Friedan, 1963: 255). He must not, by letting his wife work like a maid, run the risk of falling down the ladder of social mobility.

This chapter opened with a profile of Mr Shen to draw attention to the middle-class home – both material and imaginary – as the site of investigation. It suggests that an exploration of the social semiotics of being 'middle class' at home, including an array of new home-making practices and division of labour within one's dwelling, are crucial to the construction of a 'middle class' identity as well as the formation of middle-class subjectivity. The representation and self-representation of successful men like Shen because of their social status and economic power in the public domain entails the re-assigning of gender roles in the domestic sphere, as well as redefinition of what it means to be a 'real' man and an 'ideal' wife. The appearance of new public identities such as the 'rich man' (*dakuan*), 'full-time wife' (*quanzhi taitai*), and 'white-collar beauties' (*bailing liren*)[3] have an inevitably flow-on impact to the private and domestic sphere, whereby the meaning of housework, household consumption practices, quality of family life, and choices in parenting and filial duties, have undergone transformation. Not surprisingly, these changes invariably parallel the re-emergence of domestic workers in the post-socialist era.

The account of the middle class in the domestic sphere in this chapter draws on and juxtaposes the experiences and insights from both people who consider themselves to be middle class and their domestic servants, whose presence, as the example of Mr Shen makes clear, has become increasingly indispensable to the meaning of being 'middle class.' Although there is an inherent diversity of social experiences and formations in the problematic conceptualisation of the 'middle class' the use of the term is deliberately loose and undisciplined. In the process the chapter provides a demonstration of the argument that the formation of a 'middle class' identity is as much a discursive as a material undertaking, in the same ways that 'home' is a cultural construct as much as a physical place. Indeed, it is interested in exploring how the discourses of home in a wide array of discursive sites – urban conversations and media narratives – provide clues to how the middle-class actively engages in its own making. In other words, adopting E. P. Thompson's practical view of class, it is concerned with the ways in which people come to 'share the same categories of interest, social experiences, traditions and value system, who have a disposition to behave as a class' (Thompson, 1978: 85).

In the first part, this chapter presents a 'mise-en-scene' of the post-socialist home in the Chinese city, a new social space whereby a range of social identities and gender roles are formed and contested. Here it examines a number of ways in which the arrival of the domestic worker on the urban domestic scene is integral to such new formations. Then, against this landscape of change and transformation of the concept and practices of domesticity, the second part focuses on a 'structure of feelings' which emerges in response to the threat of eroded boundary in the domestic sphere. Here it consider a number of ways in which the 'humble little maid' simultaneously serves to address and render unrealisable a range of middle class desires, including their desire for safety, privacy, and cleanliness. Material for this chapter comes from two periods of fieldwork, each of four-month in length (May to August 2005, and June to September, 2006), when I lived, respectively, in 'Safe Lane' and 'Purple Garden', both local residential communities in districts of Beijing and interviewed and interacted with a number of property owners and the domestic workers they employed.[4]

Changes at home

In various national and social contexts, home ownership is often associated with the formation of middle class status.[5] This chapter is not concerned to use the existence of home ownership to prove the emergence of the middle class, or to gather sociological statistics on ownership to speculate on the size of the urban middle-class. It is concerned with unravelling how the paradoxical and evolved meaning of home is central to the question of the formation of middle-class subjectivity. Post-socialist urban China has witnessed the acting out of an intense desire for the privatisation of social life, whereby the home is re-imagined as a private domestic space separate from the public and social sphere.

In the socialist era, housing was state-owned and state-allocated, and one's public identity was invariably tied with one's workplace (Tomba 2004, 2005). The degree of comfort with one's accommodation was tied to dedication to the Party (CCP membership was often a point-scoring factor in housing allocation for some workplaces) and personal circumstances (married people were more likely to receive housing allocation than singles, hence the phenomenon of many singles past marriageable age still living with their parents or in dormitories) or the kind of spouse encountered (having an apartment or flat was a winning attribute in the marriage market). Housed by the socialist state, urban families were also imbued with a socialist ideology of home. Within these ideological parameters, home, the private, personal and individual sphere existed only to give meaning to the collective, public family. Members of socialist families were encouraged to subsume and suppress private interests and desires in order to serve the public and common good. The ideology of the home was also marked by a deliberate conflation of the national and socialist family with one's own home. The idea of home was associated not with the security and belonging that comes from property ownership but with a feeling of being 'owned' by and being responsible to the biggest landlord: the state, in both material and moral senses.

This idea of the home was gradually brought to an end by the development of a market economy and the subsequent state-initiated reform in housing policies, centring on privatisation in the 1980s and 1990s. For the first time since the Chinese Communist Party came to power, Chinese people could start dreaming, en masse, of owning their own home. More than anything else, home ownership and the new-fangled real estate industry have spawned endless dreams, desires and fantasies, and more than ever before, one's sense of belonging and social identity is tied to the ownership of a home. As Elisabeth Croll (Croll 2006) points out, buying an apartment, renovating it, or selling it has become the staple of everyday conversations among urban residents. Media, cashing in on the realty frenzy which has swept urban China for the last decade or so, does its share of manufacturing images of the 'perfect' home, pitched at different consumption levels. 'Property owners', a social identity that emerged in post-socialist China, command clout and respect. Regardless of one's occupation, education, and political views, ownership of a villa, an apartment or a flat, ranging from 50 to 250 square metres in size, becomes the first concrete (pun intended) signifier of one's possession of social capital and ensures membership in the newly emerged social identity commonly dubbed the 'new rich' and 'middle class'. (Tomba 2004, 2005). Whether it is villa-style (detached) housing far away from the hustle and bustle of the city or apartment living in an urban high-rise building, 'home' is built as much with the brick and mortar materiality as it is with imagination about one's social identity and sense of belonging.

Refashioning gendered identities at home

If, market economy means that masculinity is increasingly measured in terms of the amount of money he makes, it is also at the same time taking the pressure of working off many women. Urban Chinese women, particularly spouses of the new rich, find that they now have a lot more options in deciding what to do with their time, and more importantly what gendered subject positions they wish to occupy. Some women feel that their social identity is no longer contingent on them staying in the workforce. Instead, some see the family as the primary commitment, and are proud to play a supporting role to her husband. Although it is a relatively recent phenomenon, it is no longer uncommon to see 'full-time wives' in Chinese cities, particularly within the rich and privileged echelon (Wang, 2006). Although small in number, the lifestyle of this group of women has captured the imagination of the Chinese population. The reasons behind this new – new to post-socialist China – phenomenon are many and diverse. Some believe that such a trend has become possible simply because a growing number of families can afford not to have two incomes. Indeed, very few full-time wives quit jobs in order to do housework. Ms Hua, a woman I got to know during my residence in the Purple Garden was in her late 30s and had two children, 15 and 3 years old. Her husband was a real estate developer. Hua employed two full-time domestic helpers, one of whom cooked and the other who worked as a nanny. Ms Hua told me that her husband is often away on business, sometimes abroad, but she had her own network of friends. She attended adult education classes, yoga classes, and drove her children to school and childcare. When I talked to her, she was attending a year long course offered by a prestigious university in Beijing which covered a wide range of subjects including literature, history, home science, and child development. 'There is a lot of useful knowledge and information out there. I feel that I could become a more cultivated person (*ti gao xiu yang*). I also meet a lot of new friends by going to these activities.'[6]

It is beyond the scope of this chapter to discuss the pros and cons of the 'full-time housewife' phenomenon from a feminist point of view. Suffice it to say that the hyper-masculinities displayed in the grand theatre of global capitalism (Cartier 2001; Zheng 2004) also manifest themselves in the soap opera of everyday life in the familial milieu. The emergence of the middle-class or even bourgeois 'housewife' as a social category is not possible without the rapid upward mobility of the so-called 'successful businessman.' Being a 'leisured wife' practising 'female idleness' (Young 2003: 73), Ms Hua, and indeed Mr Shen's future wife, need not engage themselves in manual dirty housework, but they shoulder the responsibility of negotiating the family's middle-class status. Engaging in charity work or going to the gym as a way of spending one's time is status-conferring, whereas staying at home to clean one's toilet and scrub one's own floor is status-threatening.

Despite the glamour of the 'full-time wife', most educated, professional urban women desire to have a foot in both worlds. In constructing a profile of the archetype '*Vogue* woman,' Liu Dan, from Conde Nast, which produces the Chinese *Vogue*, has this to say, 'Vogue women are not full-time wives, nor are they stressed out with work. They want to balance work and family, and they do it successfully and effortlessly.' *Vogue* or not, women juggle work and family for a variety of reasons. Some feel that they cannot afford to have only one income in the household, or in the case of single mothers, they cannot afford not to have an income at all; others cite independence and equality as the main reason to keep working.[7] Seldom acknowledged is the fact that no matter how women choose between being full-time wives and full-time professionals, and no matter how 'effortlessly' some women balance family and work, urban middle-class women's options to pursue different kinds of motherhood and wifehood are contingent on the easy affordability of domestic help. While economic considerations drive rural women to leave home, such decision comes with high emotional cost. As the story of the Pilipino domestic workers who leave their children behind in order to work as nannies in North America powerfully suggests, love is a finite resource, and the work of carers, nannies and domestic workers in general are 'emotional work' (Hochschild 2002; Parrenas 2002). And since urban residents see their relationship to rural women as economic and contractual, they usually do not consider their business to be concerned about the latter's hardships and emotional grievances. Nor do urban mothers see much need to acknowledge the obvious fact that in order to spend more 'quality time' with their husband or children, their domestic workers have to leave their husband and children behind.

The most apt demonstration of the stratified nature of a mother's needs is the reasonably new phenomenon of wet nurses. In recent years, a new 'product' has hit the domestic service market. The *Nai ma* (wet nurse), a time-honoured profession that disappeared during the socialist era, has resurfaced. Judging by the frequency of newspaper headlines in urban newspapers and detail on Internet sites, the phenomenon, though still not common, has caught the imagination of urban residents. On 28 June 2006, *Beiijing Daily* reported that a 22-year-old peasant woman in Zhejiang Province had become the first wet nurse in the province, earning a white-collar professional's salary (4000 *yuan* a month). According to the story, growing demand for wet nurses is a result of more and more urban professional women either not having sufficient time or milk for their babies. Some women decide not to breastfeed for fear of losing their figure. An industry spokesperson is quoted as saying that the market demand for professional wet nurses is potentially large. A new echelon of rich people not only want but also can afford to hire a wet nurse; similarly, more and more women are attracted to the job due to its high income (China.com.cn 29 June 2006).

An even more controversial 'new product' in the delivery of domestic service is the 'beddable maid ' (*shangchuang baomu*) or maid-sexual partner. Around the end of the 2006, *Beijing Morning News* publicised this phenomenon. A domestic service agency in Northwest China's Xi'an (a relatively poor area) provides 'beddable maids', who are hired on the explicit agreement that the domestic worker may be expected to be a 'sexual partner' in addition to her other domestic responsibilities. The recruits are given to understand that if they are to work as 'normal maid', they will receive a wage of 800 *yuan* month; however, if they agree to be a 'beddable maid', their monthly pay will be 2,000 *yuan* a month. The agency targets married women over the age of 35 from poor rural areas, and caters to mostly widowed senior male residents who live alone (*Beijing Morning News* 7 November 2006). Since its introduction, this service has generated controversies and debates. A search on baidu.com, one of China's most widely used online websites, brings up hundreds of entries, debating the various and sundry aspects of the phenomenon.

In the same way that the figure of the wet nurse complicates and destabilises familial roles such as motherhood (Boon 1974; Drummond 1978; Moore 1994) the figure of the maid as sexual partner not only threatens to erode the concept of the wife, but also challenges the distinction between a wife, a maid, and a sex worker. To be sure, both the wet nurses and beddable maids are small in number. In comparison, the practice of outsourcing domestic work by hiring full-time live-in maids or part-time domestic helpers is more widespread. Although it is difficult to estimate the exact number of rural migrants who work as domestic workers, statistics do suggest that more and more urban families are employing domestic help and the number of vacancies urgently in need of filling is forever growing. Many young families need childcare; a growing number of Chinese families with old people need age care. Currently China has 0.13 billion people over the age of 60, and this percentage is growing at the rate of 3 percent each year. In Beijing, as many as 200,000 households are using domestic help, and within the next few years, about 230,000 families are expected to need full-time live-in maids, whereas another 220,000 families will need part-time and casual domestic help. (Beijing Baomu 2003) It is estimated that about 100,000 positions for domestic help are waiting to be filled in urban Beijing.[8] Statistically, this need translates into one in ten families in Beijing needing or employing domestic help in some form.

The increasingly common practice of outsourcing domestic work has also given rise to a new collective experience of having to live with an intimate stranger at home, imbued with anxiety, fear, ambivalence surrounding both home and this 'stranger'. These feelings are expressed in, as well as give further legitimacy to, a set of everyday practices aiming to make living with an intimate stranger a tolerable reality. These feelings are not only integral to the process of becoming middle-class, they also give shape to a set of collective social impulses and preoccupations which come to be associated with a distinctive middle-class subject.

Home a safe haven?

The relationship between spatial segregation and 'variegated citizenship' (Ong 1999) in the Chinese cities has been clearly established. Studying the spatial politics of the 'Zhejiang Village' in Beijing, Li Zhang points out a number of ways in which 'urban citizenship' vis-à-vis the household registration system discriminates against rural migrants' entitlements and rights to claim urban space (Zhang 2001, 2002). This form of spatial citizenship, or the spatialisation of class (Smart and Zhang 2006: 496) is clearly evidenced in urban middle class's tendency to build walls and hire guards in their residential compounds so as to protect residents from the increasing dangers of urban life (Tomba 2004, 2005). In particular dangers of criminality, disorder and dirt, all of which are associated with rural migrants (Zhang 2001, 2002). While significant in terms of rethinking citizenship in spatial terms, this critique of urban spatial practices in neo-liberal governance tends to omit discussion of the domestic and personal space of home. Even those studies which seek to investigate the emergence of interest groups and activism inside the gated communities sometimes give the impression that walls and gates have successfully managed to keep 'unwanted elements' outside the community (Tomba 2005). My ethnographic observation as a resident of the gated community suggests otherwise. The home within the gated community is by no means hermetic. High-density apartment living means that most residents need to rely on the effective running of property management committees (*Wuye Guanli*) not only for vital infrastructure support, such as the maintenance of gas, electricity, water, and other domestic appliances, but also for carrying out hitherto individual household responsibilities such as garbage disposal.

In comparison with many other residential communities in Beijing, Purple Garden has a much larger population of live-in domestic workers, some of whom are employed primarily to care for expensive pedigree dogs and cats. In addition, outside the residents' individual apartments, but having an essential presence to the apartment building as a whole, is typically a rural migrant worker who sweeps the foyer, corridors and stairs in the building, delivers daily newspapers, delivers bottled drinking water, collects residents' garbage, guards their bikes parked in the basement of the building, washes their cars parked in the parking lot outside the building, and weeds and tends to the flowers and grass in the communal garden outside the building. Purple Garden, home to around one thousand households, in five twenty-six storey buildings, is also serviced by two supermarkets, one of which is in the basement of one of the buildings, run by half a dozen migrant women. This supermarket was open twenty-four hours a day, seven days a week, and offered free delivery to residents. Many times while shopping there, I heard residents phone in to request delivery of a bottle of coke or half a dozen of eggs.

Despite the ease and convenience made possible by the migrant workers, urban residents' uneasiness about the presence of the 'stranger' in one's home is palpable. In fact, maids are often a source of anxiety and fear when it comes to the safety of people and the security of the properties. Domestic workers are constructed in the media not only to be inclined to petty crimes such as lying and stealing, they are also from time to time portrayed to be capable of much more horrendous crimes, such as kidnapping and murder. Media stories of the misdemeanours of the maid inevitably highlight risk, a significant trope in the middle-class narratives on home making. This discourse of risk serves a number of social purposes. Murders of employers or abductions of the employers' baby are not as frequent as, for instance, pick pocketing on the bus or smoking in prohibited areas, but they are more symbolically newsworthy. In other words, through a routine construction of the 'other', the myth of the risk both gives shape to and further validates the fear and anxiety of a cohort of otherwise disunited social group of urban residents and employers of domestic workers.

To employer Mr Sun and his wife, for instance, risk can be minimised by having a clear set of criteria in recruiting maids. Both Sun and his wife work as full-time business consultants and often travel interstate for business reasons. They have a three-year-old daughter, cared for by a full-time maid. They used no less than ten maids during only a couple of years. They lasted for as long as one year and as short as a week. One of the maids had to be let go, because she failed the 'integrity test' – Sun put a stack of 100 *yuan* bills in his coat pocket, and 'sure enough', a few of them went missing a couple of days later. Most of Sun's maids were mostly recruited through the introduction of friends or acquaintances, and very seldom did they use agencies. 'With those ones from the agencies, you don't know where they come from'. Sun professes to be quite experienced in selecting reliable maids:

> We usually look for first timers. It does mean that we need to train them a bit but as long as they are quick to learn, they should be OK. Ideally it is a woman from outside Beijing but who has no relatives or connection with people in Beijing. We usually go for women who have simple social relations. This is because you have no control over what kind of people her friends are. They may collaborate to steal from your place, and if you happen to be home, there is danger of them wanting to kill you since you know them and they don't want to be caught. Or they may make elaborate plans to steal or kidnap your child.[9]

A sense of fear of outsiders and a preoccupation with the safety and security of one's life and property is indeed real among the residents in the gated communities and the employers of domestic workers I talked to. This is only understandable, since, ironically, more so than in the socialist era, urban homes, though preciously guarded, have become more porous to and dependent on the resources from the outside world. In fact, urban homes are places and institutions where the definition of sameness in class term is made possible through the routine presence of the 'other'. Gates, walls and fences, built to confer a sense of safety and security to those living inside, as well as the ubiquitous inter-com system and security guards also have the adverse effect of heightening residents' sense of anxiety about intrusion of 'unwanted elements' from outside. As Setha Low's study of the gated communities in Los Angeles points out, gates and walls 'materially and metaphorically incorporate otherwise conflicting and in some cases polarised, social values that make up the moral terrain of middle-class life' (2003:10).

Privacy – another fetish?

Gated communities speak to – and speak of – urban residents' preoccupation with privacy as well as safety. The paradoxical process of wanting to outsource housework on one hand, and not wanting the domestic worker to intrude into one's private space on the other has engendered a profound anxiety and unease associated with home, a prevalent feeling of being not quite 'at home'. Browsing a latest issue of *Elite Shopper's Guide for Luxury Goods* (*Jingping Gouwu Zhinan*) (2005) an up-market publication which chronicles the trends and aspirations of Chinese urban consumers, I was struck by the minute detailed description of the new affluent home as well as the sense of uneasy feeling about that home:

> Think about it, folks, sure, you have just bought a spacious apartment; you have spent lots of money turning your home into a haven. You have put in the state-of-art décor, fittings and furniture. You have a flat, wide screen television, and the big shiny fridge is loaded with good food. The air-conditioner is blowing cool air, and soft music is oozing from your latest sound system. But let me ask you: who is sitting at home enjoying all these while you are slaving away in your office working long and hard? That's right: your maid (June 2005).

The fetish for privacy is a consequence of the privatisation of living space in a material sense, and as such, is by no means unique to contemporary urban Chinese residents. Tracing the evolution of the family structure and homemaking practices in England, Lawrence Stone points out that the most striking change in the lifestyle of the upper classes in the seventeenth and eighteenth centuries was in the increasing stress on personal privacy. Such emphasis was reflected in the changes in architectural design of the home, and, as Lawrence shows us, was motivated partly to obtain privacy for individual family members from the public gaze, and partly to escape from the 'prying eyes and ears of the ubiquitous domestic servants, who were a necessary evil in every middle- and upper-class household' (Stone, 1977: 254). In the Chinese context, to be able to afford both privacy and spacious living is the hallmark of modernity and good living. Real-estate advertising in Hong Kong in the 1990s identified space and privacy as the two primary selling points, and spoke to Hong Kong residents' intense desire to retreat to the private space after decades of public and co-operative housing (Cheung and Ma 2005). Similarly, the PRC urban residents, having emerged from decades of public and work-unit provided housing, where neither space nor privacy was guaranteed, embrace the concept of privacy with equal zeal. Advertisements of European-style cottages on billboards that dot the urban landscape of Beijing seduce the viewer with promises of privacy, seclusion and escape from the outside world. Apartment buildings promise that their properties will be so private that residents will 'hardly run into anyone in the elevator' as one advertisement says. They will also be exceptionally private and confidential, as the security system operates on the 'recognition of the palm and finger prints of owner-occupiers' as another advertisement promises.

On the other hand, the outsourcing of domestic work also means that more than ever before, it is impossible to keep the home 'private'. Inside the apartment building, part-time cleaners vacuum and dust your furniture, clean your toilet, and hang your laundry. Alternatively, your full-time maid not only tends to your aging parents or cares for your baby, but also cooks the meals you eat. New and recently designed urban housing has indeed taken into consideration the need and likelihood for some urban families to employ live-in maids; hence, the increasingly common storage room/maid's bedroom in most newly built apartment buildings. These are usually a pokey small room,[10] often in the middle of the apartment, with no window, and fitted with cupboards and storage spaces, the top of which can also function as a bed base. The post-socialist new urban home is not complete without the figure of its 'other' 'stranger'. A 'centrifugal' and 'peripatetic' figure in the urban middle-class home (Yan 2006: 245), the domestic worker is a threat to one's security, an intruder to their privacy, and a cleaner who ironically brings in more dirt. For instance, as Yan points out, domestic workers' tendency to 'drop in and visit each other' (*chuan meng*) is frowned upon by employers, as it potentially causes concern for one's privacy as well as security.

Measures to ensure privacy abound, ranging from restricting the maid's time outside the apartment for fear of her gossiping about one's employers, to asking one's maid to eat separately so that employers can freely carry out their dinner conversations. Many live-in domestic workers told me that they did not feel free to spend too much time talking with people outside the house; or using their employer's telephone to call someone; or inviting their own friends or relatives to visit. In some cases, such understanding is formalised in the contract signed by the employer and domestic worker; in other cases, it is a case of an employer stating or hinting at their preferences. The rationale for such practice is simple: employers value their privacy and do not want their private life to become the conversational fodder of maids and neighbours. Middle-class residents are also frustrated with their maid's inability to understand their need for privacy. One of the domestic workers I talked to got into trouble because her employers were angry upon finding out accidentally that their maid had revealed to others the private life of her dogs – indeed the maid told us the three dogs she was walking were a family consisting of the mother, the father, and the son (June 2006).

While urban employers guard their privacy preciously, they do not see it as contradictory to impose domestic chores of the most personal nature on their domestic workers. Most domestic workers accept it is part of their job to clean up the bodily fluids and excrements of the sick, the old and the children. All the same, a number of them told me that they considered it unreasonable of their employers to expect maids to wash their underwear. 'There is a washing machine but she wants me to hand wash her underwear, as it is more gentle on the fabric. I was disgusted to have to deal with the stains of her menstrual blood', a domestic worker once told me (May 2007). Ironically, while some employers would not hesitate to tell their maids to perform these 'intimate' tasks, they on the other hand display surprisingly little interest in their maid as a person. Quite often, I realised, through conversations with employers, that, apart from the name, place of origin and approximate age, they knew next to nothing about these women who cook their meals and wash their underwear. And in many cases, they justi-fied this lack of interest and knowledge about their employee in the spirit of respecting the latter's right to privacy.

Here lies a profound paradox: more and more urban residents find that a maid is indispensable to their daily life, but few people find it convenient or practical to live with one. Capitalising on this conundrum, a local neigh-bourhood committee in Shanghai came up with an innovative idea of turning a room at the back of the neighbourhood committee into a rental property, a dormitory for domestic workers who work in the neighbourhood but who come from outside Shanghai and are in need of accommodation. The room, according to the story, can sleep up to twenty people, and inha-bitants only have to pay a minimum rent. What's 'good' about these 'maid dormitories' is that urban residents can have easy access to their maid – by paging them – and at the same time keeping the maid 'out of their hair'. This, according to the story, is a very welcome phenomenon, as modern nuclear families want peace of mind – help is handy whenever called for – as well as privacy. (*Guangzhou Evening News* 21 December 2003). The employers in the story expressed some kind of discontent with the reality of having to deal with intrusion of the private and personal space. They also seemed to lament a loss of the household's self-sufficiency, a capacity which is gradually diminished with the disappearance of the traditional extended family structure. The maid is represented as a deeply problematic figure, indispensable to the smooth running of the household and yet responsible for taking away her employer's rights to privacy.

Dirt – a marker of class

In addition to a collective desire for security and privacy, an intense fetish for cleanliness also marks the middle-class's sensibility. With the improvement of living conditions and dramatic increase in the size of apartment homes comes the need to keep them clean. To property owners, the home should be safe and clean, and quarantined from the dirt and dust of the world outside. Urban middle-class residents' fetish for cleanliness manifests itself in the incessant concern with the penetration of dust into the home. It is also evidenced in their fear of dirt which domestic workers may bring from both their rural habits and through being exposed to the grime of the city. A young mother in the Purple Garden residential community related the following in the playground when our daughters were playing:

> I require my maid to live in even though she and her husband rent a room on the outskirt of Beijing. This way, I am at least able to minimise the risk of her bringing germs home. If I let her go home every day, she will need to spend a couple of hours on the road, catching buses and touching everything outside. You can also imagine how kind of hygiene standards she has in her own home. She would then come here, carry my baby and feed her food. Of course, that would be risky.

Looking at her 11-month baby girl on the slide in the playground, she then told me (8 August 2006) that she was increasingly frustrated with her maid, as the latter had made repeated requests to take a day off each week instead of each fortnight. Here there is evidence of another profound paradox. On an everyday basis it is the maid's hand that puts food in the child's or the elderly person's mouth, cleans up the mess she leaves, or wipes excrement from his bodily orifices. However, in spite of, or perhaps because of this, this direct and intimate physical interaction on a day-to-day basis has bred among employers a collective concern with what Kristeva calls the 'abject body.'[11] Media stories often carry employers' gripes about their unhygienic maids who smell of garlic, who lick the mouth of the sesame oil bottle while making salad dressing, who feed the child with food chewed and taken from their own mouth, or who inappropriately handle the pointy end of chopsticks with hands while setting the table (Wu 2005: A11).

While the migrant woman is seen to be the carrier of germs and dirt, she is at the same time thrust into the job of cleaning up someone else's dirt. Domestic cleaners are often found wanting in their cleaning skills. A university professor in Beijing told me that she had recently changed cleaners, as the former cleaner did not know how to get rid of dust:

She only dusts the surface of furniture, and when she cleans the floor with a wet mop, she simply transfers dust from here to there, and the dirt shows immediately after the floor is dry. The new cleaner is so much better. She gets down on her knees, wipes every inch of the floor with a wet rag, and rinse the dirt off after each wipe (May 2007).

As if to confirm the existence of this fetish, a few domestic workers told me that from time to time they declined to work for some employers after an initial visit, not because the apartment was too dirty but because it was too clean. 'She told me to dust the spine of each book inside all her bookcases!' While renting an apartment in the Purple Garden residential community, I rang the Property Management a few times about a blocked drain or a blown fuse. Each call was promptly attended to, with a migrant worker handy man turning up at my doorstep, specially designed plastic footwear in hand, ready to wrap around his shoes before walking in. This practice was clearly developed in recognition of property owners' fear of dirt brought into the home by 'outsiders', even though it was obvious that the household could not run smoothly without help from these same 'outsiders'. In these senses, dirt, and the work involved in removing dirt, can be seen as a primary class marker, and as such, works according to the logic of the 'semiotics of boundary maintenance'. McClintock, exploring the social meaning of housework in Victorian times, points out, 'Domestic work creates social value, segregating dirt from hygiene, order from disorder, meaning from confusion' (McClintock 1995: 170).

The urban middle-class residents' desire for order and a coherent meaning to the 'good life' manifests itself in their desire for security, privacy and cleanliness as well as in their constant complaints of their social 'other' as a source of threat to these values. Very often, one 'undesirable' attribute can become the metaphor for the other. As Yan Hairong (2003) observes, employers want their domestic workers to have 'clean hands and feet', a figurative way of expressing their desire for a maid who is not inclined to theft or other criminal conducts. What is apparent here is not simply a set of employers' views about their employees, but the systematic deployment of a discourse which establishes a structural dichotomy between 'us' and 'them'. In each case, there is a marking out in discourse of an object to be controlled and regulated and a subject who shoulders the burden of controlling and regulation. And in each case, there is a marking out in the practice of subject-making between an urban, civilised, modern, or in Yan Hairong's term, 'cosmopolitan subject', and a rural, uncivilised and backward, or again, in Yan's term, 'subaltern subject' (Yan Hairong 2006).

The making of the middle class

Increasingly in urban China the private sphere of the home has become the new semiotic battleground for the affirmation and contestation of new identities. A range of factors are at work to facilitate a shift from 'work-unit person' (*danwei ren*) to 'social person' (*shehui ren*) or community person (*shequ ren*). These factors include the state sanctioned collective pursuit of the 'good life' for 'well-to-do families' (*xiaokang zhi jia*); widespread urbanisation and entrenchment of the modern nuclear family structure; and the Chinese-style 'cult of domesticity' featuring fetishisation of security, privacy and cleanliness. These are also the most obvious reasons for turning the anthropological gaze to the 'home', an important site where gender-specific consumption activities can be studied. The home and socialisation at the domestic sphere, the neighbourhood, the residential community, and the suburb present themselves as new spaces where gender and class identities are refashioned, boundaries redrawn, and the moral hierarchy re-established, invariably in the process of resolving and interpreting competing needs and rights of the parties involved.

In other words, the making of the middle class take places not only in the realm of the economic and the material, but equally importantly, in the realm of the symbolic and the imaginary. And as this chapter demonstrates, it is in the imbrication of the two that the subject making of an urban middle-class becomes possible. Furthermore, subject making in post-socialist urban Chinese homes often involves the presence of the 'other'. Being a member of the 'middle class' in post-socialist China is not simply a matter of reaching a certain level of economic affluence or adopting a certain kind of lifestyle; it is, equally importantly, about subscribing to certain ways of talking about oneself and its 'other', as well as negotiating certain ways of living with that 'other'. Furthermore, the emergence of the middle-class, like gender and ethnicity, involves a process by which 'middle-classness' is performed, usually in the context of negotiating difference with the 'other'.

The maid is a paradoxical figure who on a daily basis reminds the employer of the difficulty, even the impossibility, of security, privacy and cleanliness, however important these things are to the middle-class residents' sense of who they are. As Yan Hairong's study of the maid-employer relationship argues eloquently, subject making, be it that of the cosmopolitan subject or the subaltern subject, is not an 'enclosed', isolated process involving a singular subject; it is a 'problematic, open-ended, and relational process relying on interplay *between* subjects' (Yan Hairong 2006: 246). Finally, what indelibly marks the middle-class sensibility is the depth of their predicaments and preoccupations as well as the scope of their ambitions and aspirations. If anything, the story of Mr Shen which started this chapter is an open-ended one, without the narrative closure of Mr Shen – or his future wife for that matter – having found happiness, order, coherence and meaning in life. What it does highlight is the fact that in a consumer society, what is on display is not only an abundance of goods and services but also, in Pun Ngai's words, a 'system of signs that codify social difference and human relationships' (Pun 2003: 479). As Pun's discussion suggests, social difference and human relationships are re-worked dramatically both in terms of gender and class. And home is one of the best places to encode and decode social difference and human relationships, as this chapter has suggested.

Notes

1 This chapter is part of a three-year project which was funded by an Australian Research Council Discovery Grant (July 2004 to June 2007). I would like to acknowledge ARC's support, which made it possible to conduct the necessary ethnographic work in China.
2 Interview, June 2005, Beijing.
3 'White-collar beauties' are young, trendy, and upwardly mobile women in post-socialist Chinese cities, working in the white collar professions.
4 Safe Lane is in Chaoyang District, northeast of Beijing, whereas Purple Garden is in Haidian District, northwest of Beijing. Pseudonyms have been used for both neighbourhoods.
5 The ownership of private property is often considered a hallmark of middle-class status: as in Victorian England (Davidoff and Hall 1987) post-socialist China (Tomba 2004) and South Korea (Lett 1998).
6 Hua and I talked often from July to September, 2006.
7 Liu Dan's comment at press conference, 28 June 2006 accompanying a workshop on consumption patterns in urban China.
8 Dr Li Tianguo, senior research fellow of the Institute for Labor, Ministry of Labour and Social Security, China, February 2004. Personal communication.
9 Interview, July 2005, Beijing.
10 I have seen the 'maid's room' in a number of apartments in Beijing. These rooms are usually no more than 4 square metres, and often have no windows.
11 Julia Kristeva draws the contrast between the 'abject body' and the 'sublime body'. She observes that the abject body is where the boundaries of the body are transgressed and when the internal becomes external. Mouth, nose, ears, eyes, anus and vagina are all sites where the outside and the internal merge. Bodily fluids – blood, urine, tears, saliva, faeces – become repellent to us when they cross the boundary of the skin. These bodily fluids inside the body, become problematic once they cross the boundary of the skin. Outside of the body, bodily fluids become divorced from their owner's body. Desire for the sublime, according to Kristeva, is symptomatic particularly of Western culture, which in seeking the sublime body, denies and hides the basic functions of the body. However, according to Kristeva (1982) the sublime body is impossible, as being 'abject' is a feature of being alive.

14 Advanced producers or moral polluters?

China's bureaucrat-entrepreneurs and sexual corruption

Elaine Jeffreys

There is a popular saying about the relationship between money, gender and sexual morality in the People's Republic of China (PRC): 'Men who get rich become immoral; women only get rich after they become immoral' (*'nanren zheng qian jiu bian hui; nüren bian hui cai you qian'*). Like most aphorisms, this observation appeals to commonsense or public perceptions of how things are. As one foreign correspondent explains:

> In China these days, people are talking about sex—extramarital affairs, prostitution and rich men taking mistresses. Many are worried that sex is becoming a commodity, leading to the exploitation of women. This comes after years of government efforts to eradicate traces of pre-communist decadence.
>
> (Kuhn 2007)

In the words of another: China's post-1978 shift from a planned to a market-based economy 'has lifted millions of people out of poverty and created a new class of millionaires'. However, unlike new freedoms and opportunities, 'get-rich-quick schemes, casual sex, and animosity between rich and poor', are worrying trends. Voices in the Chinese media and academia warn that economic progress has been accompanied by moral decay, which 'could destabilize society' (Chao 2005).

The argument that economic progress in the form of marketization sounds the death-knell for communitarian and traditional moral values is longstanding. Ever since 'Marx wrote on alienation, Durkheim on anomie, and Weber on the iron cage of capitalism', political commentators have either decried or praised the heightened individualism, secularism, and instrumental rationality, that is associated with the capitalist wage-labour system (Weller 1998: 78). Similarly, commentators have condemned or lauded the globalization of free markets, which are usually associated with Western liberal democracies, either for destroying local cultures or for bringing much-needed civilizational progress to backward, despotic, and under-developed countries (Chua 2003; Fukuyama 1992).

In the case of China, a political economy that is characterized by the marriage of communism and the market (socialism with Chinese characteristics), public discussions of the links between rising wealth and declining morals draw on similar narratives of social change, albeit with different inflections. Deng Xiaoping's advocacy of the slogan: 'Let one segment of the population get rich first and guide others along the way', and Jiang Zeming's 'Three Represents' theory, which welcomes representatives of the advanced productive forces (private entrepreneurs) into the ranks of the Chinese Communist Party (CCP) are praised by many commentators inside and outside China for promoting unprecedented economic growth and catapulting the country into a Western-orientated model of modernity (Herberer and Schubert 2006: 9–28).[1] Although Party stalwarts occasionally lament the perceived decline in socialist values that economic reform has brought in tow, those who associate market-based reforms with democratization routinely applaud private entrepreneurs for initiating a welcome rejection of the constraints associated with the former 'puritanical Confucian-socialist system' (Zheng 2006: 163–4). Indeed, for those who associate market-based reforms with political and social liberalization, China's private entrepreneurs are at the vanguard of a newly emerging middle-class that has the potential to transform China's authoritarian and traditional socio-political system into a modern and more liberal one.

Yet the Chinese public are said to mistrust China's 'brash and flashy generation' of new-rich entrepreneurs for making and spending their money in dubious ways (Toy 2007: 15). *Forbes'* 2006 China Rich List highlights the new opportunities that are available to entrepreneurs, with most of the wealth recorded coming from listed companies rather than inherited wealth, and 12 of the top 20 contenders being under 40 years of age (Gordon 2007). At the same time, such newfound wealth is not always based on the neo-liberal ideal of a combination of innovation and hard work. Wong Kwong-yu, top of the *Forbes* 2006 China Rich List, is being investigated for illegal loans; Zhang Rongkun, a real estate and highway developer who made number 16 on the *Forbes* 2005 List was arrested in relation to a Shanghai fund scandal; and Zhou Zhengyi, a real estate magnate who made number 11 on a former *Forbes* List was jailed in 2003 for fraud and security offences (Gordon 2007). Thus, contrary to President Hu Jintao's proclaimed goal of building a 'well-off and harmonious China', many commentators argue that the established links between flagrant corruption and personal wealth accumulation, as well as the growing disparity between the ostentatious high-consumption life-style of the new rich and that of the 'have-nots', are exacerbating the social tensions born of an increasingly inequitable and polarized society (Chao 2005; Gordon 2007; Kuhn 2007). These tensions are heightened by virtue of the seeming radical departure in the reform era from the characteristic egalitarianism, collectivism, and moral certainty, of the Maoist period (1949–76).

Public condemnation of China's new rich as corrupt polluters of socialist virtue is particularly pronounced in discussions of enterprising cadres or bureaucrat-entrepreneurs. Unlike cadres under the pre-reform command economy, whose main responsibility was to implement the state plan and other Party directives, bureaucrat-entrepreneurs are Party and state officials who are expected to display initiative in the marketplace, by engaging in revenue-generating and other activities directed at advancing economic development using the institutional power and resources of the communist system (Gore 1999: 30). They occupy a diverse range of positions, from mayors to provincial governors, enterprise managers to corporate CEOs, village chiefs to township directors, and 'from CCP party committee secretaries to ordinary party members holding key positions in public administration' (Gore 1997). But they are unified as a group by the fact that their positions of power and authority flow from a top-down appointment. While earning far less than private entrepreneurs, they constitute part of China's new rich because of their extraordinary access to business opportunities and state resources, including investment capital, expensive foreign cars and good accommodation. Their lower income, yet privileged access to major resources, has reportedly encouraged corruption insofar as bureaucrat-entrepreneurs 'can generate personal economic gains through illicit or illegal means more effectively than through legitimate mechanisms' (Gore 1997).

Apart from involvement in economic corruption, China's bureaucrat-entrepreneurs are said to be particularly adept at exploiting their privileged access to public resources to secure the sexual services of women. Many recent high-ranking corruption cases have been linked to the new phenomenon of '*xing huilu*' or sex-related bribery and corruption (Jeffreys 2006: 159–78; Jin 2000: 83–7). The first and most notorious case involving allegations of sex-related bribery and corruption was that of Zhang Erjiang, the former Secretary of Tianmen City in Hubei Province. On 23–25 July 2002, Zhang Erjiang was tried for accepting bribes amounting to 700,000 *yuan* and US$4,300, and for embezzling 100,000 *yuan* in public funds (Li Gang 2002). During the course of this trial, Chinese media reports focused not only on his economic crimes, but also on his arguably more serious yet 'not-punishable' moral crimes. Zhang had allegedly abused his position of power and authority to have sex with over one hundred women, including fifteen female cadres. Of these fifteen cadres, seven women had received a promotion following from their affair with Zhang, as had the husbands of two others. Extrapolating from this and other cases, media reports contend that virtually 100 percent of high-ranking corrupt officials who accept bribes and embezzle public funds either keep a mistress, exchange favours for sex, or hire the services of female sexual service providers (Dai and Lu 2000; Ji 2001; Li Zhufeng 2002: 22–3). More recent examples of bureaucrat-entrepreneurs who have been implicated in scandals involving power, sex and money include: Vice Admiral Wang Shouye, previously one of five navy deputy commanders and a member of China's legislature, for accepting bribes from property developers (Watts 2006); and Shanghai Party secretary, Chen

Liangyu, for involvement in the mismanagement of the city's social security fund (Savadove 2006).

This chapter examines the dichotomous construction of China's new (male) rich as both the most advanced productive forces and also as corrupt polluters of socialist morality. The first section provides an historical background by explaining how nineteenth century European accounts of the middle classes as the standard-bearers of enlightened progress were inverted in twentieth century China via Marxist debates on social inequality and through the actions of the early CCP. Section two discusses how the new rich have been created and framed as the simultaneous heroes and villains of economic reform via debates on socialism with Chinese characteristics and issues such as mistress-keeping and prostitution. The third section concludes that European and Atlantic constructions of China's new rich as the middle-class vanguard of progressive social change are undermined by their routine portrayal in China as both advanced economic producers and moral polluters. I argue that this particular group is currently unable to challenge one important aspect of CCP politics – it has failed to present a serious challenge to the Party-state's historic claim to represent and struggle for social *and* sexual equality.

Who are our enemies? Who are our friends?

In a 1926 article entitled, 'Analysis of the classes in Chinese society', Mao Zedong, the founder and former leader of the PRC, stated: 'Who are our enemies? Who are our friends? This is a question of the first importance for the revolution' (Mao Zedong 1926). Mao answered these questions in a 1940 article, 'On New Democracy', which was to become the political basis upon which the new state known as the People's Republic of China was founded in 1949 (Mao Tse-tung 1940). The PRC was envisioned as a 'new democratic dictatorship of the people' based on an alliance of the proletariat, the rural peasantry, and China's national and petit bourgeoisie, under the leadership of the CCP. One of its primary goals was to oppose the enemies of the revolution – big landlords, major entrepreneurs, and representatives of the rival Nationalist Party (Guomindang) – for representing exploitative feudal, capitalist and imperialist forces. Unlike the former Soviet Union, Mao maintained that the PRC could not immediately establish a dictatorship of the proletariat, because China had not yet undergone the pre-requisite Western-style bourgeois-capitalist revolution – processes of industrialization accompanied by the overthrow of the decadent upper classes by the more progressive middle classes. Instead, Mao argued that due to China's unique experience as a semi-capitalist and semi-colonial country, the Chinese proletariat should unite as friends, but without compromising their revolutionary quality, with both the rural peasantry and the Chinese middle classes to form a new democratic dictatorship.

China's commercial and middle-classes occupied an ambiguous position within Mao's New Democracy formulation of the enemy-friend dichotomy. On the one hand, they were categorized as political friends, flowing from their historical opposition to Japan's invasion of China and their inevitable displacement of old-style, feudal social relations with new style, capitalist relations of production. On the other hand, the very entanglement of China's commercial classes with 'capitalism' and the rival Nationalist Party meant that they were also defined as prone 'to conciliation with the enemies of the revolution', that is, as destined to oppose the PRC's future advance into socialism (Mao Tse-tung 1940). To restrict their inherent political conservatism, Mao proposed that the national bourgeoisie could assist the state with the goal of industrializing China, but that all large banks, and all large industrial and commercial enterprises, should be nationalized and placed under state administration, so that private capital would not be allowed to dominate the livelihood of the working people. At the same time, he advocated a land equalization policy, wherein land would be taken from the enemy landlord class and given to peasants, thereby abolishing exploitative feudal relations in the rural areas by turning the land over to the private ownership of the peasants (Mao Tse-tung 1940). This policy permitted small rich peasants or independent producers to flourish in the first instance as advanced agricultural producers who would fuel the production required to get the devastated Chinese economy back on its feet, following years of warlordism, civil war, imperialist intervention, and war with Japan. Hence, the New Democracy version of the enemy-friend dichotomy was designed to garner as many 'friends' as possible to help with the all-important task of national and economic reconstruction, whilst simultaneously introducing a Marxist-based conception of people without property as being inherently more revolutionary and politically progressive than members of the commercial classes and former social elites.

The ambiguous positioning of China's commercial classes as problematic friends was reinforced both prior to the founding of the PRC and throughout the 1950s via claims regarding the political and moral legitimacy of CCP rule, a claim which extended to the realm of sexual relations. As Gary Sigley (2006: 46) explains, the early CCP initially held radical views on sexual relations, for example, it promoted 'a romanticized view of sexual liberation as part and parcel of human liberation'. However, these views were undermined by a corollary tendency to foster the latent hostility of CCP supporters towards those defined as enemies, often by highlighting the inequality and sexual decadence wherein rich landlords, private entrepreneurs and members of the Nationalist Party kept concubines and mistresses, while 'poor men struggled to find a solitary mate' and earn a living (Sigley 2006). Augmenting its claim to political legitimacy, the early CCP maintained that New China, being based on sound material conditions of social equality, would be inevitably morally superior to Old China. Specifically, the early CCP indicated that it had the capacity not only to rescue China from foreign aggressors, but also to overturn its derogatory appellative as 'the Sick Man of Asia'. This appellative was ascribed to China by nine-teenth century Western political philosophers by virtue of its characteristic corruption, feudal-style servitude of peasants, and the debased position of women, and it was viewed as a mark of national shame by many Chinese intellectuals. According to Mao Zedong, the CCP – and only the CCP – had the political vision required to create a New China that would be poli-tically free, economically prosperous, and enlightened; that would not be kept ignorant and backward under the sway of Old China's Confucian, semi-feudal, semi-capitalist, and imperialist culture (Mao Tse-tung 1940).

Claims regarding the political and moral superiority of Chinese socialism were given concrete expression through the actions of the newly victorious CCP shortly after its assumption of political power in 1949. Following Engels (1972 [1884]), the early CCP viewed the institutions of prostitution and (Confucian-bourgeois) marriage as indicative of the debased position of women under feudal-capitalist patriarchy, and therefore as incompatible with the desired goals of building socialism and establishing more equitable socio-sexual relations (Jeffreys 2004: 76–8). Despite facing a daunting set of problems – a ruined economy, a wary population, and ongoing civil war – they implemented a series of campaigns that resulted in the virtual eradi-cation of rampant prostitution and venereal diseases, and introduced the 1950 Marriage Law. This Law was the first item of legislation to be pro-mulgated in the PRC and promoted free-choice marriage by outlawing arranged marriages and concubinage. These actions are celebrated to this day not only for demonstrating the political capacity and moral integrity of Chinese socialism, but also for effecting an 'earth-shaking historic change in the social status and condition of women' (Information Office 1994; Xin and Xiao 2000). Indeed, the revival of prostitution and mistress-keeping in the reform era is often presented as phenomena that the CCP successfully eliminated in the 1950s and must eliminate once again to demonstrate its continued moral and political legitimacy.

A combination of political events, not least of which was the advent of the Cold War and the USA's support of South Korea and Taiwan, meant that the New Democracy rendition of China's national bourgeoisie as 'friends' proved to be short-lived. Captains of industry and former Nation-alist Party-government bureaucrats were still viewed as useful members of the new state insofar as they could assist with the desired goal of advancing a nationalized programme of rapid industrialization and establishing the necessary governmental structures to do so. But, in a climate of heightened political and national insecurity, fears regarding the inherent inclination of this group towards conciliation with 'the enemies of the revolution' became more pronounced (Mao Tse-tung 1940). These fears were exacerbated by the severing of political and economic ties between the CCP and the former Soviet Union in the mid-1950s, flowing from Khruschev's unexpected denunciation of Stalin and the corollary announcement that the Soviet

Union and the USA could operate on the basis of 'peaceful coexistence', which implied the abandonment of support for international communism. The ensuing Sino-Soviet split led to accusations that the leadership of the former Soviet Union was revisionist – it was taking the revolution backwards towards capitalism (Chang 1978: 209–20).

Fears that the future of the PRC and the Chinese revolution were in jeopardy ensured that those defined as enemies or 'inclined towards conciliation' became the subject of escalating political and physical attack throughout the 1950s and 1960s. In the 1950s, a series of campaigns were launched initially against straightforward counter-revolutionary targets, such as members of the Nationalist Party, large-scale landlords and major entrepreneurs. However, as these campaigns gathered momentum they increasingly targeted fringe members of those groups – people who had thrown in their allegiances with the CCP and the new state, but whose political affiliations were viewed as suspect due to their class background and former affiliations. Associated campaigns against corruption among officialdom and economic crimes in private business during the early 1950s, and then against 'non-socialist' intellectual activity during the late 1950's anti-rightist campaign, ultimately culminated in the Great Proletarian Cultural Revolution, which is now dated as lasting from 1966 to 1976 (Strauss 2006: 891–912).

During the Cultural Revolution, members of the revolutionary classes, especially Chinese youth, were enjoined to attack China's newly engendered bourgeoisie, defined as those members of the Party and state personnel in positions of privilege and authority 'who were taking the capitalist road' (Chang 1978: 209–20). While generating widespread anarchy and personal tragedy due to the arbitrary manner in which 'the (friendly) people' chose to target and abuse others as enemies, the concept of a 'capitalist-roader' had quite specific referents at the level of Marxism-Leninism-Mao Zedong theory. It referred to members of the CCP and state personnel who were accused of leading the revolution backwards into capitalism rather than forward into communism, either by taking advantage of their position to monopolize the redistribution of wealth, or else by promoting 'capitalist' relations of production, such as small production, material incentives, and a technological and managerial elite (Chang 1978: 209–20).

The Cultural Revolution critique of corruption and capitalist relations of production also encompassed a condemnation of the 'bourgeois style of life', which included seeking and using personal advancement for individual profit and abusing state-allocated positions of power and authority to commandeer the sexual services of women (Chang 1978: 219; Honig 2003: 162–4). As with the CCP's early efforts to foster hostility towards those defined as enemies by highlighting the decadent social inequality wherein rich landlords and private entrepreneurs kept concubines and frequented prostitutes, such criticisms made sexual morality a major concern. Red Guards, in particular, often invoked charges of sexual 'errors' as part of broader political attacks on capitalist-roaders, indiscriminately targeting individual authors for promoting bourgeois (romantic) love and young, urban women for engaging in 'inappropriate' sexual relations (Honig 2003: 150–4). Concomitantly, the CCP condemned state officials accused of sexually abusing young, urban women who had been sent-down to the rural countryside to engage in productive labour alongside the peasantry. For example, a 1970 Central Committee policy document establishes legal punishments for state officials who had obliged sent-down female youth to acquiesce to rape, or enter into marriage, in order to obtain access to scarce resources such as better food and jobs, and the possibility of a transfer back to their original urban location (Honig 2003: 163–4). The Cultural Revolution attack on China's new bourgeoisie thus aimed to produce a new generation of revolutionary successors who would uphold Chinese Marxism and actively oppose feudal-capitalist practices that were deemed to foster hedonism, materialism, inequality, and sexual exploitation.

In short, the CCP's historical denunciation of the bourgeoisie runs counter not only to liberal accounts of the middle classes as the epitome of civic virtue and progressive political change, but also to popular constructions of contemporary entrepreneurs as the modern inheritors of that tradition, particularly in the context of developing countries. Simplistically speaking, Western liberal political theory describes the middle classes as emerging from the historical processes of industrialization and being at the forefront of progressive demands for franchise and liberal democracy. This account is bound-up with a theologically informed view of human nature and capacities. As Tawney (1938) explains, the liberal construction of the middle and commercial classes as the standard-bearers of enlightened progress turns on the conflation of personal character with personal success, or the assumption that the enterprising energy of the good, and implicitly godly, man will be rewarded with material success. One consequence of this liberal-protestant stress on individual character as opposed to circumstances is that poverty tends to be equated with moral failing, and individual wealth is viewed as a blessing that is occasionally abused, rather than as a natural object of moral suspicion (Tawney 1938: 227–30).

Although the genealogy of modern entrepreneurship is more nuanced than portrayed here (Wahrman 1995), popular definitions of entrepreneurship clearly draw on the liberal-protestant assumption that success is tied to individual character, a character that is assumed to be progressive and, by definition, moral (at least in terms of adhering to entrepreneurial principles). This point can be illustrated with reference to web-based definitions of entrepreneurship. To summarize some standard examples: entrepreneurship is a mindset, personality is the key. An entrepreneur is an habitually creative, innovative and educated risk-taker, someone who is the master of their own fate because they seek opportunities and exploit contacts and resources that other people do not see ('Entrepreneur' (n.d.); 'The entrepreneur' (n.d.)). These innovating entrepreneurs have a 'very American [read democratic] virtue': they 'want to make it possible for the whole population to enjoy products previously available only to the elite' (Pascall 2005).

In contrast, the early CCP followed the broad parameters of Marxist theory by repudiating the liberal-protestant ethos of nineteenth century Europe – that wealth is intrinsic to the individual and a fitting reward for civic and private virtue – and by condemning capitalism as being equivalent to theft and slavery (Marx 1967). Convinced that human nature is a product of the particular system of political and economic relations that a society establishes for itself, the CCP set about smashing China's old owners of the means of production, replacing them with a new bureaucratic and managerial group of Party-state personnel that was supposed to work selflessly in the interests of nationalized industry, the revolution, and the people. Yet, having created this group, the CCP promptly proceeded to denounce many of its members for constituting a new bourgeoisie, accusing them of promoting capitalist relations of production and perpetuating the feudal-Confucian exploitation of women (Chang 1978: 209–20).

Reference to these different genealogical underpinnings helps to explain why business people and individuals engaging in economic activities for personal profit continue to be viewed as morally suspect in economic-reform China, despite state-led efforts to improve the reputation of China's new rich by promoting provincial and national model entrepreneurs. It also helps to explain why bureaucrat-entrepreneurs, especially those whose lifestyles are associated with high-level consumption practices and extra-marital affairs, are routinely exposed to public scandal on the grounds of economic and sexual corruption. Indeed, to the extent that media accounts of the links between the new rich and corruption in China are apposite, corrupt bureaucrat-entrepreneurs continue to be condemned as enemies of 'the people with no property' for abusing their positions of power and privilege to gain unfair access to public resources and female sexual services.

Socialism with Chinese characteristics

China's post-1978 shift to a market economy and the recent popularization of Jiang Zeming's 'Three Represents' theory has overturned the Maoist enemy-friend dichotomy by actively encouraging members of the commercial classes to join the CCP in building socialism with Chinese characteristics. According to Jiang Zemin (2002), the Three Represents is about 'keeping pace with the times and blazing new trails for the development of Marxist theory': it means uniting with the innovative, advanced productive forces to make China strong and the Chinese people rich. Members of this group include: freelance professionals; private entrepreneurs; managerial and technical staff employed by non-public and overseas-funded enterprises; and bureaucrat-entrepreneurs as a matter of course. Jiang concludes that 'the people' – members of the working class, farmers and intellectuals – should unite with the pioneering, advanced productive forces, because: 'it is improper to judge whether people are politically progressive or backward simply by whether they own property or how much property they own'. Instead of equating personal wealth with political incorrectness, Jiang suggests that the Chinese public should judge members of new rich based on whether they uphold Chinese Marxism, how they have acquired and used their property, and how their work has contributed to the goal of building socialism with Chinese characteristics (Jiang Zemin 2002).

While displacing the Maoist dichotomy of 'the people' versus 'the bourgeoisie', the concept of socialism with Chinese characteristics does not so much sever previous links between political and moral sensibility as reactivate them under the rubric of socialist spiritual civilization. In the words of Jiang Zemin (2002), the task of building socialism with Chinese characteristics requires attaching equal importance to material, economic development and spiritual civilization and therefore running the country 'by combining the rule of law with the rule of virtue'. Although the precise nature of such civic virtues is debated, they clearly refer to principles enshrined in the PRC Constitution and education system such as the 'Five Loves' – love of the motherland, the people, labour, science and socialism, and ultimately love of Chinese Marxism and the CCP (Li Ping *et al.* 2004: 449–64; Jiang 2002). They also refer to the historical accomplishments and renewed goals of the CCP in terms of eliciting public support for campaigns against the resurgent phenomena of corruption and prostitution, and, by implication, an incorrect preference for bourgeois, Western lifestyles.

Hu Jintao, for example, prescribed a socialist concept of honour and disgrace at the Tenth National People's Congress in 2006 as follows: 'know plain living and hard struggle, do not wallow in luxuries and pleasures' ('President Hu' 2006). Hu's virtuous living list was upheld by the *China Daily* as offering a positive contribution to China's efforts to produce an advanced socialist culture by trying to combat corruption and 'close the gap' between the elite who have profited from economic reforms and the poor majority ('President Hu' 2006). His prescription revives calls associated with the early campaigns of the reform era which aimed to reinvigorate public belief in the historical accomplishments and values of Chinese socialism, in the form of late 1980s and early 1990s campaigns against spiritual pollution, bourgeois liberalization, and the 'six evils' (prostitution, trafficking in women and children, producing and disseminating pornography, manufacturing and trafficking in narcotics, illegal gambling, and swindling others through superstition). The dual advocacy of material and socialist spiritual civilization is therefore intended to expand the membership base of the CCP, whilst simultaneously inducing compliance from local networks of officials and entrepreneurs by encouraging them to act as model citizens and stopping them from engaging in corrupt and morally unacceptable behaviours.

Hu's promotion of civic virtue is intended to counter new and controversial expressions of cadre corruption and misconduct, including the phenomenon of sex-related bribery and corruption (*xing huilu*). Jin Wei-dong, a former MA student from the Law Faculty at Nanjing University, is credited with inventing the term *xing huilu* when he presented a paper on the subject of sex-related bribery and corruption to the 'Jiangsu Province Seminar on Criminal Law Research' on 6 December 2000 (Meng 2001). In this paper, Jin acknowledges that the trade in power and sex (*quanse jiaoyi*) had taken place in Mao's China, in the form of both high and low-ranking cadres abusing their positions of power and authority to have sex with women in exchange for the promise of work transfers and promotions (Zhi 2001). However, such practices remained highly restricted due to the tight social control networks that were exercised through the regulation and development of the household registration and work-unit systems. In contrast, the practice of businessmen using or hiring female sexual service providers to bribe bureaucrat-entrepreneurs into giving them favourable business deals or protection has become commonplace in the reform era. Hence, Jin concludes that the Chinese penal code should be amended to criminalize the activities of Party and government officials who accept or solicit a bribe in the form of sexual services (Dai and Lu 2000).

Jin Weidong's call to criminalize the phenomenon of sex-related bribery and corruption sparked widespread debate due to the perception that this particular form of corruption is increasing, despite the introduction of new legal sanctions. In China, the Communist Party's Central Commission for Discipline Inspection is responsible for handling corruption cases. Historically, this meant that high-ranking officials remained outside of the reach of the *Criminal Law*, being dealt with by Party disciplinary regulations and other administrative sanctions. However, since September 1997, when Chen Xitong's case was handed over to the courts, a growing number of high-ranking officials have been tried for corruption by the state procuratorial organs (Hao 1999: 414). Chen Xitong, former Mayor and Communist Party Secretary of the city of Beijing, was sentenced by a Chinese court in 1998 to 16 years imprisonment on charges of corruption and dereliction of duty. The public trial of this senior official coincided with the introduction of the PRC's revised *Criminal Law* of 1997, signifying a new understanding that all citizens are equal under the 'rule of law'.

China's revised 'Communist Party discipline regulations' (1997: 15–16) also explicitly penalize cadre involvement in the trading of power and sex. Article 132 of these regulations, under the heading 'Mistakes that seriously violate socialist ethics', states that any Party member who has sexual intercourse with others by 'using their powers, their superior or senior positions, seduction, cheating, or other means, shall be dismissed from their party posts'. Concomitantly, the Chinese government has sought to ban cadre involvement in the running of public entertainment venues and practices such as the use of public funds to cover entertainment costs that may also involve sex-related services. In the early 1990s, the National Bureau of Statistics estimated that between 60 and 70 percent of the income accruing to high-grade hotels, guesthouses, restaurants and karaoke/dance venues, came from male bureaucrat-entrepreneurs spending public funds to wine, dine, and purchase the company of women, at an estimated annual cost to the public of around 800 billion *yuan* (Jeffreys 2006: 168–9). Hence, during the mid to late 1990s, China's relevant authorities introduced a whole host of regulations designed to curb the spending of public funds within such venues and to ban members of the public security forces, and other kinds of government employees, both from running recreational and entertainment venues and from protecting illegal business operations in this connection. These measures are now being enforced, not strictly on the basis of police-led campaigns and information derived from public informants, but also on the basis of disciplinary procedures that are integral to the reform era itself, namely, via the practice established in 1998 of auditing government officials, and thereby combining the resources of the CCP's disciplinary committees with those of the State Auditing Administration (Jeffreys 2006: 168–9).

Yet the majority of high-ranking corruption cases are still linked to the trade in power and sex. According to an unspecified investigation conducted in Guangzhou, Shenzhen and Zhuhai during 1999, more than 95 percent of 102 high-ranking government officials who were tried for corruption had a 'mistress or second wife' (*bao ernai*), and some even had three or four mistresses (Shao 2002; Wang and Liu 2000). Investigations conducted by the Chinese Communist Party's Central Commission for Discipline Inspection and the All-China Women's Federation similarly suggest that virtually every corrupt official has a mistress or second wife (Xie Donghui 2003; Zhao 2001: 7). Given that the cost of keeping such women allegedly comes from public monies at an estimated cost of US$700–1,000 per mistress per month, or else from funds provided by another party with the anticipation of obtaining illegitimate benefits, it is not surprising that the issue of sexual bribery and corruption has been publicly condemned as yet another instance of the perceived manifest abuse of power in China, and one that adds to the PRC's growing number of social problems relating to the family and marriage (Jeffreys 2006: 162).

A standard explanation for China's renewed trade in power and sex is that increased public tolerance of pre-marital and extra-marital affairs in the post-Mao era has meant that sexual affairs outside of marriage are no longer viewed as a political matter. Instead, sex between consenting adults is increasingly understood as a private affair, with practices relating to the selling and buying of sex and the keeping of a mistress being viewed as a moral or lifestyle problem, not as a legitimate target of punitive governmental intervention (Wang and Liu 2000). Concomitantly, the ostentatious lifestyles associated with China's newly rich class of private business entrepreneurs have become the paradoxical focus of public praise and condemnation, with many people desiring a taste of the 'good life' for themselves, and others criticizing the new rich for transgressing socialist values. Media reports, for instance, frequently condemn the high-consumption lifestyles of China's business entrepreneurs, whilst simultaneously regaling their readers with voyeuristic stories of how such men can be recognized instantly by the presence of beautiful young women by their sides (Wang and Liu 2000).

Media reports suggest that growing public tolerance of extra-marital and commercial sex has encouraged the unlawful practice of businessmen using or hiring female sexual service providers to bribe party officials and company managers into giving them favourable business deals or protection (Li Zhufeng 2002: 22–3). As they argue, veteran cadres who have dedicated their life to the revolution are neither easily seduced by the offer of material forms of bribery, nor are they overly willing to engage in outright acts of embezzlement or graft (Meng 2001; Wang Jin 2002). The introduction of economic reforms has undoubtedly opened the window for a small if highly corrupt number of government officials to accept bribes and appropriate state resources on a grand scale. But the introduction of harsh legal sanctions against such measures, combined with the traditional Maoist condemnation of such activities and the raising of cadre salaries, has ensured that most Party members and working personnel of the state still view such activities as morally and politically reprehensible. Consequently, most working personnel of the state will reject offers of bribery unless the offer involves extraordinary sums of money or property (Wang Jin 2002). However, when it comes to the issue of sex, the story is reportedly different. Cadres who would otherwise resist involvement in bribery and corruption are easily led on to the path of 'moral decay' because they no longer see the provision of sexual services as a political and social order problem (Zhao 2001). Recent cases therefore have involved not only young bureaucrat-entrepreneurs (predominantly men between 29–49 years of age), but also veteran cadres of 59 years of age or older (Wang and Liu 2000; Watts 2006).

Media reports further insist that China's rapidly changing sexual culture has led to an increase in the practice of women offering themselves as a bribe to bureaucrat-entrepreneurs in return for work promotions and other opportunities (Watts 2006). An oft-cited example in this regard is the case of Jiang Yanping, who was tried on 20–23 March 2001 for embezzlement and abusing her official position to gain favourable business deals for members of her family (Da 2002). Although Jiang was subsequently castigated in the press as an example of an 'upstart official' who obtained a senior position by sleeping with her superiors, she is also claimed to have defended her actions by stating: 'In a male-dominated world, a smart woman has to exploit the value that men place on the female sex' (Li Zhufeng 2002: 22–3). Following from an examination of this and other cases, media reporters maintain that the motivations for offering sex-related bribes have also proliferated. Apart from longstanding factors such as obtaining employment, promotion or a work transfer, they now include: gaining Party membership; obtaining housing; facilitating business deals; avoiding legal punishment; and promoting smuggling operations (Feng 2001: 93–6).

In sum, there is a broad consensus that something has to be done about the phenomenon of sexual bribery and corruption in China, but the question of whether that problem should be resolved by recourse to the 'rule of law' or the 'rule of virtue' is disputed. Those who oppose the criminalization of this phenomenon claim that it is essentially a moral issue, and therefore an inappropriate target of legally based governmental intervention (Jeffreys 2006: 159–78). They argue that recourse to the time-honoured method of seeking compliance through the provision of ideological and moral education, which now includes supervision by 'the masses' in the form of exposés in the media, constitutes a more appropriate response. Conversely, those who support the criminalization of sexual bribery and corruption tend to focus on legal and judicial reform in the name of consolidating China's post-Mao shift to a rule of law. They insist that counter-arguments based on notions of mutual consent and privacy function to excuse the existence of sex-related bribery and corruption by portraying it as a 'life-style problem' of the propertied classes, rather than a serious social order problem (He 2002). What contributors to both sides of this debate have in common is a belief that the 'sex' in sex-related bribery and corruption is neither moral nor right. It is an expression of bourgeois right insofar as the privileged access of bureaucrat-entrepreneurs to public resources and the commodified sexual services of women are viewed as an unfair display of their inequitable share of personal wealth proportional to the work they contribute to the development of socialism with Chinese characteristics.

The challenge to social and sexual equality

Western constructions of China's new rich as the middle-class vanguard of progressive social change are undermined by the routine portrayal of this group in the Chinese media as both advanced economic producers and polluters of socialist virtue. Despite state-led efforts to improve the reputation of China's new rich, in the form of promoting provincial and national model entrepreneurs, the Chinese public reportedly still assumes that 'no rich man is a good man' and that private entrepreneurs are particularly prone to displays of extra-marital sexual impropriety in the form of hiring the services of female prostitutes and keeping 'second wives' (Toy 2007: 15). The ostentatious consumption of sexual services by private entrepreneurs as a means to affirm their wealth and privileged social status is also blamed for leading bureaucrat-entrepreneurs on the road to moral decline. Such criticisms turn on the reactivation of former CCP claims to guarantee social and sexual equality, and, in doing so, offer both support and a challenge to the legitimacy of continued one-party rule.

Public condemnation of China's so-called 'mistress and prostitution boom' entails an explicit criticism of the CCP for creating the market conditions in which such phenomenon can flourish in the first place, whilst simultaneously upholding the Party-state's historically proven capacity and hence assumed ability to redress them in the future. Indeed, although the Chinese media often portray female sex sellers as 'fallen women' who will happily forsake their virtue for money, they also routinely present them as young, poor and rural women who are disadvantaged by the reform process, and who therefore deserve to be treated with sympathy and concern. Beijing lawyer, Zheng Baichun, for example, has recently established a website that provides legal advice to 'second wives' and advocates for 'mistress rights' on the grounds that such women are victimized by society, when they are themselves the victims of social and gendered inequalities (www.2n88.com). The perceived decline in social and sexual equality in reform-era China is also integral to arguments that the existence of commercial sexual services in entertainment and leisure venues stems from the ongoing demand for such services by male members of the new rich, including private and bureaucratic entrepreneurs.

However, to the extent that voices in China's media and academia call on the Chinese government to realize prosperity for all, and to resolve the interlinked problems of declining moral standards and sex-related corruption, it appears that China still needs the Chinese Communist Party. Media accounts of the dubious ways in which the new rich obtain and spend their wealth fuel public discontent over the growing chasm between the 'haves' and the 'have-nots', even as stories of corrupt cadres point to the CCP's declining legitimacy as the (moral) vanguard party. But the PRC Government and concerned academics are also portrayed as more determined and innovative than ever before in terms of creating new ways of preventing and controlling cadre corruption. More than 846,000 CCP members were penalized for corruption of various forms from 1988 to 2002. Stricter legal sanctions have been accompanied by the introduction of auditing and other practices designed to encourage governmental transparency, including establishing public accounts for repentant corrupt officials to return bribes. Government officials in Nanjing City, Jiangsu Province, are now required to register details both of their marital circumstances, and any long-term extra-marital relationship, in a move to curb sex-related bribery and corruption ('New anti-corruption method' 2005). The All-China Women's Federation has also launched a nationwide project to educate wives of leading officials about how to build a 'family firewall' against corruption ('China promotes anti-graft' 2006).

Viewed from this perspective, the modernizing mantra that 'economic reform demands (Western-style) political reform' not only ignores the evident and ongoing capacity of the CCP to transform itself by demanding political transparency and accountability within the parameters of one-party rule, it also overlooks the other myriad ways in which democratic political reform can be effected. Most notably, it discounts the diverse ways in which voices in the Chinese media and academia have both drawn on and reinvented the historical legacy of the CCP to demand a form of political liberalization that includes issues of social and sexual equality as a matter of course. Social and gender equity is a component of modern democratic change that is given scant attention in most accounts of 'why China does not need the Chinese Communist Party'. If criticisms of the sex-consumption practices of the new rich are anything to go by, then this omission may be misplaced.

Note

1   The 'productive forces' is a central concept in Marxism. It refers to the combination of the means of production with human labour power and encompasses all those forces that are applied by people in the production process. The productive forces are thus the unity of the means of production – the tools (instrument) and the raw material (subject) used to create something – and human labour (Marxists.org n.d.).

Bibliography

Abercrombie, N. and J. Urry (1983) *Capital, Labour, and the Middle Classes* London: Allen & Unwin.

Adelmen, Irma and David Sunding (1987) 'Economic Policy and Income Distribution in China' in *Journal of Comparative Economics* 11/3, pp. 444–61.

Aitchison, Jim (2002) *How Asia Advertises: The Most Successful Campaigns in Asia-Pacific and the Marketing Strategies Behind Them* Hong Kong: John Wiley (Asia).

All-China Federation of Industry and Commerce (2005) *Shiwu Qijian Minying Jingji Xingshi Fenxi Baogao* (An Analysis on the Situation of the Private Economy during the 'Tenth Five-Year-Plan').

All-China Women's Federation (2005) *Zhongguo Xingbie Pingdeng yu Funü Fazhan Zhuangkuang* (Gender Equality and Situation of Women's Development in China), at www.gov.cn/zwgk/2005-/content_25813.htm.

Amen, Mark, Kevin Archer and Marin Bosman (eds) (2006) *Relocating Global Cities. From the Centre to the Margin* Lanham: Rowman and Littlefield.

Anagnost, Ann (1997) 'Constructions of Civility in the Age of Flexible Accumulation' in Ann Anagnost (ed.) *National Past-Times: Narrative, Representation and Power in Modern China* Duke University Press, pp. 75–97.

Anagnost, Ann (2004) 'The corporeal politics of quality (*suzhi*)' in *Public Culture* 16/2, pp. 189–208.

Atkinson, Rowland and Gary Bridge (eds) (2005) *Gentrification in a Global Context. The New Urban Colonialism* London and New York:Routledge.

Aristotle (1992) *The Politics* (translated by T.A. Sinclair and revised by T.J. Saunders), London: Penguin Books.

Arole, Sanjiv (1999) 'Indian diamentaires losing out to the Chinese' in *Indian Express* [Mumbai] 11 May, p. 1.

AWE website, China Association of Women Entrepreneurs, at www.cawe.org.cn.

Bai, Chong-En, Jiangyong Lu and Zhigang Tao (2006) 'Property Rights Protection and Access to Bank Loans—Evidence from Private Enterprises in China' in *Economics of Transition* 14/4, pp. 611–28.

Bakken, B½rge (2000) *The Exemplary Society. Human Improvement, Social Control and the Dangers of Modernity in China* Oxford: Oxford University Press.

Bakshi, Gurdip and Zhiwu Chen (1996) 'The Spirit of Capitalism and Stock Market Prices' in *American Economic Review* 86/1, pp. 133–57.

Banerjee, Swapna (2004) *Men, women and domestics: Articulating middle-class identity in Colonial Bengal* New Delhi: Oxford University Press.

Bardhan, Pranab (1997) 'Corruption and Development: A Review of Issues' in *Journal of Economic Literature* 35/3, pp. 1320–46.

Barkow, Jerome (1989) *Darwin, Sex, and Status* University of Toronto Press.

Barmé, Geremie R. (1999) *In the Red: On Contemporary Chinese Culture* New York: Columbia University Press.

Barnett, A. Doak (1967) *Cadres, Bureaucracy and Political Power in Communist China* Columbia University Press.

Batjargal, Bat and Mannie Liu (2004) 'Entrepreneurs' Access to Private Equity in China: The Role of Social Capital' in *Organization Science* 15/2, pp. 159–72.

Beijing Baomu (2003) 'Beijing baomu shichang duandang' ('Beijing maid market supply too low'), at www.cctv.com/news.society/20031126/100610.shtml.

Beijing Morning News (7 November 2006) 'Tongchuang baomu youbei meifeng' ('"Beddable maids" violate public morality') in *Beijing Chengbao* (Beijing Morning News) 7 November 2006, p. 6.

Beijing Review (14 June 2007) 'Enterprise Income Tax Law of the People's Republic of China', at www.bjreview.com/document/txt/2007-/content_71269_2.htm.

Beijing University (1987) 'Shehuizhuyi chuji jieduan songjiao qingkuang diaochagao jituan' ('Report on the religious situation in the primary stage of socialism') volume 3, Beijing University Philosophy Department.

Beijing Youth Daily (*Beijing qingnian bao*) (2005) 'Zhongguo nianqingren cheng sheqipin xiaofei zhulijun' ('China's youth are becoming the leading forces of luxury goods consumers') 19 July 2005.

Bendix, R. and S. M. Lipset (1967) 'Karl Marx's Theory of Social Class', in R. Bendix and S. M. Lipset (eds), *Class, Status and Power* (2nd edition), London: Routledge.

Benewick, Robert, Irene Tong and Jude Howell (2004) 'Self-Governance and Community: A Preliminary Comparison between Villagers' Committees and Urban Community Councils' in *China Information* 18/1, pp. 11–28.

Bernstein, Thomas P. (1977) *Up to the Mountains and Down to the Villages* Yale University Press.

Berger, Joseph and Morris Zelditch (1998) *Status, Power, and Legitimacy* New Brunswick: Transaction.

Bian, Yanjie (1996) 'Chinese Occupational Prestige' in *International Sociology* 11/2, pp. 161–86.

Bian, Yanjie (2002) 'Chinese Social Stratification and Social Mobility' in *Annual Review of Sociology*, pp. 91–116.

Bian, Yanjie and John R. Logan (1996) 'Market Transition and the Persistence of Power: The Changing Stratification System in Urban China' in *American Sociological Review* 61/5, pp. 739–58.

Bishop, Ryan, John Phillips and Wei-Wei Yeo (eds) (2003) *Post Colonial Urbanism. Southeast Asian Cities and Global Processes* London and New York: Routledge.

Blauer, Ettagale (2007) 'Christie's Hong Kong sets record' in *Rapaport Diamond Report* 30/3, pp. 80–1.

Blecher, M. (1989) *China: Politics, Economics and Society* London: Frances Pinter.

Blecher, Marc (1991) 'Development State, Entreprenuerial State: The Political Economy of Socialist Reform in Xinju Municipality and Guanghan County' in Gordon White (ed.) *The Chinese State in the Era of Economic Reform* London: Macmillan, p. 265.

Blecher, Marc (1999) 'Strategies of Chinese State Legitimation among the Working Class', paper presented to the Workshop on Strategies of State Legitimation in Contemporary China, Centre for Chinese Studies, University of California at Berkeley, 7–9 May 1999.

Blecher, Marc (2002) 'Hegemony and Worker's Politics in China', *The China Quarterly*, No. 170, p. 283.

Blecher, Marc and Vivienne Shue (1999) *Tethered Deer: Government and Economy in a Chinese County* Stanford University Press.

Bloom, Gerald, Han Leiya and Li Xiang (2000) 'How Health Workers Earn A Living In China' in *Institute of Development Studies Working Paper 108* (March), at www.ids.ac.uk/ids/bookshop/wp/wp108.pdf.

Bo, Zhiyue (2002) *Chinese Provincial Leaders: Economic Performance and Political Mobility since 1949* New York: M E Sharpe.

Bolton, Gary E. and Axel Ockenfels (2000) 'ERC: A Theory of Equity, Reciprocity and Competition' in *American Economic Review* 90/1, pp. 166–93.

Boon, J. (1974) 'Anthropology and nannies' in *Man* 9, pp. 137–40.

Bourdieu, P. (1987) 'What Makes a Social Class?', *Berkeley Journal of Sociology* 22, p. 1–18.

Bourdieu, Pierre. (1989) *Distinction: a Social Critique of the Judgement of Taste* trans. Richard Nice, London: Routledge & Kegan Paul.

Bourdieu, Pierre. and Jean-Claude Passeron. (1979) *The Inheritors: French Students and Their Relation to Culture* Trans. Richard Nice, University of Chicago Press.

Boxer, Marilyn J. (2007) 'Rethinking the Socialist Construction and International Career of the Concept of "Bourgeois feminism"' in *American Historical Review*, February, pp. 131–58.

Braester, Yomi (2005) '"A Big Dying Vat": The Vilifying of Shanghai during the Good Eighth Company Campaign' in *Modern China* 31/4, pp. 411–47.

Braudel, Fernand (1992) *Civilization and Capitalism, 15th–18th Century* 3 vols. University of California Press.

Bray, David (2005) *Social Space and Governance in Urban China* Stanford University Press.

Brodsgaard, Kjeld Erik (1983) 'Paradigmatic Change: Readjustment and Reform in the Chinese Economy, 1953–1981, Part 1' in *Modern China* 9/1, pp. 37–83.

Brown-Humes, Christopher (2005) 'China's rising middle classes to outstrip Japan on spending' in *Financial Times* 21 September, p. 42.

Brugger, Bill and David Kelly (1990) *Chinese Marxism in the Post-Mao Era* Stanford University Press.

Bu Wei and Mi Xiaolin (Cecilia Milwertz) (2005) 'Yi xiao zhi da – tantao minjian funü zuzhi fandui jiating baoli de xingdong zhuyi jiqi chuanbo zhanlüe' ('Popular Organizing to Combat Domestic Violence – Activism and Media Interaction') in *Shehui Xingbie* (Gender Studies) 3.

Buckley, Christopher (1999) 'How a Revolution Becomes a Dinner Party: Stratification, Mobility and the New Rich in Urban China' in M Pinches (ed.) *Culture and Privilege in Capitalist Asia* London: Routledge.

Burnham, James (1972) *The Managerial Revolution* Greenwood Press, 1972 (Reprint of 1940 original edition.)

Burriss, Scott C. and Shen, Weixing (2005) *Emerging Issues in Chinese Health Law* Peking University Press.

Business Week (6 February 2006) 'In China Getting Rich is Glorious', at www.businessweek.com/magazine/content/06_06/b3970072.htm.

Cai, Yongshun (2002) 'The Resistance of Chinese Laid-off Workers in the Reform Period' in *The China Quarterly* 170, pp. 327–44.

Cai, Yongshun (2005a) *State and Laid-off Workers in Reform China* London: Routledge.

Cai, Yongshun (2005b) 'China's Moderate Middle Class' in *Asian Survey* 45/5.

Callick, Rowan (2007) 'All the Coal in China' in *The American* May/June, at www.american.com/archive/2007/may-june-magazine-contents/all-the-coal-in-china.

Cao, Yang (2004) 'Behind the Rising Meritocracy: Market, Politics, and Cultural Change in Urban China' in *Social Science Research* 33/3, pp. 435–63.

Carrillo, Beatriz (2008) *A North China Town: Social inclusion and social change* London: Routledge.

Cartier, Carolyn (2001) *Globalizing South China* Blackwell.

Cartier, Carolyn (2005) 'City-space. Scale Relations and China's Spatial Administrative Hierarchy' in Ma, Lawrence J. C and Fulong Wu (eds) *Restructuring the Chinese City: Changing Society, Economy and Space* London and New York: Routledge.

Cartier, Carolyn and Jessica Rothenberg-Aalami (1999) 'Empowering the "Victim"' in *The Journal of Geography* 98/6, pp. 283–94.

Castells, Manuel and Peter Hall (1994) *Technopoles of the World: The Making of 21st Industrial Complexes* London and New York: Routledge.

CDB (*China Development Brief*) (2006) 'Education in limbo between state and market' 1 June 2006, at www.chinadevelopmentbrief.com.

CDB (*China Development Brief*) (2007) 'Non-profit sector: The management scientists are coming' 19 April 2007, at www.chinadevelopmentbrief.com.

Chan, Anita and Jonathan Unger (1982) 'Grey and Black: The Hidden Economy of Rural China' in *Pacific Affairs* 55/2, pp. 452–71.

Chang, Chun-chiao (1978) 'On exercising all-round dictatorship over the bourgeoisie', in Raymond Lotta (ed.) *And Mao Makes Five* Chicago: Banner Press, p. 209–20.

Chao, J. (2005) 'Rise of wealth; fall of morals' in *Washington Times* 6 May 2005.

Chen, An (1999) *Restructuring Political Power in China: Alliances and Opposition, 1978–1998* Boulder: Lynne Rienner.

Chen, An (2002) 'Capitalist Development, Entrepreneurial Class, and Democratization in China' in *Political Science Quarterly* 117/3.

Chen, An (2003a) 'The New Inequality' in *Journal of Democracy* 14/1, p. 54.

Chen, An (2003b) 'Rising-Class Politics and Its Impact on China's Path to Democracy' in *Democratization* 10/2.

Chen, Chien-Hsun and Hui-Tzu Chen (2005) *High-Tech Industries in China* Cheltenham, UK: Edward Elgar.

Chen, Chin-Jou Jay (2004) *Transforming Rural China* London: RoutledgeCurzon.

Chen, Chin-Jou Jay (2006) 'Elite Mobility in Post-Reform Rural China' in *Issues & Studies* 42/2, pp. 53–83.

Chen Dongdong (2004) 'Woguo zhongchan jieji yanjiu de xianzhuang, yiyi ji xuyao tuzhan de jige wenti' ('The State and Significance of the Research on the Middle Class in China and they Way Forward') in *Hubei jingji xueyuan xuebao* (*Journal of the Hubei Economic Institute*) 2/4, pp. 112–117.

Chen Feng (2000) 'Subsistence Crises, Managerial Corruption and Labour Protests in China' in *The China Journal* 44, pp. 41–63.

Chen Feng (2006) 'Privatization and Its Discontents in Chinese Factories' in *The China Quarterly* 185, pp. 42–60.

Chen Guangjin, Li, Jun and Matlay, Harry (2006) 'Who are the Chinese private entrepreneurs? A study of entreprenurial attributes and business governance' in *Journal of Small Business and Enterprise Development*, 13/2, pp. 148–160.

Chen, Guanren *et al.* (2004) *Zhongguo zhongchanzhe diaocha* (*A Survey of China's Middle Class*) Beijing: Tuanjie chubanshe.

Chen, Mingyuan (2006) *Zhishi fenzi yu Renminbi shidai* (*Intellectuals and the Era of the PRC Dollar*) Shanghai: Wenhui Publishing House.

Chen, Shuhong (2004) 'Xin zhongchan jieji he minzhu' ('The New Middle Class and Democracy') in *Zhejiang xuekan* (*The Zhejiang Journal*) 4, pp. 36–38.

Chen Shujuan *et al.* (2005) 'Zhongguo zhongjian jieceng de xianzhuang ji shehui peiyu' ('The Shape of China's Middle Stratum and its Development') in *Chuanshan xuebao* (*The Chuanshan Journal*) 2, pp. 162–164.

Chen, Wenling (2005) 'Yaopin jiage jugao bu xia jiujing yuanyin hezai?' ('What is the reason behind high drug prices?') in *Zhongguo jingji shibao* (*China Economic Times*) 10 January.

Chen Xiaoya (2002a) 'Zhongchan jieceng Jiang chengqi Zhongguo weilai' ('China's Future Belongs to the Middle Stratum') in *Jingji yuekan* (*Economic Monthly*) 3, p. 37–38.

Chen Xiaoya (2002b) 'Zhongguo zhongchan jieji fuchu shuimian' ('The Emergence of a Middle Class in China') in *Juece tansuo* (*Policy Research & Exploration*) 2, p. 32–34.

Chen, Zhenggao (2005) 'Jianshe senlin chengshi jiasu tuijin shenyang laogongye diqu quanmian zhenxing' ('Build a forest city, speed up the transformation of Shenyang's industrial base') in *Zhongguo Chengshi linye* (*Journal of Chinese Urban Forestry*) 3/4, pp. 7–10.

Chen Ziwu (2007) 'Chanquan baohu shi yizhong ji weimiao de shehui zhuangtai' ('Protection of private properties is a very delicate social issue') 27 February 2007, at www.ceceo.cn/Detail.asp?II_ID=19259&CLS=105.

Cheung, Sidney and Eric Ma (2005) 'Advertising Modernity: Home, Space and Privacy' in *Visual Anthropology* 18/1, pp. 65–80.

Children (2006) 'Zhongguo yiwan fuhao 9 cheng yishang shi gaogan zinü' ('Over 90 percent of the rich in China are children of high ranking officials') 19 October 2006, at www.financenews.sina.com/ausdaily/000-000-107-105/202/2006-10-.shtml.

Chin, Christine. B. N. (1998) *In Service and Servitude: Foreign Female Domestic Workers and the Malaysian "Modernity" Project* Columbia University Press.

China.com.cn (29 June 2006) 'Zhi ye nai ma chong xia ying zheng yi' ('The controversial reappearance of professional wet nurses'), at www.china.com.cn.

China Daily (3 December 2002) *Blueprint for an Overall Xiaokang Society in China*.

China Daily [Hong Kong edition] (25 September 2003) 'Focus: China's gold rush', at www.chinadaily.com.cn/en/doc/2003-/content_267390.htm.

China Daily (6 September 2004) 'Surge in gold demand expected', at www.english. people.com.cn/200409/06/eng20040906_156020.html.

China Daily (9 October 2004) 'Year of events brings a lot of France to China', at www.chinadaily.com.cn/english/doc/2004-/content_380591.htm.

China Daily (30 January 2007) 'Diamonds demand set to continue', at www.en.ce.cn/ stock/marketnews/200701/30/t20070130_10259591.shtml.

China Daily (22 March 2007) 'China seeks private health input', at www.china.org. cn/english/health/203919.htm.

China Daily (20 July 2007) 'China now No 3 gold consumer and producer', at www. news.xinhuanet.com/english/2007–07/20/content_6403870.htm.

China Enterprise Confederation (n.d.) 'Mingxing qiyejia: Liu Suisheng' ('Star Entrepreneurs: Liu Suisheng'), at www.cec-ceda.org.cn/huodong/mxqyj/liushuisheng/index.htm.

China needs (2004) 'Liangxing fuhao ji dai zhongguo zao, zhongguo shi furen de tiantang' ('China needs good rich people, China is the heaven of the rich') 7 January 2004, at www.news.xinhuanet. com/fortune/2004–/content_1267972.htm.

China.org.cn (30 November 2005) 'Breaking the Public Hospital Monopoly', at www.china.org.cn/english/2005/Nov/150402.htm.

China.org.cn (20 June 2006) 'Ding Zuyi: Pioneering Private Education in China', at www.china.org.cn/english/2006/Jun/172102.htm.

China's Problems (2006) 'Wenti zhongguo zhi "riqu yanzhong de pinfu liangji fenhua" pian' ('China's problems: Chapter on rising inequalities') 13 October 2006, at blog.chinesenewsnet.com/?p=16662.

China promotes anti-graft (2006) 'China promotes anti-graft by educating officials' wives', Xinhua News Agency, 28 October 2006, at www.china.org.cn/english/MATERIAL/186577.htm.

CRI (China Radio International) (11 June 2007) 'China's New-Rich makes it the World's No. 3 Luxury Market', at english.cri.cn/4406/2007/06/11/1181@237088.htm.

China Unicom (n.d.) 'Dang he guojia lingdaoren tici' ('Inscriptions by Party and State Leaders'), at www.chinaunicom.com.cn/profile/gsjs/file10.html.

Chinese Communist Party (1993) 'Zhonggong zhongyang guanyu jianli shehuizhuyi shichang jingji tizhi ruogan wenti de jueding' ('Decision on Several Issues Relating to Building a Socialist Market Economic System'), at china.com.cn/ch-80years/lici/14/14–.htm.

Chinese Entrepreneurs Poetry Anthology Editorial Committee (2005) 'Zhongguo qiyejia shixuan zhenggao qishi' ('Call for Manuscripts for the Chinese Entrepreneurs Poetry Anthology') posted on Beijing Six Books website, at www.6book.com.cn/Article/ShowArticle.asp?ArticleID=220.

Chongqing Daily (2006) 'Chongqing qiong fu lushi shouru xianzhuang' ('The incomes of poor and rich lawyers in Chongqing') in *Chongqing ribao* (*Chongqing Daily*) 31 March 2006.

Chow Tai Fook (2006) 'Chow Tai Fook officially opens its 500th branch in Greater China' 14 September Press release, at www.chowtaifook.com/EN/Press%20Release/Chow%20Tai%20Fook%20Officially%20Opens%20Its%20500th%20Branch%20in%20Greater%20China2.htm.

Christiansen, Flemming (1992) 'Market Transition in China' in *Modern China* 18/1, pp. 72–93.

Chua, A. (2003) *World on Fire: How Exporting Free Market Democracy Breeds Ethnic Hatred and Global Instability* New York: Doubleday Books.

Chua, Beng-Huat (ed.) (2000) *Consumption in Asia: Lifestyles and Identities* London: Routledge.

Chua, Beng-Huat and Tan, Joo Ean (1999) 'Singapore: Where the New Middle Class sets the Standard' in M. Pinches (ed.) *Culture and Privilege in Capitalist Asia* London: Routledge, pp. 137–158.

Cody, Edward (2004a) 'China's Land Grabs Raise Specter of Popular Unrest: Peasants Resist Developers, Local Officials' 5 October 2004, at www.rrojasdatabank.org/chinpo03.htm.

Cody, Edward (2004b) 'Workers in China Shed Passivity: Spate of Walkouts Shakes Factories' in *Washington Post* 27 November 2004.

Colin, Finn (1997) *Social Reality* London and New York: Routledge.

Commentary (2006) 'Zhongguoren bixu zhi rong chi' ('Chinese people must learn what integrity and shame are') posted on 22 March 2006, at gb.chinareviewnews.com/doc/1001/1/3/3/100113388.html?coluid=5&kindid=110&docid=100113388.

'Communist Party discipline regulations' (1997) *Xinhua News Agency*, Beijing, 10 April, trans. *Selected World Broadcasts—China* 14 April, FE/2892 S2/1–18.

Cong Zhiguo (2004) 'Shenyang Zhongyi yuan "erci jixiao kaohe fenpei" zhengduan diaocha' ('Investigation of "redistribution according to second performance assessment" of Shenyang TCM Hospital') in *Huasheng chenbao* (*Huasheng Morning News*) 7 June 2004.

Courage, James (2004) 'Growing the jewelry market' in *Proceedings of The LBMA Precious Metals Conference*, 5–7 September, Shanghai, pp. 111–14, at www.lbma.org.uk/conf2004/2004proceedings.html.

Criticisms of wealth (14 July 2005) 'Xiaomi kaiche, jiao wo ruhe bu choufu' ('I cannot help but hate rich people—look, their mistresses come to work with fancy cars'), at news.sohu.com/ 20050714/n226304438.shtml.

Criticisms of wealth (29 September 2005) 'Li Yifu de "choufulun" rang ren chijing' ('It is unbelievable that Professor Li Yifu asks us not to hate rich people'), at big5.southcn.com/gate/big5/www.southcn.com/opinion/pe/200509290 386.htm.

Criticisms of wealth (7 February 2006) 'Zhuanjia: chengshi jumin shouru chaju pianda jiang daozhi "choufu"' ('Experts advise: increasing income inequality in urban China will lead people to hate the rich'), at big5.xinhuanet.com/gate/big5/news.xinhuanet.com/politics/2006–02/07/content_4145435.htm.

Criticisms of wealth (18 July 2006) 'Buxiang 'choufu', naihe wenti fuhao taiduo' ('I do not want to hate well-off people, but I cannot help since many of them are problematic rich'), at big5.southcn.com/gate/big5/www.southcn.com/opinion/pe/200607180422.htm.

Criticisms of wealth (12 February 2007) 'Zhongguoshi caifu shenhua, jiao wo ruhe bu choufu' ('How can I possibly not hate rich people given the ways they make money?'), at big5.southcn.com/gate/big5/www.southcn.com/opinion/pe/200702120375.htm.

Croll, E. (1995) *Changing Identities of Chinese Women: Rhetoric, Experience and Self-perception in Twentieth-Century China* Hong Kong University Press.

Croll, Elisabeth (2006) *China's New Consumers: Social Development and Domestic Demand* London: Routledge.

Crompton, Rosemary (1993) *Class and Stratification: An Introduction to Current Debates*, Cambridge: Polity Press.

Da, Yang (2002) *Zhongguo diyi nü tanguan Jiang Yanping* (*China's 'Number One' Corrupt Female Official, Jiang Yanping*) Beijing: Jincheng chubanshe.

Dai, Jinhua (1999) *Yinxing shuxie* (*The Hidden Script: Studies of Chinese Culture of the 1990s*) Nanjing: Jiangsu People's Press.

Dai, Yuanzhi and Lu, Zhijian (2000) 'Jiang "xing huilu" zhiyu xingfa shecheng zhinei' ('Talking about putting 'sex-related bribery and corruption' within the effective range of the criminal code') in *Zhongguo qingnian bao* (*China Youth Daily*) 15 December.

Davidoff, Leonora and Catherine Hall (1987) *Family Fortunes: Men and Women of the English Middle-Class, 1780–1850* London: Hutchison.

Davies, David J. (2005) 'Old Zhiqing Photos: Nostalgia and the "Spirit" of the Cultural Revolution' in *The China Review* 5/2 (2005), pp. 97–123.

Davies, Gloria (ed.) (2001) *Voicing Concerns: Contemporary Chinese Critical Inquiry* Lanham: Rowman & Littlefield.

Davis, Deborah (2000a) 'Social Class Transformation in Urban China: Training, Hiring, and Promoting Urban Professionals and Managers after 1949' in *Modern China* 26/3, pp. 251–275.

Davis, Deborah S. (ed.) (2000b) *The Consumer Revolution in Urban China* Berkeley: University of California Press.

Davis, Deborah S (2000c) 'A Revolution in Consumption' in Deborah S Davis (ed.) *The Consumer Revolution in Urban China* University of California Press, p. 1.

Davis, Deborah S., Richard Kraus, Barry Naughton and Elizabeth J. Perry (eds) (1995) *Urban Spaces in Contemporary China: The Potential for Autonomy and Community in Post-Mao China* Cambridge University Press.

Davis-Friedmann, Deborah (1985) 'Intergenerational Inequalities and the Chinese Revolution' in *Modern China* 11/4, pp. 177–201.

Deng Liqun (2001) cited in Willy Wo-Lap Lam, 'China's Struggle for "Democracy"', at www.cnn.com/Asia, 1 Aug. 2001.

Deng Liqun (1991) 'Have a Correct Understanding of Contradictions in Socialist Society, Grasp Initiative in Handling Contradictions' *The People's Daily* 23 Oct. 1991, p. 5, trans. FBIS-CHI, 29 Oct.1992, pp. 22–9.

Deng, Xiaoping (1993) 'Zai Wuchang, Shenzhen, Zhuhai, Shanghai dengdi de tanhua yaodian' ('Essential points from talks in Wuchang, Shenzhen, Zhuhai, Shanghai and other places'), in *Deng Xiaoping wenxuan* (*Selected Works of Deng Xiaoping*), Vol. III, Beijing: Foreign Languages Press.

Deng, Xiaoping (1994) *Selected Works of Deng Xiaoping* Vol. III, Beijing: Foreign Languages Press.

Deng, Xiaoping (1995) *Selected Works of Deng Xiaoping* Vol. II, Beijing: Foreign Languages Press.

Devine, Fiona (2004) *Class Practices: How Parents Help their Children Get Good Jobs* Cambridge University Press.

Diamond, N. (1975) 'Collectivization, kinship and the status of women in rural China' in *Bulletin of Concerned Asian Scholars* 7/1.

Dickson, Bruce J. (2003a) *Red Capitalists in China: The Party, Private Entrepreneurs, and Prospects for Political Change* Cambridge University Press.

Dickson, Bruce J. (2003b) 'Threats to Party Supremacy' in *Journal of Democracy*, 14/1, pp. 27–35.

Dickson, Bruce (2004) 'Dilemmas of Party Adaptation: the CCP's Strategies for Survival' in Peter Hays Gries and Stanley Rozen (eds) *State and Society in 21st-Century China: Crisis, Contention, and Legitimation* New York and London: RoutledgeCurzon.

Di Maggio, Paul J. and Walter W. Powell (1983) 'The iron cage revisited: institutional isomorphism and collective rationality in organizational fields' in *American Sociological Review* 48/2, pp. 147 – 160.

Ding, Lechao and Yao Zhenxing (eds) (1987) *Jingji fanzui yinan anli fenxi* (*Analysis of complicated cases of economic crimes*) Changchun: Dongbei Shifandaxue Chubanshe.

Ding Ling (1942) 'Thoughts on March 8' in Tani E. Barlow with Gary J. Bjorge (eds) *I Myself am a Woman: Selected Writings of Ding Ling* (Reprint and translation 1989) Boston: Beacon Press, pp. 316–21.

Dirlik, Arif (1994) *After the Revolution: Waking to Global Capitalism* Hanover, NH: Wesleyan University Press.

Djankov, Simeon, Yingyi Qian, Gerard Roland and Ekaterina Zhuravskaya (2006a) 'Who Are China's Entrepreneurs?' in *American Economic Review* 96/2, pp. 348–52.

Djankov, Simeon, Yingyi Qian, Gerard Roland, and Ekaterina Zhuravskaya (2006b) 'Entrepreneurship in China and Russia Compared' in *Journal of European Economic Association* 4/2–3, pp. 352–65.

Donald, Stephanie H. (2000) *Public Secrets, Public Spaces: Cinema and Civility in China* Lanham: Rowman & Littlefield.

Donald, S. H. and R. J. Benewick (2005) *The State of China Atlas* Sydney: UNSW Press; Berkeley: University of California Press.

Donald and Yi (2008) 'Richer than before – the cultivation of middle-class taste: education choices in urban China' in David S. G. Goodman (ed.) *The New Rich in China* Routledge.

Dong, Ming (2003) 'Jianshe xiaokang sehui yu kuoda zhongdeng shouru zhe bizhong' ('The Construction of a Xiaokang Society and the Expansion of the Middle-Income Strata') in *Zhonggong Zhejiang shengwei dangxiao xuebao* (*Journal of the Zhejiang Party School*) 6, pp. 17–22.

Drummond, L. (1978) 'The transatlantic nanny: notes on a comparative semiotics of the family in English-speaking societies' in *American Ethnologist* 5/1, pp. 30–43.

Du, Bessie (2005) 'Land Grab in China' 6 August 2005, at www.peacehall.com/news/gb/english/2005/08/200508060006.shtml.

Duan Yali (2007) 'Yisheng jishu jiazhi bi bu shang xiaoshi gong' ('The value of doctors' technical expertise is lower than the hour rate of casual workers') in *Jiankang bao* (*Health News*) 8 March 2007.

Duckett, Jane (1998) *The Entrepreneurial State in China* London: Routledge.

Dutton, Michael (1998) *Streetlife China* Cambridge University Press.

Edwards, Louise (2004) 'Constraining Women's Political Work with "Women's-Work": The Chinese Communist Party and Women's Participation in Politics' in Anne E. McLaren (ed.) *Chinese Women—Living and Working* London: RoutledgeCurzon, pp. 109–30.

Edwards, Louise (2006) 'Sport, Fashion and Beauty: New Incarnations of the Female Politician in Contemporary China' in F. Martin and L. Heinrich (eds) *Embodied Modernities: Corporeality, Representation and Chinese Cultures* Hawaii University Press, pp. 146–61.

Edwards, Louise (2007) 'Strategizing for politics: Chinese women's participation in the one-party state' in *Women's Studies International Forum* 30/5 (September–October) pp. 380–90.

Edwards, Louise (2008a) *Gender, Politics and Democracy: Women's Suffrage in China* Stanford University Press.

Edwards, Louise (2008b) 'Diversity and Evolution in the State-in-society: International influences in combating violence against women' in Linda Chelan Li (ed.) *The State in Transition: Processes and Contests in Local China* London: Routledge.

Edward, Peter (2006) 'Examining Inequality: Who Really Benefits from Global Growth?' in *World Development* 34/10, p. 1,679.

Ehrenreich, Barbara (1990) *Fear of Falling: The Inner Life of the Middle Class* New York: Harper Collins.

The Electric Canvas (2004), at www.theelectriccanvas.com.au/showcase/cartier1243.htm.

Elite Shoppers Guide for Luxury Goods (*Jingping Gouwu Zhinan*) (2005) at www.csonline.com.cn.

Engels, F. (1934) *Anti-Dühring* Moscow: Co-operative Publishing Society.

Engels, Friedrich (1972 [1884]) *The Origins of the Family, Private Property and the State* New York: International Publishers.

Ensler, Eve (1998) *The Vagina Monologues* New York: Villard.

'Entrepreneur: what's in a definition?' (n.d.), at www.hcmpublishing.com/Essays/entrepreneur-definition.html.

Entwisle, B. and G. E. Henderson (eds) (2000) *Re-Drawing Boundaries: Work, Households, and Gender in China* Berkeley: University of California Press.

Esherick, J, P. Pickowicz and A. Walder (eds) (2006) *China's Cultural Revolution as History* Stanford University Press.

Evans, Harriet and S. Donald. (eds) (1999) *Picturing Power in the People's Republic of China: Posters of the Cultural Revolution* Lanham: Rowman and Littlefield.

Fan, Chengze S. (2000) 'Economic Development and the Changing Patterns of Consumption in Urban China' in Chua, Beng-Huat. (ed.) *Consumption in Asia: Lifestyles and Identities* London: Routledge, pp. 82–97.

Fan, C. Cindy (2004a) 'The State, the Migrant Labour Regime, and Maiden Workers in China' in *Political Geography* 23/3, pp. 283–305.

Fan, C. Cindy (2004b) 'Out to the City and Back to the Village' in Arianne M. Gaetano and Tamara Jacka (eds) *On the Move: Women and Rural-to-Urban Migration in Contemporary China* Columbia University Press, pp. 177–206.

Fang Tong (2004) 'Zhiji yi jie guai xianzhuang zhi huikou' ('Kickbacks, an abnormal phenomenon in medicine') in *Jiankang bao* (*Health News*) 12 May.

Fang, Y., C. S. Granrose and R. V. Kong (2005) 'National Policy Influence on Women's Careers in the People's Republic of China' in Cherlyn Skromme Granrose (ed.) *Employment of Women in Chinese Cultures: Half the Sky* Cheltenham: Edward Elgar Publishing, pp. 49–83.

Feng, Xiang (2001) 'Xing huilu weishenme busuan huilu?' ('Why is sex-related bribery and corruption not treated as a crime?') in *Dushu* (*Reading*) November, p. 93–6.

Feng, Shuquan (2005) 'Goujian Hexie Shehui Bixu Jiejue Ruoshi Qunti Wenti' ('The Construction of a Harmonious Society Must Solve the Problem of the Disadvantaged Groups') in *Renmin Ribao* (*The People's Daily*) 21 July.

Fewsmith, Joseph (2001) *China since Tiananmen* Cambridge: Cambridge University Press.

Fish, M. Steven and Omar Choudhry (2007) 'Democratization and Economic Liberalization in the Postcommunist World' in *Comparative Political Studies* 40/3, pp. 254–82.

Five Groups (2002) 'Five groups', at www.china.org.cn/english/2002/Dec/50803.htm.

Flannery, Russell (2006) 'Private wealth—China's Richest' in *Forbes* 178/11, 27 November 2006, p. 56.

Ford, Peter (2007) 'Consumer tidal wave on the way: China's middle class' in *The Christian Science Monitor 2 January.*

Forden, Sara Gay (2006) 'New wealth in Asia lifts jewelers' outlook' in *The International Herald Tribune* 2 January, p. 11.

Frank, Robert H. (1985) *Choosing the Right Pond: Human Behavior and the Quest for Social Status* New York: Oxford University Press.

Fraser, David (2000) 'Inventing Oasis: Luxury Housing Advertisements and Reconfiguring Domestic Pace in Shanghai' in Deborah S Davis (ed.) *The Consumer Revolution in Urban China* University of California Press, p. 25.

Friedan, Betty (1963) *The Feminine Mystique* New York: Norton.

Frykman, Jonas and Orvar Lofgren (1987) *Culture Builders: A Historical Anthropology of Middle-Class Life* Rutgers University Press.

Fukuyama, F. (1992) *The End of History and the Last Man* London: Penguin.

Fung, Vigor (1987) 'China Lawyers, Once Banned, Grapple With Government Hostility and Low Pay' in *Wall Street Journal* (Eastern edition) 14 April, p. 1.

'Funü yingdang' (1939) 'Funü yingdang zuo funü gongzuo' ('Women must undertake women's work') in *Zhongguo funü (China's Women)* 1/2 (1 July), p. 19.

Gabriel, Satyananda J. (2006) *Chinese Capitalism and the Modernist Vision* London and New York: Routledge.

Galbraith, John K. (1967) *The New Industrial State* Hamish Hamilton.

Gallagher, M. (2001) 'Women and gender' in H. Giskin and B. S. Walsh (eds) *An Introduction to Chinese Culture through the Family* Albany: State University of New York, p. 89–105.

Gao Qiang (2005) 'Fazhan yiliao weisheng shiye, wei goujian shehui zhuyi hexie shehui zuo gongxian' ('Develop medical and health enterprise, and contribute to the construction of a socialist harmonious society'), at www.moh.gov.cn/public/.

Gardner, John (1969) 'The *Wu-fan* Campaign in Shanghai: A Study in the Consolidation of Urban Control' in A Doak Barnett (ed.) *Chinese Communist Politics in Action* University of Washington Press.

Garnaut, Ross and Ligang Song (2003) *China's Third Economic Transformation: The Rise of the Private Economy* London: Routledge.

Gates (2005) 'Bi'er Gaici weihe zai zhongguo liulei?' ('Why did Bill Gates cry for China?') 13 October 2005, at www. chinaxq.com/forum/read_art_display.asp?boardid=135&bbsid=417.

Gates, Hill (1985) 'Money for the gods' in *Modern China* 13/3, pp. 259–77.

Gaubatz, Piper Rae (1995a) 'Changing Beijing' in *Geographical Review* 85/1, pp. 74–96.

Gaubatz, Piper Rae (1995b) 'Urban Transformation in post-Mao China: impacts of the reform era on China's urban form' in Deborah S. Davis, Richard Kraus, Barry Naughton and Elizabeth J. Perry (eds) *Urban Spaces in Contemporary China. The potential for Autonomy and Community in Post Mao China* Cambridge University Press.

Gibb, Allan and Jun Li (2003) 'Organizing for Enterprise in China: What Can We Learn from the Chinese Micro, Small, and Medium Enterprise Development Experience' in *Futures* 35/4, pp. 403–21.

Giddens, A. (1973) *The Class Structure of Advanced Societies.*

Giga-Catholic Information (n.d.), at www.gcatholic.com/dioceses/diocese/hung1.htm.

Giles, John, Albert Park and Fang Cai (2006) 'How Has Economic Restructuring Affected China's Urban Workers' in *The China Quarterly* 185, pp. 61–95.

Gillin, Donald G. (1967) *Warlord Yen Hsi-shan in Shansi Province 1911–1949* Princeton University Press.

Gilmartin, Chris (1984) 'Recent developments in research about women in the PRC' in *Republican China* 10/1 B (November) pp. 57–66.

Gilmartin, Christina K. (1995) *Engendering the Chinese Revolution: Radical Women, Communist Politics and Mass Movements in the 1920s* California University Press.

Glassman, R M. (1991) *China in Transition: Communism, Capitalism and Democracy* New York: Praeger.

Gold, Thomas B. (1990) 'Urban Private Business and Social Change' in Deborah Davis and Ezra F. Vogel (eds) *Chinese Society on the Eve of Tiananmen* Harvard University Press, pp. 157–78.

Gold, Thomas B. (1991) 'Urban Private Business and China's Reforms' in Richard Baum (ed.) *Reform and Reaction in Post-Mao China* London and New York: Routledge, pp. 84–103.

Goldman, Merle (2005) *From Comrade to Citizen: The Struggle for Political Rights in China* Harvard University Press.

Gong, Xiantian (2006) 'Yibu feibei xianfa he beili shehuizhuyi jiben yuanze de "wuquanfa" cao'an' ('The draft law on property rights is unconstitutional and deviates from socialist principles') 10 February 2006, at www.lawyerstown.com/newlaw/news_page.asp?id=0000000031&lawid=0000000020.

Gong, Xiaobing (2005) 'Zhongguo lushi ye xianzhuang, wenti ji duice yanjiu' ('A study of the current conditions of China's lawyers, and their problems and solutions') in *Shijiao* (*Perspectives*) 5/2.

Goodman, David S. G. (1980) 'The Provincial First Party Secretary in the People's Republic of China, 1949–1978: A Profile' in *The British Journal of Political Science* 10/1, p. 39.

Goodman, David S. G. (1994a) *Deng Xiaoping and the Chinese Revolution: A Political Biography* London: Routledge.

Goodman, David S. G. (ed.) (1994b) *China's Quiet Revolution: New Interactions between State and Society* Melbourne: Longman Cheshire.

Goodman, David S. G. (1994c) 'The Political Economy of Change' in David S. G. Goodman (ed.) *China's Quiet Revolution: New Interactions between State and Society* Melbourne: Longman Cheshire.

Goodman, David S. G. (1995) 'Collectives and connectives, capitalism and corporatism: structural change in China' in *Journal of Communist Studies and Transition Politics*, 11/1, pp. 12–32.

Goodman, David S. G. (1996) 'The People's Republic of China: the party-state, capitalist revolution and new entrepreneurs' in R. Robison and D. S. G. Goodman (eds) *The New Rich in Asia: Mobile phones, McDonalds and middle class revolution* London: Routledge, pp. 225–242.

Goodman, David S. G. (1998) 'In Search of China's New Middle Classes: the Creation of Wealth and Diversity' in *Asian Studies Review* 22/1, pp. 39–62.

Goodman, David S. G. (1999a) 'The New Middle Class' in Merle Goldman and Roderick MacFarquhar (eds) *The Paradox of China's Post-Mao Reforms* Harvard University Press, pp. 241–61.

Goodman, David S.G. (1999b) 'King Coal and Secretary Hu: Shanxi's Third Modernisation' in Hans Hendrischke and Chongyi Feng (eds) *The Political Economy of China's Provinces* Routledge, pp. 211–244.

Goodman, David S. G. (2000) 'The Localism of Local Leadership: Cadres in Reform Shanxi' in *Journal of Contemporary China* 9/24, p. 159.

Goodman, David S. G. (2001) 'The interdependence of state and society: the political sociology of local leadership' in Chien-min Chao and Bruce J. Dickson (eds) *Remaking the Chinese State: Strategies, Society and Security* London: Routledge, p. 132.

Goodman, David S.G. (2002) 'Revolutionary Women and Women in the Revolution: The Chinese Communist Party and Women in the War of Resistance to Japan, 1937–1945' in *The China Quarterly* 164 (December), pp. 915–42.

Goodman, David S. G. (2005) 'Exiled by Definition: The Salar and Economic Activism in Northwest China' in *Asian Studies Review* 29/4 (December), pp. 325–343.

Goodman, David S. G. (2006) 'Shanxi as translocal imaginary: reforming the local' in Tim Oakes and Louisa Schein (eds) *Translocal China* London: Routledge, p. 56.

Goodman, David S. G. (2007) 'Narratives of Change: Culture and Local Economic Development' in Barbara Krug and Hans Hendrsichke (eds) *The Chinese Economy in the 21st Century: Enterprise and Business Behaviour* Cheltenham: Edward Elgar, pp. 175–201.

Goodman, David S. G. (2008) 'News from the Front: The State in Transition' in Li, Linda Chelan (ed.) *The State in Transition: Processes and contests in local China* London: Routledge.

Goodman, David S. G. and Richard Robison (1992) (eds) *The New Rich in Asia* Special issue of *The Pacific Review* 5/4.

Gordon, J. (2007) 'To get rich is glorious, but not harmonious' in *China Business Blog*, 30 January, at www.chinabusinessservices.com/blog.

Gore, L. L. P. (1997) 'Bureaucratic entrepreneurs: politically and socially embedded economic actors' *Working Paper No. 83*, National Library of Australia, at wwwarc.murdoch.edu.au/wp/wp83.rtf.

Gore, L. L. P (1999) 'The communist legacy in post-Mao growth' in *The China Journal*, 41, pp. 25–54.

Gore, L. L. P. (2000) 'A Meltdown with Chinese Characteristics?' in Kanishka Jayasuriya, Richard Robison, Mark Beeson and Hyuk-Rae Kim (eds) *Politics and Markets in the Wake of the Asian Crisis* London: Routledge, pp. 130–150.

Gray, Jack (1974) 'Politics in Command' in *Political Quarterly* 54/1, pp. 26–48.

Greenlees, Donald (2005) 'The subtle power of Chinese tourists' in *The International Herald Tribune* 6 October.

Gregory, Neil and Stoyan Tenev (2001) 'China's Home-Grown Entrepreneurs' in *The China Business Review* January–February 2001, at www.chinabusinessreview.com/public/0101/gregory.html.

Gries, Peter Hays and Stanley Rosen (2004) 'Introduction: popular protest and state legitimation in 21st-century China' in Peter Hays Gries and Stanley Rosen (eds) *State and Society in 21st century China* London: RoutledgeCurzon, pp. 1–24.

Groves, Richard, Alan Murie and Christopher Watson (eds) (2007) *Housing and the new welfare state: perspectives from East Asia and Europe* Aldershot, Hampshire, England; Burlington, Vermont: Ashgate.

Gu, Edward and Merle Goldman (eds) (2004) *Chinese Intellectuals between State and Market* London: Routledge Curzon.

Gu, Mingyuan (2001) 'Zhongguo dalu guocheng shezhi gaige yaozhi' ('The Spirit of Curriculum Reform in Mainland China') in *Jiaoyu Shiji* (*Educational Century*) 3, pp. 21–23.

Gu, Xin and David Kelly (1994) 'New Conservatism: Intermediate Ideology of a "New Elite"' in Goodman (ed.) *China's Quiet Revolution: New Interactions between State and Society* Melbourne: Longman Cheshire, pp. 219–233.

Gu, Yining (2003) 'Zhejiang dui 32 jia yiyuan diaocha biaoming: yiyuan shoushu fei guodi yao jia tai gao' ('Investigation of 32 hospitals in Zhejiang shows: surgical fees are too low while drug prices are too high') in *Qianjiang wanbao* (*Qianjiang Evening News*) 27 September.

Guanghui Group (2005a) 'Qiye ge' ('Corporate Songs'), at www.guanghui.com/culture/whjs/sbxt.asp.

Guanghui Group (2005b) 'Wenhua huodong' ('Cultural Activities'), at www.guanghui.com/culture/whjs/whhd.asp.

Guangzhou Evening News (21 December 2003) 'Baomu shushe shequ xian shen, ci ju rang shanghai ju min gandao heng fang bian' ('Maid dormitories appear in residential communities, bringing convenience to Shanghai residents') originally from *Yangcheng Wanbao* (*Guangzhou Evening News*) 21 December 2003, at www.sina.com.cn.

The Guardian (14 January 2006) 'China's new rich learn to flaunt it—Jonathan Watts in Shanghai.'

Guo, Gang (2004) 'Review of Red Capitalists in China: The Party, Private Entrepreneurs, and Prospects for Political Change' in *Comparative Political Studies* 37/8, pp. 986–9.

Guo Zhenshu (2003) 'Dangdai Zhongguo shehui jieji jieceng jiegou de fenxi fangfa' ('Class and Stratum Analysis in Contemporary China') in *Zhonggong zhongyang dangxiao xuebao* (*Journal of the Party School of the Central Committee of the CCP*) , pp. 36–38.

Guthrie, Doug (1999) *Dragon in a Three-Piece Suit: The Emergence of Capitalism in China* Princeton University Press.

Habermas, Jürgen (1992) *The Structural Transformation of the Public Sphere* Oxford: Polity.

Hai'er Group (n.d.) 'Haier qiye wenhua' ('Haier's Corporate Culture'), at www.haier.com/cn/haier/culture/faith1_01.asp.

Hall, David L. and Roger T. Ames (1987) *Thinking Through Confucius* New York: SUNY Press.

Han, Jun (1995) 'Zhongguo xin shiqi gongren jieji neibu jieceng liyi geju baogao' ('A Report on the Patterns of Interests of the Chinese Working Class in the New Era') in Li Peling (ed.) *Zhongguo xin shiqi jieji jieceng baogao* (*Social Stratification during China's Market Transition in China*) Shenyang: Liaoning renmin chubanshe.

Han, Rongliang (2002) 'China becomes world biggest platinum consumer' in *People's Daily Online*, 21 May, at www.english.peopledaily.com.cn/200205/21/eng20020521_96118.shtml.

Hann, C. M. (ed.) (2002) *Postsocialism: Ideals, Ideologies and Practices in Eurasia* London: Routledge.

Hao, Yufan (1999) 'From rule of man to rule of law: an unintended consequence of corruption in China in the 1990s'in *Journal of Contemporary China* 8/22, pp. 405–23.

Hare, Paul G. (1990) 'From Central Planning to Market Economy' in *Economic Journal* 100/401, pp. 581–95.

Harris, Lloyd C. and Kai Yi Cai (2002) 'Exploring market driving: a case study of De Beers in China' in *Journal of Market-Focused Management* pp. 171–96.

Harrison, Carol E. (1999) *The Bourgeois Citizen in Nineteenth-Century France: Gender, Sociability, and the Uses of Emulation* Oxford: Oxford University Press.

Harvey, David (2006) *A Brief History of Neoliberalism* Oxford: Oxford University Press.

Hasan, Shela Raza (2006) 'China a golden opportunity for Indian jewelers' in *Asian Times Online*, 25 February, at www.atimes.com/atimes/China_Business/HB25Cb05.html.

He, Jingwen (ed.) (2002) '"Xing huilu" falü gai bugai guan?' ('Can the law control "sex-related bribery and corruption" or not?') in *Nangfang wang*, 23 October, at www.southcn.com/news/gdnews/chuamei/200210230695.html.

He Li (2006) 'Emergence of the Chinese Middle Class and Its Implications' in *Asian Affairs* 33/2, pp. 67–83.

He Qinglian (1998) *Xiandaihua de xianjing: Dangdai Zhongguo de jingji shehui wenti (The Pitfalls of Modernization: The Economic and Social Problems of Contemporary China)* Beijing: Jinri chubanshe.

He Qinglian (2007) '"Yuanzui" zhi zheng houmian yincang de shehui jinzhang' ('Social tensions as reflected in the debate on "the original sin of the rich"') 10 February 2007, at www.epochtimes.com/b5/7/2/10/n1619404.htm.

He, Xinyi (2004) 'Ye tan peiyang yu zhuangda zhongchan jieceng' ('On the Expansion of the Middle Stratum') in *Jingji luntan (Economic Forum)* 13, pp. 152–153.

He, Zhongzhou (2007) 'Gaoxiao de "Zhongguo shi fuzhai": Jilin Daxue qianzhai yangben diaocha' ('University's "Chinese style debts": a sample investigation of Jilin University's debts') in *Zhongguo xinwen zhoukan (China News Weekly)* 6 April.

Hearn, Francis (1978) 'Rationality and Bureaucracy: Maoist Contributions to a Marxist Theory of Bureaucracy' in *The Sociological Quarterly* 19/1, pp. 37–54.

Heberer, Thomas (2003) *Private Entrepreneurs in China and Vietnam: Social and Political Functioning of Strategic Groups* Leiden and Boston: Brill.

Herberer, T. and G. Schubert (2006) 'Political reform and regime legitimacy in Contemporary China' in *Asien* 99, April, pp. 9–28.

Henan Renmin Zhengfu (Heman People's Government) (2005) 'Guanyu guanche 2005(3) hao wenjian guli zhichi he yindao feigongyouzhi jingji fazhan de shishi yijian' ('Opinions regarding carrying out 2005(3) document by State Development and Reform Commission on encouraging, supporting and directing the development of non-state owned economy'), at www.smehen.gov.cn/info/Show.aspx?id=87070.

Hendrischke, Hans (1994) 'Expertocracy and Professionalism' in Goodman (ed.) *China's Quiet Revolution: New Interactions between State and Society* Melbourne: Longman Cheshire, 144–161.

Henriot, Christian (1993) *Shanghai 1927–1937: Municipal Power, Locality, and Modernization* University of California Press.

Henriot, Christian and Shi Lu (1996) *La Réforme des Entreprises en Chine: Les entreprises shanghaiennes entre État et marché (Enterprise Reform in China: Shanghai Enterprises between State and Market)* Paris: L'Harmattan.

Hershkovitz, Linda (1985) 'The Fruits of Ambivalence: China's Urban Individual Economy' in *Pacific Affairs* 58/3, pp. 427–50.

Hewitt (2006) *2006 Hewitt TCM^{TM} Study.*

Hirsch, Fred (1976) *Social Limits to Growth* Harvard University Press.

HKTB (Hong Kong Tourism Board) (2007a) *Hong Kong Tourism Board Annual Report 2005–06* Hong Kong: Hong Kong Tourism Board.

HKTB (Hong Kong Tourism Board) (2007b) *HKTB Departing Visitor Survey* Hong Kong: Tourism Research, Hong Kong Tourism Board.

HKTB (Hong Kong Tourism Board) (2007c) *Tourism Overview 2007: Market Presentation – Mainland China* Hong Kong, at www.partnernet.hktb.com/pnweb/jsp/comm/index.jsp?charset=en&pageContent=//jsp/doc/docMain.jsp&cat_id=5080&menu_cat_id=5079.

HKTB (Hong Kong Tourism Board) (2007d) *Hong Kong Tourism Statistics in Brief 2006* Hong Kong: Hong Kong Tourism Board.

HKTDC (Hong Kong Trade and Development Council) (2002) *Jewelry Shoppers in Major Chinese Cities* Hong Kong: Hong Kong Trade and Development Council.

Hochschild, Arlie Russell (2002) 'Love and Gold' in Barbara Ehrenreich and Arlie Russell Hochschild (eds) *Global Woman: Nannies, Maids and Sex Workers in the New Economy* New York: Metropolitan Books, pp. 15–30.

Hoffman, Lisa (2006) 'Autonomous choices and patriotic professionalism: on governmentality in late-socialist China' in *Economy and Society* 35/4, pp. 550 – 570.

Holmstrom, Nancy and Richard Smith (2000) 'The Necessity of Gangster Capitalism, in *Monthly Review* 52/2, pp. 1–15.

Holton, R. J. and B. Turner (1989) *Max Weber on Economy and Society* London: Routledge.

Hong, Zhaohui (2004) 'Mapping the Evolution and Transformation of the New Private Entrepreneurs in China' in *Journal of Chinese Political Science* 9/1, pp. 23–42.

Honig, E. (2003) 'Socialist sex: the Cultural Revolution revisited' in *Modern China* 29/2, pp. 143–75.

Honig, E. and G. Hershatter (1988) *Personal Voices: Chinese Women in the 1980's,* Stanford University Press.

Hooper, Beverley (1984) 'China's Modernization: Are Young Women Going to Lose Out?' in *Modern China* 10/3, pp. 317–43.

Horscroft, Elizabeth (2007) 'Sector shines on' in *South China Morning Post* 3 March, Supplement section, p. 7.

Howell, J. (2002) 'Women's political participation in China: struggling to hold up half the sky' in *Parliamentary Affairs* 55/1, pp. 42–56.

Howell, Jude (2003) 'Women's Organizations and Civil Society in China' in *International Feminist Journal of Politics* 5/2 (July), pp. 191–215.

Hsiao, Hsin-Huang Michael (ed.) (1993) *Discovery of the Middle Classes in East Asia* Taipei: Institute of Ethnology, Academica Sinica.

Hsiung, Ping-Chun, Maria Jaschok and Cecilia Milwert (eds) (2001) *Chinese women organising: Cadres, feminists, muslims, queers* Oxford, New York: Berg.

Hsu, Carolyn L. (2006) 'Cadres, *getihu*, and good businesspeople: making sense of entrepreneurs in early post-socialist China' in *Urban Anthropology and Studies of Cultural Systems and World Economic Development* 35/1.

Hsüeh Feng-hsüan (Victor F. S. Sit) (1995) *Beijing: The Nature and Planning of a Chinese Capital City* Chichester, New York: Wiley.

Hu, Fox Yi (2007) '"Star of Stanley Ho" a heavy dose of bling' in *South China Morning Post* 19 July, p. 2.

Hu, Jintao (2005) *Zai Sheng Buji Zhuyao Lingdao Ganbu Tigao Goujian Shehui Zhuyi Hexie Shehui Nengli Zhuanti Yantaoban Shang De Jianghua* (Speech at the Special Meeting of Provincial Cadres to Discuss the Construction of a Socialist Harmonious Society) Beijing: Renmin chubanshe.

Hu, Xiaopeng (2004)'Zhuanxingqi shouru de chuci fenpei he zaifenpei wenti yanjiu' ('A study of resource allocation and redistribution during market transition') 10 December, at sym2005.cass.cn/file/ 2004121027769.html.

Hu, Xiuhong and David H. Kaplan (2001) 'The Emergence of Affluence in Beijing: Residential Social Stratification in China's Capital City' in *Urban Geography* 22/1, pp. 54–77.

Huaixiang Education Park (*Huaixiang Jiaoyuan*) (10 September 2005) '2005 nian bai jiao weifang gaizao dahui zhanbiaoying mingdan' ('In 2005 a hundred dangerous classrooms are repaired by a group of highly commended people').

Huang, Xianghuai (2003) 'Dangdai Zhongguo zhongjian jieceng de zhengzhixue jiedu' ('Political Implications of the Middle Stratum in Contemporary China') in *Kexue shehuizhuyi (Scientific Socialism)* 2, pp. 13–16.

Huang, Yasheng (2002) 'Two Cheers for Jiang Zemin's Three Represents' in *Project Syndicate* November 2002, at www.project-syndicate.org/commentary/1038/1.

Huang, Yi (2006) *Chengshi shehui fenceng yu Juzhu geli (Urban Social Stratification and Residential Segregation)* Shanghai: Shanghai Tongji Daxue Chubanshe.

Huawei Technologies (2006) 'Chanwu guanli' ('Management through Zen Enlightenment') in *Huawei People* 179 (August), at www.huawei.com/cn/publications/view.do?id=1112&cid=1222&pid=87.

Huberman, Bernardo A., Christoph H. Loch and Ayse Önçüler (2004) 'Status as a Valued Resource' in *Social Psychology Quarterly* 67/1, p. 103.

Hudson, Christina (2007) 'Bumper year for weddings fuels diamond growth in China' in *Diamond: Diamond Federation of Hong Kong 2007 Yearbook* Hong Kong: Diamond Federation of Hong Kong, China Ltd, pp. 48–51.

Hung, Eva P.W. and Stephen W.K. Chiu (2003) 'The Lost Generation' in *Modern China* 29/4, pp. 204–36.

Hunter, Ian (1988) *Culture and Government: The Emergence of Literary Education* Houndmills: Macmillan Press.

Huters, Theodore (2003) 'Introduction' in Wang Hui, T. Huters and R. Karl (eds) *China's New Order: Society, Politics, and Economy in Transition* Harvard University Press, pp. 1–40.

Inequality (2005) 'Pinglun: suoxiao pingfu chaju diyibu' ('Commentary: The first step towards reduction in inequality') 6 September 2005, at paowang.com/blog/langege/archives/007294.html.

Information Office of the State Council of the People's Republic of China (1994) 'Chapter 1: Historic liberation of Chinese women' in *The Situation of Chinese Women*, at www.china.org.cn/e-white/chinesewoman/11–2.htm.

Insecurity (7 February 2005) 'Woguo zhongdeng pianshang shouru renqun anquangan zuidi, nongmingong zuigao' ('In cities, rural migrant laborers have a good sense of safety, the well-off do not'), at news.sohu.com/20050207/n224267820.shtml.

Insecurity (13 July 2005) 'Zhongguo shehui fencing yanzhong shiheng rang qiongren furen dou meiyou anquangan' ('Both the rich and the poor have a sense of insecurity due to inequality'), at news.sohu.com/20050713/n226284899.shtml.

Insecurity (19 July 2006) '"Cishan" shi yizhi fuhao xinling bu'an de yi wei liangyao' ('"Charity" is a good cure for the rich to feel peace again'), at old.racszh.net/NewsView.Asp?classid=5&id=432.

Insecurity (20 July 2006) 'Zai jufu zhong bu'an yeshi yizhong chiru' ('The rich feel unsafe, which in fact shows how guilty they are'), at big5.xinhuanet.com/gate/big5/news.xinhuanet.com/comments/2006–/content_4858180.htm.

Interviews (2007) *A series of 15 interviews conducted with principals of family-owned diamond jewelry firms*, Hong Kong and Shenzhen, May–July (Carolyn Cartier.)

Ip, Hung-Yok (1994) 'The Origins of Chinese Communism: A New Interpretation' in *Modern China* 20/1, pp. 34–63.

Jacka, T. (1997) *Women's Work in Rural China: Change and Continuity in an Era of Reform* Cambridge University Press.

Jacka, Tamara (2000) '"My life as a migrant worker": Women in Rural-Urban Migration in Contemporary China' in *Intersections* 4 (September), at wwwsshe.murdoch.edu.au/intersections/issue4_contents.html.

Jacka, Tamara (2006) *Rural Women in Urban China* Armonk NY: M.E. Sharpe.

James, Jeffrey (1987) 'Positional goods, conspicuous consumption and the international demonstration effect reconsidered' in *World Development* 15/4, pp. 449–62.

Jeffreys, E. (2004) *China, Sex and Prostitution* London; New York: Routledge-Curzon.

Jeffreys, E. (2006) 'Debating the legal regulation of sex-related bribery and corruption in the People's Republic of China' in Elaine Jeffreys (ed.) *Sex and Sexuality in China*, London, New York: RoutledgeCurzon, pp. 159–78.

Ji, Wenhai (2001) 'Shui shi "xing huilu" de shouhaizhe' ('Who is the victim of 'sex-related bribery and corruption'?') in *Zhongguo jingji shibao* (*China Economic Daily*) 9 January.

Jia Gaojian (2005) 'Jiejie fenxi and jieceng fenxi: liangzhong butong fangfa de bijiao yanjiu' ('Class analysis and stratum analysis: two different approaches compared') in *Xinshiye* (*New Perspectives*) 1.

Jiang, Wenran (2006) 'The Dynamics of China's Social Crisis' in *Jamestown's China Brief* 6/2, pp. 1–3.

Jiang Zemin (1995) quoted in Zhang Weiping (ed.) *Dangwu gongzuo shouce* (*A New Work Manual for Party Affairs*) Beijing: Zhongguo yanshi chubanshe.

Jiang Zemin (2001) 'Zai qingzhu Zhongguo gongchandang chengli bashi zhouniandahu shang de jianghua' ('Speech at the Celebration of the Eightieth Anniversary of the Founding of the Chinese Communist Party') in Jiang Zemin *Lun Sange daibiao* (*On the Three Represents*) Beijing: Zhongyang wenxian chubanshe, p. 169.

Jiang Zemin (2002) 'Quanmian jianshe xiaokang shehui, kaichuang Zhongguo tese shehui zhuyi shiye xin jumian – zai Zhongguo gongchandang di shiliu ci quanguo daibiao dahui shang de baogao' ('Build a Comprehensive Xiaokang Society and Create a New Order of Socialism with Chinese Characteristics') in *The People's Daily*, 18 November 2002.

Jiang Zemin (2003) cited in Will Wo-Lap Lam 'Prospects for Reform under the Fourth Generation Leadership' in Joseph Cheng (ed.) *China's Challenges in the Twenty-First Century* City University of Hong Kong Press.

Jiangnan shibao (*South of the Yangtze Times*) (2005) 'Ming jiaoshou yici jiangzuo baochou da ba wan yuan' ('Payment for a lecture by a reputable professor can reach 80,000 dollars') 21 September, p. 12.

Jiangsu Xinhua Net (8 July 2005) 'Nanjing Changjiang Daqiao ri tongche 6.6 wan liang yi bukan zhongfu', at www.js.xinhuanet.com/xin_wen_zhong_xin/2005–/content_4596878.htm.

Jilin Daily (2007) 'Changchun qiyejia shishe jiepai' ('Changchun Entrepreneurs Poetry Society Established') 11 June, at www.jlsina.com/news/jlrb/2007-06-.shtml.

Jin, Weidong (2000) 'Ying sheli "xing huilu zui"' ('"Sex-related bribery and corruption" should be a crime') in *Jiangsu gongan zhuanke xuexiao xuebao* (*Jiangsu Public Security College Journal*) 7 June, pp. 83–7.

Jing, Jun (2003) 'Environmental Protest in China' in E. J. Perry and Mark Selden (eds) *Chinese Society: Change, Conflict and Resistance* London: Routledge Curzon, pp. 204–222.

Jingji da cankao (July 2000) (Major Reference on the Economy) 18, p. 23–24.

Johnson, Chalmers (1966) *Revolutionary Change* Boston: Little, Brown and Company.

Johnson, David, Andrew J. Nathan and Evelyn S. Rawski (eds) (1985) *Popular Culture in Late Imperial China* University of California Press.

Jones, Richard (2007) 'Conspicuous Consumption' in *PostMagazine* (Hong Kong) 4 February, pp. 16–20.

Joshi, Sanjay (2001) *Fractured Modernity: Making a Middle Class in Colonial North India* Oxford: Oxford University Press.

Ju, Xuewei (2005) 'Shehui xinli chengshouli yu shehui jiazhi xuanze' ('The aggregate levels of collective tolerance and the societal choices of values') 20 May 2005, at www.sociologybar.com/index. asp?xAction=xReadNews&NewsID=228.

Judd, E. R. (2002) *The Chinese Women's Movement between State and Market* Stanford University Press.

Kapp, Robert A. (1973) *Szechwan and the Chinese Republic: Provincial Militarism and Central Power, 1911–1938* Yale University Press.

Keane, Michael (2003) 'Creativity and complexity in post-WTO China' in *Continuum* 17/3, pp. 291–302.

Kidd, Alan J. and K. W. Roberts (eds) (1985) *City, Class, and Culture: Studies of Social Policy and Cultural Production in Victorian Manchester* Manchester University Press.

Kim, Jae Cheol (2005) 'From the Fringe to the Center: The Political Emergence of Private Entrepreneurs in China' in *Issues & Studies* 41/3, pp. 113–43.

Kipnis, Andrew (2006) '*Suzhi*: A keyword approach' in *The China Quarterly* 186, pp. 295–313.

Kipnis, Andrew (2007) 'Neoliberalism reified: *suzhi* discourse and tropes of neoliberalism in the People's Republic of China' in *Journal of the Royal Anthropological Institute* 13/3, pp. 383–400.

Ko, Dorothy and Wang Zheng (2006) 'Introduction: Translating Feminisms in China' in *Gender and History* 18/3 (November), pp. 463–71.

Kolo, Vicent (2007) 'Privatisation and greedy officials responsible for coal mining accidents!' in *China Worker* 28 May 2007, at www.chinaworker.org/en/content/news/191/.

Kong, Qingjiang (2003) 'Quest for Constitutional Justification: privatization with Chinese characteristics' in *Journal of Contemporary China* 12/36, pp. 537–551.

Kong, Shuyu (2002) 'Between a Rock and a Hard Place: Chinese Literary Journals in the Cultural Market' in *Modern Chinese Literature and Culture* 14/1, pp. 93–140.

Konrad, George and Ivan Szelenyi (1979) *The Intellectuals on the Road to Class Power* New York: Harcourt Brace Jovanovich.

Korabik, K. (1994) 'Managerial women in the People's Republic of China: the Long March continues' in Nancy J. Adler and Dafna N. Izraeli (eds) *Competitive Frontiers: Women Mangers in A Global Economy* Cambridge: Blackwell, pp. 114–126.

Kornhauser, William (1959) *The Politics of Mass Society* Glencoe: Free Press.

Korzec, Michel and Martin King Whyte (1981) 'Reading Notes: The Chinese Wage System' in *The China Quarterly* 86, p. 248–273.

Kracauer, Siegfried (1998) *The Salaried Masses: Duty and Distraction in Weimar Germany* trans. Quintin Hoare, New York: Verso.

Kraus, Richard Curt (1991) *Brushes with Power: Modern Politics and the Chinese Art of Calligraphy* University of California Press.

Kristeva, Julia.(1982) *Powers of Horror: An Essay on Abjection* trans. Leon S. Roudiez Columbia University Press.

Kroll, Luisa and Allison Fass (2007) 'The World's Billionaires' posted on 8 March 2007, at www.forbes.com/2007/03/07/billionaires-worlds-richest_07billionaires_cz_lk_af_0308billie_land.html.

Krug, Barbara (ed.) (2004) *China's Rational Entrepreneurs: The development of the new private business sector* London: Routledge.

Krug, Barbara and Laszlo Polos (2004) 'Emerging Markets, Entrepreneurship and Uncertainty: The emergence of a private sector in China' in Barbara Krug (ed.) *China's Rational Entrepreneurs: The development of the new private business sector* London: Routledge, pp. 72–96.

Kuhn, A. (2007) 'China debates morality, exploitation of women' in *NPR* (*Weekend Edition Saturday*) 20 January.

Kurth, James (1979) 'Industrial Change and Political Change' in David Collier (ed.) *The New Authoritarianism in Latin America* Princeton University Press, p. 319.

Kwaku, Atuahene-Gima, Haiyang Li and Luigi M. De Luca (2006) 'The Contingent Value of Marketing. Strategy Innovativeness for Product Development Performance in Chinese New Technology Ventures' in *Industrial Marketing Management* 35/3, pp. 359–72.

Lam, Willy Wo-Lap (2001) 'China's Struggle for "Democracy"', at www.cnn.com/ Asia, 1 Aug. 2001.

Lan, Xinzhen (2004) 'China's Biggest Reform Challenge' in *Beijing Review* 47/18, 6 May.

Lang, Larry Hsien Ping (2003) 'Tanqiu minqi "yuanzui" chulu' ('How could we forgive "the original sin" of private business') 6 August 2003, at 210.51.178.2/ztpd/ hqmt/gnmt/nfc/more/t20031204 _235311.shtml.

Lang, Larry Hsien Ping (2004) 'Zhongguo minying qiye de chuntian lailin le?' ('Has the spring of Chinese private businesses come?') 10 September 2004, at www.chinabrand.net.cn/wwww2222/ nang0013.htm.

Lardy, Nicholas R (2007) 'China's Economy: Problems and Prospects' in *Footnotes* (The Newsletter of the USA Foreign Policy Research Institute's Marvin Wachman Fund for International Education) 12/4.

Latham, Kevin (2002) 'Rethinking Chinese Consumption: Social Palliatives and the Rhetorics of Transition in Postsocialist China' in C. M. Hann (ed.) *Postsocialism: Ideals, Ideologies and Practices in Eurasia* London: Routledge, pp. 217–237.

Latham, Kevin (2006) 'Introduction: consumption and cultural change in contemporary China' in K. Latham, S. Thompson and J. Klein (eds) *Consuming China: Approaches to Cultural Change in Contemporary China* London and New York: Routledge, p. 1–21.

Latham, Kevin, Stuart Thompson and Jakob Klein (eds) (2006) *Consuming China* London: Routledge.

Lee, Chin-Chuan (ed.) (2003) *Chinese Media Global Contexts* London: Routledge.

Lee, Ching Kwan (1999) 'From Organized Dependency to Disorganized Despotism: Changing Labour Regimes in Chinese Factories' in *The China Quarterly* 155, p. 44–71.

Lee, Ching Kwan (2000) 'The Revenge of History: Collective Memories and Labour Protests in North-Eastern China' in *Ethnography* 1/2, pp. 217–237.

Lee, Ching Kwan (2002) 'From the Specter of Mao to the Spirit of the Law' in *Theory and Society* 31/2.

Lee, Ching Kwan (2003) 'Pathways of Lobor Insurgency' in E. J. Perry and Mark Selden (eds) *Chinese Society: Change, Conflict and Resistance* London: Routledge Curzon, pp. 71–92.

Lee, Ching Kwan (2007) *Against the Law: Labor Protests in China's Rustbelt and Sunbelt* University of California Press.

Lee, Duke (2004) 'Competing for Chinese consumers' in *Proceedings of The LBMA Precious Metals Conference*, 5–7 September, Shanghai, pp. 111–14, at www.lbma. org.uk/conf2004/2004proceedings.html.

Lee, Hong Yung (1978) *The Politics of the Cultural Revolution* University of California Press.

Lee, Hong Yung (1991) *From Revolutionary Cadres to Party Technocrats in Socialist China* University of California Press.

Legg, Stephen (2007) *Spaces of Colonialism: Dehli's Urban Governmentalities* Malden: Blackwell.

Lei, Guang (2003) 'Rural Taste, Urban Fashions: The Cultural Politics of Rural/ Urban Difference in Contemporary China' in *Positions* 11/3, pp. 613–646.

Lett, Denise Potrzeba (1998) *In Pursuit of Status: The making of South Korea's "New" Urban Middle Class* Harvard University Asia Center.

Levy, Ariel (2006) *Female Chauvinist Pigs: Women and the Rise of Raunch Culture* New York: Simon and Schuster.

Li Bin (2002) 'Zhongguo zhufang gaige zhidu de fengexing' ('The distinctive features of China's housing reform system') in *Shehuixue Yanjiu (Sociological Research)* 2, pp. 80–7.

Li, Bobai and Andrew G. Walder (2001) 'Career Advancement as Party Patronage' in *American Journal of Sociology* 106/5, p. 1,371–408.

Li Chunling (2005) *Duanlie yu suipian: dangdai Zhongguo shehui jieceng fenhua shili fenxi (Cleavage and Fragmentation: An Empirical Analysis of Social Stratification in Contemporary China)* Beijing: Shehui kexue chubanshe.

Li Fan (2006) 'Unrest in China's Countryside' in *Jamestown's China Brief* 6/2, pp. 6–8.

Li Gang (2002) 'Xian "shui" hou tiba bufanfa? "Xing huilu"—feizui qi da liyou' ('Shouldn't "sleeping" with someone first and then getting promoted be illegal? Seven reasons why sex-related bribery and corruption cannot be considered a crime') in *Beijing qingnian bao (Beijing Youth News)* 30 July.

Li Gang and Zhao Xinpei (2004) 'Weisheng bu, Guowu yuan Jiufeng ban zuo qi yancha Jingcheng yiyuan hongbao' ('Ministry of Health and the Practice Rectifying Office of the State Council start to meticulously investigate red packets in Beijing hospitals') in *Beijing qingnian bao (Beijing Youth News)* 23 November, p. A3.

Li Guoping and Huang Qing (2003) 'Siying qiyezhu de xingqi: yanjiu zhongguo shehui de bianqian de yige shijiao' ('The rise of private entrepreneurs: a perspective to look at China's social change'), at www.usc.cuhk.edu.hk/wk_wzdetails.asp? id=3835.

Li Haiyang (ed.) (2006) *Growth of New Technology Ventures in China's Emerging Market* Northampton: Edward Elgar.

Li Haiyang and Michael A. Hitt (2006) 'Growth of New Technology Ventures in China: an Introduction' in Li Haiyang (ed.) *Growth of New Technology Ventures in China's Emerging Markets* Cheltenham, UK: Edward Elgar.

Li He (2001) '"Qiong jiaoshu de" we he bei shuiwu ding shang le?' ('How come the tax office is targeting the "poor teachers"?'), at www.people.com.cn/GB/kejiao/41/ 20010924/568197.html.

Li, Hongbin, Lingsheng Meng and Junsheng Zhang (2006) 'Why do entrepreneurs enter politics? Evidence from China' in *Economic Enquiry* 44/3, pp. 559–578.

Li, Huajie and Li, Yongjie (1991) 'Lun er yuan jizhi xia gongwu yuan gongzi shuiping de tiaoshi' ('Adjustment of the wage levels of public employees under a dual track system') in *Nanfang jingji (Southern Economy)* 2, pp. 27–30.

Li, Jian and Niu, Xiaohan (2003) 'The New Middle Class(es) in Peking: A Case Study' in *China Perspectives* 45, pp. 4–20.

Li Ka Shing (26 August 2006) 'Juan 500 yi yuan yu gongyi, Li Jiacheng: huikui shehui caishi zhen caifu' ('A $50 billion donation to his charitable trust, Li Ka Shing said that private assets became wealth only when they were used to increase social welfare'), at news.xinhuanet.com/overseas/2006–/content_5009196.htm.

Li Ka Shing (2006) 'Li Ka Shing 480 yi cishan juankuan de yiyi' ('Li Ka Shing discusses the purposes of his donation of $48 billion'), at www.njcharity.org/cps/ site/ njcs/ywyj-mb_a20061108691.htm.

Li Ka Shing (20 January 2007) 'Junheng yu caifu he gongyi de Li Jiacheng' ('Li Ka Shing pursues both empathy for the needy and search for private wealth'), at finance.sina.com.cn/g/20070120/12393266235.shtml.

Li Lihui (2005) 'Zhongguo jieding gao shouru hangye, dianxin gaoxiao jiaoshi shang bang' ('China defines high income occupations, telecommunication [employees and] university teachers are on the list') in *Remin ribao* (*The People's Daily*) 29 August, p. 6.

Li, Lin (2005) '"Zhongchan jieji" shuzihua jieding' ('The Digital Definition of "Middle Class"') in *Zhongguancun* 25 (May), pp. 62–65.

Li Peilin (1995) *Zhongguo xin shiqi jieji jieceng baogao* (*Social Stratification during China's Market Transition in China*) Shenyang: Liaoning renmin chubanshe.

Li Peilin (2004) *Zhongguo Shehui Fenceng* (*Social Stratification in China Today*) Beijing: Shehui Kexue Wenxian Chubanshe.

Li Peilin, Li Qiang and Sun Liping (2004) *Zhongguo Shehui Fenceng* (*Social Stratification in China Today*) Beijing: Shehui kexue xueshu chubanshe.

Li Pelin *et al.* (2007) '2006 nian Zhongguo shehui hexie wending zhuangkuang diaocha baogao' ('A Report on Social Harmony in 2006') in Ru Xin *et al.* (eds) *2007: Zhongguo shehui xingshi fenxi yu yuce* (*Analysis and Forecast on China's Social Development*) (Blue Book of China's Society).

Li Ping, Zhong Minghua, Lin Bin and Zhang Hongjuan (2004) ' "Deyu" as Moral Education in Modern China' in *Journal of Moral Education* 33/4, pp. 449–64.

Li Qiang (1996) '"Nao ti dao guan" yu wo guo shichang jingji fazhan de liangge jieduan' ('Reverse wage disparity between mental and manual labourers and the two stages in the development of our country's market economy') in *Shehuixue yanjiu* (*Sociological Research*) 6, pp. 5–12.

Li Qiang (2001) 'Guanyu zhongchan jieji he zhongjian jieceng' ('On the Middle Class and the Middle Stratum') in *Zhongguo remin daxue xuebao* (*Academic Journal of People's University*) 2, p. 17–20.

Li Qiang (2007) 'Cong shehuixue jiaodu kan "goujian shehui zhuyi hexie shehui"' ('A sociological account of how to build a socialist harmonious society in China'), at www.usc.cuhk.edu.hk/wk_wzdetails.asp?id=4724.

Li, Si-ming (2000) 'Housing Consumption in Urban China: A Comparative Study of Beijing and Guangzhou' in *Environment and Planning A* 32/6, pp. 1115–34.

Li, Si Ming (2005) 'China's Changing Urban Geography: A Review of Major Forces at Work' in *Issues & Studies* 41/4, pp. 67–106.

Li, Si-ming and Doris K.W. Fung (2001) 'Housing Tenure and Residential Mobility in Urban China: Analysis of Survey Data' in *Occasional Papers Series of Hong Kong Baptist University, Centre for China Urban and Regional Studies*.

Li Weizuo (1998) 'Jintian zenyang kandai "nao ti dao gua"' ('How to regard "reverse wage disparity" between mental and physical labours') in *Zhongguo tongji* (*China Statistics*) 4, pp. 16–17.

Li Xiaojiang and Zhang Xiaodan (1994) 'Creating a space for women: Women's studies in China in the 1980s' in *Signs* 20/1 (Autumn), pp. 137–51.

Li Yi (2005) *The Structure and Evolution of Chinese Social Stratification* Lanham, Maryland: University Press of America.

Li Zehou and Liu Zaifu (eds) (1995) *Gaobie geming: huiwang ershi shiji Zhongguo* (*Farewell to revolution: Looking Back on Twentieth-Century China*) Hong Kong: Tiandi tushu youxian gongsi.

Li Zehou (1994) 'Guanyu wenhua xianzhuang daode chongjian de duihua' ('A dialogue about moral reconstruction in contemporary culture') in *Dongfang* (*The East*) 5, extracted in *Zhongliu* (*Midstream*) 10, p. 29.

Li, Zhang (2006) 'Contesting Spatial Modernity in Late-Socialist China' in *Current Anthropology* 47, pp. 461–484.

Li Zhigang and Fulong Wu (2006) 'Socio-spatial Differentiation and Residential Inequalities in Shanghai: A Case Study of Three Neighbourhoods' in *Housing Studies* 21/5, pp. 695–717.

Li Zhufeng (2002) 'Qianxi xing huilu fanzui lifa de biyaoxing' ('A brief discussion of the need to legislate against the crime of sex-related bribery and corruption') in *Keshan shizhuan xuebao* (*Keshan City College Journal*) 4, pp. 22–3.

Liao Huailing and Gan Yuanhong (2005) 'Quan sheng 1490 suo yiyuan 3.6 wan yisheng shangjiao 636 wan hongbao huikou' ('Thirty-six thousand doctors from 1490 hospitals in the province hand in 6.36 million *yuan* of red packets and kickbacks') in *Yangcheng wanbao* (*Yangcheng Evening News*) (Guangdong)18 January.

Lieberthal, Kenneth (1995) *Governing China: From Revolution Through Reform* New York: Norton.

Lim, Meng-Kin, Hui Yang, Tuohong Zhang, Wen Feng and Zijun Zhou (2004) 'Public Perceptions of Private Health Care in Socialist China' in *Health Affairs* 23/6, pp. 222–234.

Lin, Chun (2001) 'Whither Feminism: A Note on China' in *Signs* 26/4 (Summer), pp. 1281–86.

Lin, George C S. and Samuel P S. Ho (2005) 'The State, Land System, and Land Development Processes in Contemporary China' in *Annals of the Association of American Geographers* 95/2, pp. 411–36.

Lin, Jing (1999) *Social Transformation and Private Education in China* Westport. Conn: Praeger.

Lin, Mei (2004) 'Guangzhou Daxue chutai xin zhengce: 1000 wan zhuankuan yinjin youxiu rencai' ('Guangzhou University formulates new policy: 10 million *yuan* special fund to attract top talents') in *Nanfang wang* (*Southern Net*) 18 March.

Lin, Nan (1990) 'Social Resources and Social Mobility' in Ronald L. Breiger (ed.) *Social Mobility and Social Structure* Cambridge University Press, pp. 247–71.

Lin, Nan and Wen Xie (1988) 'Occupational Prestige in Urban China' in *American Journal of Sociology* 93/4, pp. 793–832.

Lin Xiaolei (2007) 'Heilongjiang weisheng xitong quan nian chachu 460 ming weiji zhe, shangjiao hongbao 190 wan' ('Heilongjiang healthcare system investigates and punishes 460 wrongdoers; 190 million *yuan* red packets handed in') in *Dongbei wang* (*Northeast Net*) 1 March.

Lin Yanzhi (2001) 'How the Communist Party Should Lead the "Capitalist Class"' in *Shehui kexue zhanxian* (*Social Sciences Frontline*) 20 June 2001, trans. in FBIS, 14 July 2001.

Lin Zhangjie (ed.) (1999) *Lun xinshiqi Zhongguo de zhishi fenzi wenti* (*Issues about Chinese intellectuals in the new era*) Shanghai: Shanghai Jiaotong Daxue Chubanshe.

Link, Perry, Paul G. Pickowicz and Richard P. Madsen (eds) (2002) *Popular China: Unofficial Culture in a Globalizing Society* Lanham: Rowman & Littlefield.

Liu, Changjiang (2006) '"Zhongchan jieji" yanjiu: yiwen yu tanyuan' ('Studies of the Middle Class: Questions and Origins') in *Shehui* (*Society*) 4, pp. 43–56.

Liu, Gordon, Liu Xingzhu and Meng Qingyue (1994) 'Privatization of the medical market in socialist China: A historical approach' in *Health Policy* 27/2.

Liu Jing (2005) 'Quanguo gongshanglian shoufa niandu minying jingji fazhan fenxi baogao' ('All-China Federation of Industry and Commerce published its first analysis on the development of China's private economy'), at www.gov.cn/jrzg/2005-/content_123447.htm.

Liu, Kang (2004) *Globalization and Cultural Trends in China* Honolulu: University of Hawaii Press.

Liu Lanbiao and Cai Jiming (1998) 'Zhongguo nao ti laodong de shouru chabie: shizheng fenxi he jiazhi panduan' ('The income disparity between mental and physical labours in China: an empirical study and value assessment') in *Nankai jingji yanjiu* (*Nankai University Economic Studies*) 5, pp. 10–16.

Liu Liping *et al* (eds) (1989) *Zhongguo dangdai qiyejia mingdian – Shanxi tao* (*Contemporary Entrepreneurs in China – Shanxi volume*) Beijing: Gongren chubanshe.

Liu, Serena (2006) 'Toward an Analytical Theory of Social Change' in *The British Journal of Sociology* 57/3.

Liu, Xingzhu, Liu Yuanli and Chen Ningshan (2000) 'The Chinese experience of hospital price regulation' in *Health Policy and Planning* 15/2.

Liu, Yuanli, Peter Berman, Winnie Yip, Haocai Liang, Qingyue Meng, Jiangbin Qu and Li Zhonghe (2006) 'Health care in China: The role of non-government providers' in *Health Policy* 77/2.

Liu, Yuting and Wu Fulong (2006) 'The State, Institutional Transition and the Creation of New Urban Poverty in China' in *Social Policy and Administration* 40/2, pp. 121–37.

Lo, Ping (1994) 'The Anti-Deng Meeting Incident in Hebei' in *Zhengming* 205, 1 November, p. 9–14; trans. FBIS-CHI, 17 November 1994, pp. 16–18.

Loch, Christoph, Bernardo Huberman and Suzanne Stout (2000) 'Status Competition and Performance in Work Groups' in *Journal of Economic Behavior and Organization* 43/1, pp. 35–55.

Low, Setha (2003) *Behinds the Gates: Life, Security, and the Pursuit of Happiness in Fortress America* New York: Routledge.

Lu, Hanlong (2000) 'To Be Relatively Comfortable in an Egalitarian Society' in Deborah S Davis (ed.) *The Consumer Revolution in Urban China* University of California Press, p. 124.

Lu, Hanlong (2005) '"Zhongchan jieji" yu xiaokang shehui' ('The "Middle Class" and Xiaokang Society') in *Shehui guancha* (*Social Observation*) 1, pp. 9–11.

Lu, Xueyi (ed.) (2002) *Dangdai Zhongguo shehui jieceng yanjiu baogao* (*Research Report on the Social Stratification of Contemporary China*) Beijing: Shehui kexue wenxian chubanshe.

Luo, Biliang (2002) 'Zhongchan jieji zai jueqi' ('The Middle Class Is Rising') in *Shangye shidai* (*Commercial Times*) 233 (25 November 2002) p. 43–44.

Luo Guifen, and Bai Nanfeng, Chou yulin (1994) 'Shehui xinli chengshouli de shenceng fenxi'('An in-depth analysis of the aggregate levels of collective tolerance') in *Shehuixue Yanjiu* (*Sociological Research*) 4, pp. 56–66.

Luo, Jun and Yehua Dennis Wei (2006) 'Population distribution and spatial structure in transitional Chinese cities: a study of Nanjing' in *Eurasian Geography and Economics* 47/5, pp. 585–603.

Ma Dali and William L. Parish (2006) 'Tocquevillian Moments: Charitable Contributions by Chinese Private Entrepreneurs' in *Social Forces* 85/2, pp. 943–64.

Ma, Deyong (1999) 'Zhuanxing shehui zhong de zhongjian jieceng' ('The Middle Strata during China's Transition') in *Jinyang xuekan* (*The Academic Journal of Jinyang*) 5, pp. 109–110.

Ma, Hong *et al.* (ed) (1990) *Quanguo gesheng, zizhiqu, zhixiashi lishi tongji ziliao huibian 1949–1989* (*Collection of Historical Statistics on all China's Provinces, Autonomous Regions and Centrally Directed Municipalities, 1949–1989*) Beijing: Zhongguo tongji chubanshe.

Ma, Laurence J. C. (2002) 'Urban Transformation in China, 1949–2000: A Review and Research Agenda' in *Environment and Planning A* 34, pp. 1545–69.

Ma, Lawrence J. C and Fulong Wu (eds) (2005a) *Restructuring the Chinese City. Changing Society, Economy and Space* London and New York: Routledge.

Ma, Lawrence J. C and Fulong Wu (2005b) 'Restructuring the Chinese city. Diverse processes and reconstituted spaces' in Lawrence Ma and Fulong Wu (eds) *Restructuring the Chinese City: Changing Society, Economy and Space* London and New York: Routledge.

MaBelle (2005) 'History of the group', at www.mabellelife.com/help/en/aboutus. aspx?section=history.

McBride, Theresa M. (1976) *The Domestic Revolution: The Modernisation of Household Service in England and France 1820–1920* London: Croom Helm.

McCann, Leon and Gregory Schwartz (2006) 'Terms and conditions apply: management restructuring and the global integration of post-socialist societies' in *International Journal of Human Resource Management* 17/8, pp. 1339 – 1352.

McClintock, Anne (1995) *Imperial Leather: Race, gender and sexuality in the colonial contest* New York: Routledge.

MacFarquhar, R. and M. Schoenhals (2006) *Mao's Last Revolution* Harvard University Press.

McGregor, James (2005) *One Billion Customers: Lessons from the Front Lines of Doing Business in China* New York: Free Press-Simon & Schuster.

McGregor, Richard (2005) 'Private sector "in control of China economy"' in *Financial Times* 13 September, at www.ft.com/cms/s/27ecf9fa-23fc-11da-b56b-00000e2511c8.html.

The McKinsey Quarterly (June 2007) 'The Middle Kingdom's middle class', at www. mckinseyquarterly.com/newsletters/chartfocus/2007_06.htm.

McLaren, Anne (1979) 'The Educated Youth Return' in *Australian Journal of Chinese Affairs* 2, pp. 1–20.

McMillan, John and Christopher Woodruff (2002) 'The Central Role of Entrepreneurs of Transition Economics' in *Journal of Economic Perspectives* 16/3, pp. 153–70.

Macroeconomic Research Group, State Planning Commission (2000) 'Establishing a Social Protection System Is the Key to Our Country's Social Stability' in *Neibu canyue* (*Internal Consultations*) 5 May 2000, cited in Dorothy Solinger 'The New Crowd of the Dispossessed: The Shift of the Urban Proletariat from Master to Mendicant' in Peter Gries and Stanley Rosen (eds) *State and Society in 21st-Century China: Crisis, Contention, and Legitimation* New York and London: RoutledgeCurzon, pp. 51–52.

Mailliard, Pierre (2004) 'The cultural strategy of Richemont in China' in *Europa Star*, 16 November, at www.europastar.com/europastar/magazine/article_display.jsp?vnu_content_id=1000720088.

Mamo, David (1981) 'Mao's Model for Socialist Transition Reconsidered' in *Modern China* 7/1, pp. 55–81.

Martin, John Levi (2002) 'Power, Authority, and the Constraint of Belief Systems' in *American Journal of Sociology* 107/4, p. 864.

Mao Zedong (1926) 'Zhongguo shehui ge jieji de fenxi' ('An Analysis of the Social Classes of China') in *Mao Zedong xuanji* (*Selected Works of Mao Zedong*) vol. 1, Beijing: Renmin chubanshe, 1991, at www.marxists.org/reference/archive/mao/selected-works/volume-1/mswv1_1.htm.

Mao Tse-tung (January 1940) *On New Democracy*, at www.rrojasdatabank.org/mao13.htm#s5.

Marx, K. (1955) *The Poverty of Philosophy* Moscow: Foreign Languages Publishing House.

Marx, K. (1967) *Capital Vol. 1*, trans. Samuel Moore and Edward Aveling, New York: International Publishers.

Marx, K. and F. Engels (1962) *Manifesto of the Communist Party*, in K. Marx and F. Engels, *Selected Work*, vol.1, Moscow: Foreign Languages Publishing House.

Marx, K. and F. Engels (1968) *The German Ideology* Moscow: Progress Publishers.

Marxists.org (n.d.) 'Productive Forces', at www.marxists.org/glossary/terms/p/r.htm.

Mayer, Margit (1994) 'Post-Fordist City Politics' in Ash Amin (ed.) *Post Fordism: A Reader* Oxford; Cambridge, Mass.: Blackwell.

Melikian, Souren (2005) 'Some surprising new facets to the art jewelry market' in *The International Herald Tribune* 29 October, p. 9.

Meng, Qingyue, Liu Xingzhu and Dhi Junshi (2000) 'Comparing the services and quality of private and public clinics in rural China' in *Health Policy and Planning* 15/4.

Meng, Yasheng (2001) 'Timing: "xing huilu"' ('Jin Weidong: the man who coined the term "sex-related bribery and corruption"') in *Dangdai gongren* (*Contemporary Worker*), at www.v2000.com.cn/lmdx/fasc/2001.11/tm.html.

Mianyang Tongjiju (Mianyang Statistics Bureau) (2005) *Mianyang Tongji Nianjian* (*Mianyang Statistical Yearbook*) Mianyang: Mianyang Tongjiju.

Michelson, E, and William L Parish (2000) 'Gender differentials in economic success: rural China in 1991' in Barbara Entwisle and Gail E. Henderson *Re-Drawing Boundaries* University of California Press, pp. 134–56.

Middle Stratum (2004) 'Dissecting China's Middle Stratum' 27 October 2004, at www.china.org.cn/english/ China/110521.htm.

Milwertz, Cecelia (2002) *Beijing Women Organising for Change: A new wave of the Chinese women's movement* NIAS Press.

Min Jie and Wang Xinxin (2007) 'Wanshan nongcun zhongxin yiyuan "kaidan ticheng" diaocha' ('Investigation of "prescription commissions" in Wanshan Village Centre Hospital') in *Zhongguo qingnian bao* (*China Youth*) 7 February.

Ministry of Education (1981) 'Guanyu shixing gaodeng xuexiao jiaoshi gongzuoliang zhidu de tongzhi' ('Circular regarding evaluating the workload system of tertiary school teachers'), at www.fz.jxmu.edu.cn/policy/workliang.htm.

Ministry of Education (1999) 'Guanyu dangqian shenhua gaodeng jiaoyu renshi fenpei zhidu gaige de ruogan yijian' ('Some proposals on deepening the reform of personnel and redistribution systems in tertiary education'), at www.edu.cn/gao_jiao_/t20060323_110108.shtml.

Ministry of Education, Ministry of Finance and National Bureau of Labour (1978) 'Guanyu gaodeng xuexiao jianke jiaoshi choujin he jiaoshi bianyi jiaocai gaochou de zanxing guiding' ('Provisional Regulations on remuneration for tertiary school part-time teachers and payments for teachers compiling textbooks'), at www.scrs. gov.cn:8080/was40/detail?record=253&channelid=42486.

Ministry of Health (1985) 'Guanyu weisheng gongzuo gaige ruogan zhengce wenti de baogao' ('Report regarding several policy issues in health reform'), at www. china.com.cn/law/flfg/txt/2006–/content_7060220.htm.

Ministry of Health (2004) 'Quan guo weisheng xitong kaizhan jiuzheng yiliao fuwu zhong buzheng zhi feng zhuanxiang zhili shishi fang'an' ('Implementing plans to rectify inappropriate conduct in healthcare delivery in the national health system'), at www.moh.gov.cn/newshtml/7823.htm.

Ministry of Health (2007) '2007 Chinese Health Statistical Digest', at www.moh.gov. cn/open/2007tjts/P16.htm.

Ministry of Health, Ministry of Finance, and Ministry of Personnel (1986) 'Guanyu yeyu yiliao weisheng fuwu shouru ticheng de zanxing guiding' ('Provisional regulations on the commission of after-hour medical and health services'), at www.law-lib.com/law/.

Ministry of Health, Ministry of Finance, Ministry of Personnel, State Price Administration, and State Taxation Administration (1989) 'Guanyu kuoda yiliao weisheng fuwu youguan wenti de yijian' ('Proposals on issues regarding expanding medical and health services'), at www.law-lib.com/law/.

Ministry of Justice (1984) 'Guanyu jiaqiang he gaige lushi gongzuo de yijian' ('Opinions on strengthening and reforming lawyers' work'), at www.mylaw.com/.

Ministry of Justice (1988) 'Hezuo zhi lushi shiwusuo shidian fang'an' ('Plan for the trial of cooperative law firms'), at www.law-lib.com/law/.

Ministry of Justice (1993) 'Guanyu shenhua lushi gongzuo gaige de fang'an' ('Plan to deepen the reform of lawyers' work'), at www.icncn.com/Law/Show.asp?id=197900.

Ministry of Labour and Social Security, National Bureau of Statistics (2001) '2000 nian laodong baozhang fazhan tongji baogao' ('Statistical Report of the Developments in Labour and Social Security for 2000') in *Laodong baozhang tongxun* (Labour and Social Security Bulletin) 6, p. 36.

Ministry of Personnel (1983) 'Guanyu 1983 nian qiye tiaozheng gongzi he gaige gongzi zhidu wenti de baogao' ('Report on issues in the reform of wage readjustments and wage reform in enterprises in 1983'), at www.article.zhaopin.com/pub/ print.jsp?id=24265&DYWE=1187147560765.460322.1187147561.1187307704.2.

Ministry of Personnel (1988) 'Guanyu "lushi zhiwu gongzi biaozhun" de fuhan' ('Reply to "wage standards for lawyers"'), at www.law-lib.com/law/.

Ministry of Personnel (2000) 'Guanyu jiakuai tuijin shiye danwei renshi zhidu gaige de yijian' ('Advice on speeding up the progress of the reform of the personnel system of institutional work-units'), at www.cws.net.cn/wsc/policy/f17.html.

Ministry of Personnel and Ministry of Finance (2006) 'Shiye danwei gongzuo renyuan shouru fenpei zhidu gaige fang'an' ('Reform Plans for income and redistribution system for institutional work-unit personnel'), at www.rsc.hnxwxy.com/ News/UploadFile/2006119154040513.doc.

Misra, Kalpana (1998) *From Post-Maoism to Post-Marxism* New York and London: Routledge.

Mok, Ka-Ho (2005) 'Riding over socialism and global capitalism: changing education governance and social policy paradigms in post-Mao China' in *Comparative Education* 41/2.

Mok, Ka-Ho and Yat-Wai Lo (2007) 'The Impacts of Neo-Liberalism on China's Higher Education' in *Journal for Critical Education Policy Studies* 5/1.

Moore, Henrietta (1994) *A Passion for Difference* Cambridge: Polity Press.

Nanfang Weekend (23 November 2003) '*Nanfang zhoumo* jiang chu fuhao bang yi yulun cu qiyejia dan shehui zeren' ('*Nanfang Weekend* will publish a list of the rich to encourage their willingness to shoulder social responsibilities'), at news. xinhuanet.com/newmedia/2003–/content_1183673.htm.

Nanfang Weekend (17 November 2004) 'Ruhe kandai choufu xintai yu furen yuan-zui' ('How to diagnose people's hatreds toward rich people and the original sin of the rich'), at news.xinhuanet.com/comments/2004–/content_2227331.htm.

Nanfang Weekend (12 July 2006) 'Zhongguoren kangkai dan bu cushan' ('Chinese are generous but do not care about charities'), at old.racszh.net/NewsView.Asp? classid=5&id=423.

Nanfang Weekend (17 July 2006) 'Chonggou zhongguo cishan wenhua hexin jiazhi-guan' ('Let's rebuild the core values for philanthropy in China'), at old.racszh.net/ NewsView.Asp?classid=5&id=427.

Nanfang Weekend (17 September 2006) 'Cishan lengmo kaowen zhongguo fuhao: weihe ningke huihuo buyuan juanzeng' ('The rich are interrogated in the court of benevolence: why do they spend money on lavish consumptions instead making some donations to charitable organizations?'), at old.racszh.net/NewsView.Asp? classid=5&id=47.

Nee, Victor (1989) 'A Theory of Market Transition: From Redistribution to Markets in State Socialism' in *American Sociological Review* 54/5, pp. 663–81.

Nee, Victor (1991) 'Social Inequalities in Reforming State Socialism' in *American Sociological Review* 56/3, pp. 267–282.

Nee, Victor (1992) 'Organizational Dynamics of Market Transition: Hybrid Forms, Property Rights, and Mixed Economy in China' in *Administrative Science Quarterly* 31, p. 1.

Nee, Victor (1996) 'The Emergence of a Market Society' in *American Journal of Sociology* 101/4, pp. 908–49.

Nee, Victor (2005) 'Organizational Dynamics of Institutional Change: Politicized Capitalism in China' in Victor Nee and Richard Swedberg (ed.) *The Economic Sociology of Capitalism* Princeton University Press, pp. 53–74.

Nee, Victor and Yang Cao (1999) 'Path Dependent Societal Transformation' in *Theory and Society* 28/6, p. 799–834.

Nee, Victor and Rebecca Matthews (1996) 'Market Transition and Societal Transformation in Reforming State Socialism' in *Annual Review of Sociology* 22, pp. 401–35.

'New anti-corruption method sparks debate' (2005) *China Daily*, 20 April.

Ning, Gaoning (2006) 'Zhongguo qiye de wenxue siwei yinggai gaibian' ('The Literary Thinking of Chinese Corporations Should Be Changed') in *Zhongliang People* 10/1, at cofcomag.cofco.com/cn/periodical/index.aspx?con_id=180.

Niu Dao (2006) 'Gao fangjia xia wen zhongguo, ni xiang hechu qu?' ('Is there hope for China given unaffordable housing?') 15 November 2006, at vip.bokee.com/ 190178.html.

North China University of Technology (2002) 'Guanyu yinjin boshi, shuoshi yan-jiusheng de youguan guiding' ('Rules of attracting (academics with) PhD and Masters degrees') in *Renshi zhengce fagui huibian* (*Collection of personnel policies, laws and regulations*) Taiyuan: Huabei gongxueyuan renshichu.

NPC Standing Committee (1980) 'Lushi zanxing tiuli' ('Provisional Regulations on Lawyers'), at www.law-lib.com/law/.

NPC Standing Committee (1996) 'The Law of the People's Republic of China on Lawyers', at www.asianlii.org/cn/legis/cen/laws/ll1996129/.

Ockey, Jim (1999) 'Creating the Thai Middle Class' in M. Pinches (ed.) *Culture and Privilege in Capitalist Asia* London: Routledge.

O'Connell, Rhona (2003) 'The de-regulation of the Chinese gold market' London: World Gold Council Research Study, at www.gold.org/rs_archive/.

OECD (2007) *SourceOECD*, masetto.sourceoecd.org.

Oi, Jean C. (1989) *State and Peasant in Contemporary China* University of California Press.

Oi, Jean C. (1999) *Rural China Takes Off: Institutional Foundations of Economic Reform* University of California Press.

Oi, Jean C. and Andrew G. Walder (eds) (1999) *Property Rights and Economic Reform in China* Stanford University Press.

Olins, Wally (2003) *On Brand* London: Thames and Hudson.

Ollivier, Michele and Viviana Friedman (2004) 'Taste/Taste Culture' in N. Smelser and P. B. Baltes (eds) *International Encyclopedia of the Social and Behavioral Sciences* Elsevier, pp. 15442–15447.

O'Loughlin, John and Jurgen Friederichs (1996) *Social Polarization in Post-Industrial Metropolis* Berlin and New York: Walter de Gruyter.

Ong, Aihwa (1999) *Flexible Citizenship: the Cultural Logics of Transnationality* Duke University Press.

Overholt, William (1999) 'China in the Balance' Nomura Strategy Paper, Hong Kong, 12 May.

Owensby, Brian P. (1999) *Intimate Ironies: Modernity and the Making of Middle-Class Lives in Brazil* Stanford University Press.

Pahl, R. E. (1989) '"Is the Emperor Naked?" Some Questions on the Adequacy of Sociological Theory in Urban and Regional Research' in *International Journal of Urban and Regional Research* 13/4, pp. 711–20.

Pan, Shiyi (n.d.) *Pan Shiyi de BLOG* (Pan Shiyi's Blog) at blog.sina.com.cn/panshiyi.

Pan, Shiyi (2007) 'Chuangzaoli de qishi' ('The Revelation of Creativity') in *SOHO Journal*, at www.sohoxiaobao.com/chinese/index.php.

Pang, Yuanzheng (1989) 'Jiejue nao ti dao gua wenti shi jianchi shengchanli biaozhun de biran yaoqiu' ('Solving the problem of reverse wage disparity between mental and manual workers is required to ensure productive forces maintain the highest standard') in *Zhongguo dangzheng ganbu luntan* (*Forum for Chinese political and administrative cadres*) 6, pp. 24–28.

Parish, William and Ethan Michelson (1996) 'Politics and Markets: Dual Transformations' in *American Journal of Sociology* 101/4, pp. 1042–59.

Parker, D. S. (1998) *The Idea of the Middle Class: White-Collar Workers and Peruvian Society, 1900–1950* Pennsylvania State University Press.

Parrenas, Rhacel Salazar (2002) 'The Care Crisis in the Philippines: Children and Transnational Families in the New Global Economy' in Barbara Ehrenreich and Arlie Russell Hochschild (eds) *Global Woman: Nannies, Maids and Sex Workers in the New Economy* New York: Metropolitan Books, pp. 39–54.

Pascall, G. (2005) 'America's entrepreneurial spirit rides to rescue' in *San Jose Business Journal*, 28 January, at www.bizjournals.com/sanjose/stories/2005/01/31/editorial3.html.

Pearson, Margaret M. (1997) *China's New Business Elite: The Political Consequences of Economic Reform* University of California Press.

Peerenboom, Randall (2002) *China's Long March toward Rule of Law* Cambridge: Cambridge University Press.

Pei, Minxin (2006a) 'The Dark Side of China's Rise' in *Foreign Policy* 153 (March/April), pp. 32–40.

Pei, Minxin (2006b) *China's Trapped Transition. The Limits of Developmental Autocracy* Harvard University Press.

Peng, Mike W. (2001) 'How Entrepreneurs Create Wealth in Transition Economies' in *Academy of Management Executive* 15/1, pp. 95–108.

Peng, Yusheng (2004) 'Kinship Networks and Entrepreneurs in China's Transitional Economy' in *American Journal of Sociology* 109/5, pp. 1045–74.

People (2005) '*Ren yao zhi jian* yu guandao' ('*People or monsters?* and guandao') 23 December 2005, at blog.chinesenewsnet.com/?p=5790.

The People's Daily (24 March 2004) 'China ponders reform of government-run public service agencies', at english.people.com.cn/200403/24/eng20040324_138315.shtml.

The People's Daily (26 March 2004) 'China has more than 70,000 private schools', at english.people.com.cn/200403/26/eng20040326_138601.shtml.

The People's Daily (23 December 2004) 'Jewelry becomes hot item of consumption in China.', english.people.com.cn/200412/13/eng20041213_167098.html.

The People's Daily (17 January 2005) 'China becomes largest jewellery consumer.', english.people.com.cn/200501/17/eng20050117_170871.html.

The People's Daily (*Remin ribao*) (21 December 2005) 'Yiyao daibiao pu heimu: jiaoshou ji yisheng yue huikou da shi wan' ('Drug representative lifts the black curtain: professor-level doctor pockets 100,000 *yuan* in kickbacks a month') p. 2.

The People's Daily (2006) *The People's Daily*, at english.people.com.cn/200601/13/eng20060113_235266.html.

The People's Daily (16 March 2007) 'China's top legislature adopts landmark property law', at english.people.com.cn/200703/16/eng20070316_358242.html.

People's Daily Online (3 January 2007) 'Foreign invested firms to lose tax and land use privileges', english.peopledaily.com.cn/200701/03/eng20070103_337789.html.

Perez, Carlota (1985) 'Microelectronics, long waves and world structural change: New perspectives for developing countries' in *World Development* 13/3.

Perry, Elizabeth J. (2002) *Challenging the Mandate of Heaven: Social Protest and State Power in China* Armonk: M. E. Sharpe.

Perry, Elizabeth J. and Merle Goldman (2007) 'Introduction: Historical Reflections on Grassroots Political reform in China' in Perry and Goldman (eds) *Grassroots Political Reform in Contemporary China* Harvard University Press, pp. 1–19.

Perry, Elizabeth J. and Xun Li (1997) *Proletarian Power* Boulder: Westview.

Pinches, Michael (1999) 'Cultural Relations, Class and the New Rich of Asia' in M. Pinches (ed.) *Culture and Privilege in Capitalist Asia* London: Routledge, pp. 1–55.

Polanyi, Karl (1957) *The Great Transformation* Boston: Beacon Press.

Pow, Choon-Piew (2007) 'Securing the Civilised Enclaves: Gated Communities and the Moral Geographies of Exclusion in (post)-Socialist Shanghai' in *Urban Studies* 44/8, pp. 1539–1558.

'President Hu preaches morality to the Chinese' (2006) *China Daily*, 16 March.

Private entrepreneurs (2007) 'Guanzhu minying qiyejia' ('Let's pay attention to private entrepreneurs') 7 January 2007, at blog.sina.com.cn/u/4b7c03de010006wv.

Pun, Ngai (2003) 'Subsumption or Consumption? The Phantom of Consumer Revolution in Globalizing China' in *Cultural Anthropology* 18/4, pp. 469–492.

Qian, Yingyi (2000) 'The Process of China's Market Transition (1978–1998): The Evolutionary, Historical, and Comparative Perspectives' in *Journal of Institutional and Theoretical Economics* 156/1, pp. 151–71.

Qiao Farong (2005) 'Chengyan: Goujian Hexie Shehui De Daode Jichu' ('Truth: The Moral Foundation of a Harmonious Society') in *Renmin Ribao* (*The People's Daily*) 19 July.

Qin, Yan (1999) *Zhongguo zhongchan jieji* (*The middle class in China*) Beijing: Zhongguo Jihua Chubanshe.

Qin, Yan (2002) *Zhongguo zhongchan jieji: weilai shehui de zhuliu* (*The Chinese Middle Class: The Mainstream of the Future Society*) Beijing: Zhongguo jihua chubanshe.

Qing Lianbin (2001) 'Woguo shehui shifou you yige "zhongchan jieji?"' ('Is There a "Middle Class" in China?') in *Zhongguo dangzheng ganbu luntan* (*Forum for Party and Government Cadres*) 3, pp. 24–26.

Radway, Janice A. (1997) *A Feeling for Books: the Book-of-the-Month Club, Literary Taste, and Middle-class Desire* The University of North Carolina Press.

Read, Benjamin L. (2000) 'Revitalizing the State's Urban 'Nerve Tips'' in *The China Quarterly* 163, pp. 806–20.

Read, Benjamin L. (2003) 'Democratizing the Neighborhood? New Private Housing and Home-Owner Self-Organization in Urban China' in *The China Quarterly* 49, pp. 31–59.

Reed, Gay Garland (1995) 'Moral/Political Education in the People's Republic of China: Learning through Role Models' in *Journal of Moral Education* 24/2, pp. 99–111.

Reports of violence (27 July 2004) 'Yiwan fuhao pinpin sangming, choufu jihua maodun hou quefa youxiao tiaojie' ('Several billionaires killed, clearly there are no workable mechanisms to re-conciliate the rich and the poor'), at news.sohu.com/20040727/n221212495.shtml.

Reports of violence (12 July 2005) 'Zhongguo furen zaoyu "choufu xinli", qiyejia zhifu shici beibang' ('The rich in China are hated—a private entrepreneur's father kidnapped ten times'), at news.sohu.com/20050712/n226277540.shtml.

Reports of violence (6 July 2006) 'Xinwen zongshen: choufu xinli yanshi xia de Wangfujing xue'an' ('In-depth news: a murder in Wangfujing and the hatred against the rich'), at big5.xinhuanet. com/gate/big5/news.xinhuanet.com/legal/2006-/content_4800784.htm.

Research Office, State Council (2002) *Zhongguo nongmin gong diaoyan baogao* (*A Report on China's Rural Migrant Workers*).

Research Team (1993) 'Gaige de shehui chengshouli yanjiu' ('A study of the aggregate levels of collective tolerance during market transition') in *Guanli Shijie* (*Journal of Management Science*) 5, pp. 189–98.

Richardson, Philip (2005) *Economic Change in China 1800–1950* Cambridge University Press.

Ridgeway, Cecilia L. et.al. (1998) 'How Do Status Beliefs Develop?' in *American Sociological Review* 63/3, p. 331.

Ritzer, George (2004) *The Globalization of Nothing* Thousand Oaks: Pine Forge Press.

Roberts, Dexter and Frederik Balfour (2006) 'In China, to Get Rich is Glorious' 6 February, at biz.yahoo.com/special/chinarich06_article1.html.

Robison, Richard and David S. G. Goodman (1996a) (eds) *The New Rich in Asia: Mobile-phones, McDonalds and Middle Class Revolution* London: Routledge.

Robison, Richard and David S. G. Goodman (1996b) 'The new rich in Asia: economic development, social status and political consciousness' in R. Robison and D. S. G.Goodman (eds) *The New Rich in Asia: Mobile phones, McDonalds and middle class revolution* London: Routledge, pp. 1–16.

Rocca, Jean-Louis (1999) 'Old Working Class, New Working Class: Reforms, Labour Crisis and the Two Faces of Conflicts in Chinese Urban Areas' paper presented at the 2nd Annual Conference of the European Union-China Academic Network, 21–22 January 1999, Centro de Estudios de Asia Oriental, Universidad Autonoma de Madrid, Spain.

Rodan, Garry. (ed.) (1996) *Political Oppositions in Industrialising Asia* London: Routledge.

Rodan, Garry (1998) 'Seeking Theory from Experience: Media Regulation in China' in Vicky Randall (ed.) *Democratization and the Media* London: Frank Cass.

Rohlen, Thomas (2002) 'Cosmopoloitan Cities and Nation States. Open Economics, Urban Dynamics and Government in East Asia' in Luigi Tomba (ed.) *East Asian Capitalism: Conflicts, Growth and Crisis* Milan: Feltrinelli, pp. 01–148.

Root, Hilton (1996) 'Corruption in China: Has It Become Systemic?' in *Asian Survey* 36/8, pp. 741–57.

Rosen, Daniel H. (1999) *Behind the Open Door: Foreign Enterprises in the Chinese Marketplace* Washington, DC: Institute for International Economics.

Rosen, Stanley (1982) *Red Guard Factionalism and the Cultural Revolution in Guangzhou* Boulder: Westview Press.

Rosen, Stanley (1994) 'Chinese women in the 1990s: images and roles in contention' in Tsu-chien Lu and Maurice Brosseau (eds) *China Review 1994* Hong Kong: Chinese University Press.

Rosen, S. (1995) 'Women and political participation in China' in *Pacific Affairs* 68/3.

Rosen, Stanley (2004) 'The state of youth/youth and the state in early 21st century China: the triumph of the urban rich?' in Peter Hays Gries and Stanley Rosen (eds) *State and Society in 21st Century China* New York and London: Routledge-Curzon, pp. 159–179.

Saich, Tony (2000) 'Negotiating the State: The Development of Social Organizations in China' in *The China Quarterly* 161 (March), pp. 124–141.

Santoro, Michael A. (2000) *Profits and Principles: Global Capitalism and Human Rights in China* Cornell University Press.

Sassen, Saskia (2001) *The Global City: New York, London, Tokyo* Princeton University Press, Second Edition.

Savadove, B. (2006) 'Shanghai party chief sacked in graft probe: downfall of Chen Liangyu is linked to allegations of pension fund mismanagement, abuse of power' in *South China Morning Post*, at www.hkhkhk.com/engpro/messages/2169.html.

Schurmann, H. Franz (1968) *Ideology and Organization in Communist China* University of California Press, 2nd edition.

Segal, Adam (2003) *Digital Dragon: High-Technology Enterprises in China* Ithaca: Cornell University Press.

Shandong People's Government (n.d.) 'Shandong sheng zhi: nongye ku' ('Shandong Provincial Annals: Agriculture'), at www.shandong.gov.cn/art/2005/12/20/art_6327_145327.html.

Shanghai Daily (26 June 2007) 'Exchange starts gold trading via local banks.', at news.xinhuanet.com/english/2007–/content_6291900.htm.

Shanghai Daily (17 September 2007) 'China may take No. 1 position in gold output.', at www.shanghaidaily.com/article/?id=331117&type=Business.

Shanghai Morning Post (*Xinwen chenbao*) (17 June 2006) 'Huangpu: wu ge huangjin xiaofeiqu yu san ge sheji shenchang jidi' ('Huangpu: five gold consumption districts and three design production bases').

Shanghai University, Personnel Department (2003) 'Shanghai Daxue yinjin gao cengci rencai gongzuo tiaoli' ('Shanghai University working rules for attracting high level talented people'), at www.hr.shu.edu.cn/show.aspx?ID=223.

Shao, Daosheng (2002) '95 % de tanguan dou you qingfu: falü gai bugai guanguan xing huilu?' ('95 per cent corrupt officials have a mistress: should the law be used to govern sex-related bribery and corruption?') 23 October, at www.163.com/editor/021023/021023_550346.html.

Shen, Shunjing (2003) 'Yunyong jieceng fenxi de fangfa renshi dangqian Zhongguo de shehui jiegou' ('Understanding China's Current Social Structure through Stratum Analysis') in *Xuexi luntan* (*Study Forum*) 10, pp. 93–94.

Shen, Xiaojie (2006) 'Shi shui daoqu he daomai le women de jiben juzhu quan' ('Who stole and sold our housing rights?') 8 March 2006, at finance.sina.com.cn/review/observe/20060308/11302400815.shtml.

Sheng Li (2005) 'Jini xishu, zhongchan jiejie yu minzhu fazhi' ('The GIBI Index, the Middle Class, Democracy and *the Rule of Law'*) in *Dangdai jingli ren* (*Contemporary Manager*) 17, pp. 174–175.

Shenzhen Entrepreneurs (n.d.) *Shenzhen qiyejia shuhua xuehui* (*Shenzhen Entrepreneurs Society for the Study of Calligraphy and Painting*), at www.qyjsh.com/.

Sheridan, James E. (1975) *China in Disintegration: The Republican Era in Chinese History, 1912–1949* London: The Free Press, Macmillan.

Shi Xiuyin (1995) 'Zhongguo saying qiye gugong ji laozi guanxi baogao' ('A Report on Labour Relations in Private Enterprises') in Li Peling (ed.) *Zhongguo xin shiqi jieji jieceng baogao* (*Social Stratification during China's Market Transition in China*) Shenyang: Liaoning renmin chubanshe.

Shirk, Susan (1982) *Competitive Comrades* University of California Press.

Shue, Vivienne (1998) 'State Power and the Philanthropic Impulse in China Today' in Warren Ilchman, Stanley Katz and Edward Queen (eds) *Philanthropy in the World's Traditions* Bloomington: Indiana University Press, p. 382.

Shue, Vivienne (2004) 'Legitimacy crisis in China?' in Peter Hays Gries and Stanley Rosen (eds) *State and Society in 21st century China* London: RoutledgeCurzon, pp. 24–49.

Sichuansheng Tongjiju (Sichuan Provincial Bureau of Statistics) (2005) *Sichuan Tongji Nianjian* (*Sichuan Statistical Yearbook*) Beijing: Zhongguo tongji chubanshe.

Sigley, G. (2006) 'Sex, politics and the policing of virtue in the People's Republic of China' in Elaine Jeffreys (ed.) *Sex and Sexuality in China* London; New York: RoutledgeCurzon, pp. 43–61.

SinoCast China Business Daily News (23 August 2007) 'Nokia Siemens to Create Largest R&D Center in Chengdu', at www.sinocast.com.

Slaves (2007) 'Fangnu gongfang bugan shengzi, gao fangjia jiang rang zhongguo shehui duanzi juesun' ('Slaves of the housing market dare not bear children, there will be no children in the future due to unaffordable housing') 5 March 2007, at sh.focus.cn/news/2007-03-.html.

Smart, Alan and Li Zhang (2006) 'From the Mountains and the Fields: The Urban Transition in the Anthropology of China' in *China Information* 20/3, pp. 481–518.

Smith, Neil (1996) *The New Urban Frontier: Gentrification and the Revanchist City* London and New York: Routledge.

So, Alvin (2003) 'The Making of the Cadre-Capitalist Class in China' in Joseph Cheng (ed.) *China's Challenges in the Twenty-First Century* City University of Hong Kong Press.

So, Bennis Wai-yip (2002) 'The Policy-Making and Political Economy of the Abolition of Private Ownership in the Early 1950s' in *The China Quarterly* 171, pp. 682–703.

SOHO China [a] 'SOHO Xiandaicheng meishuguan' ('SOHO New Town Art Gallery'), at www.sohochina.com/xiandai/art.asp.

SOHO China [b] 'Zhang Xin yu Pan Shiyi' ('Zhang Xin and Pan Shiyi'), at www.sohochina.com/about/zhangxin.asp.

SOHO Journal Editorial Board *SOHO Xiaobao* (*SOHO Journal*), at www.sohoxiaobao.com/chinese/index.php.

SOHO Journal Editorial Board (ed.) (2005) *Quanzi* (*Urban Circles*) Wuhan: Changjiang wenyi chubanshe.

Solinger, Dorothy J. (1984) *Chinese Business under Socialism: The Politics of Domestic Commerce, 1949–1980* University of California Press.

Solinger, Dorothy J. (1991) *From Lathes to Looms: China's Industrial Policy in Comparative Perspective, 1979–1982* Stanford University Press.

Solinger, Dorothy J. (2002) 'Labour Market Reform and the Plight of the Laid-off Proletariat' in *The China Quarterly* 170, pp. 304–26.

Solinger, Dorothy (2004) 'The New Crowd of the Dispossessed: The Shift of the Urban Proletariat from Master to Mendicant' in Peter Gries and Stanley Rosen (eds) *State and Society in 21st-Century China: Crisis, Contention, and Legitimation* New York and London: Routledge-Curzon.

Southern Weekend (*Nanfang zhoumo*) (17 August 2007) 'Zhongguo shi 'shenji': renhai zhanshu shuoming shenme?' (The China model of 'seeking fortune': what do sea of people tactics tell us?')

Spence, Jonathan D. (1990) *The Search for Modern China* New York: Norton and Co.

State Council (1956) 'Guanyu gongzi gaige de jueding' ('Resolution regarding wage reform'), at www.news.xinhuanet.com/ziliao/2004–/content_2393793.htm.

State Council (1957) '"Guanyu shengji gongzuo yilu dingzhi" de jieshi' ('An explanation of "About stopping all promotion-related work"'), at www.labournet.com.cn.

State Council (1982) 'Guanyu tiaozheng guojia jiguan, kexue wen jiao weisheng deng bumen bufen gongzuo renyuan gongzi de jueding' ('Resolution regarding adjusting the wages for some staff working in state organs and agencies of science, culture, education and health'), at www.fm120.com/zt/law/laws/1/YYWSZHFLFG/XZFG/XZFG1003.htm.

State Council (1985) 'Guojia jiguan he shiye danwei gongzuo renyuan gongzi zhidu gaige wenti de tongzhi' ('Circular about wage reform issues in relation to personnel in state organs and institutional work-units'), at www.cneduinfo.cn/fagui/Class1187/200611/1065075.html.

State Council (1993) 'Guanyu jiguan he shiye danwei gongzuo renyuan gongzi zhidu gaige wenti de tongzhi' ('Circular regarding wage reform issues in relation to personnel of state organs and institutional work-units') in *Renshi zhengce fagui huibian* (*Collection of personnel policies, laws and regulations*) Taiyuan: Huabei gongxueyuan renshichu (North China University of Technology) 2003.

State Council, Bureau of Technical Cadres (1982) 'Guanyu shixing kexue jishu renyuan jianzhi, jiaoliu de zanxing banfa de tongzhi' ('Circular regarding experimental implementation of provisional regulations of technical personnel taking and exchanging second jobs'), at www.21wecan.com.cn/zcfg/4/4_33.htm.

State Council, General Office (1986) 'Zhuanfa Sifa bu guanyu jiaqiang he gaige lushi gongzuo de baogao de tongzhi' ('Circular notice: Report from the Ministry of Justice on strengthening and reforming lawyers' work'), at www.law-lib.com/law/.

State Council, General Office (1994) *Zhongguo Funu de Zhuangkuang* (Women's situation in China), at www.china.com.cn/ch-book/funvzhuangkuang/woman.htm.

State Council, Personnel Bureau (1957) 'Guanyu gaodeng xuexiao he zhongdeng zhuanye xuexiao biye fenpei gongzuo yihou gongzi daiyu deng wenti de zonghe dafu' ('Comprehensive reply on issues regarding salaries and benefits for graduates of tertiary and middle level specialized schools after they have been assigned jobs'), at www.fagui.findlaw.cn/plus/view.php?aid=58114.

State Council, Research Office (2006) *Zhongguo nongmin gong diaoyan baogao* (A Report on China's Rural Migrant Workers).

Stone, Lawrence (1977) *The Family, Sex and Marriage in England 1500–1800* London: Weidenfeld and Nicolson.

Strauss, J. (2006) 'Morality, coercion and state building campaign in the early PRC: regime consolidation and after, 1949–1956' in *The China Quarterly* 188, pp. 891–912.

Su Rongcai and Wu Tao (2005) 'Shenzhen shi lushi ren jun nian shouru 35 wan' ('The average annual income of Shenzhen lawyers is 350,000 *yuan*') in *Xinhua wang Guangdong pindao* (*Xinhua Net Guangdong Channel*) 14 April, at www.gd.xinhuanet.com/newscenter/2005-/content_4058392.htm.

Su, Xueqin (2004) 'Zhongguo shehui zhuanxing shiqi jieji he jieceng zhuangkuang fenxi' ('An Analysis of the Situation of Classes and Strata during China's Transitional Period') in *Qinghai minzu xueyuan xuebao* (*Journal of Qinghai Nationalities Institute*) 30/3 (July), pp. 17–20.

Sull, Donald N. with Yong Wang (2005) *Made in China: What Western Managers Can Learn from Trailblazing Chinese Entrepreneurs* Harvard Business School Press.

Sun Liping (1994) 'Pingmin zhuyi yu Zhongguo gaige' ('Populism and China's Reforms') in *Zhanlue yu guanli* (*Strategy and Management*) 5 (October) pp. 1–10.

Sun Liping (1996) 'Huiru shijie wenming zhuliu: minzuzhuyi santi' ('Join the Mainstream of World Civilization: Three Questions Regarding Nationalism') in *Dongfang* (*Eastern*) 1, pp. 19–30.

Sun Liping (2003) *Duanlie: ershi shiji jiushi niandai yilai de Zhongguo shehui* (*Rupture: Chinese Society since the 1990s*) Beijing: Shehui kexue wenxian chubanshe.

Sun Liping (2005) 'Zhongguo ziben yuanshi jilei de sanzhong leixing ji qi yinfa de wenti' 7 April 2005, at blog.sociology. org.cn/ thslping/archive/2005/04/07/1375. aspx.

Sun, Yan (1999) 'Reform, State, and Corruption: Is Corruption Less Destructive in China than in Russia' in *Comparative Politics* 32/1, pp. 1–20.

Sun, Yifei, Maximilian Von Zedtwitz and Denis Fred Simon (2007) 'Globalization of R&D and China: An Introduction' in *Asia Pacific Business Review* 13/3, pp. 311–319.

SYNJ (2006) *Shenyang Nianjian 2006* (*Shenyang Yearbook, 2006*) Beijing: Zhongguo Tongji Chubanshe.

Szelenyi, Ivan (1978) 'Social Inequalities in State Socialist Redistributive Economies' in *International Journal of Comparative Sociology* 19/1–2, pp. 61–87.

Szelenyi, Ivan and Eric Kostello (1996) 'The Market Transition Debate: Toward a Synthesis?' in *American Journal of Sociology* 101/4, pp. 1082–96.

Szelenyi, Ivan and Robert Maunchin (1987) 'Social Policy under State Socialism' in Martin Rein, Gosta Esping-Andersen and Lee Rainwater (eds) *Stagnation and Renewal in Social Policy: The Rise and Fall of Policy Regimes* Armonk: M.E. Sharpe, pp. 102–39.

Tan Ying (2001) 'Dangdai Zhongguo zhongjian jieceng de jueqi jiqi shehui xiaoying' ('The Rise of the Middle Stratum and Its Social Effects') in *Shehui* (*Society*) 2, pp. 11–13.

Tang, Changli (1989) 'Shidai tezheng yu rujia gongneng' ('Characteristics of the times and the function of Confucianism') in *Dongyue luncong* (*Shandong Forum*) 1, p. 5.

Tang, Xiangyue (2004) 'Ta weihe likai zhe jia yiyuan' ('Why he left that hospital') in *Guangming ribao* (*Guangming Daily*) 16 December.

Tang, Xiaobing. (2000) *Chinese Modern: the Heroic and the Quotidian* Duke University Press.

Tanner, Murray Scot (2004) 'China Rethinks Unrest' in *The Washington Quarterly* 27/3, pp. 137–56.

Tao, Xidong (2005) 'Jiakuai Chengshi Hexie Shequ Jianshe Jizhi De Chongjian Yu Zaizao' ('Accelerate the Reconstruction of the Mechanisms for the Edification of Harmonious Communities in the Cities') in *Renmin ribao* (*The People's Daily*) 21 June.

Tawney, R. H. (1938) *Religion and the Rise of Capitalism: A Historical Study* Harmondsworth, England; New York: Penguin.

Teiwes, Frederick C. (1967) *Provincial Party Personnel in Mainland China* East Asia Institute, Columbia University.

Tengen Group (n.d.) 'Tianzhengren xuanyan' ('Tengen Declaration'), at www.tengen.com.cn/wenhua/tzrxy.asp.

Tengen Group (2005) 'Huore de Tianzheng, huore de qing' ('Passionate feelings for a passionate Tengen') in *Tengen People* 1, at www.tengen.com.cn/news/tzr/index.asp?bt.

The entrepreneur (n.d.) 'The key personality, environmental, and action factors' at 1000ventures.com/ten3_operations/customized/entrepreneur_eu.html.

Thomas, Dana (2007) *Deluxe: How Luxury Lost its Luster* New York: The Penguin Press.

Thompson, E. P. (1966) *The Making of the English Working Class* New York: Vintage Books.

Thompson, E. P. (1978) 'The Peculiarities of the English' in *The Poverty of Theory* London: Merlin.

Thorne, Susan (2002) 'Shanghai chic: makeover will bring high-end retail to China's No.1 shopping street' in *Shopping Centers Today*, December, at www.icsc.org/srch/sct/sct1202/page79a.php.

Thye, Shane R. (2000) 'A Status Value Theory of Power in Exchange Relations' in *American Sociological Review* 65, pp. 407–32.

Tianjin Municipal Government (1988) 'Pi zhuan shi sifa ju "guanyu wo shi lushi tizhi gaige de jidian yijian"' ('Approval and circulation of the Bureau of Justice "Several opinions on the reform of the lawyer system in our city"'), at www.lawlib.com/law/.

Tomba, Luigi (2004) 'Creating an Urban Middle Class. Social Engineering in Beijing' in *The China Journal* 51, pp. 1–32.

Tomba, Luigi (2005) 'Residential Space and Collective Interest Formation in Beijing Housing Disputes' in *The China Quarterly* 184, pp. 934–951.

Tomba, Luigi (2008) 'Of Quality, Harmony and Community: Civilization and the Middle Class in Urban China' in *positions*.

Tompson, William (2002) 'Was Gaidar Really Necessary?' in *Problems of Post-Communism* 49/4, pp. 12–21.

Torri, Michelguglielmo (1991) '"Westernized Middle Class": Intellectuals and Society in Late Colonial India' in John L. Hill (ed.) *The Congress and Indian Nationalism: Historical Perspectives* London: Curzon Press.

Toy, M. A. (2007) 'China's young high-flyers in crash-landing' in *Sydney Morning Herald*, 17–18 February: World, p. 15.

Tsai, Kellee S. (2002) *Back-Alley Banking: Private Entrepreneurs in China* Cornell University Press.

Tsai, Kellee S. (2005) 'Capitalists without a Class: Political Diversity among Private Entrepreneurs in China' in *Comparative Political Studies* 38/9, p. 1, 130–58.

Tsai, Kellee S. (2006) 'Changing China: Private Entrepreneurs and Adaptive Institutions' presented at the conference *Capitalism with Chinese Characteristics: China's Political Economy in Comparative and Theoretical Perspective* Indiana University, May 19–20, 2006.

Tsai, Kellee S. (2007) *Capitalism Without Democracy: The Private Sector in Contemporary China* Cornell University Press.

Tsang, E. W. K. (1996) 'In search of legitimacy: the private entrepreneur in China' in *Entrepreneurship: Theory and Practice* 21/1.

Tsang, Shu-Ki and Cheng Yuk-Shing (1997) 'Evasion and Supply Instability in a Double-track System' in *Economics of Planning* 30/1, pp. 1–16.

Unger, Jonathan (1994) '"Rich Man, Poor Man": the Making of New Classes in the Countryside' in David S. G. Goodman (ed.) (1994) *China's Quiet Revolution: New Interactions between State and Society* Melbourne: Longman Cheshire, pp. 43–64.

Unger, Jonathan and Anita Chan (2004) 'The Internal Politics of an Urban Chinese Work Community: A Case Study of Employee Influence on Decision-making at a State Owned Factory' in *The China Journal* 52, pp. 1–26.

Van Dijk, Meine Pieter (2005) 'Nanjing. Promoting the ICT sector' in Peter J. M. Nas (ed.) *Directors of Urban Change in Asia* London: Routledge.

Vanke Film and TV Corporation 'Niumeng' ('The Gadfly') at mt.vanke.com/index.php?id=124.

Vanke Company, website at mt.vanke.com/index.php?id=101.

Vanke Group, Wanke (*Vanke Weekly*), at www.vankeweekly.com/main/.

Veblen, Thorstein (1939) *The Theory of the Leisure Class* New York: The Modern Library.

Wahrman, Dror (1995) *Imagining the Middle Class: the Political Representation of Class in Britain, c. 1780–1840* Cambridge University Press.

Walcott, Susan M. (2003) *Chinese Science and Technology Industrial Parks* Ashgate.

Walder, Andrew G. (1984) 'The Remaking of the Chinese Working Class, 1949–1981' in *Modern China* 10/1, pp. 3–48.

Walder, Andrew G. (1986) *Communist Neo-traditionalism* University of California Press.

Walder, Andrew G. (1994) 'Evolving Property Rights and their Political Consequences' in David S. G. Goodman (ed.) *China's Quiet Revolution: New Interactions between State and Society* Melbourne: Longman Cheshire.

Walder, Andrew (1995) 'Career Mobility and the Communist Political Order' in *American Sociological Review* 60/3, pp. 309–28.

Walder, Andrew (1996) 'Markets and Inequality in Transitional Economies: Toward Testable Theories' in *American Journal of Sociology* 101/4, pp. 1060–73.

Walder, Andrew G. (ed.) (1998) *Zouping in Transition: The Process of Reform in Rural North China* Harvard University Press.

Walder, Andrew (2002a) 'Markets and income inequality in rural China' in *American Sociological Review* 67/2, pp. 231–53.

Walder, Andrew (2002b) 'Income Determination and Market Opportunity in Rural China, 1978–1996' in *Journal of Comparative Economics* 30/2, pp. 354–75.

Walder, Andrew (2006) 'The party elite and Chinas trajectory of change' in Kjeld Erik Brodsgaard and Zheng Yongnian (eds) *The Chinese Communist Party in Reform* London: Routledge, pp. 15–32.

Walder, Andrew and Litao Zhao (2006) 'Political Office and Household Wealth' in *The China Quarterly* 186, pp. 357–76.

Walder, Andrew, Bobai Li and Donald J. Treiman (2000) 'Politics and Life Chances in a State Socialist Regime' in *American Sociological Review* 65/2, pp. 191–209.

Walfish, Daniel (2001) 'China's Private Schools. Lessons in Profits' in *Far Eastern Economic Review*, 14 June.

Walker, Kathy Le Mons (2006) '"Gangster Capitalism" and Peasant Protest in China: The Last Twenty Years' in *Journal of Peasant Studies* 33/1, p. 4.

Walsh, Kathleen A. (2007) 'China R&D: A High-Tech Field of Dreams' in *Asia Pacific Business Review* 13/3, pp. 321–335.

Wang, Bing (2004) *Tiexi qu* (A L'Ouest de Rails – West of the Tracks) Documentary in four parts, MK2, Allumettes Films.

Wang, Chaohua (ed.) (2003) *One China, Many Paths* London: Verso.

Wang, Gan (2006) 'Net-moms – a new place and a new identity: parenting discussion forums on the Internet in China' in Tim Oakes and Louisa Schein (eds) *Translocal China* London: Routledge, pp. 155–165.

Wang Jianbing (2001) 'Beida nan qiang you qi shang le' ('The south wall of Beijing University was put up again') in *Beijing chenbao* (*Beijing Morning News*) 15 July.

Wang Jin (2002) 'Xing huilu gaizhi shui de zui: baixing daduo zancheng lifa zhicai "quanse jiaoyi"' ('Who are the criminal offenders in sex-related bribery and corruption? Most people want the "trading of power and sex" to be punished by law') in *Beijing qingnian bao* (*Beijing Youth News*) 19 December.

Wang, Jing (1996) *High Culture Fever: Politics, Aesthetics, and Ideology in Deng's China* University of California Press.

Wang, Jing (2004) 'The Global Reach of a New Discourse: How Far can "Creative Industries" Travel?' in *International Journal of Cultural Studies* 7/1, pp. 9–19.

Wang Jun 2007 'Private Entrepreneurs More Elite' in *Beijing Review* no. 11 (15 March), at www.bjreview.com.cn/business/txt/2007-/content_58874.htm.

Wang Junxiu *et al.* (2007) '2006 nian Zhongguo shehui xintai diaocha baogao' ('A Report on Social Perceptions – 2006') in Ru Xin *et al.* (eds) *2007: Zhongguo shehui xingshi fenxi yu yuce* (*2007: Analysis and forecast on China's Social Development*) (Blue Book of China's Society) pp. 68–69.

Wang Lei (2004) 'Zhongguo Yiyao Shangye Xiehui mishuzhang Wang Jingxia: yi yao yang yi tizhi bu gai, yiliao fubai manman bu jue' ('Wang Jinxia, Secretary of China's Pharmaceutical Industry Association: if the system of "financing-hospitals-with-drug-sales" does not change, medical corruption will be endless') in *Zhongguo qingnian bao* (*China Youth Daily*) 23 July.

Wang Lei (2007) 'Jilin Daxue fuzhai zongliang da 30 yi yuan, xiaozhang fengming "du qiangyan"' ('The total debt of Jilin University reached 3 billion *yuan*. Its President ordered to "plug the hole"') in *Nanfang dushi bao* (*Southern Metropolitan News*) 9 April.

Wang, Lei and Liu, Ke (2000) 'Xing huilu yueyan yuelie, faxue zhuanjia huyu lifa zhicai' ('The more sex-related bribery and corruption develops the stronger it becomes: lawyers appeal for legal punishments') in *Qingnian shixun* (*Youth News*) 14 December.

Wang, Mark (2004) 'New Urban Poverty in China' in *International Development Planning Review* 26/2, pp. 117–139.

Wang Shaoguang and Hu Angang (1999) *The Political Economy of Uneven Development: The Case of China* Armonk, New York: M E Sharpe.

Wang, Shi (2006) *Daolu yu mengxiang* (*Roads and Dreams*) Beijing: Zhongxin chubanshe.

Wang, Shi (n.d.) *Shan zai na: Wang Shi BLOG* (*Mountains over there: Wang Shi's blog*), at blog.sina.com.cn/wangshi.

Wang Ya Ping (2000) 'Housing Reform and Its Impact on the Urban Poor' in *Housing Studies* 15/6, pp. 845–64.

Wang Ya Ping and Alan Muric (1999) 'Commercial Housing Development in Urban China' in *Urban Studies* 36/9, pp. 1475–94.

Wang, Yongyang and Margaret Secombe (2004) 'A Study of People-Run Tertiary Education in South and west China' in *International Education Journal* 4/4, p. 21–29.

Wang Zheng (1997) 'Maoism, feminism and the UN conference on women: Women's studies research in contemporary China' in *Journal of Women's History* 8/4 (Winter), pp. 126–52.

Wang Zheng (2003) 'Gender, Employment and Women's Resistance' in E. J. Perry and M. Selden (eds) *Chinese Society: Change, Conflict and Resistance* London: Routledge, pp. 158–182.

Wang Zheng (2006) 'Dilemmas of Inside Agitators: Chinese State Feminists in 1957' in *The China Quarterly* 188, pp. 913–32.

Wang Zhuoqiong 2007 'Nation's Rich Have Poor Reputation' in *China Daily* 12 September, at www.chinadaily.com.cn/china/2007–/content_6098768.htm.

Wank, David (1999) *Commodifying Communism: Business, Trust, and Politics in a Chinese City* Cambridge University Press.

Watkins-Mathys, Lorraine and M. John Foster (2006) 'Entrepreneurship' in *Entrepreneurship and Regional Development* 18/3, pp. 249–74.

Watson, James (ed.) (1984) *Class and Social Stratification in Post-Revolution China* Cambridge University Press.

Watts, J. (2006) 'Mistress turns in "corrupt" Chinese vice admiral' in *Guardian*, 15 June.

Wealth Forum (2005) 'Beijing caifu luntan' ('Forum on wealth in Beijing') 18 August 2005, at www.und. cn/news.do?act=detail&newsid=2005081817374896.

Weber, Max (1946) Hans H. Gerth and C. Wright Mills (eds) *From Max Weber: Essays in Sociology* New York: Oxford University Press.

Webster, Murray and Stuart J. Hysom (1998) 'Creating Status Characteristics' in *American Sociological Review* 63/3, pp. 351–2.

Wei Caihong (2004) 'Shanghai lushi xinchou diaocha' ('An investigation of Shanghai lawyers' salaries') in *Xinwen chenbao* (*Morning News*) 18 June.

Wei Xinghua and Huang Taiyan (1993) 'Lun naoli laodong shouru fenpei tizhi de gaige' ('Reform of the income and redistribution system for mental labour') in *Jingji lilun yu jingji guanli* (*Economic theory and economic management*) 1, pp. 34–38.

Weller, R. P. (1998) 'Divided market cultures in China: gender, enterprise, and religion' in Robert P. Hefner (ed.) *Market Cultures: Society and Morality in the New Asian Capitalisms*, Boulder, CO: Westview Books, pp. 78–103.

Wesoky, S. (2002) *Chinese Feminism Faces Globalisation* New York and London: Routledge.

White, Gordon (1974) *The Politics of Class and Class Origins* Contemporary China Centre, The Australian National University.

White, Gordon Jude Howell and Shang Xiaoyuan (1996) *In Search of Civil Society: Market Reform and Social Change in Contemporary China*Oxford: Clarendon Press.

White III, Lynn T (1998) *Unstately Power* White Plains, New York: M E Sharpe.

Whiting, Susan (2001) *Power and Wealth in Rural China: the Political Economy of Institutional Change* Cambridge University Press.

Whyte, Martin King and William L Parish (1984) *Urban Life in Contemporary China* University of Chicago Press.

Wolf, M. (1985) *Revolution Postponed: Women in Contemporary China* Stanford University Press.

Wolff, Janet and John Seed (eds) (1988) *The Culture of Capital: Art, Power, and the Nineteenth-century Middle Class* Manchester University Press.

Wong, Chack Kie and Lee, Nan Shong Peter (2000) 'Popular Belief in State Intervention for Social Protection in China' in *Journal of Social Policy* 29/1, pp. 109–116.

Wright, E. O. (1979) *Class Structure and Income Determination* New York: Academic Press.

Wright, Teresa (2004) 'Contesting state legitimacy in the 1990s: the China Democratic Party and the China Labor Bulletin' in Peter Hays Gries and Stanley Rosen (eds) *State and Society in 21st century China* London: RoutledgeCurzon, pp. 123–40.

Wu, Fulong (1997) 'Urban Restructuring in China's Emerging Market Economy: Towards a Framework for Analysis' in *International Journal of Urban and Regional Research* 21/4, pp. 640–63.

Wu, Fulong (1998) 'The New Structure of Building Provision and the Transformation of the Urban Landscape in Metropolitan Guangzhou' in *Urban Studies* 35/2, pp. 277–83.

Wu, Fulong (1999) 'The "Game" of Landed-Property Production and Capital Circulation in China's Transitional Economy, with Reference to Shanghai' in *Environment and Planning A* 31/10, p. 1,757–71.

Wu, Fulong (2002) 'Sociospatial Differentiation in Urban China: Evidence from Shanghai's Real Estate Markets' in *Environment and Planning A* 34/9, pp. 1591–615.

Wu, Fulong (2004) 'Urban Poverty and Marginalization under Market Transition' in *International Journal of Urban and Regional Research* 28/2, pp. 401–23.

Wu, Fulong and Shenjing He (2005) 'Changes in traditional urban areas and impacts of urban redevelopment: a case study of three neighbourhoods in Nanjing, China' in *Tijdschrift voor Economische en Sociale Geografie* 96/1, pp. 75–95

Wu, Fulong, Jiang Xu and Anthony Gar-On Yeh (2007) *Urban Development in Post-Reform China* London: Routledge.

Wu, Jinglian (1987) 'The Dual Pricing System in China's Industry' in *Journal of Comparative Economics* 11/3, pp. 309–318.

Wu, Jixue (2006) 'Ziben yuanshi jilei zai zhongguo jiushi guozi de liushi' ('Primitive accumulation of capital and the transfer of state properties into the private sector') 8 February 2006, at finance.sina.com.cn/review/zlhd/20060208/09322325142.shtml.

Wu, Wenjie (2005) '*Baomu*, guzhu "chengjiao" za zhenme nan?' ('Why is it so hard for the maid and the employer to reach an agreement?') in *Jingji Ribao* (*Economy Daily*) 18 April, p.A11.

Wu, X. and Perloff, J. (2004) *China's Income Distribution Over Time: Reasons for Rising Inequality* CUDARE Working Papers 977, Berkley: University of California.

Wu, Xiaogang (2006) 'Communist Cadres and Market Opportunities: Entry into Self-employment in China, 1978–1996' in *Social Forces* 85/1, pp. 389–411.

Wu, Xiaogang and Xie, Yu (2003) 'Does the market pay off? Earning returns to education in urban China' in *American Sociological Review* 68/3.

Wu Yan (2000) 'Liaokai gaojia yao heimu' ('Lift up the black curtain of highly priced drugs') in *Renmin ribao* (*The People's Daily*) 22 September.

Wu, Yanrui (1999) *China's Consumer Revolution* Cheltenham: Edward Elgar.

Xia Yunfan (2004) 'The Great Chinese Land Grab Is On' in *Asian Times Online* 17 July 2004, at www.atimes.com/atimes/China/ FG17Ad03.html.

Xiang Jingyu (1923) 'Zhongguo funü yundong zaping' ('Notes on the Chinese Women's Movement') in *Qianfeng* (*The Vanguard*) 1/2 (1 December), pp. 51–56.

Xiao Gongqin (2003) 'The Rise of the Technocrats' in *Journal of Democracy* 14/1.

Xiao Wentao (2001) 'Zhongguo zhongjian jieceng de xianzhuang he weilai fazhan' ('The Current State of the Chinese Middle Stratum and Its Future Development') in *Shehuixue yanjiu* (*Sociological Research*) 3, pp. 93–98.

Xiao, Xianfu, Ouyang Tao and Cheng Jian (eds) (1986) *Yinan jingji fanzui anli xi* (*Analysis of complicated economic criminal cases*) Nanning: Guangxi Renmin Chubanshe.

Xie Donghui (2003) 'Jianlun xing huilu fanzui lifa' ('A brief discussion on the criminalization of sex-related bribery and corruption') in *Anhui lüshi wang* (*Anhui Lawyer's Website*) 29 May 2003, at www.ahlawyer.com.cn/kanwu/2003/lx2/more.html.

Xie, Shusen and Chen Bing (1989) 'Gaige gongben zhidu shi jiejue nao ti dao gua de genben chulu' ('Reform of the cost system is the fundamental solution for reverse wage disparity between mental and manual labour') in *Jingji lilun yu jingji guanli* (*Economic theory and economic management*) 2, pp. 60–65.

Xin Zhigang (2004) 'Dissecting China's "middle class"' 27 October 2004, at www. China-daily.com.cn/english/doc/2004-/content_386060.htm.

Xinhua (1 December 2001) 'Long Yongtu: Zhongguo jiang chengwei 21 shiji shijie zuida shichang' ('Long Yongtu: China Will Be the World's Biggest Market in the 21st Century'), at www.china.com.cn/chinese/kuaixun/81814.htm.

Xinhua (10 November 2002) 'All About "Xiaokang"'.

Xinhua (29 March 2004) 'Chinese Middle Class Covers 19 Percent by 2003, Up One Percent Per Year'.

Xinhua (3 October 2004) '"Golden Week" tourists help boost HK's retail trade', at english.peopledaily.com.cn/200410/03/eng20041003_159003.html.

Xinhua (20 May 2005) '"Social entrepreneurs" to play a bigger role in China, experts', at news.xinhuanet.com/english/2005-/content_2982164.htm.

Xinhua (18 June 2005) 'China Has 80 Million Middle Class Members', at www.chinaview.cn/index.htm.

Xinhua (30 September 2005) 'HK ready to receive "Golden Week" tourists', at english.peopledaily.com.cn/200509/30/eng20050930_211847.html.

Xinhua (12 January 2006) 'Natural diamond 'Siam star' to stage at Shanghai auction', at english.people.com.cn/200601/12/eng20060112_234707.html.

Xinhua (27 January 2006) 'Leaders underline social harmony in New Year speech', at www.chinadaily.com.cn/english/doc/2006-/content_516221.htm.

Xinhua (11 October 2006) 'Communiqué of the Sixth Plenum of the 16th CPC Central Committee', at chinadigitaltimes.net/2006/10/communique_of_the_sixth_plenum_of_the_16th_cpc_central.php.

Xinhua (17 January 2007) 'China suffers widening income gap', at http://english.cri.cn/3130/2007/01/07/262@ 182284.htm.

Xinhua (3 March 2007) 'Sessions focus on harmony, pollution', at www.chinadaily.com.cn/china/2007–/content_ 818905.htm.

Xinhua (28 April 2007) 'China reports jump in diamond imports', at english.peopledaily.com.cn/200704/28/eng20070428_370657.html.

Xinhua (10 May 2007) 'Scholar: Middle Class Develops Slowly in China', at www.chinaview.cn/index.htm.

Xinhua (18 June 2007) 'China Has 80 Million Middle Class Members: Official'.

Xin, Pu and Xiao, Juan (eds) (2000) *Dangdi huanghuo: gongheguo 50 nian saohuang douzheng jishi* (*Wash Away the Yellow Peril: A Record of the 50 Year Anti-Yellow Struggle in the People's Republic of China*) Guangzhou: Guangdong jingji chubanshe.

Xinxi shibao (*The Information Times*) (21 July 2001) 'Weilai wunian woguo zhongchan jieji da liangyi' ('The Capacity of China's Middle Class in the Next Five Years').

Xiu Yangfeng (2005) 'Li Yifu de biejiao bianhu xituo bu liao furen yuanzui' ('The original sin of the rich cannot be covered by Li Yifu's poor arguments') 19 October 2005, at finance.sina.com.cn/review/ 20051019/09322045382.shtml.

Xu Binglan (2007) 'China's GDP grows 10.7% in 2006, fastest in 11 years' in *China Daily* 26 January 2007.

Xu, Chi, Maosong Liu, Cheng Zhang, Shuqing An, Wen Yu and Jing M. Chen (2007) 'The spatiotemporal dynamics of rapid urban growth in the Nanjing metropolitan region of China' in *Landscape Ecology* 22, pp. 925–937.

Xu Guosheng and Chen Ninghua (eds) (1992) *Shanxi xianqu jingji fazhan shilue* (*Historical Outline of the Economic Development of Counties and Regions in Shanxi*) Taiyuan: Shanxi jingji chubanshe.

Xu Jiang (2002) 'Xin zhongchan jieji jueqi: Zhongguo fuyu shidai dekaishi' ('The Rise of a New Middle Class: The Beginning of China's Prosperity') in *Jingmao shijie* (*The World of Economics and Trade*) 8, pp. 43–47.

Xu, Xinxin (2000) 'Cong zhiye pingjia yu fanye quxiang kan Zhongguo shehui jigou bianqian' ('Changes in the Chinese Social Structure as Seen from Occupational Prestige Ratings and Job Preferences') in *Shehuixue yanjiu* (*Sociology Research*) 3, at www.sociology.cass.cn/pws/xuxinxin/rwjxuxinxin/P020040721335850156349.pdf.

Xu, Yingbao (2006) 'Shouru cen ci bu qi gao di chaju jiao da: guanzhu Guilin lushi hangye' ('Incomes are unequal and disparity is huge: concerns about Guilin lawyers') in *Guilin ribao* (*Guilin Daily*) 14 December.

Yan, Fengqiao and Daniel C. Levy (2003) 'China's New Private Education Law' in *International Higher Education* (Spring), at www.bc.edu/bc_org/avp/soe/cihe/newsletter/News31/text005.htm.

Yan, Hairong. (2003) 'Neoliberal Governmentality and Neohumanism: Organising *Suzhi*/Value Flow through Labor Recruitment Networks' in *Cultural Anthropology* 18/4, p.493.

Yan, Hairong (2006) 'Self-Development of Migrant Women and the Production of Suzhi (Quality) as Surplus Value' in Madeleine Yue Dong and Joshua Goldstein (eds) *Everyday Modernity in China* University of Washington Press.

Yan Tan, Graeme Hugo and Lesley Potter (2005) 'Rural Women, Displacement and the Three Gorges Project' in *Development and Change* 36/4, pp. 711–34.

Yang, Dali L. (2006) 'Economic Transformation and its Political Discontents in China' in *Annual Review of Political Science* 9, pp. 143–64.

Yang, Guobing (2003) 'China's Zhiqing Generation: Nostalgia, Identity, and Cultural Resistance in the 1990s' in *Modern China* 29/3, pp. 267–96.

Yang, Jingqing (2006) 'The privatisation of professional knowledge in the public health care sector in China' in *Health Sociology Review* 15/1, pp. 16–28.

Yang, Keming (2004) 'Institutional Holes and Entrepreneurship in China' in *The Sociological Review* 52/3, pp. 371–89.

Yang, Mingli (1989) '"Nao ti dao gua" wenti de jiezheng hi jiejue tujing' ('The crux of the problem of "reverse wage disparity between mental and manual labour" and solutions) in *Renwen zazhi* (*Journal of the Humanities*) 3, pp. 18–23.

Yao Haiying (2004) 'Fengyu bianhuan 50 nian, "di yi ci guanxiang" quan jilu' ('Changes in salaries of university graduates over 50 years, a complete record of "the first official pay") in *21 Shiji rencai bao* (*21st Century Talented People*), at www.usc.cuhk.edu.hk/wk_wzdctails.asp?id=2819.

Yao, Shujie, Zongyi Zhang and Lucia Hanmer (2004) 'Growing Inequality and Poverty in China' in *China Economic Review* 15/2, pp. 145–63.

Ye Xiaonan (2007) 'Zhongguo xin shehui jicceng yinqi guanzhu' ('New Social Strata in China Have Attracted Attention') in *The People's Daily* 13 February, p.1.

Yeh, Anthony G. O. (1995) 'The Social Space of Guangzhou City, China' in *Urban Geography* 16, pp. 595–621.

Yeh, Anthony Gar-On and Fulong Wu (1996) 'The New Land Development Process and Urban Development in Chinese Cities' in *International Journal of Urban and Regional Research* 20/2, pp. 400–21.

Yep, Ray (2003) *Manager Empowerment in China: Political implications of rural industrialization in the reform era* London: Routledge.

York, Geoffrey (2007) 'The New China: Keeping Track of Tycoons' in *The Globe and Mail* 26 May, at www.theglobeandmail.com/servlet/ArticleNews/freeheadlines/LAC/20070526/CHINA26/international/?pageRequested=2.

You Ji (1998) *China's Enterprise Reform* London: Routledge.

Young, Ken (1999) 'Consumption, Social Differentiation and Self-definition of the New Rich in Industrializing Southeast Asia' in M. Pinches (ed.) *Culture and Privilege in Capitalist Asia* London: Routledge, pp. 56–85.

Young, Linda (2003) *Middle-Class culture in the Nineteenth Century America, Australia and Britain* New York: Palgrave Macmillan.

Young, Matt (2006) 'Industry eyes China's "failed" health care reform' in *Asia Times*, 7 February, at www.atimes.com/atimes/China_Business/HB07Cb05.html.

Young, Nick (2002) 'Three "C"s: Civil Society, Corporate Social Responsibility, and China' in *The China Business Review* (January–February), at www.chinabusinessreview.com/public/0201/young.html.

Young, Susan (1995) *Private Business and Economic Reform in China* New York: M E Sharpe.

Yu Chunlai (2006) 'Zhongguo furen caifu zong'e da 1.59 wanyi meiyuan' ('The total assets of rich people in China are estimated to be $1.59 trillion') 13 October, at www.taiwaner.org/forums/showthread. php?t=16902.

Yu, Hongmei (2000) 'Dujie women shidai de jingshen zhenghou' ('Clarifying the Spiritual Malaise of Our Times') in Dai Jinhua (ed.) *Shuxie wenhua yingxiong: shiji zhi jiao de wenhua yanjiu* (*Writing Cultural Heroes: Cultural Research at the Turn of the Century*) Nanjing: Jiangsu renmin chubanshe, pp. 192–227.

Yu Wei (2005) 'Beijing lushi nian jun shouru 50 wan' ('Average annual income of Beijing lawyers 500,000 *yuan*') in *Fazhi wanbao* (*Evening Legal News*) 20 June, p.A11.

Yu, Zhou (2006) 'Heterogeneity and Dynamics in China's Emerging Urban Housing Market: Two Sides of a Success Story from the Late 1990s' in *Habitat International* 30/2, pp. 277–304.

Yuan, Caroline (2005) 'Diamond demand buoyant' in *Rapaport Diamond Report* 28/9, p. 77.

Zang, Xiaowei (1995) 'Industrial Management Systems and Managerial Ideologies in China' in *Journal of Northeast Asian Studies* 14/1, pp. 80–104.

Zang, Xiaowei (2001) 'Educational Credentials, Elite Dualism, and Elite Stratification in China' in *Sociological Perspectives* 44/2, pp. 189–205.

Zang, Xiaowei (2002) 'Labor Market Segmentation and Income Inequality in Urban China' in *Sociological Quarterly* 43/1, pp. 27–44.

Zang, Xiaowei (2003) 'Network Resources and Job Search in Urban China' in *Journal of Sociology* 39/2, pp. 115–29.

Zang, Xiaowei (2004) *Elite Dualism and Leadership Selection in China* London and New York: Routledge.

von Zedtwitz, Maximilian (2004) 'Managing foreign R&D laboratories in China' in *R&D Management* 34/4, pp. 439 – 452.

Zhan, Ni (2003) 'Pan Shiyi: Avant-garde Real Estate Developer' in *China Today* (March 2003), at www.chinatoday.com.cn/English/e20033/pan.htm.

Zhang Dajun (1997) 'Guanyu shehui xinli chengshou nengli de jige jiben wenti' ('Some issues about the aggregate levels of collective tolerance') in *Xinan Shifan Daxue Xuebao* (*Journal of Southwest Normal University*) 4, p. 7–13.

Zhang, De (ed.) (2003) *Qiye wenhua jianshe* (*Building Corporate Culture*) Beijing: Tsinghua University Press.

Zhang Jinrong (2004) 'Peiyang zhongjian jieceng, jianshe xiaokang shehui' ('Nurture the Middle Stratum and Build a Xiaokang Society') in *Zhanlue yu guanli* (*Strategy and Management*) 3, pp. 80–83.

Zhang, Jingxiang and Fulong Wu (2006) 'China's changing economic governance: administrative annexation and the reorganization of local governments in the Yangtze River Delta' in *Regional Studies* 40/1, pp. 3–21.

Zhang, Li (2001) *Strangers in the City: Reconfigurations of space, power, and social networks within China's floating population* Stanford University Press.

Zhang, Li (2002) 'Spatiality and Urban Citizenship in Late Socialist China' in *Public Culture* 14/2, pp. 311–334.

Zhang Liang (2001) *Zhongguo 'liu si' zhenxiang* (*June Fourth: The True Story*) Hong Kong: Mirror Books.

Zhang Lijing (2005) 'Yenei renshi suan xizhang: jiedu Jingcheng lushi shouru' ('People from all walks of life do accounts in detail: understanding Beijing lawyers' incomes') in *Fazhi wanbao* (*Evening Legal News*) 2 August, p.B14.

Zhang Na (2006) 'Zhongguo lushi zhidu 20 nian bianqian: cong tongyi bianzhi dao ziyou fazhan' ('Changes in China's lawyer system over 20 years: from unified quota to free development') in *Fazhi zaobao* (*Morning Legal News*) 20 August.

Zhang Xuemei (2005) 'Beijing shi Weisheng ju zhili luan shoufei: shi jia da yiyuan faxian duo shou fei' ('Beijing Health Bureau regulates arbitrary charges: ten major hospitals found overcharging') in *Beijing wanbao* (*Beijing Evening News*) 26 May.

Zhang, Wanli *et al.* (2005) 'Yingyun er sheng de Zhongguo "xin zhongjian jieceng"' ('The Emergence of China's "New Middle Stratum"') in *Shehui guancha* (*Social Observation*) 1, pp. 3–5.

Zhang, Xiaoguang (1998) 'Modeling Economic Transition: A Two-Tier Price Computable General Equilibrium Model of the Chinese Economy' in *Journal of Policy Modeling* 20/4, pp. 483–511.

Zhang, Xudong (ed.) (2001) *Whither China: Intellectual Politics in Contemporary China* Duke University Press.

Zhang Yirong (2007) 'Qinli zhe shuo lushi zhidu chongjian hou de 28 nian' ('People with personal experiences tell the stories of the 28 years since the re-establishment of the lawyer system') in *Fazhi ribao* (*Legal Daily*) 2 July.

Zhang Yin and Wan Guanghua (2006) 'The Impact of Growth and Inequality on Rural Poverty in China' in *Journal of Comparative Economics* 34/4, pp. 694–712.

Zhao Anping (2004) 'Ruian Shi Renmin Yiyuan yaopin huikou an haizai deng chuli' ('Drug kickback case of Ruian People's Hospital awaiting processing') in *Renmin ribao* (*The People's Daily*) 2 June, p.5.

Zhao, Beihai (2005) 'Goujian Hexie Shehui Er San Yan' ('A Few Words on Harmonious Society') in *Renmin Ribao* (*The People's Daily*) 14 July.

Zhao, Chengliang (2001) 'Tanguan nanguo nüren guan' ('Corrupt officials find it difficult to get past women') in *Fazhan daobao* (*Development Times*) 23 January.

Zhao, Liming and John D. Aram (1995) 'Networking and Growth of Young Technology-intensive Venture in China' in *Journal of Business Venturing* 10/5, pp. 349–70.

Zhao Xiao (2006) 'Jianshe jiankang de shichang he caifu lunli' ('Let's build a healthy market economy and good ethics about wealth') 4 April, at www.Nanfang daily. com. cn/southnews/sjjj/chanjing/200604240493.asp.

Zhao, Xiaohui and Jiang Xueli (2004) 'Coal mining: Most deadly job in China' in *China Daily* 13 November, at www.chinadaily.net/english/doc/2004-/content_391242.htm.

Zhao Yandong *et al.* (2007) 'Xibu chengxiang jumin de pinkun zhuangkuang' ('Poverty in Urban and Rural Areas in Western China') in Ru Xin *et al.* (eds) *2007: Zhongguo shehui xingshi fenxi yu yuce* (*Analysis and forecast on China's Social Development*) (Blue Book of China's Society).

Zhao, Yuezhi (1998) *Media, Market, and Democracy in China* University of Illinois Press.

Zheng Bijian (2001) '"Sange daibiao"' sixiang shi xin shiji dangjian de weida gangling' ('The Theory of "Three Represents" Is a Great Guiding Principle for Building the Party in the 21st Century') in *Guangming ribao* (*Guangming Daily*) 11 July.

Zheng, Hangsheng (2002) 'Guanyu woguochengshi shehui jieceng huafen de jige wenti' ('A Few Questions Concerning the Classification of Strata in China') in *The People's Daily* 9 February.

Zheng, Hangsheng (2004a) *Dangdai Zhongguo Chengshi Shehui Jiegou* (*Social Structure of Cities in Contemporary China*) Beijing: Zhongguo Renmin Daxue Chubanshe.

Zheng, Hangsheng (ed.) (2004b) *Zhongguo Shehui Jiegou Bianhua Qushi Yanjiu* (*Studies of Changing Trends in China's Social Structure*) Beijing: Zhongguo Renmin Daxue Chubanshe.

Zheng, Hangsheng and Li, Lulu (2004) *Dangdai Zhongguo chengshi shehui jiegou* (*Social Structure of Cities in Contemporary China*) Beijing: Zhongguo Renmin Daxue Chubanshe.

Zheng, Jianjiang (n.d.) 'Zongcai zhi dao' ('The Way of the CEO') AUX Group website, at www.auxgroup.com/about/zongcai.asp.

Zheng, Tiantian (2004) 'From Peasant Women to Bar Hostesses: Gender and Modernity in Post-Mao Dalian' in Arianne M. Gaetano and Tamara Jacka (eds) *On the Move: Women in Rural-to-Urban Migration in Contemporary China* Columbia University Press, pp. 80–108.

Zheng, Tiantian (2006) 'Cool masculinity: male clients' sex consumption and business alliance in urban China's sex industry' in *Journal of Contemporary China* 15, pp. 161–82.

Zheng, Yefu (2004) *Zhishi fenzi yanjiu* (*A study of intellectuals*) Beijing: Zhongguo Qingnian Chubanshe.

Zheng, Yi. (2003) 'Cultural Traditions and Contemporaneity—the Case of the New Confucianist Debate' in Wolf Lepenies (ed.) *Entangled Histories and Negotiated Universals: Centers and Peripheries in a Changing World* Frankfurt and New York: Campus Verlag.

Zhi, Gang (2001) 'Kankan gudai de xing huilu' ('Sex-related bribery and corruption in traditional China') in *Renmin fayuan bao* (*People's Courts Daily*) 18 January.

Zhi Jian (2002) 'Chong huo ziyou shen, Jing cheng ming yi jiang cheng "jianghu Bian Que"?' ('Regain freedom: will reputable Beijing doctors become "Bian Que" of the rivers and lakes"?') in *Qianlong wang* (*Qianglong Net*) 17 December.

Zhongguo Guojia Tongjiju (The National Statistical Bureau of China) (2005) 'Diyici quanguo jingji pucha zhuyao shuju gongbao' ('A report on the major figures obtained in the first national economic survey'), at www.stats.gov.cn/ZGjjpc/cgfb/t20051206_402294807.htm.

'Zhongguo renkou xianzhuang' ('The current situation of China's population') (2005), at www.gov.cn/test/2005–/content_17363.htm.

Zhong Xueping (2006) 'Who is a feminist? Understanding the Ambivalence towards *Shanghai Baby*, "Body writing" and Feminism in Post-Women's Liberation China' in *Gender and History* 18/3 (November) pp. 635–660.

Zhou, Xiaohong (ed.) (2005) *Zhongguo zhongchanjieceng diaocha* (*Survey of the Chinese Middle Classes*) Beijing: Shehui kexue wenxian chubanshe.

Zhou, Xueguang (2000) 'Economic Transformation and Income Inequality in Urban China' in *American Journal of Sociology* 105/4, p.1,135–74.

Zhou, Xueguang (2004) *The State and Life Chances in Urban China* Cambridge University Press.

Zhou, Xueguang (2005) 'The Institutional Logic of Occupational Prestige Ranking' in *American Journal of Sociology* 111/1, p.90.

Zhu, Bian and Hao Keming (2001) *Dangdai zhongguo jiaoyuj iegou tixi yanjiu* (*A Study on the Structural System of Contemporary Chinese Education*) Guangzhou: Guangdong Educational Press.

Zhu, Jieming (2005) 'A Transitional Institution for the Emerging Land Market in Urban China' in *Urban Studies* 42/8, p.1,369–90.

Zhu Jintao *et al.* (eds) (1989) *Jingji fanzui bianhu anli xuan bian* (Selected cases in defending economic crimes) Changsha: Hunan Daxue Chubanshe.

Zhu Qingfang (2007) 'Jingji shehui hexie fazhan zhibiao tixi zonghe pingjia' ('An Integrated Evaluation of the Indexes of Harmonious Socio-economic Development') in Ru Xin *et al.* (eds) *2007: Zhongguo shehui xingshi fenxi yu yuce* (*Analysis and forecast on China's Social Development*) (Blue Book of China's Society).

Zhu Yaoqun (2005) *Zhongchan jieceng yu hexie shehui* (*Middle strata and Harmonious Society*) Beijing: Zhongguo renmin gong'an daxue chubanshe.

Zhu Yu (2002) 'Weisheng bu biaoshi: jianjue fandui yisheng "zouxue" xingwei' (Ministry of Health: firmly oppose doctors "moonlighting"'), at www.people.com. cn/GB/shenghuo/78/1933/20021227/897137.html.

Zimmerman, D. and D. L. Wieder (1971) 'Ethnomethodology and the Problem of Order' in J. Douglas (ed.) *Understanding Everyday Life* London: Routledge and Paul Kegan.

Zurndorfer, Harriet T. (2004) 'Confusing Confucianism with Capitalism: Culture as Impediment and/or Stimulus to Chinese Economic Development' paper presented at the Third Global Economic History Network Meeting, Konstanz, Germany, 3–5 June 2004.

'2005 Zhongguo siying qiye diaocha baogao' ('2005 investigation of China's private enterprises') (2005), at www.southcn.com/finance/gdmqgc/gdmqyyrl/200502030218.html.

Index